A History of Political Th

A History of Political Thought

From Antiquity to the Present

Bruce Haddock

polity

First published in 2008 by Polity Press

Polity Press
65 Bridge Street
Cambridge CB2 1UR, UK

Polity Press
350 Main Street
Malden, MA 02148, USA

ISBN-13: 978-07456-4084-6
ISBN-13: 978-07456-4085-3 (pb)

A catalogue record for this book is available from the British Library.

Typeset in 10pt on 11.5pt Palatino
by Servis Filmsetting Ltd, Stockport, Cheshire
Printed and bound in Great Britain by
Biddles Ltd, Kings Lynn, Norfolk

The publisher has used its best endeavours to ensure that the URLs for external
websites referred to in this book are correct and active at the time of going to
press. However, the publisher has no responsibility for the websites and can
make no guarantee that a site will remain live or that the content is or will
remain appropriate.

Every effort has been made to trace all copyright holders, but if any have been
inadvertently overlooked the publishers will be pleased to include any necessary
credits in any subsequent reprint or edition.

For further information on Polity, visit our website: www.polity.co.uk

320.01
R S9095F

Contents

Acknowledgements

This book has a complicated history. I began working on a comprehensive history of political thought in 2000 during an intense period of study at Emory University. Don and Molly Verene ensured that I had ideal working conditions and were delightful hosts throughout the year. Soon after that Louise Knight invited me to contribute the modern volume to a planned series on history of political thought for Polity. An author could not ask for a more supportive publisher. I essentially broke off from the Emory manuscript to work on the modern material, eventually published by Polity in 2005.

I found myself wondering what to do with the early material. A timely conversation with Louise Knight encouraged me to go back to something like my original plan, incorporating some of the material from the 2005 volume in condensed and radically reworked form. I am very grateful for the opportunity to present history of political thought in broad terms, counter-balancing the many fine treatments of more restricted periods and thinkers that have emerged over the last thirty years. Staff at Polity have been wonderfully helpful throughout this project. I am grateful, too, for the constructive comments of anonymous readers for Polity.

I have worked on the issues in this book throughout my career and gladly acknowledge the help I have received from countless people. More specifically, I must thank teachers and colleagues at Leicester, Oxford, Swansea and Cardiff. I have grown ever more conscious of the debt I owe to my first teachers, Christopher Hughes, John Day and Maurice Keens-Soper, as my thinking has progressed. My immediate colleagues at Cardiff, David Boucher, Peri Roberts, Peter Sutch and Paul Furlong, have helped me in a bewildering variety of ways. And I am also grateful for timely support and encouragement from Ovidiu Caraiani and Rex Martin.

As ever, my family have given me unstinting support over the years. Simon, Jessica, Lizzie and Nellie have kept me going in their different ways through the usual trials and tribulations of writing. The support and encouragement of my wife, Sheila, is too deep and complex to be adequately expressed.

I have drawn on and developed some of my earlier work in this volume. Chapters 8–11 cover some of the ground of *A History of Political Thought: 1789 to the Present* (Polity, 2005) in condensed and revised form. My thanks also go to the editors and publishers of the following: *A Guide to the Political Classics* (Oxford University Press, 1988); *The Political Classics: Hamilton to Mill* (Oxford University Press, 1993); *The Political Classics: Green to Dworkin* (Oxford University Press, 1996); *Themes in Modern European History: 1830– 1890* (Unwin Hyman, 1990); *History of Political Thought*, 20 (1999); *The Edinburgh Companion to Contemporary Liberalism* (Edinburgh University Press, 2001); *Multiculturalism, Identity and Rights* (Routledge, 2003); and *Principles and Political Order: The Challenge of Diversity* (Routledge, 2006).

Chronology

625BC   Estimated birth of Thales
610BC   Estimated birth of Anaximander

545BC   Estimated death of Thales
540BC   Estimated death of Anaximander
540BC   Estimated birth of Heracleitus
525BC   Birth of Aeschylus

496BC   Estimated birth of Sophocles
485BC   Estimated birth of Protagoras
484BC   Estimated birth of Herodotus
483BC   Estimated birth of Gorgias
480BC   Estimated death of Heracleitus
469BC   Birth of Socrates
460BC   Estimated birth of Thucydides
456BC   Death of Aeschylus
428BC   Birth of Plato
420BC   Estimated death of Herodotus
415BC   Estimated death of Protagoras
406BC   Death of Sophocles
400BC   Estimated death of Thucydides

399BC   Death of Socrates
384BC   Birth of Aristotle
376BC   Death of Gorgias
356BC   Birth of Alexander the Great
347BC   Death of Plato
341BC   Birth of Epicurus
331BC   Birth of Zeno
323BC   Death of Alexander the Great
322BC   Death of Aristotle

271BC	Death of Epicurus
261BC	Death of Zeno
106BC	Birth of Cicero
43BC	Death of Cicero
40	Estimated birth of Dio Chrysostom
120	Estimated death of Dio Chrysostom
354	Birth of Augustine
360	Estimated birth of Pelagius
410	Sack of Rome by Alaric
420	Death of Pelagius
430	Death of Augustine
533	Promulgation of the *Corpus juris civilis* by Justinian
1126	Birth of Averroes
1198	Death of Averroes
1224	Birth of Aquinas
1270	Birth of Marsilius
1274	Death of Aquinas
1342	Death of Marsilius
1469	Birth of Machiavelli
1517	Luther initiates his formal challenge to the Church
1527	Death of Machiavelli
1530	Birth of Bodin
1557	Birth of Althusius
1566	Birth of James I
1583	Birth of Grotius
1588	Birth of Filmer
1588	Birth of Hobbes
1596	Death of Bodin
1625	Death of James I
1632	Birth of Pufendorf
1632	Birth of Locke
1632	Birth of Spinoza
1638	Death of Althusius
1645	Death of Grotius

1647	Birth of Bayle
1648	Treaty of Westphalia
1649	Execution of Charles I
1653	Death of Filmer
1668	Birth of Vico
1677	Death of Spinoza
1679	Death of Hobbes
1688	Glorious Revolution
1689	Birth of Montesquieu
1694	Death of Pufendorf
1694	Birth of Voltaire
1704	Death of Locke
1706	Death of Bayle
1711	Birth of Hume
1712	Birth of Rousseau
1713	Birth of Diderot
1717	Birth of d'Alembert
1724	Birth of Kant
1729	Birth of Burke
1737	Birth of Paine
1744	Death of Vico
1744	Birth of Herder
1745	Birth of Jay
1748	Birth of Sieyes
1748	Birth of Bentham
1751	Birth of Madison
1753	Birth of Maistre
1755	Death of Montesquieu
1755	Birth of Hamilton
1758	Birth of Robespierre
1760	Birth of Siant-Simon
1760	Birth of Babeuf
1762	Birth of Fichte
1767	Birth of Constant
1770	Birth of Hegel
1771	Birth of Owen
1776	Death of Hume
1778	Death of Voltaire
1778	Death of Rousseau
1783	Death of d'Alembert
1784	Death of Diderot
1789	Outbreak of the French Revolution
1789	Inauguration of the federal constitution in the United States
1793	Execution of Louis XVI

1794	Death of Robespierre
1797	Death of Burke
1797	Death of Babeuf
1803	Death of Herder
1804	Death of Kant
1804	Death of Hamilton
1805	Birth of Tocqueville
1805	Birth of Mazzini
1806	Birth of Mill
1809	Death of Paine
1814	Death of Fichte
1815	Defeat of Napoleonic France
1818	Birth of Marx
1820	Birth of Engels
1821	Death of Maistre
1825	Death of Siant-Simon
1829	Death of Jay
1830	Death of Constant
1831	Death of Hegel
1832	Death of Bentham
1836	Death of Madison
1836	Death of Sieyes
1836	Birth of Green
1843	Birth of Labriola
1844	Birth of Nietzsche
1847	Birth of Sorel
1848	European revolutions
1848	Birth of Pareto
1850	Birth of Bernstein
1858	Death of Owen
1859	Death of Tocqueville
1864	Birth of Hobhouse
1866	Birth of Croce
1870	Birth of Lenin
1872	Death of Mazzini
1873	Death of Mill
1875	Birth of Gentile
1882	Death of Green
1883	Death of Marx
1888	Birth of Schmitt
1895	Death of Engels
1899	Birth of Hayek

1900	Death of Nietzsche
1901	Birth of Oakeshott
1902	Birth of Popper
1904	Death of Labriola
1909	Birth of Berlin
1914	Outbreak of the First World War
1917	Russian Revolution
1918	End of the First World War
1921	Birth of Rawls
1922	Death of Sorel
1923	Death of Pareto
1924	Death of Lenin
1926	Birth of Foucault
1929	Death of Hobhouse
1932	Death of Bernstein
1938	Birth of Nozick
1939	Outbreak of the Second World War
1944	Death of Gentile
1945	End of the Second World War
1952	Death of Croce
1984	Death of Foucault
1985	Death of Schmitt
1989	Fall of the Berlin Wall
1990	Death of Oakeshott
1992	Death of Hayek
1994	Death of Popper
1997	Death of Berlin
2002	Death of Rawls
2002	Death of Nozick

1

Introduction

Political thought is in one sense as old as organized communities. At the very least, groups of people have had to provide for their mutual security and to establish sustainable terms of social co-operation. This is true of all communities, whether or not they have left a formal record of political theorizing. Anthropologists have told us a great deal about pre-literate modes of political organization. As political theorists or philosophers, however, we are interested not so much in the fact that specific social and political arrangements have been established in communities as in the arguments that have been devised to justify particular institutional schemes. And it is simply a fact about our political education and the historical development of our culture that we have learned to think about these issues through disciplined reflection on what are taken to be canonical texts. To be sure, fashions change in relation to 'classic' texts, as with everything else. For the moment I want to focus not on specific texts that might be included in the classical canon, but rather on the way our thinking revolves around points of reference. These points of reference have changed significantly over time; yet without some shared points of reference, we cannot engage in disciplined argument or reflection at all.

This point holds for thinking of any kind, not simply for political theorizing in its various guises. What distinguishes political philosophy, however, is the public dimension in which it operates. Arguments about social co-operation have necessarily to be projected to whomever might be expected to engage in or be subject to a given set of arrangements. It does not follow that everybody in a community would be entitled to the same sort of consideration. Consensual persuasion may be reserved for a select few, while a majority may be coerced or manipulated. How the balance is struck in a particular community will be a matter of political argument. The point remains that the effective exercise of power presupposes minimally shared objectives and values among relevant groups. And these objectives and values can be challenged by the disgruntled, excluded and disappointed.

It would be foolish to suppose that consensus on objectives and values is always and everywhere a direct consequence of disinterested intellectual assent. Political arguments always come with 'baggage'; and it may not always be possible or desirable to insist on 'transparency' as an ideal value. At one level we may think of arguments as tokens which we exchange with one another in order to get our own way as often as possible. At another level, however, the clash of interested parties invites a more rigorous reformulation of the form and content of an argument. To be sure, political leaders in all ages have had many more resources at their disposal than intellectual ingenuity. The point is simply that the pursuit of coherence constitutes a point of reference for subsequent argument.

It is important to stress that arguments can be effective without necessarily being based on objective truth claims. In the course of this book we will see that foundational truth claims have often been made in the history of political thought. But they are always contentious; and none of them have proved to be universally acceptable. In modern political thought it is widely assumed that it makes no sense to advance 'objective' truth claims at all. Yet it does not follow that all we are left with in the appraisal of political thought is rhetorical effectiveness. We can make internal judgements of the coherence or consistency of arguments, without invoking an external or objective criterion. What we cannot do, however, is to assume that 'anything goes' in a text or argument.

Political arguments, like conversations, are intelligible because participants share more or less specific assumptions. For the most part we do not need to specify what these assumptions might be or how far they extend. The fact remains that something must be shared for an utterance to be intelligible. Sometimes what we say or do may only be intelligible to cultural insiders. The formal procedures for the state opening of parliament, for example, may not be immediately intelligible to everyone. And we know that we cannot appreciate or play a game until we have grasped at least some of the rules and practices that constitute the game. Yet in other contexts we may need to learn little or nothing of a language or culture in order to understand that someone is in acute distress and in need of assistance. Precisely what we may feel called upon to do in such circumstances will depend upon a host of factors. At the very least, we will have something to think about.

The thinking involved in the pursuit of immediate practical objectives is not sophisticated. Matters become much more complex, however, when medium or long term objectives are involved, requiring co-operation with groups and individuals on a consistent basis. And if the people involved happen to be strangers, whose preferences and predilections are unknown to us, then the considerations that are likely to be practically effective will be very different from the stratagems that may secure the co-operation of friends and acquaintances. In the history of political thought, a great deal hinges on the way we portray the people we expect to co-operate with in our regular dealings. Do we have special obligations only to family and friends? Do the people with whom we share a language and culture have particular claims on our loyalty? What can strangers expect from us? Do we have any responsibilities for people remote from us? Do we have any obligations to ancestors or future generations? These are not easy questions to answer in abstract terms. Yet whenever we establish co-operative practices we are assuming that answers to some of these questions can be given. Practices involve at least a tacit specification of roles, responsibilities and objectives. Unspoken ground rules will be amended in response to new circumstances. The distribution of rights and duties may be challenged, prompting a reformulation or refinement of shared understandings. And shared understandings need to be justified to a relevant audience.

Political philosophy as a specialized pursuit grows out of the ordinary business of maintaining and justifying social co-operation. I have nothing to say in this book about the anthropological or strictly historical beginnings of organized political practices. It is important to be clear, however, about the problems political philosophy seeks to resolve. These problems arise (historically) as communities establish specialized institutions for maintaining effective co-operation. And because these institutions are deemed to be important for the lives of everyone within a community, they become a focus for energetic individuals seeking power, influence or (in the Greek sense) glory. For the moment we need not specify the precise form a community might take. The point to stress is that the community will be characterized in terms of normative commitments made by individuals in competitive and (potentially) dangerous circumstances. Political orders are coercive. Specific forms of social co-operation will distribute benefits and burdens in ways which impinge differently on individuals and groups. Access to power and influence, however it is managed institutionally, may have a dramatic impact on life (or sometimes survival) chances. Political office will thus be seen as a resource which can be used and abused. A political role is necessarily contentious. It cannot be exercised without the co-operative commitment of others, and yet that commitment will seldom be given unconditionally.

Establishing acceptable conditions of co-operation is a messy and murky business. At one level we are dealing with a game of power and mutual accommodation played out with a ruthlessness that is unlikely to appeal to philosophers. But it does not follow that what goes on at the political level has no philosophical implications, nor that philosophical arguments might not modify the way interests are pursued. We can imagine anyone, anywhere, asking searching questions about acceptable conditions for mutual accommodation. What should be noticed here is the imperceptible shift from balance of power to balance of argument. These things are not worked out in a seminar. But questions are raised that are distinctly philosophical in character.

No matter how political order is actually established, it makes sense for philosophers to ask why order is desirable. And when they speak about desirability, they mean not desirability from the perspective of someone located specifically within an institutional hierarchy but from the perspective of anyone who might be minded to consider the question. Whether or not the question has a precise answer, it is couched in general terms. The philosopher tries to make a general, though necessarily qualified, case for order; he is not interested in order as a means of pursuing personal objectives.

There is in fact a consistent tradition in political philosophy, extending from the ancient Greeks all the way through to modern political theorists, which focuses on the basic dilemmas that oblige us to think philosophically about order. In the first place, we need to remind ourselves of the contingent predicament that all societies find themselves in. When we think about moral, political and legal questions, we are responding to background circumstances shared by all communities, anywhere. It is easy to forget certain facts about human life sitting in a warm seminar room after a good lunch. No matter who we are or where we are, it is foolish to disregard the constraining circumstances that shape our lives. We are all vulnerable to personal attack, our position vis-à-vis other people is always one of relative equality (for even the weak can threaten the strong through stealth), we have to accept that there are limits to our altruism, resources and understanding. In these circumstances, social co-operation is not an optional extra but a basic necessity for a sustainable life. We can imagine situations in which these restrictions would not apply. We can fantasize about heaven on earth, where both resources and goodwill are superabundant. But whatever arrangements people in that happy situation might devise for their delight, we can assume that distributive and coercive procedures would not be among them. Politics as we know it would simply not be necessary. Nor, at the other extreme, can we envisage regular civil life in conditions of absolute scarcity. Where starvation is a likely prospect, we cannot assume that the laws of property would be greatly respected. In the ordinary way of things, of course, we are not faced with such stark dilemmas, except in cases where regimes actually break down. What we have to accept, however, is that our practical lives are necessarily rendered problematic because of the circumstances in which we live.

We may say, at the very least, that recognition of mutual vulnerability commits us to the adoption of some rules of social co-operation. These rules may be many and varied and could in substance be wholly arbitrary. But that there should be some rules may be said to be a defining characteristic of a society. Given that societies with (necessarily) limited understanding and scarce resources will have to make hard choices, we must assume that they will have authoritative procedures for allocating resources. Government of some kind will have to be carried on, even if a formal specification of institutional roles is not developed. But, of course, to recognize the philosophical necessity of government in certain circumstances is not to endorse any particular kind of government.

At this stage our philosophical interest is in the general predicament that all schemes of institutional order must respond to. We are concerned with viability rather than desirability. The key issue here is not how particular practices and institutions might be justified but what makes practices and institutions possible. Argument at this level of abstraction seldom surfaces in conventional discussions of policy. At times of crisis, however, when the existence or functional relevance of a political order is threatened, basic questions about the point of schemes of institutional co-operation have necessarily to be confronted.

Our concern as philosophers, then, before we consider the institutions and practices we might happen to prefer, is to explore the necessary requirements which enable practices to flourish. We must assume that these requirements will be very general indeed since we know from ordinary experience that different cultures pursue all manner of ends in a variety of ways. Our starting point is to focus on what people need to acknowledge in order to attain any satisfaction at all rather than on the things they happen to want. Recognition of mutual vulnerability commits us to establishing acceptable terms of social co-operation. If you do not accept this point, you can have no interest in normative political philosophy. And, indeed, in the history of political philosophy, the validity of this assumption has often been challenged. From Callicles and Thrasymachus in ancient Greece, through to Nietzsche, Carl Schmitt and their modern followers, the arbitrariness of initial assumptions has been forcefully argued. Yet it has never proved to be possible to remain satisfied with this position as a stable solution to the dilemma posed by the need for social co-operation. From a certain perspective, normative political philosophy may be treated as a mistake; yet it seems to be a mistake we are compelled to keep repeating in different forms.

The point may be put more strongly. Social co-operation is indispensable to human flourishing, though it can clearly be generated in all manner of ways. In fact the sheer diversity of experience invites us to think critically about the way we actually do things. Circumstances constrain what we do and how we do it. Just as the technology of daily life has to be adapted to fit changing circumstances, so we might have to think in more abstract terms about the schemes of social co-operation that underpin our daily lives. Critical reflection is thus inescapable once we recognize that things can go better and worse.

Modern citizens have grown accustomed to the (near) universality of diverse styles of critical thinking as an important dimension of their self-understanding. The fact that things could be different commits them (at least in principle) to formal justification of the practices they choose to endorse. Even to decide to carry on in the same old way is to exercise political (and theoretical) discretion. In (what we are still pleased to call) the

'West', we have refined this critical reflection from selective engagement with seminal arguments in political philosophy. This book focuses on texts in political philosophy (contentious in their own terms) that constitute building blocks in a long (but sporadic) history of reaction and response to radically changing social, economic and cultural circumstances. In an important sense our political thinking is framed by shifting demands in a bewildering variety of contexts, yet it also displays structural features that are remarkably stable over time. An important theme in this book is the need to see political philosophy, even in its most abstract formulations, as a response to historically contingent circumstances, without limiting its relevance to those initial circumstances. The emphasis throughout is on political thinking as a response to hard choices. And we continue to exploit and develop that experience as our circumstances change.

2

Nature and Convention

This book takes the beginnings of political thought seriously. The prehistory of political philosophy is crucial for understanding the distinctive features of the tradition of reflection that Plato and Aristotle have handed down to us. Yet it would be a Herculean task (not attempted here) to chart the beginnings of the western tradition of political thinking in any detail. It is worth stressing, however, that critical reflection on political ends has not occurred everywhere. We may assume that personal conflict and rivalry has always been a feature of human life, but there are many more straightforward means of containing such pressures than elaborate theoretical argument. Families, tribes and clans have ritual means of reinforcing the *status quo* within their ranks. And while these may not be successful in individual cases, the likely consequence is ostracism or death for individuals who step out of line, or a parting of the ways if larger groups are involved. What we do not see in typical family 'squabbles' (at least in hypothetical 'prehistorical' contexts) is a sustained challenge to the authority of the family or group. The missing dimension here is any awareness of an alternative to the tried and trusted means of managing daily life. Note that these comments are conjectural rather than anthropological or historical in any strict sense. We are simply trying to envisage conditions that might transform personal conflict into political argument.

At the very least, we can say that critical political reflection presupposes the possibility of change. It would make no sense to ask oneself how social co-operation might best be managed if in fact we could not envisage alternative ways of life. But nor would such reflection make much sense if change were seen as the product of dark, inscrutable forces over which human beings had no control. If the gods or the fates are seen as the instigators of events, and their motives are beyond human comprehension, then people can at best adopt a passive attitude to their life chances. Exhortation and ritual propitiation might make sense; justification of different courses of human conduct would not.

Note that we are still engaged in conceptual clarification rather than historical analysis here. We can assume that the gods or fates would be invoked in personal rivalries, with individuals claiming to be inspired, cursed or whatever. The portrayal of these rivalries could well be richly ingenious and striking. But it would still not amount to political philosophy or political theory, no matter how far these terms are stretched. The symbolism of political conflict in such contexts would provide rich material for the historian or anthropologist. And it would certainly make sense to see a certain kind of symbolism as a first step on a road that might lead to political philosophy. An essential dimension, however, would still be lacking: the formal justification of ends that human beings might plausibly adopt.

The detailed story of the transition from polytheistic clientelism to an awareness of social co-operation as a political achievement is too complex to be told here. Remarkably, however, at least for the beginnings of formal politics in the western tradition, we have a set of texts and fragments that enable us to document at least the rudiments of the story of speculative development. From the eighth century BC in archaic Greece down to the death of Alexander the Great of Macedon in 323 BC, we can trace a series of intellectual and cultural engagements which finally culminated in the self-conscious political theorizing that we associate with Socrates, Plato and Aristotle in the fifth and fourth centuries.

To be sure, the circumstances that facilitated this level of political awareness were unique. In the first place, the scale of the Greek *polis* (or city-state) enabled a distinctive style of politics to develop. Athens, the largest of the *poleis*, probably did not exceed 300,000 at its peak; and that figure would include women, slaves and foreigners who could take no active part in politics. Other *poleis*, of which we know much less, were much smaller. Each would be large enough, however, to enable it to satisfy the basic criterion laid down by Aristotle in the *Politics*, that it should be 'nearly or quite self-sufficing', and that it should cater not simply for the 'bare needs of life' but should exist 'for the sake of a good life'.[1] The good life in question here focuses largely on the requirements of the citizen elite. It is their recognition that they cannot flourish collectively if they manipulate one another as slaves that obliges them to engage in elaborate public justifications of proposals for the proper conduct of life. They owe one another public accounts; and their individual prospects and esteem within the community depend upon their command of argument.

How far does the situation depicted by Aristotle in the fourth century differ from that depicted by Homer in the eighth? In the *Iliad* and *Odyssey* it is clear that heroic king-like figures need to attract allies and seek advice.[2] They cannot be effective in the chaotic circumstances of practical life on their own. Their ability to command and retain followers seems to depend in the poems on their personal effectiveness in confronting and overcoming opponents. Personal charisma is the key to practical success.

The formal quality of the case being made for a particular course of action is treated as secondary.

It would be misleading to claim that the Homeric heroes had no conception of justice. They are acutely aware of the due consideration that goes with their personal status. The plot of the *Iliad* is driven by jealousies and resentments. Achilles comes close to undermining the Greek cause in his response to a personal slight from Agamemnon. Homer accepts that Achilles's withdrawal from the fray is a deep misfortune and that Achilles himself bears the primary responsibility. But he also acknowledges that a hero's wounded pride will necessarily have an unpredictable impact on any co-operative venture.

In a world of heroic confrontations, reflective politics or ethics is out of place. That such a world is intelligible to us at all is largely due to the role accorded to the gods. They are powerful, partisan and interventionist. They are also all too human, pursuing goals obsessively and displaying pique in their turn if things go badly for them. Like the heroes themselves, they seem to be engaged in a game of clientelistic confrontation. The crucial difference is that they operate in a more clearly defined hierarchy. Zeus is not so far above the other gods that he cannot be irritated and frustrated. In the last resort, however, he is powerful enough to get his way.

In one sense, this resembles nothing so much as the world of politics as we know it with the theory removed. Individuals compete desperately for status and followers; but their triumphs and disasters are treated almost exclusively in personal terms. The upshot is that when co-operation occurs it is generally unstable. Achilles and Agamemnon are always aware that a co-operative engagement is secondary to the pursuit of personal glory. The paradox is that heroes need one another's endorsement if they are to bask in glory. The rivalry between them is such, however, that that endorsement will be given grudgingly. Demonstrable personal success is so important that cheating and betrayal are encouraged. Homeric politics has little attraction for the cautious or fastidious.

The Homeric world view, as it has come down to us, is theoretically fractured and politically unstable. The attempt to fashion a coherent view out of the melange of archaic Greek culture is a dramatic story that takes us way beyond the history of political thought. What made the Homeric position so difficult to defend was its essential wilfulness. No doubt this is why Homeric poetry retains its appeal. We understand caprice very well indeed. It is the attitude of mind that comes most easily to us. It makes it very difficult, however, for us to deal with one another in other than a coercive fashion. It makes consensual co-operation among equals very difficult; among strangers it is simply impossible.

The 'natural' philosophers take the first decisive steps away from Homeric polytheism. In their different ways, Thales (*c*.625–*c*.545), Anaximander (*c*.610–*c*.540) and Heracleitus (*c*.540–*c*.480), among many others, sought a unifying principle that might make the chaotic world of appearances intelligible. They each try to depict a primary material foundation beneath the shifting world that is revealed to the senses. In retrospect, their efforts seem somewhat primitive to us. It is difficult for us to appreciate the significance of attributing primacy to water (in the case of Thales) as the basic constituent of all material things, or a boundless and unlimited matter that is modified into the forms that we recognize with our senses (in the case of Anaximander), or that changes in the world can be interpreted in terms of an ever-living fire that assumes different guises in specific conditions (in the case of Heracleitus). What is being claimed in each of these views, however, is that an intelligible principle underpins everything that exists or occurs. From the perspective of the history of philosophy, the specific principle defended is less important than the claim that a specific principle should be sought.[3]

Greek efforts to establish intelligible principles for the comprehension and management of practical life have proved to be a more lasting achievement, in terms of both method and substantive conclusions. Indeed it used to be claimed, with a forgivable hint of exaggeration, that political philosophy in the western tradition amounts to a series of footnotes to the Greeks. Such a claim would be absurd in relation to Greek natural philosophy, mathematics, or even metaphysics, and it is doubtless a gross distortion of the history of political philosophy. But there is no doubt that Socrates, Plato and Aristotle established terms of reference that are still indispensable when we do our own philosophical thinking about politics.

It is worth asking ourselves why Greek political philosophy should continue to be so relevant. Certainly the formal structure of the *polis* is so very different from our modern states that the immediacy of Plato's dialogues (in particular) is remarkable. The background cultural assumptions that informed political life were also so different from our own that we should pause before assuming that Plato was addressing anything remotely like our problems. We do not read Plato as his contemporaries would have read him. Yet there remains something in what Plato was trying to do that is indispensable for us if we are to make our own political experience intelligible.

It is significant that the period we take to be the high point in Greek political philosophy occurs as Athenian culture in particular, and the form of the *polis* more generally, was already in decline. Socrates, Plato and Aristotle, in their different ways, were commenting on a world that seemed to be threatened. They had personal experience of traumatic crises in various *poleis* that rendered the way of life they valued precarious. The corruption of the political culture of the *polis* is a leading theme in their thought. They propose different remedial strategies; but they share a common view of political life as a predicament that demands a reflective response.

Awareness of the theoretical significance of change had been gradually building in Greek culture. Herodotus (*c*.484–*c*.420) provides a cornucopia of traditions, stories and anecdotes gathered during travels throughout the Greek world, ranging as far afield as Asia Minor, Egypt, Syria and the Black Sea.[4] The focus of his *Histories* is the clash between Greeks and Persians; and though theoretical analysis is not his principal concern, he presents his readers (or listeners) with rich insight into possible ways of life. The practical imperative is inescapable. Once the Greeks had been confronted with plausible evidence of the sustainability of a variety of cultures, they clearly had to adopt a theoretical view of what might be ideally desirable. The basic distinction between Greek and barbarian culture is obviously loaded with normative significance. Yet even if attention is restricted to the customs and practices Greeks themselves had devised for the ordering of their affairs, it is difficult to evade the conclusion that a way of life is something that can change and may have to be endorsed, defended or challenged.

Conflicting values were most vividly illustrated in Greek drama. Aeschylus (525–456) in the *Oresteia* trilogy highlights the (potentially destructive) tension between the fated course of events ordained by the gods and human responsibility for the consequences of actions freely undertaken.[5] Aeschylus clearly envisages cosmic harmony beneath the fractured lives of his characters; but the drama is driven by the tragedy of individuals pursuing irreconcilable moral imperatives.

The same basic structure is evident in Sophocles's *Antigone* (441), in which Antigone defies the ruling of Creon, king of Thebes, that she should not bury her brother. Antigone claims that she has done what the gods would demand. Creon insists upon his prerogative. The upshot is a series of deaths which finally undermine the peace of mind of Creon himself. Creon bemoans at the end of the play that 'all that is in my hands has gone awry, and fate hard to deal with has leapt upon my head'.[6] In both Aeschylus and Sophocles a chorus is employed to provide running commentary and summary judgement. These glosses do not resolve conflict at the level of the individual. The implication is that nothing can do that. What is emphasized, instead, is the inescapable personal agony of trying to live a morally coherent life.

All this is food for thought in a literal sense. The fact that lives seem to be fragmented invites deeper reflection about principles that might make ordinary experience more intelligible. Nor is this merely a theoretical imperative. Deciding what to do is not something that can be put off indefinitely. Inaction, quite as much as action, is a consequence of decisions made after due reflection. In a more narrowly political context, action necessarily involves a public audience, no matter how narrow the relevant conception of a 'public' might be. When different courses of action are available, argument counts. What makes argument effective became an almost obsessive concern among the Greek (and especially Athenian) elite. In the process they devised political philosophy as a public practice, along lines that are instantly recognizable to modern philosophers. The *polis* may have become a historical curiosity; the controversial culture it generated, however, has continued to animate public life wherever consensual co-operation is recognized as a public ideal.

The elements were in place in fifth century Athens for sustained philosophical reflection on moral and political issues. The sheer contingency of these circumstances is worth dwelling on for a moment. Political activity of some kind (though not as Aristotle would understand it) may be regarded as a feature of any organized society. High-level theoretical analysis of politics most decidedly is not. If we want to understand what is distinctive about political theory or political philosophy, it helps if we can highlight circumstances which impel people to take a considered view. Political instability in the Greek world meant that change could not be ignored. It could, of course, be deplored. Such negative judgements constitute a leading theme in Greek political reflection. The point to stress here is that condemnation invites the articulation of cogent reasons.

The plausibility of particular views of politics will clearly depend upon issues that go beyond the specific values or preferences that people happen to have. What we want or expect from life will be informed by what we regard as possible for human beings. Where values are contested, knowledge claims are likely to be challenged. Disputes about what is actually the case will get tied up in arguments about the status and validity of knowledge claims. The fact that values and preferences differ, or that individuals have immense problems ranking the values that are simply current within a community, encourages reflection on the status of values themselves. In simpler times it may have been possible for us to assume that values are ordained by the gods. But if Homer is to be believed, different gods endorse different values, and Aeschylus and Sophocles show how these psychological conflicts can destroy individuals. As things stood for the Greeks in the fifth century, and as they stand for us today, reflective individuals are compelled to try to find a way through a moral and political thicket that initially appears to be impenetrable. Changing and disturbing times commit us to thinking hard.

Where thinking hard might lead us, of course, remains an open question. One response to the manifest variety of customs among the Greeks was to argue that rules, procedures and practices are conventions. They are devised within particular communities to satisfy particular purposes. According to this argument, conventions cannot be judged against an ideal theoretical standard because any such standard would itself be merely a convention. The position is epitomized in the claim by Protagoras that 'man is the measure of all things'.[7] The practical political implications of this view remain entirely open. Recognizing that all values, practices and laws are conventional, we may decide that we are happy to persist with the conventions that happen to prevail within our communities. Alternatively we may argue that conventions which have been devised to cater for particular needs and conveniences should be changed to reflect other needs and conveniences. Within these terms of reference, arguments about the desirability of change could never be theoretically resolved. It would leave the laws and institutions of a community vulnerable to passing fashion and factional advantage.

From the perspective of Socrates, Plato and Aristotle (albeit in significantly different ways) the adoption of theoretical relativism had contributed signally to what they perceived as a serious decline in public culture in Athens. What they sought to defend, instead, was a 'natural' or 'ideal' standard against which particular conventional settlements could be assessed. Within this remarkable period, we see terms of reference being established which have continued to structure a good deal of our political thinking. Substantive arguments about justice or virtue or righteousness were linked specifically with the wider question of whether judgements of value were natural or conventional. It marks the beginning of political philosophy as a self-conscious engagement.

The original significance of the emergence of political philosophy is easily missed because of the massive influence that Plato and Aristotle have exercised on subsequent thinkers. Both articulated rich and complex views of the world that made sense of politics and morality in relation to a wider metaphysical system. Their thinking was thus holistic in the literal sense, inviting us as students and scholars to master the system in order to understand specific dimensions of human experience. From a philosophical point of view, however, this is almost certainly a misleading approach. Especially in Plato's early dialogues, philosophical problems are portrayed as arising from the ordinary dilemmas we face in daily life. Athens in the fifth and fourth centuries BC, we must remember, was a cosmopolitan society, acutely aware of other ways of life and the cultural gulf that separated contemporary Athens from the Homeric world. In these circumstances, it was by no means clear how an ideal (or even the best possible) life should be understood. The Homeric preoccupation with personal glory had given place to a much broader (though still fiercely competitive) conception of intellectual, cultural and political life. Personal advancement depended upon highly refined intellectual skills. And a group of teachers (the Sophists) had emerged to cater for the needs and aspirations of the children of the wealthy.

The Sophists did not constitute a school or movement in a strict philosophical sense. Even if we restrict our attention to the ethical and political questions that are central to this book, it is clear from the evidence we have that they defended a range of different positions.[8] As a group, however, they emerged precisely because ethical and political questions had become problematical. Hence it makes sense to identify them with sceptical positions on these matters, though it would be wrong to see them all as moral or cultural relativists. Even Protagoras, whose man-measure dictum was cited earlier, should not be dismissed as a straightforward relativist. But they all regard customary received culture as an inadequate preparation for an active and successful life.

Here we come to the crux of a question that occupied Plato throughout his career. If we are to assume that an active and successful life requires preparation, then it follows that we should be able to specify what constitutes a successful (or good) life. It would certainly make little sense to present ourselves as teachers of the art of practical success if we could not give a defensible account of the criteria that should guide our 'art'. We may think of teachers as experts. With specific arts (like medicine, carpentry, cookery or playing the flute) we may have some idea of the technical skills that are indispensable to a competent practitioner, though we may still have disputes about what constitutes excellence. Argument makes sense in these contexts because we assume that a criterion of excellence can be invoked, even if it is controversial.

Practical success, however, is far too slippery a concept to serve as an effective criterion. We can envisage a ruthless and manipulative person exploiting the gullibility of other people in order to advance his personal interests. He may be acclaimed for his ingenuity. People who know the truth about his methods may nevertheless defer to him in fear and awe. Does this amount to success? In several dialogues (*Protagoras*, *Gorgias* and *Meno* in particular) Plato, through the person of Socrates, throws this question out to defenders of the Sophists without getting a coherent or consistent reply. Gorgias is portrayed as advancing a purely instrumental art which enables his students to present the most persuasive possible arguments, irrespective of the intrinsic merits of the particular causes they seek to promote. Indeed Gorgias is presented as being entirely agnostic on the question of what might constitute a good cause. People will always disagree about such matters. All he claims is that through his teaching he can 'make clever speakers'.[9] Protagoras is depicted as making a stronger case for the progressive adoption of laws, practices and procedures in response to the problems encountered in fashioning a maximally co-operative social life. He argues that 'respect for others and a sense of justice' are indispensable to human beings if they are to flourish.[10] These qualities are the achievements of custom and convention. But Protagoras is unable to specify in detail what they might involve. He is alleged to have been content simply to argue 'that whatever practices seem right and laudable to any particular state are so, for that state, so long as it holds by them'.[11] All that Sophists can teach, within these terms of reference, are the requisite oratorical and other skills that might enable their pupils to advance themselves within particular cultures. They can say nothing about the quality of the values that happen to be upheld within these cultures.

Great care must be taken in interpreting the positions of Protagoras, Gorgias or any of the other Sophists against whom Socrates clarifies his own arguments in the dialogues. Though Protagoras and Gorgias, in particular, are treated with respect by Plato, they are very much supporting figures in a drama dominated by Socrates. We simply do not have enough independent evidence to question seriously the accuracy of Plato's accounts of their views. It is nevertheless clear, especially in the case of Protagoras, that supporting arguments can be produced which can fill out his position in ways that would make it less vulnerable to Socrates's criticisms. The idea that any viable community will have to have a conception of justice is not incompatible with a recognition that substantive conceptions of justice will vary widely in response to cultural circumstances. There is a hint in Protagoras of a core idea of justice that can be developed in different ways to meet the needs of particular communities.[12] The core idea will not be sufficiently detailed to function as a practical political code; but it might still serve as a formal criterion to distinguish justice from injustice.

To be sure, the fragmentary nature of the texts available to us leaves us with too much conjectural work to do for comfort.[13] Plato's main concern in these texts is to highlight the baleful ethical consequences that follow if knowledge is simply treated as a matter of belief. If we accept the Sophist position, Plato argues that we have no theoretical criterion to help us to make difficult choices about the way we should live. Yet from the fact that we might find it hard to discriminate between different values in theoretical terms, it does not follow that we cannot devise procedural means of managing the consequences of the contrasting values that happen to prevail within or between communities. Scepticism about values should not necessarily be equated with scepticism about procedures. In the absence of a demonstrable conception of virtue that everyone in a community can be expected to adhere to, an open ('discursive') politics may be the best theoretical option for citizens who accept that social co-operation is essential if they are to flourish together. And, of course, they cannot flourish on their own.

Plato portrays Protagoras and Gorgias as theoretically misguided but decent men. His real concern is with the implications of the loss of a theoretical criterion of judgement for social stability. And, in characteristic fashion, he dramatizes the issue in the persons of two alarming but memorable figures, Callicles and Thrasymachus. Callicles in the *Gorgias* argues not only that laws are mere conventions, but that they are conventions devised by the weak majority in order to restrain the strong, able and audacious minority. In this view of things, moral principles will appear persuasive only to the gullible or timorous. We are all naturally competitive, assertive and manipulative. Rulers disguise this truth from us while continuing to exploit us for their ends. We are a party to the deception because we dare not confront them directly and are content to settle for mediocre hypocrisy.

A similar argument is presented by Thrasymachus in the *Republic* from the perspective of the ruling elite. Justice, he argues, is 'nothing else than the advantage of the stronger' and simply expresses the interest of the 'established government'.[14] Socrates delights in showing that even within these terms of reference, government can be well or ill conducted. There is a world of difference between a cunning and effective tyrant who pursues self-interested policies and a capricious individual who follows his passing whims. A successful tyrant creates stable expectations. Even if we take him as a hypothetical limiting case, he still depends on social co-operation in order to flourish, though it will be based upon fear and deception rather than adherence to a set of defensible principles. Impulsive tyranny simply does not pay. If we grant that it makes sense to ask how a tyrant might best manage his affairs, then the door is opened once again to the introduction of a criterion of judgement.

Thrasymachus is in many ways an easy target for Socrates. He is presented as personally aggressive and abusive and it is certainly the case that Plato has not made the best possible defence of Thrasymachus's position. In a crucial passage in the *Republic* the argument is reformulated by Glaucon in a form that has continued to be influential to this day.[15] Glaucon argues that in the best of all possible worlds, we would each do as we pleased if we could be assured that no harmful consequences would follow from our actions. In reality, however, we are constrained by the fact that we need the co-operation of others if we are to flourish and fear their hostile reactions. What justice amounts to, in this view, is 'a compromise between the best, which is to do wrong with impunity, and the worst, which is to be wronged and be impotent to get one's revenge'.[16] In effect, Glaucon accepts the view of human nature implicit in the arguments of Callicles and Thrasymachus, but recognizes that a gambler's luck is always likely to run out. I cannot cheat effectively at poker if it is common knowledge that I am an inveterate cheat. Nobody would play with me. I would be left playing patience on my own.

Despite the brevity with which it is presented, this is a formidable argument. Themes drawn from it continue to resonate in modern liberalism, in the form of both social contract and rational choice theory. The stress on the individual, too, links this argument with a good deal of contemporary political philosophy. Why is Plato unhappy with it? We should be clear that, despite appearances to the contrary in the way the argument develops in the *Republic* and the received view of the implications of the text, Plato accepts that the fulfilment of the individual must be a central concern of any defensible theory. And in terms of the view he attributes to Socrates in other writings, he is not always hostile to rudimentary versions of social contract theory. In the *Crito* one of the central arguments Socrates uses to justify his decision not to escape from prison is that he has enjoyed a lifetime of benefits from the laws and institutions of Athens and should not, simply because it happens to suit his purposes for the moment, breach his tacit agreement to abide by the laws in expectation of reciprocal benefits.[17] To be sure, the *Crito* is among the earliest dialogues and probably reflects rather more the historical position of Socrates than the mature view of

Plato. But a commitment to the mutuality of a flourishing society remained a central theme throughout Plato's career.

Individual fulfilment, then, is a relevant criterion for Plato. Where he differs from the Sophists is in his account of what constitutes individual fulfilment. If you ask Protagoras how people should live, he is likely to say it depends who you are and where you are. Scepticism about the intrinsic value of particular ways of life left Callicles and Thrasymachus free to argue that whatever you happen to want, you will be better off having more of it than less. Glaucon moderates the position by emphasizing the prudential value of social co-operation. The criterion of value, however, remains an individual choice. The hedonistic pursuit of one thing after another is as worthwhile as a considered commitment to mutually compatible goals. The stress is on what individuals choose, not on what they may have good reason to choose.

Plato's concern, instead, is to specify what it might mean to have a good reason to lead one's life in a particular way. He takes it for granted that when we are engaged in any activity (making pots, wrestling, demonstrating mathematical hypotheses) we are applying criteria in such a way that it would make sense to say that we had made a mistake. His claim is that when we think about our lives in a rounded way, we still need to invoke criteria, even though the grounds for invoking one criterion rather than another may be obscure to us. Note that Plato insists that there must be a criterion, not that we should necessarily be aware of it. Not everyone will be able to live a fully self-conscious and transparent life. But they will still be able to lead a good life, provided that their best efforts are not dissipated in counter-productive ways. The key to fulfilment, for Plato, is harmony, both within the personality of the individual and in the wider society. Harmony, however, cannot be attained in all conditions and on any terms. It depends upon balancing needs and priorities that may only be apparent to the philosopher. Hence the philosopher is (in principle) in the privileged position of being able to specify terms for the fulfilment of everyone within a society.

The philosopher's claim to political authority depends upon his access to moral knowledge which is timeless in quality, valid for anyone, anywhere. In our day it has become extraordinarily difficult to defend such a position, especially in secular terms. Claims to eternal righteousness can more easily be made in religious terms, though the foundation in such cases is faith rather than argument, and there is no expectation that people who lack faith will find the spectacle persuasive.

For Plato, however, it is crucial that moral knowledge should be demonstrable. One of Plato's tactics is to argue from analogy with our classification of ordinary objects. We have an idea in our minds of what tables and chairs are; and we use that idea in assessing the adequacy of actual tables and chairs. An elegant 'chair' that could not bear weight might at best be described as a model. It might also be a practical joke. At all events, it would not satisfy all the criteria we invoke when we describe something as a chair.

If we are to talk about moral knowledge at all, Plato argues that we must similarly invoke a commanding or over-arching idea, though he is aware that its detailed specification will be deeply contentious. His claim is not that he (or any other philosopher) is actually in a position to give a definitive account of moral knowledge, rather that the idea of moral knowledge presupposes a certain structure of argument. He can thus refer to 'the idea of good by reference to which just things and all the rest become useful and beneficial'.[18] When Socrates is pressed by his interlocutors to be more specific, Plato (revealingly) allows him to resort to metaphor. In an image that is still central to our portrayal of knowledge, Socrates likens the relationship between the form of the good and specific good qualities to the relationship between the sun as a source of light and the specific things that are illuminated. In each case, if we try to dispense with the source of light or goodness, we will cease to understand how we can actually see or make judgements of value. And Plato takes it that Socrates has shown in his responses to Thrasymachus and Glaucon that judgements of value are essential to intelligible agency.

It is crucial for Plato that judgements of value should be based on knowledge and not personal preference. To make his point he envisages a divided line depicting stages of enlightenment. Initially we encounter casual opinions that have simply been picked up in the course of our daily pursuits. These opinions are based upon little more than sense perception. By degrees, however, we learn to classify and generalize. We are still dealing with the world as it appears to us, but we are at least beginning to build up a body of systematically ordered perceptions. A qualitative change occurs when we progress beyond perceptions to the structures that enable us to think constructively. We make this transition in our thinking through exposure to the hypothetical abstractions of mathematics. Plane geometry, in particular, enables us to picture the idea of the form of an object as clearly distinct from the image of an actual object. The culmination of the process is our recognition that through 'dialectic' (or pure reason) we can portray a world of ideas that is not dependent on the vagaries of sense perception but which nevertheless makes our experience intelligible.[19]

Plato does not claim that we can describe the world in terms of the categories of pure reason. It is significant that when he tries to give an account of the idea of the good, he has to resort to elaborate metaphors. His point, however, is that our ability to discriminate intellectually depends upon the fact that we can envisage a hierarchy of levels of understanding. He describes a conceptual journey from 'picture thinking', through belief, to understanding and finally reason, arguing that differences in degree of clearness and precision should be seen as proportionate to differences in degrees of 'truth and reality'.[20]

What are the political implications of this distinction between knowledge and opinion? To make his point, Plato again resorts to metaphor. In the famous allegory of the cave, Plato pictures men chained to fixed positions watching the images of shadows cast by a fire. Because they are unable to view these images from any other perspective, they take them for reality. Liberation from these illusions initially generates more confusion. An individual compelled to confront the source of the images would no longer be able to use the distinctions that had previously made his world intelligible. If he were forced to leave the cave and to face the sun as the real source of light and life, he would literally be blinded by the intensity of the glare. But learning to see by the light of the sun would amount to learning to see things as they really are. If our newly enlightened philosopher were obliged to return to the cave, we cannot expect him to be enthusiastic. Nor can we expect his erstwhile colleagues, still chained to their positions and taking shadows for reality, to be best pleased when told that their world is merely a series of illusory images. Enlightenment is not always welcomed.

It is nevertheless the case that the philosopher sees things aright. And he may well feel obliged to dispel the illusions of those who can come to know. Many people will find the demands of philosophy too arduous and complex. They will have no choice but to remain in the realm of illusions. At the very least, however, philosophers who do know the truth will be able to manipulate opinions in such a way that individuals will be able to live the most fulfilling life available to them. They will not be able to choose that life freely because they do not know how things really stand. The best they can hope for is that the crude ideas they live by (presented to them by the philosophers) will be fitted to their functional needs.

Plato developed the institutional implications of his theoretical position with astonishing imagination and insight. He endorsed authoritarianism as a natural corollary of his philosophical stance. Yet for all their intrinsic interest, these institutional details need not detain us here. We do not read Plato as political philosophers today because he defended authoritarianism; our interest is focused instead on his defence of an objective criterion of value. In all sorts of spheres we accept (something like) Plato's argument with barely a moment's hesitation. If we need major surgery, we are likely to feel most comfortable in the hands of a recognized expert. Expertise does not worry us in specialized spheres. We may even be happy to follow the advice of a psychiatrist in the approach we adopt to resolve some of our most intimate problems. Plato simply extends these arguments to embrace our moral and political lives more broadly. Some of us, argues Plato, understand better than others how human beings should lead their lives. He treats philosophers as experts in the art of living well. If fulfilment and a good life are important to us, it follows that we should accept the political authority of those who know best.

We should be clear that Plato was proposing a radical break with Athenian political practice. He had seen democratic politics transformed into faction-ridden populist tyranny. What value should be placed on a style of government that could endorse the execution of Socrates? For all that free enquiry and discussion may be regarded as the life-blood of philosophy, Plato could not support openness as a political ideal. His position may best be described as a pessimistic elitism. Even the very best are likely to be tempted by the status, power and riches that may accrue to the ruthlessly ambitious in a popular regime. In his own ideal polity in the *Republic*, the ruling class of guardians would be denied the opportunity to develop private and family interests. Their own satisfactions as individuals must be subordinated to the well-being of the community. The guiding principle of the community is to be the specialized fulfilment of functional roles. Ruling in the public interest is simply incompatible with the pursuit of private economic advantage. But by the same token, merchants and workers could not be expected to assume the responsibilities of government.

In one sense, Plato's recipe for a flourishing community is simple. He accepts that no one can flourish alone. We are each dependent upon one another for the satisfaction of any number of mundane needs. The community as a whole is best off if individuals specialize in the spheres in which they excel. Ruling itself is a specialized skill which requires unusual intelligence and self-restraint. Hence the worst fate that can befall a community is for governing responsibilities to fall into the wrong hands. One of Plato's arguments against democracy is precisely that desirable outcomes cannot be guaranteed in the cut and thrust of political competition. Given his assumption that only a small elite really understands the demands of ruling, there is always the prospect that clever but unscrupulous individuals would offer sops to the people as a mask for the pursuit of their own advantage. The Sophists accepted that this is the way the political game is always played. Plato, by contrast, argued that even shoddy politicians invoke a criterion of value. Once it is granted that standards can be good or bad, better or worse, it makes sense (at least theoretically) to envisage the very best standard as a measure against which practical choices and judgements might be assessed.

The most startling omission from Plato's theory is any conception of a positive role for political authority itself. This is especially surprising in the light of Plato's frank admission that he cannot present a definitive philosophical account of his view of the good. In these circumstances, we might have expected some discussion of procedural means that would make sound political decisions most likely. What we find in the *Republic*, instead, is a detailed account of a system of education aimed at the cultivation of philosophical excellence. Nor is Plato's system designed to open minds. He knows how he wants people to think. He has no regard whatever for the autonomous choices that individuals might make after careful and conscientious reflection.

What the *Republic* justifies, in the end, is manipulation of the members of a community by an intellectual elite. To be sure, he thinks this is the best way to defend the real interests of both individuals and the community. If ill-informed individuals are left to make public decisions for themselves, they are likely to make mistakes that will undermine their own prospects for happiness. He is even prepared to allow his philosopher-kings to propagate 'opportune falsehoods' in order to encourage people who cannot appreciate the philosophical justification for political order to keep to their appropriate roles in society.[21] He develops the practical implications of his claim that certain values are objectively defensible unwaveringly, without pausing to ask what philosophers should do if they are genuinely unsure of the truth of their doctrines.

Plato's most able pupil and follower, Aristotle, proved to be his most perceptive critic on precisely this question. The supposition behind the *Republic* is that the harmony of the community is a necessary condition for the individual members of the community to flourish in their different ways. In Plato's ideal polity, argues Aristotle, the pursuit of harmony actually becomes an obsession. What Plato seeks is not harmony but unity, of a kind that we might suppose would be possible or desirable within the family or a military alliance. But this is to mistake the nature of the state altogether. Aristotle contends that 'the nature of a state is to be a plurality'.[22] If in fact anything approaching Plato's *Republic* were ever to be realized in practice, it would amount to 'the destruction of the state'.[23] The crucial point, for Aristotle, is that the state is necessary precisely because it is made up of 'different kinds of men' whose interests will naturally differ.[24] In a properly constituted polity, they will each recognize that the harmony of the community is a necessary condition for each and every one of them to flourish individually. But that awareness will be the consequence of their coming together to discuss matters of mutual public concern. Recognition of the good that is common between them depends upon an institutional and cultural context that facilitates discussion and deliberation.

Where Plato had tried to defend an ideal theory that made politics as an activity redundant, Aristotle argued, in a celebrated phrase, 'that man is by nature a political animal'.[25] What he means by this deeply ambiguous phrase is that distinctively human capacities are stunted unless there is scope for discussion and mutual resolution of public affairs. He certainly does not mean that a life dedicated to public affairs is the most rewarding or fulfilling. Indeed in the *Nicomachean Ethics* he argues quite specifically that the contemplative life is superior to the practical life because it enables man to develop his distinctive capacities in the most complete way. '. . . reason more than anything else is man', says Aristotle, while the exercise of the moral virtues depends upon contingent circumstances that can never be entirely under our control.[26] In order to display generosity we need sufficient resources. Pure contemplation, by contrast, is self-generating, self-sustaining and intrinsically rewarding. Yet if practical life does not represent the height of human achievement, it nevertheless remains indispensable to the enjoyment of a full and reflective life. Even if we put a purely theoretical question to ourselves ('what is the best life for a human being?'), we cannot begin to make progress in our reflections until we envisage something like a conversation. Problems arise for us and can be considered from a number of different perspectives. What we call 'truth' is disclosed to us in the course of actual or hypothetical conversations.

Aristotle sees the capacity for considered reflection as the distinctive human attribute. Other creatures (bees, ants, cows, dolphins) may be said to be gregarious. But, argues Aristotle, rightly or wrongly in relation to the 'higher' gregarious animals, only human beings have the 'gift of speech'.[27] Other creatures may be able to give voice to their pleasures and pains, and their bellowing may constitute warnings to herd-members that a predator is at hand, but they are not capable of discussion. It is only through considered discussion that distinctions between the 'expedient and inexpedient' or between 'just and unjust' can be specified.[28] For Aristotle, 'it is characteristic of man that he alone has any sense of good and evil'.[29] He can thus come to awareness of the bonds of dependence that bind him to others, but at the same time use that understanding of natural necessity as a criterion to fashion the best possible life.

The stress in Aristotle is always on what is possible. He is not sympathetic to theoretical schemes that treat the constraints of practical life as somehow unnecessary or dispensable. We may deplore, with Plato, the fact that political life creates dissension and animosity. But it is deeply dangerous to suppose that in an ideal world we would all think with the same mind. A community is a coming together of people with different needs, skills and attributes. A properly constituted community fosters shared understandings that enable people to celebrate their common life as intrinsically valuable. Celebrating what is valued in common, however, involves recognition of the irreducible plurality of the constituents of the community. Aristotle never loses sight of the fact that human beings come to an understanding of the finer things in life through reflection on the bonds of necessity that link them together.

A capacity for reflection is not a universal blessing. Though human beings are naturally sociable, they are not naturally clear sighted. Thinking about the demands of social life is hard work and can be done well or ill. The fact that we are not self-sufficient creates endless possibilities for mutual irritation and conflict. Practical and political life is essentially problematic. If we need to think hard in order to live well, it follows that intellectual confusion can do a great deal of harm both to individuals and communities. Worst of all, ill-will coupled with intelligence sets the scene for the kind of tyrannical exploitation that Thrasymachus and Callicles had argued was the natural form of political life. Aristotle is aware that political acumen can be abused; but he does not accept that it will be abused everywhere and always.

Civilized politics is an intellectual achievement. It enables human beings to perfect themselves, to make themselves 'the best of animals', but only so long as they respect law and justice.[30] If human beings do not apply their intelligence for good ends, they become the 'most unholy and the most savage of animals, and the most full of lust and gluttony'.[31] Their capacity for self-deception means that even a discursive politics may be abused. Thinking clearly, however, enables them to recognize the significance of justice as the 'principle of order in political society'.[32]

Moving from theory to practice may still pose problems. Aristotle does not share Socrates's optimism (at least as portrayed by Plato in the early and middle dialogues) regarding the tight relationship between thinking about the right thing to do and then actually doing it. In imperfect situations, all sorts of contingent circumstances have to be taken into account before we can happily embark on a particular institutional course. Aristotle's crucial point, however, is that thinking seriously about how we should live is an integral part of the good life for us, given our needs and capacities. It is the exercise of practical reason, rather than specific preferences, that he values.

Aristotle's celebration of politics as an activity can be made to sound strikingly modern and has been a prime source for recent 'civic republicans' who see mutual involvement in matters of public concern as a crowning human achievement.[33] Indeed it is sometimes argued that we cannot develop our full potential as agents unless we take our turn in exercising public responsibilities. Arguments along these lines can certainly be drawn from Aristotle, though he did not share the enthusiasm for politics displayed in Pericles's famous funeral oration in Thucydides's *History of the Peloponnesian War*.[34] Political involvement was necessary for citizens in Aristotle's ideal scheme of things, but the rewards to be gained from it could not match the intrinsic satisfactions of pure contemplation. The active life, for Aristotle, important though it was, could not match the contemplative life.

The practice of both politics and philosophy, however, depended upon leisure. Aristotle had no sympathy for the egalitarian assumptions of the democrats of his day and we must assume that he would have found the interest-based politics of modern democracies equally distasteful. He was clear that deliberative politics was only possible for a small elite. Relations in other domains of life were hierarchical and authoritarian. The family was structured in terms of the 'natural' superiority of parents over children and husbands over wives. Households would also be able to call upon slaves to perform menial tasks. Indeed the Athenian economy as a whole would not have functioned without a large substratum of slaves. Aristotle's elite were able to cultivate a conversational ideal precisely because other people were obliged to work.

Aristotle's discussion of slavery is ambivalent and complex. He describes a slave as 'a living possession' or 'instrument' for the fulfilment of his master's wants and needs.[35] He justifies the relationship 'on grounds both of reason and of fact' because he regards it as self-evident that 'some should rule and others be ruled'.[36] Some people are naturally fitted to make choices and to give orders and instructions. Others (natural slaves) are able to interpret instructions and (sometimes) to engage in complex technical tasks. But they cannot initiate projects and will always tend to be dominated by appetite rather than reason.

This is a hoary argument that elites have found convenient in one form or another throughout the history of political thought. In Aristotle's day it functioned as part of the received wisdom of Athenian political life. A citizen would no more have regarded a slave as his equal than an orthodox white in apartheid South Africa would have accepted that a black should share the expectations and entitlements of a common life. For all that the argument is largely discredited, something like it can be discerned whenever peoples or classes are divided hierarchically according to their presumed natures. Racists in the southern states of the USA in the 1950s could appeal to a doctrine of separate but equal treatment in order to justify the exclusion of blacks from positions of authority or privilege. If the nature of peoples can be shown to be different, it follows that in equity they should be afforded appropriately different treatment. We would not dream of burdening a child with the responsibilities of an adult. Nor would it be fair to insist that everyone should take their turn at the most rigorous intellectual occupations, irrespective of their preparation or disposition. In these situations, respecting a person's fitness for a task is crucial to equitable treatment. What we find unpalatable is the assumption that whole groups should be barred from certain roles as a matter of principle.

It is clear from the qualifications that Aristotle introduces into the discussion that he recognized some of the weaknesses of the received Athenian view of slavery. Captives in war, for example, who may be coerced into slavery in return for their lives, owe their status to a tacit agreement. They can be described as slaves only by 'convention'.[37] They are forced to lead a life that does not accord with their natures. Aristotle does not try to stretch his defence of 'natural' slavery to cover this case. Indeed he has deep misgivings about the propriety of Greek enslaving Greek, since anything approaching parity of status undermines the basic claim that 'it is better . . . for all inferiors that they should be under the rule of a master'.[38] Problems arise for Aristotle because he finds it extraordinarily difficult to specify what it means to be inferior in a relevant sense. He was aware that slaves performed many sophisticated roles (in banking, commerce and public service) in addition to manual labour. The citizen elite were in fact dependent upon the expertise of slaves for the efficient pursuit of very many of their own interests. Yet Aristotle cannot allow that natural slaves are entitled to the deliberative respect that is appropriate for fellow citizens.

This issue brings us to the heart of Aristotle's account of political association. We stand before one another as citizens when we accept that coercion is not an appropriate means of facilitating collective endeavours. This is not to say that citizens will always be self-governing in a literal sense. Typically they will be involved in complex public relationships characterized by reciprocity, knowing 'how to govern like a freeman, and how to obey like a freeman'.[39] The point is that exercising authority is specifically on behalf of a wider citizen body. Citizens are answerable to each other in their efforts to fashion a good life for the community.

The principle at work here may sound like something a modern democrat could endorse. Yet the modern conception of citizenship embracing all adult members of a community is much broader than anything Aristotle defended. Citizens are defined as those who have 'the power to take part in the deliberative or judicial administration of any state'.[40] Their qualification is that they are best able to serve the good of the community. Adults who lack a capacity to serve that good would be excluded from citizenship in a properly constituted polity, no matter how numerous they may be.

Like Plato, then, Aristotle appealed to an objective notion of the good in order to legitimize political association, though he discarded the theory of forms as its ideal foundation. He did not see the objectively good as something that philosophers can grasp and then impose. The good life involves, among other things, thinking about the good among equals. A constitutional framework is essential for this activity, though it can take a number of forms. Aristotle argues that 'true forms of government . . . are those in which the one, or the few, or the many, govern with a view to the common interest'.[41] Each of these forms (kingship, aristocracy and polity) will involve a number of public roles for citizens, even if executive responsibility is focused in the hands of a single individual. When government goes wrong it is not the constitutional form that is necessarily to blame but the motivating spirit behind it. Kingship or monarchy degenerates into tyranny when the ruler puts his private interest before the public interest, just as aristocracy degenerates into oligarchy and polity into democracy.

Aristotle's dismissive treatment of democracy will surprise modern readers. What he fears is that government of the many will in practice amount to government of the poor in their own interest. It is the least bad of the degenerate forms of government, but nevertheless loses sight of the purpose of government which is to secure 'the common good of all'.[42] Our thinking about how we should govern ourselves should always be focused on this criterion. If citizens collectively feel that one among them is pre-eminently qualified to carry the burden of public responsibility, Aristotle thinks it would be absurd for them to settle for rule by the second best. More likely, however, we will find ourselves meeting as citizens with a range of skills and abilities, none of which would set us as individuals so

distinctively apart from our colleagues to justify the institution of monarchy in ordinary circumstances. For Aristotle kingship is more than a theoretical possibility. Yet his political thinking always starts from the practical
circumstances in which we find ourselves. We cannot rule out pre-
eminent goodness; but we may be wise to remain suspicious of its practical viability.

Aristotle was clear that theoretical prescriptions had to be attuned to a
prevailing political culture and circumstances. Thinking about what might
be the ideally best form of constitution, whether kingship, aristocracy or
polity should be preferred, had to be tempered by awareness of the political limitations of an active citizenry. As things stood in the Athens of his
day, he argued that a version of 'polity' or constitutional government was
the best practical option, combining (in different formulations) a balance
between oligarchy and democracy, rich and poor.

The constitutional detail need not detain us here. The principle at issue,
however, is of the first importance, and has been adapted in various representative schemes throughout the history of political thought. The
crucial point is that a political elite should be selected according to a relevant criterion and should then remain answerable to a wider body of citizens. The criterion invoked may not be the most ideally desirable. In an
oligarchy it would typically be wealth rather than merit. But the impact of
oligarchy is tempered by the need to retain the approval of citizens. The
different groups involved in political life would have to accommodate (at
least some of) the demands of opponents. The successful politician would
serve as a broker, fashioning a moderate course that would command the
widest possible support.

Aristotle accepted that the politics of compromise was second best. Yet
it served to preserve a fundamental condition for the continued enjoyment
of political association. The state, says Aristotle, 'is a partnership'; and,
more specifically, it is 'a partnership of citizens in a constitution'.[43] Political
association is to be contrasted with coercive relationships where the wiser
or stronger will always prevail. The state is not like a family or military
unit or limited organization focused on narrow goals. It is an association
of equals who regard coercion as an inappropriate means of pursuing the
ordinary business of public life among themselves. Procedures will be
available for coercive measures to be used in exceptional circumstances.
But these procedures will be publicly agreed by citizens in such a way that
the respect they owe each other will be reinforced.

Aristotle's focus on deliberative politics retains its attraction for many
of us today. Indeed we still use a political vocabulary that owes a great deal
to Aristotle and his predecessors. Our stress on public justification structured by a constitutional form is very much an Aristotelian ideal. At a more
basic level, our conception of a reflective politics has drawn heavily on
Aristotelian assumptions. We have largely accepted that a viable politics
must take the mutual needs and necessities of human life very seriously

indeed. Unrealistic assumptions about what is possible can have disastrous consequences for the well-being of communities. But we are not entirely constrained by necessity. In fashioning a scheme of workable institutions and practices, we also focus attention on what is desirable for people such as ourselves. None of this can be done alone. We flourish collectively and co-operatively or not at all.

Participatory politics, however, is desperately demanding, both intellectually and culturally. Aristotle was happy to use different notions of friendship as a way of characterizing the relations between citizens. More recent political traditions have focused on notions of fraternity or comradeship. In each of these formulations, citizens are defined in terms of qualities that are not universally shared, either within or between communities. Active citizens form a self-conscious and exclusive elite. They may be expected to have a sophisticated understanding of what they owe to each other. Yet within Aristotle's terms of reference, it is not at all easy to specify what is owed to strangers. The style of political life advocated by Aristotle depended upon assumptions that had begun to appear quaintly old-fashioned even as he wrote. Greek communities had ceased to be culturally homogeneous or economically self-sufficient. The *polis* was giving place to different forms of empire as an institutional norm. And new forms of political association would require a new political vocabulary.

3

Law

It is one of the most intriguing paradoxes of the history of political thought
that Plato and Aristotle in particular, and the political life of the Athenian
polis more broadly, should have exercised such a magnetic hold on the
political imagination for so many centuries. The *polis*, after all, was a
unique institution, offering a degree of political involvement for citizens
that has never been matched. Measured by its standards, the political life
of empires and states is bound to appear remote and disappointing. In
practical terms, we have all accepted that the political intimacy of the *polis*
cannot be replicated, that if we take our ideal of participatory democracy
from Pericles we are bound to regard the representative democracy of
modern times as a rather dull affair.[1] Hierarchies, bureaucracies, political
parties and interest groups estrange us from the large questions about the
good life that had so occupied Plato and Aristotle. The press of information available to us makes it very difficult for the ordinary citizen to grasp
even the contours of a political order. And, of course, information is often
presented from the perspective of political interest groups, which have
their own story to tell. In these circumstances, it is not surprising that few
of us can wholeheartedly endorse Aristotle's positive portrayal of man as
a political animal. Indeed we may regard scepticism about the political
virtues as a mark of personal distinction.

Disenchantment with politics, however, is not a modern phenomenon.
Even as Plato and Aristotle were writing, the political world they immortalized was drawing to a close. Aristotle actually served as tutor to
Alexander of Macedon, whose conquests effectively ended the political
autonomy of the *polis*. Rivalry between the Greek city-states had always
rendered them vulnerable to attack by a determined outside power. The
expansion of Macedonia had begun under Alexander's father, Philip. The
military exploits of Alexander extended Macedonian power beyond
Greece to embrace much of Asia and Egypt. The Macedonian empire itself
was not to prove long-lasting. After Alexander's death in 323 BC rivalries
almost immediately arose and the empire was to fragment. But there

would be no return to the *polis* as an autonomous political entity in Greece. City-states could no longer muster the economic resources to secure their positions militarily. For the Greek city-states the choice was between either a military confederation or domination by an outside power. The confederal experiment had been tried, but internal rivalries made it unworkable. In the event, the political problems of the Macedonian empire gave place not to a resurgence of the *polis* but to the emergence of a new hegemon. The territorial expansion of the Roman Republic left no scope for the independence that Greece had enjoyed in the period of Athenian/Spartan rivalry described by Thucydides. And with the triumph of Octavian in 31 BC the political fate of Greece was sealed for centuries to come as an integral part of the Roman Empire.

If the Greek city-states lost their independence, it should not be supposed that all aspects of life were suddenly transformed. Imperial governance in ancient times necessarily involved a good measure of local discretion in the conduct of daily business. In some ways the Macedonian empire served to reinforce the special role of Athens because Greek language and culture became the medium for elite groups throughout the empire. Plato, Aristotle and other classic writers were thus introduced to what amounted to an international audience. The intellectual legacy of Greece was secured precisely as its political autonomy was lost.

What could not be sustained, however, was the immediate urgency that informs the political writings of Plato and Aristotle. Schools of philosophy might pass on a technical language, but not the commitment to political philosophy as a means of shaping the conduct of political life. Indeed in the Hellenistic period (extending from the death of Alexander the Great to the consolidation of the Roman Empire under Octavian) ethical reflection ceased to treat the political order as the necessary focus of attention. The *polis* had embraced so much that was important in life that Socrates could not bear to leave Athens even to save his life. Aristotle in the *Politics* extols the friendship of citizens as the most rewarding relationship that we could expect to encounter. All this was lost in the Hellenistic period. Henceforth the satisfactions that had been gained from politics had to be sought in other fields. Community as the embodiment of all that was worthwhile no longer made the same sense to people living under distant (and alien) imperial authorities. The restricted circumstances of public life obliged thinkers to fashion a new political vocabulary.

The classic critical discussion of this development is to be found in Hegel's condensed account of the emergence of individualistic styles of thought in the *Phenomenology of Spirit*.[2] In a remarkable phrase, he describes the various philosophies of the Hellenistic period as the response of the 'unhappy consciousness' to the feeling of estrangement from the public world. In a quite literal sense, people had ceased to feel at home in a world framed by public institutions that were not their own. Public life, in other words, was no longer an expression of their cultural self-understanding. In these circumstances, detachment from public life was seen to be indispensable to personal well-being. One could not, of course, flourish alone. But it would be folly to identify one's most important interests with the fulfilment of a public role within the life of a community. To engage in public life at all was to risk frustration, disappointment or worse at the hands of strangers. A wise man would not expose himself to such hazards unnecessarily. If he had to commit himself to public business, it would always be with a mental reservation. However his public interests might suffer, he retained the option of withdrawing from the hurly-burly of practical affairs, satisfying himself that his capacity to make personal judgements was more important than the adventitious fate of his projects.

This negative attitude was clearly not fertile ground for political philosophy. The Hellenistic period did not yield any classics of political philosophy. And the only unambiguous classic of the later Roman period was produced by Augustine as the empire in the West was on the verge of collapse.[3] What we have, instead, are a series of ethical and cultural responses to the perceived inadequacies of politics as an activity. A common theme is clear. We would become politicians in the broadest sense only out of necessity. When attention is turned to what it might mean to lead a good life, it would be in terms of the satisfactions that could be secured for us as individuals. In a very important sense, the community is now regarded as a fiction that might very well beguile and deceive us. Personal well-being is a product of clear thinking. We should focus on our physical and social needs, taking care not to be misled by the conventional wisdom of the community. We may well come to different conclusions about how important social co-operation is to our personal satisfactions. But only fools would gullibly accept that personal interests should be sacrificed or subordinated to the greater good of the community.

Individualism became the dominant *motif* of social and political discourse. Yet it came in a variety of forms, some of them starkly opposed on specific issues, despite common adherence to a set of fundamental assumptions. Hellenistic individualism was a direct continuation of the sophistic style which we associate with Plato's portrayals of Protagoras, Thrasymachus, Callicles and others. What is missing, however, is the stress on individual assertion for political ends that both Plato and Aristotle identified with democracy as a political form. Without a *demos*, there simply would be no scope for such activity. Narrowly self-interested individuals would seek, instead, to secure themselves in a much more amorphous world that they could not expect to control.

We seek in vain for a full-fledged political philosophy in the Hellenistic individualists. Interpretation of their positions is, in any case, made more difficult because so few of their texts have survived. In the case of two of the major figures, Epicurus (341–271 BC) and Zeno (331–261 BC), we are dependent on such sources as Diogenes Laertius's *Lives of Eminent Philosophers* for reasonably accurate accounts of their leading ideas.[4] In what is often an uncritical compilation of anecdote and quotation, we have to proceed very cautiously before advancing strong interpretative claims. We have to search for corroboration of Diogenes Laertius in more fragmentary quotations from other surviving texts. This is a painstaking and highly specialized form of philosophical scholarship. The kind of textual analysis that has been devoted to the works of Plato and Aristotle is simply not possible when our primary objective is to piece together a coherent position from the fragments that may be available to us. But we do at least have the parameters of Hellenistic individualism in place.

Epicureanism and stoicism constitute the currents that have had the most lasting impact on Western political thought, though the late connotations of these traditions are significantly different from the earliest forms. Epicureanism, in particular, is often misleadingly caricatured. Epicurus's hedonism is not a justification of indulgent gratification. His point is simply that whatever satisfactions we may derive from life come to us as individuals. Our primary concern should be not to maximize the passing pleasures that come our way but rather to ensure the stable enjoyment of our minds and bodies. The wise man, in Epicurus's view, does not take chances. He is most certainly not a gambler. He will ask himself what is most vital to the continued enjoyment of his own existence. For Epicurus, it is fear of death that torments most people above all else. But what is it about death that people actually fear? They may be terrified by the prospect of ghastly punishment in *hades* after they die, but they have no grounds whatever for supposing that the stories they find so disconcerting are actually true. If they think about themselves as physical beings, they will have to accept that death is simply the absence of life. In a positive sense, it is not anything at all. And it makes no sense to be terrified by nothing. If we focus on the satisfaction of minimal necessities, we avoid the frustration, disappointment and fear that dominate life for the gullible. Our happiness is best attained through presence of mind. Serenity should be our goal, not the hectic pursuit of one pleasure after another.

The political implications of Epicurus's thought are nowhere developed in any detail. Diogenes Laertius, however, provides us with a series of maxims that are highly suggestive in relation to the later history of political philosophy. The most that we can expect from Epicurus is a conception of institutions and practices that enable us to minimize the risks of social life. He rejects the teleological treatment of justice out of hand. If it means anything at all, natural justice should be seen as 'a symbol or expression of expediency', designed 'to prevent one man from harming or being harmed by another'.[5] Thus justice cannot be regarded as an absolute value. At most, it is the product of 'an agreement made in reciprocal intercourse'.[6] The sole objective is the avoidance of 'the infliction or suffering of harm'.[7] As individuals, we are always self-interested, though not always enlightened. We may be tempted in our folly to treat one another unfairly. Indeed Epicurus accepts that 'injustice is not in itself an evil'.[8] A wise man, however, should recognize that a consequence of treating people unfairly will very likely be hostile reactions from them. Acting 'unjustly' (in the conventional sense) exposes us to the machinations of those we may have harmed. We may fear for our lives or interests. We will certainly not be able to guarantee even minimal social co-operation. If, as Epicurus argues, fear is the sentiment most disruptive to the quiet enjoyment of our lives, it follows that we should always have a prudent regard for other people's expectations.

Anyone familiar with Hobbes may be tempted to read more into Epicurus's position than the texts available to us strictly warrant. What we have is certainly an incipient version of social contract theory, but it has no place for anything remotely resembling a foundational contract. The Epicurean wise man treats his engagements on an *ad hoc* basis. He will argue only that justice is 'something found expedient in mutual inter-course'.[9] When he considers his obligations to specific people on particular occasions, he will always be aware of the circumstances in which he committed himself. As circumstances change, so will commitments. There can be no talk here of a social contract (whether actual or hypothetical) as a basis for political obligation. At best, Epicurus urges us to guard against the reactions of those we cannot expect to control; at worst, he suggests we should avoid company altogether.

The stoics developed a much more complex and flexible view of the appropriate response of a wise man to the vagaries of the world. They endorsed the individualism and materialism of the Epicureans, but contended that individuals were an integral part of a natural order that is fundamentally rational and benign. In reflecting on his own best interest, the wise man would be led ineluctably to see himself in relation to the material world, including other people. Peace of mind remained an ideal, but it could not be attained by means of detachment and withdrawal. Individuals were neither self-contained nor self-sufficient. The wise man used nature as his guide in striving to understand where he stood in a complex system of relations. He treated his own well-being as a function of a proper understanding of a wider whole.

The stoics remained much closer to Plato and Aristotle than the Epicureans. Yet though they stress the significance of connection for a good life, there is no sense that individual well-being is subordinate to the common good of the community. Individuals pursue their myriad projects in unimaginably complex ways. Whatever they want, however, they are going to need the co-operation of other people if they are to achieve lasting satisfaction. They will also need to understand how the natural world works. At each step, the stoic wise man will strive to go with the grain of events and natural forces.

The stoics embrace a reflective politics that takes seriously the 'natural' ties of family, friendship and locality. But they try to avoid treating these attachments as abstract ideals. They constitute the complex backdrop against which we must lead our lives. Just as it would be foolish to suppose that we could flourish without attachments, so we should take care not to identify ourselves exclusively with any specific attachment. It would not do, for example, to imagine that we could only lead a worthwhile life in Athens, or to lament that all would go well for us if only circumstances were different. We must accept the world, though it may not be intelligible to us at first glance. Above all, however, we must avoid being swept away by enthusiasms that distract our attention from the way the world functions. Considered judgement after rational reflection is the key to human flourishing.

It should be clear that within stoic terms of reference no especial significance should be attached to the fact that we are members of one political community rather than another. A political community or 'city', argues Dio Chrysostom (circa 40–120), is simply 'a group of men living in the same place who are administered by law'.[10] Whether or not we happen to be living in a community that is 'administered by law' in the proper sense is entirely adventitious. When we see rights, duties, privileges and burdens being distributed within communities by rich and powerful individuals to reward followers or to marginalize opponents, then we can assume from the outset that the natural harmony of reasonable relations has been distorted by malice and folly. In these circumstances, no-one can flourish, least of all those who assume they are rich and powerful. At each turn their fortune is dependent upon an ability to pre-empt opposition. Yet there can be no grounds for trusting anyone. And enjoyment is always vitiated by the dread fear of being out-manoeuvred at any moment.

Whatever else we might want to say about life on such terms, we would have to accept that it is unreasonable. It could only be willingly embraced by someone who had failed to understand how human beings flourish. A cynic might claim that the city is like a bazaar; we have to learn to live on our wits. But that, according to the stoic, would be to confuse the city with (what would later be termed) a state of nature. Dio Chrysostom says that if what the poets report of Ninevah is true, then it should not be regarded as a city at all 'since it is mad'.[11] If arbitrariness is the rule, then nature's basic precept has been breached. The regularity of nature should serve as an ideal for the rulers of cities; the temporary order that may be attained coercively is merely a simulacrum.

In the last resort, stoic commitment is not to persons or places but to values. These values are open to anyone, anywhere, though it is likely that they will be realized most effectively in a community with a vibrant intellectual culture. What binds individuals together, finally, is a shared commitment to the pursuit of virtue. This is precisely what would be lacking in Ninevah, where fear and opportunity guided people's conduct. Crucially for the stoic, personal well-being is enhanced if we can enlighten others. Without such a meeting of minds, genuine fellowship is impossible. Indeed Dio Chrysostom goes so far as to suggest that it makes more sense to treat the universe as a whole as a city than the paltry places where individuals take advantage of one another's weaknesses.[12] Reason enables us to discover 'the only strong and indissoluble principle of the community and justice'; and anyone capable of reason may be regarded as a member of an ideal community.[13]

The cosmopolitan theme fitted perfectly the circumstances of the Roman Republic as it expanded its dominance in Europe, Asia and north Africa. Over time Rome was transformed from a city state to the centre of a cosmopolitan empire, effectively the centre of a world system in the estimation of educated people throughout its jurisdiction. Judgements which identified cultural, moral or political excellence with the contingent circumstances of a particular community would clearly be unworkable in an empire on this scale. Roman pre-eminence would only be effectively maintained if means were found to accommodate (at least some of) the ambitions and aspirations of disparate individuals and communities. The successive extensions of Roman citizenship to embrace conquered peoples, initially in relation to private law and civil obligations in the second century BC but finally involving full citizenship rights, was crucial in this development. It marked a radical breach with the idea of the *polis*, in which citizens could be presumed to share language, culture and folk memories. The contrast with Aristotle is instructive. He had agonized about the appropriate qualities citizens might need in order to qualify them for public responsibilities. In one form or another, the distinction between Greek and barbarian continued to do a great deal of work in his political philosophy. In a Roman imperial context, by contrast, it made no sense to characterize citizens in terms of the special qualities that distinguished them from outsiders. The empire was a world system. The specification of roles and responsibilities was entirely an internal matter.

The institutional history of Rome is too complex to be closely examined here.[14] Constitutional procedure, in any case, was something of a façade concealing a desperate factional politics that has been portrayed vividly by the great Roman historians.[15] The celebrated struggle of the orders between patricians and plebs served as a backdrop for personal rivalries, often involving access to lavish military and economic resources. It seems to be very remote indeed from the principled criteria of Greek political philosophy. Yet questions of legitimacy could not always be equated with power in its various forms. The Romans themselves were acutely aware that the precarious institutional balance could easily be upset by the ambitions of powerful figures. Indeed the personal rivalry between Caesar and Pompey was among the factors that precipitated the collapse of the republic in the first century BC. The formal establishment of the empire in 31 BC, however, did not mark the emergence of an untrammelled military dictatorship. Very many of the institutional arrangements were initially maintained, including crucially the semblance of an advisory role for the senate. Empires, like republics, have to accommodate a wide range of interests in order to function effectively. The military is one among many means of maintaining order. It is also one of the most expensive in terms of resources and opportunity costs.

The cosmopolitan perspective was thus a response to necessity. In its stoic form it was widely shared among the Roman intellectual elite down to the collapse of the empire in the West in the fifth century AD. The political principle at the heart of the doctrine, however, has continued to be a vital dimension of attempts to mediate cross-cultural disputes. The point is succinctly expressed in Cicero's treatise *The Laws*. He dismisses out of hand the claim 'that everything decreed by the institutions or laws of a particular country is just'.[16] How should we respond, he asks, if the laws have been imposed by a tyrant? Would it make any difference if the entire population welcomed tyrannical laws? Cicero argues that unanimous agreement is irrelevant if the laws in question are intrinsically unjust. To use his own example, a constitutionally 'correct' procedure cannot authorize the execution of a citizen without trial. 'There is one, single, justice. It binds together human society and has been established by one, single, law. That law is right reason in commanding and forbidding.'[17] Note that in this passage Cicero does not specify precisely what 'right reason' is. He simply regards it as an implication of the fact that people separated by cultural circumstances nevertheless share something important in their humanity. This has nothing to do with the particular agreements that groups of citizens may have come to in their assemblies or gatherings. Questions of justice cannot be decided in terms of the law that happens to have been enacted. Justice, says Cicero, 'is completely non-existent if it is not derived from nature'.[18] To be sure, this does not help us very much if we are genuinely puzzled about what justice prescribes. But it sets us on our guard against the complacent assumption that shared opinion may be taken to be a sufficient indication of right thinking.

Cicero's defence of the role of reason in politics is in many respects philosophically disappointing. He simply asserts that the 'virtues are rooted in the fact that we are inclined by nature to have a regard for others; and that is the basis of justice'.[19] He does not explain why, if this is the case, we should find ourselves so often ensnared in intractable conflicts. If we are all so well-disposed towards each other naturally, we may wonder why we need coercive institutions at all. Yet this is to approach the issue from the wrong perspective. We know from ordinary experience (even among well-intentioned people) that disagreements occur naturally. Our concern should not be how these disagreements may ideally be eradicated, but rather how we should respond when we find ourselves in disagreement over fundamental issues. Cicero's supposition is that agreement is possible if we think hard enough about these difficult cases, at least in principle. He assumes that coming to agreement does not depend upon the accident of happening to share certain values. The claim here is that our capacity for rational reflection is no more tied to contingent circumstances than the laws of the natural world itself. Reason is a natural faculty. We may see the precepts we can rationally defend as equivalent to articles of natural law. Cicero barely hints at the implications of this position. However he effectively highlights assumptions that may be said to be implicit in the fact that we can establish co-operative relations in culturally diverse circumstances.

Cicero's discussion of natural law is significant as a measure of the conventional wisdom of his day. His position is best seen as a filtering of Greek theory to suit the concerns of a much more narrowly practical culture. Indeed no Roman figures attained anything approaching the philosophical stature of the Greeks. They were exceptionally clear-sighted, however, in their grasp of the practical measures necessary to sustain a diverse empire. Greek theory was not rejected so much as set on one side. The idea of the collective good of a discrete community had ceased to be relevant in Roman politics. Roman ethics, too, was preoccupied with the idea of a good man rather than a good community. What remained, given the facts of cultural diversity, was the urgent practical question of how social co-operation among strangers may be facilitated. The stress here had necessarily to be on the framework within which people worked, rather than the particular goals they sought to achieve. Given the paucity of philosophical defences of the idea of law in Roman literature, we have to be careful not to read more into their positions than the texts warrant. By the same token, however, it would be misleading not to highlight the philosophical significance of practical developments that have had a lasting impact on political life in the West.

Our principal source for Roman law is the remarkable *Corpus juris civilis* promulgated by the emperor Justinian in 533 AD. The date here is significant. The Roman empire in the West had already collapsed. The capital in the east, Constantinople, was open to a range of cultural influences that changed the way law was understood in important ways. Most significantly, increased exposure to Greek philosophy and religious metaphysics led to concerted efforts to see law as a system rather than a series of authoritative pronouncements. In the eyes of later commentators, this is often seen as a corruption of the limpid style characteristic of the (so-called) classical period of Roman law in the second and third centuries AD.[20] However that may be, our knowledge of Roman law would have been impoverished had it not been for the systematic obsession of Justinian's Code. Few works from the classical period have survived intact, with the exception of Gaius's *Institutes*.[21] We are often dependent on what has been preserved in the *Corpus juris civilis* for a balanced understanding of the earlier period.

The *Corpus juris civilis* is essentially a compilation of authoritative legal opinion from the second to the sixth century, together with an analytical introduction to the law derived largely from Gaius's *Institutes*.[22] A group of leading jurists, headed by Tribonian, worked for three years to draw up a definitive codification of law. The purpose was made clear by Justinian himself in a preface. The military extension of the empire had involved peoples from disparate cultures being 'governed by the laws which we have made or settled'.[23] But how could this law be made intelligible to the many peoples who were subject to it? Roman law had developed through more than 400 years of learned comment from jurists, coupled with the authoritative endorsement of consuls and emperors. The situation had become so complex that the ordinary subject could not be sure what the law prescribed in specific contexts without consulting an expert. And experts themselves would often disagree about the interpretation of points of detail. Justinian urged that 'the august constitutions which were previously in disarray' should be reduced to 'lucid harmony'.[24] He also charged that Tribonian and his colleagues should 'compose Institutes' so that people might acquire the 'first rudiments of law not from ancient stories but through the splendour of the Emperor' in such a way that they might 'receive the truth in these matters without that which is unnecessary or erroneous'.[25] Justinian's Code purported to contain 'the first elements of the whole of legal knowledge'.[26] Legal opinion that was not preserved in the Code was regarded as irrelevant for practical purposes. Here was a definitive statement of the requirements of the law. No other text was accorded any authority.

Detailed treatment of the *Corpus juris civilis* would be out of place here. As a source for understanding both Rome as a legal order and the minutiae of private life, it is unparalleled. Yet the weight of four centuries of outstanding scholarship makes this a difficult text for philosophers to handle.[27] The opening sections of the *Institutes* establish philosophical terms of reference without actually defending them.[28] And in the body of the text important philosophical issues (for example, regarding the idea of legal personality) are lost in a welter of detail. Read in conjunction with other contemporary texts, however, and with half an eye on legal practice, it is possible to discern the rudiments of a theory that modern legal scholars would describe as an early version of legal positivism.[29] It would be deeply misleading to identify Roman legal theory too closely with legal positivism in its developed forms. But within the riches of the text we can gather materials to construct (something like) a 'pure' legal theory.

Students coming to the *Institutes* for the first time should not expect to find a fully worked out philosophical position. As a compilation reflecting views drawn from four centuries, Justinian's Code inevitably has flaws as a theoretical statement. But even the *Institutes*, which were designed as an introduction to the body of the law, leave crucial problems unresolved. In the event, the twin aims of being comprehensive in scope and systematic in treatment could not be fulfilled. The initial characterization of the distinct spheres of the *jus naturale*, the *jus gentium* and the *jus civile*, for example, are left in confusion because different authorities have been followed. Thus, following Ulpian, natural law (*jus naturale*) is defined as that law 'which nature instils in all animals', extending the scope of law far beyond the jurist's sphere of competence to include not only 'humankind' but also 'all animals which are born on land or in the air or sea'.[30] While this formulation might seem to be close to the stoic view of a law regulating the operations of the universe as a whole, the important contrast between man-made law and immutable law is drawn in rather different terms. Gaius is the source in a passage which draws the essential line of demarcation in the *Corpus juris civilis*. Immediately after the characterization of natural law, the text focuses instead upon the distinction between the *jus gentium* (the law of nations) and the *jus civile* (the civil law). 'Civil law and the law of nations . . . are distinguished in this way. All peoples who are governed by law and customs use law which is in part particular to themselves, in part common to all men: the law which each people has established for itself is particular to that state and is styled civil law as being peculiarly of that state: but what natural reason has established among all men is observed equally by all nations and is designated *jus gentium* or the law of nations, being that which all nations obey.'[31]

It is clear that the *jus gentium*, like the *jus civile*, serves both descriptive and prescriptive purposes. Any organized community will be seen to have adopted a common core of legal practices; and, because it is deemed to be the rationality of such practices that recommends their universal acceptance, there is a *prima facie* case for the arbitrary enactments of the *jus civile* to defer to the *jus gentium* in the event of conflict between them. Conflict is generally avoided because the *jus gentium* came to be regarded simply as law that gained universal currency. Thus a civil law that ran counter to the *jus gentium* could be accommodated by conceptually modifying the content of the latter.

The theoretical uncertainty in the specification of the two spheres reflects the practical pressures that led to the emergence of the *jus gentium*. As Rome's political and commercial importance grew, so dealings with foreigners increased; and hence there was an urgent need for a code pliable enough to regulate the transactions between Roman citizens and subjects of other legal systems. The law that developed was a simplification of Roman practice rather than a synthesis of contemporary codes. In effect the *jus gentium* acquired two distinct characters: the one theoretical, as the expression of natural reason, barely distinguishable from the *jus naturale*; the other practical, as a rudimentary system of international law.

The compilers of the *Corpus juris civilis* left the further refinement of these categories to later commentators. For most practical purposes, the *jus naturale* and the *jus gentium* could be identified. It was accepted that some institutions (like slavery) had flourished in all communities 'through force of circumstances and human needs' but yet remained 'contrary to natural law' which specified that 'all men are originally born free'.[32] But this was not allowed to blur the fundamental distinction between the *jus naturale* and the *jus gentium* on the one hand (which gave expression to the

universal features that would be evident in the arrangements of any organized society) and the *jus civile* on the other (which was the sum of the
enactments that a particular society had been able to devise in response to
fluctuating circumstances). The position is classically summed up in a
passage that conflates the earlier characterizations of the *jus naturale*
and the *jus gentium*: 'Natural laws which are followed by all nations
alike, deriving from divine providence, remain always constant and
immutable. But those which each state establishes for itself are liable to frequent change whether by the tacit consent of the people or by subsequent
legislation.'[33]

The *jus naturale, jus gentium* and *jus civile* provided a framework which
enabled Romans to pursue their affairs in essentially legal fashion. Yet the
distinctions in themselves do not furnish a philosophical defence of legal
order. We have to go beyond the *Corpus juris civilis* to find anything along
these lines in Roman literature. Cicero, as is so often the case, proves to be
a treasure trove for these purposes. Not only did he have a glittering career
in law and politics, including a tempestuous period as consul in 63 BC, but
he was also assiduous in preserving his major speeches as a record of his
career. It can be said without exaggeration that we know more about
Cicero than any other figure from the ancient world. Even his biography
comes vividly to light in the remarkable set of letters that have been preserved.[34]

In a defence of the rightful inheritance of Aulus Caecina, the details of
which do not concern us here, Cicero advances a perceptive argument in
defence of the idea of legality.[35] How, he asks, is property secured and
enjoyed in Roman society? Not, certainly, through the generosity of benefactors, who are in no position to ensure that their instructions are in fact
followed. '. . . the property which any of us enjoys', he argues, 'is to a
greater degree the legacy of our law and constitution than of those who
actually bequeathed it' to us.[36] Without implicit reliance on the law, we are
all vulnerable to the machinations of others when we try to secure an
appropriate disposition of our properties. 'The law is that which influence
cannot bend, nor power break, nor wealth corrupt; if law be overthrown,
nay, if it be neglected or insufficiently guarded, there will be nothing which
anyone can be sure either of possessing himself or of inheriting from his
father or of leaving to his children.'[37] The point, of course, is broader than
our right to dispose of, hold or inherit property. What the law provides is
'freedom from anxiety and litigation'.[38] Neglect of specific rights to private
property should thus be seen in the broadest context, for though 'the individual only is affected if he abandons his inheritance, . . . the law cannot
be abandoned without seriously affecting the community'.[39]

The crucial issue to focus on is the significance of stable expectations in
a flourishing polity. Cicero broadens the discussion in *On Duties*, which
was his last work and provides something of an overview of his moral and
political ideas.[40] In relation to benefits which the state confers directly on

individuals, Cicero stresses that they should be 'both practicable for the state and necessary for the commons'.[41] In this way public benefits are sustainable and predictable.

The position is similar with regard to property rights. Cicero argues that private citizens should 'suffer no invasion of their property rights by act of the state'.[42] In a passage that would later be developed by John Locke, Cicero describes 'the chief purpose in the establishment of constitutional state and municipal governments' as the maintenance of individual property rights.[43] He does not treat the right to property as a natural right, but he is categorical that a state cannot flourish unless such rights are secured.

Cicero singles out arbitrary policy initiatives as a principal source of disorder and confusion. Agrarian laws, for example, which in Roman politics were urged on leaders as a means of redistributing wealth and rewarding followers, especially among the army, Cicero contends have served to reduce politics to factional accommodation rather than deliberation for the public good. Rewarding friends and followers involves driving occupants 'out of their homes'.[44] Public measures to relieve the burdens of borrowers can only be effective if the expectations of lenders are threatened, creating what modern economists would describe as 'moral hazard'. Individuals are encouraged to take unreasonable chances because they assume that the state (or a particular influential faction) will intervene to save them from the consequences of their own folly. The upshot is that projects are planned with an eye on personal and clientelistic factors rather than the tangible benefits that may accrue from a course of action. If individuals are powerful enough, they will sell their support to the highest political bidder.

Cicero's discussion of justice is contained within very narrow parameters. He accepts that 'harmony' and 'equity' are the 'foundations of the commonwealth', but in effect argues that neither can be attained without scrupulous respect for property rights.[45] Again, when he defends an inclusive rather than exclusive polity, it is in terms of the 'interests of citizens' united on the 'basis of impartial justice'.[46] In this argument, however, impartiality is specifically contrasted with arbitrary liberality. Cicero's response to Caesar's dictum, 'let them live in their neighbour's house rent-free', is to ask who precisely is paying the bills.[47] If 'I have bought, built, kept up, and spent my money upon a place', do you have a right to 'enjoy what belongs to me' without my consent?[48] According to Cicero, this amounts to no less than 'to rob one man of what belongs to him and to give to another what does not belong to him'.[49] On this basis, the only criterion in public life would be which thief is the strongest.

It would be rash to read more into Cicero's defence of legality than his texts warrant. Nor is it necessary to endorse the narrowness of his preoccupation with property rights. What we can begin to see in his writings, however, is an incipient philosophy of law that the Roman jurists themselves nowhere provide. Roman law was, of course, to serve as a template for legal reflection in the West for centuries to come. But to this day political philosophers seldom do justice to the riches at their disposal.

The Italian philosopher Giambattista Vico (1688–1744) is an exception to this rule. His political philosophy was steeped in jurisprudential literature. And in a major but neglected treatise, *Il diritto universale* (Universal Law) of 1720–2, he developed a philosophy of law drawn largely from Roman sources.[50] Vico went back beyond the *Corpus juris civilis* to chart a developmental account of the way Roman law had developed over the centuries. His concern was to characterize the function of law in changing social circumstances.

From Cicero's account we can see that the relationship between natural law and civil law is still uneasy. Vico focuses directly on this problem. He argues that the categorical separation of natural law from civil law has severed a connection which is essential to a proper understanding of the basis of an ordered social life. Civil law is often portrayed as a framework imposed to facilitate the ordinary conduct of affairs. Seen in this light, it might be regarded as little more than an arbitrary assertion of authority. Vico treats that as only a part of the story. A particular regime might seem to be little more than a vehicle serving the interests of the most powerful family, group or class. Certainly Cicero's position is (quite rightly) associated with the interests of the patrician order. The point to stress, however, is that an established order functions as a point of reference for subject groups and furnishes its own set of moral and procedural criteria.

Vico distinguishes three related dimensions that must be taken into account in the consideration of any regime: (1) a group will need to exercise power in order to enforce its rule; but (2) in justifying and explaining its policy a limited conception of political legitimacy will necessarily be invoked; and (3) in providing a viable framework a regime will actually be advancing wider moral and political interests that can emerge only in an organized society. The essential contrast for Vico is between the chaos which is a consequence of man's corrupt and fallen nature and the benefits that derive from living under legal restraint. Hence it would be a mistake to equate the advantages which follow from the rule of law with the intentions and purposes of specific (necessarily fallible) lawgivers. And enactment should be considered both as an assertion of authority, much as the Roman jurists had treated the *jus civile*, and as an expression of reason, along lines similar to those sketched by Cicero in his discussion of natural law. Vico's point is that an adequate understanding of law depends upon showing how the ends of natural law have to be achieved through the civil law. In Vico's terminology, the ideal purpose of law, the 'true' (*verum*), has to be grasped in the context of individuals trying to establish a semblance of order, the 'certain' (*certum*).[51] In specific cases, one or other dimension might be uppermost. In the establishment of a political regime all efforts might be focused on the consolidation of power to the exclusion of a wider consideration of the ends that a community was designed to serve. But, despite appearances to the contrary, some of those wider ends would in fact be served. The task of the philosopher is to balance both *verum* and *certum* in the appraisal of a particular system.

Vico's point is aptly illustrated in his repeated references to Ulpian's dictum, *lex dura est, sed scripta est* ('the law is harsh, but it is written').[52] If we think of civil law only as an arbitrary assertion of authority, then we miss the crucial reliance of any system of law on stable expectations. To be sure, stable expectations are not everything. There are stable expectations in prison.[53] But we can only make plans for ourselves if we can reasonably assume that people whose views are entirely unknown to us are likely to respond in predictable ways. Our expectations are often disappointed in specific cases. Practical misjudgement leads to frustration, as anyone who has tried to organize a public event can attest. Yet the law provides a framework that enables us to structure our strategies and responses. We can take certain things for granted while pursuing our more important projects. I am unlikely to be assaulted if I contradict a colleague in a departmental meeting.

Vico expresses the point in his own technical language. We may think of certainty as the 'proper and perpetual attribute of voluntary law'; yet in that certainty there is in fact an 'impression of truth'.[54] If we lack sufficient self-control or foresight to follow regular rules, we are at least obliged to obey determinate laws through the authority of a legislator. Indeed it is only through experience of living under fixed laws that we later acquire the subtlety to insist upon good ones. Thus if our choice is between a law that is known and obeyed or one that is morally sound but unintelligible in the context of a given way of life, then the weight of justification is entirely behind the former. In order to be classed as law at all (rather than arbitrary coercion) certain criteria have to be satisfied. Whether we like the specific provisions of a legal system or not, we all benefit (though in different degrees) from the form of legality.

Among modern philosophers the position is best defended by Hart in *The Concept of Law*.[55] Following Wittgenstein and Winch, he adopts a rule-following model of law as a practice, highlighting the rules (formal or tacit) that enable agents to set themselves standards in the conduct of their business.[56] An agent can only ask herself what she should do (whether as a judge, a lawyer or a litigant) within the context of a practice constituted by procedural rules. This is not to say that the idea of law as an authoritative command backed by coercive power is wholly redundant. This may well be how law is regarded by people who do not acknowledge the authority of a legal system or who see themselves as free-riders prepared to exploit the passive obedience of others; but it certainly does not help us to explain what makes conduct within a legal practice intelligible.

Hart draws a distinction between purposive (rule-following) behaviour and habitual behaviour, though he is very cautious about drawing out normative implications. He is interested in law as such, and not in any particular variety of law that may have emerged in a given context. A theory of law that simply reflected the culture and values of a particular community would (in Hart's terms) be no theory at all. He avoids reference to substantive conceptions of the good life which have been the stock-in-trade of the traditional theory of natural law. He accepts that a formally viable legal system may be morally reprehensible. The fact that legal rules are always grafted on to a moral context has (for Hart) no implications for the specification of the formal requirements of a legal system.

Hart makes the point emphatically in his insistence that 'criteria of validity in any given legal system' are actually matters of fact, stemming from the 'rule of recognition' that happens to be endorsed.[57] A rule of recognition may be complex (as in an elaborate juridical culture such as the United States) or formally straightforward (whatever the Queen in Parliament enacts will be recognized as law in the United Kingdom) or crude (the tyrant's will, Rex I in Hart's example, will be taken to be law).[58] Hart's point is that we can make sense of each of these legal systems in terms of criteria furnished by a rule of recognition, though in each case the rule of recognition may be arbitrary. Yet it makes the world of difference that what we are talking about here is a rule. To be sure, the whim of Rex I constitutes a rule only in the most primitive sense. But recognizing that it is the existence of a rule that makes public co-operation possible gives us grounds, all other things being equal, to prefer a rule which is more predictable in its operation rather than less. It is certainly what the plebeians sought in the celebrated struggle of the orders that culminated in the Law of the Twelve Tables in Rome in the fifth century BC.[59] And it was precisely the loss of that certainty that Cicero and others deplored as the Roman Republic tottered towards terminal crisis in the first century BC.

The crucial distinction at work in Hart's argument is between 'primary' and 'secondary' rules of obligation.[60] It is perfectly possible to envisage a community in which dealings between people would be regulated in terms of customary rules. Social ostracism clearly constitutes a powerful coercive constraint in contexts where alternative life-styles are not available. In a purely customary society one is not faced with choices between options but with more or less reluctant compliance. But, as Hart makes clear, such arrangements of unofficial rules can only work in 'a small community closely knit by ties of kinship, common sentiment, and belief, and placed in a stable environment'.[61] Customary rules are simply given. As soon as we start wondering about their desirability, we introduce hypothetical considerations that may be contentious. The need to accommodate change of any kind obliges us to make judgements. Our concern here is with the most rudimentary level of social organization. The point to stress is simply that a (hypothetical) customary society ceases to function effectively when alternative possibilities are made available. Disputes about ends have to be settled somehow (through fighting, ritual manipulation, social pressure or whatever). But it soon becomes evident that ordinary business requires authoritative procedures. Considered practical judgement cannot be made in chronically uncertain situations. The introduction of these authoritative procedures (or 'secondary rules') constitutes, for Hart, 'a step from the pre-legal into the legal world'.[62]

Analytical focus on the idea of a legal order should not be confused with defence of a polity providing a minimal institutional framework. A pure legal order is neither possible nor desirable. What the Roman example serves to highlight is the role legal order plays in enabling other values and activities to flourish. Significantly, the most lasting Roman achievement was in the sphere of private law. In the imperial period, rights under private law had been extended to all free men. It is, of course, a vexed philosophical issue to specify what free status might involve. The point to stress here is that it was seen by the Romans as a matter of legal stipulation. Free men enjoyed private rights under the law. Slaves did not, though they enjoyed some legal protection as the property of free men. Anyone who had been specified as a full bearer of legal rights was thus enabled to call on the institutional defence of his interests, irrespective of the particular values he may endorse.

The specific provisions of Roman law are only of incidental interest here. Details of family life, property relations, contractual obligations and so on necessarily reflect the substantive values of the period, though in the imperial period the law had to be flexible enough to embrace a bewildering array of cultural practices. The narrowly Roman legal inheritance always occupied a privileged position in the body of the law, but it was not the particular values of Rome that made the law effective.

In the last resort, law is important because it enables strangers to engage in predictable co-operative practices. A full philosophical defence of law would have to focus much more on the character of human agency than any discussion we find in the *Corpus juris civilis*. Stoic philosophy had provided the essential ingredients for such a theory, though it was not to be fully articulated until the early modern period. Where the Greeks had been pre-occupied with political identity and engagement, the Romans had a sophisticated grasp of the practical requirements of agency. If Roman theory is wanting, experience of legal order has undoubtedly been a major factor in the development of civil philosophy.

4

The Earthly City

Roman legal culture was highly specialized. It provided a framework which enabled individuals to go about their business, despite the immense cultural and linguistic divisions that the empire had never sought to bridge. Unlike the intense experience of the Greek *polis*, life viewed in purely legal terms had a necessarily mundane quality. It did not encompass the finest things people were capable of, but they were at least left in relative peace to pursue their many and varied concerns. Indeed the longevity of Roman hegemony led educated people to assume that its dominance was a permanent feature of any conceivable practical life.

These assumptions were shattered in the most dramatic fashion by the sack of Rome by Alaric in 410. The Roman Empire had not, of course, crumbled with the one assault. There had been complaints since Cicero's days that all was not well with the culture of the Roman elite. Corruption and decadence had taken lurid forms in the personal conduct of some of the emperors. Sophisticated critics could argue that the public culture of the empire had been undermined by its own notional guardians. The fact remained, however, that the empire had survived three centuries of cultural decadence. Alaric's triumph administered a symbolic shock that obliged the elite to re-examine some of their most fundamental values. For pagan traditionalists, the Roman Empire had come to be identified with civilization itself. And the very idea that it could be successfully assailed by barbarians led people to ask themselves why a vigorous (and seemingly invincible) regime should now be so weak and divided. A convenient scapegoat could be found in the Christian religion. The conversion of the empire to Christianity by imperial edict under Constantine in 310 had led to a neglect of traditional pagan rites and practices; and it was no accident that the administrative and military prowess of the empire should reach its nadir as the influence of Christianity approached its zenith. Or so the argument ran. What we see among the far-flung Roman aristocracy is a self-conscious return to the roots of pagan culture, a cultivation of habits of mind which had never, in fact, been wholly abandoned.

The rise of religion in late Roman culture is a complex story that cannot be told here. At one level, it may be seen as a response to the limited satisfactions afforded by public political culture in the imperial period. One cannot live by legal rules alone. Religion, in various forms, enabled individuals to cultivate a rich 'interior' life that was untouched by the shortcomings of public culture. What mattered most to them could be best expressed in terms of their identification with God, or a set of ceremonial practices, or close fellowship with a community of believers. This opened up new possibilities for judgement and appraisal. Fresh ways of describing the significance of human life had become available. And it was by no means clear that conventional political values would survive close scrutiny from this perspective.

The focus in this chapter is specifically on the Christian contribution to political thought. It will necessarily involve consideration of theological issues that modern political theorists may find disconcerting. Yet the theological context highlights an issue that is easily forgotten if our attention is concentrated too narrowly on the political realm. Early Christian thinkers were clear that the significance of politics had to be seen in relation to wider assumptions about the value of human life. In modern theoretical debates these assumptions may not be shared. But when we think about the place of politics in our daily lives, we too bring to the discussion a host of assumptions drawn from the different facets of our experience. Most of us would find it very difficult to talk about these assumptions in a systematic way. The strength of medieval theology is precisely that it had a clearly articulated view of the importance that should be attributed to the various dimensions of our experience. The fact that we tend not to think about these things theologically should not excuse us from thinking about them systematically.

Christian politics was from the outset informed by theology, but it was not simply deduced from Christian doctrine. A Christian politics, indeed, has always been the product of complex arguments, drawn from both philosophy and theology, designed to make the contingent circumstances that shape our experience intelligible in relation to a wider scheme of ideas. Theory is thus elaborated as (necessarily unpredictable) events unfold.

It is barely possible to imagine circumstances more dramatic than the imminent collapse of the Roman Empire in the West. For Christian theorists, the matter is complicated because the 'official' status accorded to the Christian religion was seen in influential quarters as a signal factor that had rendered traditional Roman values politically ineffective. Christianity, no less than the Roman Empire, had to confront a moment of acute crisis. Indeed Christians found the decline of Rome especially difficult to accommodate within their own scheme of things. The conversion of the empire to Christianity had seemed to fit perfectly with a providential view of history, extending the influence of the Church to the furthermost limits of the civilized world. With the demise of the empire an imminent possibility,

Christian thinkers had to seek a fresh understanding of the Church's relationship with the secular world. Not only had they to exonerate themselves from the charge that their beliefs and practices had undermined the foundations of the empire; but they had to discern a meaning or significance in the traumatic events which had shaken the civilization they had all taken for granted.

St Augustine of Hippo was ideally qualified to address these tasks. As the product of a mixed marriage, with a pagan father and Christian mother, he had a solid grounding in both the secular and religious dimensions of the Roman tradition. Indeed, before his baptism in 387 (at the age of thirty-three), he had been thoroughly eclectic in his intellectual and spiritual tastes, flirting at different times with Stoicism, Manichaeism and neo-Platonism. In his professional career, as a teacher of rhetoric, he had shown outstanding promise, earning advancement to a prestigious post at Milan in 384. After his baptism, however, all his intellectual energies would be marshalled in the cause of the Church. By the time he was consecrated as bishop of Hippo in 395, he had a considerable reputation as a philosopher, theologian and controversialist. Uniquely among his contemporaries, he had mastered both the pagan and Christian intellectual traditions. When he came, then, in the *City of God*, to state the case for Christianity against a resurgent paganism, he could exploit an insider's knowledge of Roman culture in order to expose its shortcomings.[1]

The *City of God* poses special problems for political theorists. Not the least of these difficulties concerns the organization of the text itself. Written in instalments between 413 and 426, the work is both immensely long and discursive. Far from following a distinctive line of argument throughout, Augustine gives us absorbing accounts of a host of issues which preoccupied him. Nor did Augustine conceive the text as a treatise on political theory. His principal concern was rather to highlight the gulf that separated two world views, Christian and pagan, at a time when there was still a tendency to treat Christianity as an ambiguous offshoot from the common stock of classical culture. This, in itself, was a task with profound political implications. The burden of the argument, especially when set against the classic texts of Greek theory, was deeply negative. Augustine contended that the political world had no intrinsic significance. He regarded the state itself (and the various institutions of social life) as a series of constraints imposed upon men and women because of their sinful natures. The truly significant relationship in any individual's life was not between himself and the state but between himself and God. One's appraisal of political institutions, in this scheme of things, could not be in terms of their intrinsic merits but rather in terms of their providential role in the fulfilment of God's design for humankind.

This attribution of a limited and derivative significance to political life is Augustine's distinctive contribution to political thought. We should be clear, however, that in reacting against the state or *polis* as the ideal focus for our actions and deliberations, he was not simply denying the validity of secular institutions. Unlike the Stoics, Cynics and Epicureans, Augustine was not arguing for a radical individualism. His claim was not simply that the state could not embody the highest aspirations of life; but rather that human reason itself was an inadequate instrument for the fashioning of a way of life. We need the state and its institutions to restrain us, reprehensible though the values of any specific state might be. Given our predicament, we cannot flourish without the state; yet neither can we find fulfilment in it. What we need, above all, is to see the state aright, in relation to matters of permanent value. It was precisely this perspective that Augustine sought to provide in the *City of God*.

The contrast at the core of the *City of God* is between the eternal values enshrined in God's ordered universe and the transience and fickleness of all human endeavour. What makes the *City of God* so distinctive as a theological treatise, however, is its penetrating account of human motivation. We are portrayed as wretched creatures tossed by impulses which we can struggle to subdue but will never finally master. The lust for power and sex are given special prominence. But even in the finer details of life we are liable to find our judgement distorted by greed, envy or vainglory. In his portrayal of the darker side of human nature, Augustine draws very much upon his own observations of affairs. Indeed as a stylist he is often singled out for the vividness and realism of his descriptions. It gives his writing an immediacy that is lacking in later scholastic theology. For the political theorist who may be diffident about theology, it is some comfort to know that the individual portrayed in the *City of God* is a close relation of the creature we have grown accustomed to in the writings of Machiavelli, Hobbes and Hume.

Noting the affinity between Augustine's account of human nature and that of later (more secular-minded) pessimists is no more than a beginning. What has to be grasped is that the distinctive cast of political pessimism in the Western tradition has theological roots; and Augustine's remains the most authoritative statement of the view that has come down to us. Here was a man straddling the pagan and Christian worlds, thoroughly versed in Roman literature, who was anxious to specify precisely where Christianity stood in relation to classical culture. It is a measure of his achievement that Christian writers would approach Greek and Roman philosophy within his frame of reference for the next 800 years. Indeed his reading of Plato as the classical philosopher who had most nearly grasped the essentials of the Christian position persisted until the eighteenth century. All this must be borne in mind when we come to consider Augustine's importance in the history of political thought. It is something of a commonplace to describe the Western tradition as a synthesis of classical and Christian culture. But if we want to understand that tradition, it is essential that we grasp precisely how the two cultures were mutually absorbed. Seen in this light, Augustine assumes a double significance: not only is his synthesis of pagan and Christian thought worthy of attention in its own right, it also set the parameters for Christian reactions to the classical world.

Augustine's strategy is to establish a providential framework which highlights the positive significance of the series of events that had shaken the confidence of Christian and pagan alike. Behind his concern with the historical record lurked a larger philosophical purpose. His intention was not only to stress the futility of hoping to influence a course of events but also to sever the connection in conventional attitudes between virtue and desert. The virtuous and the wicked are equally vulnerable in the face of the vagaries of experience. The distribution of worldly felicity between individuals was something that simply had to be accepted as a datum, susceptible of neither theoretical nor moral justification. But there was a lesson to be learned from our responses to fortune. The proper reaction to life's variable prospects was a disdain for the goods it provided. One could, of course, seek comfort and well-being; but it should not have a moral significance attached to it. This was the flaw at the heart of pagan religious culture. The equation of practical success with civic or religious virtue had led to an undue importance being attributed to occurrences that would always be beyond human comprehension. We may exult in the world's goods or be overwhelmed by its ills, thereby identifying our conceptions of ourselves with the shifting fortunes of daily life. Yet there was an alternative view. The apparent unfairness of events could be seen as a sufficient reason for seeking one's criteria of significance elsewhere, in a world of eternal values disclosed by reason or faith. Such a perspective had the obvious merit of accepting the transience of affairs without relapsing into scepticism. Not the least of the advantages of what is usually regarded as a thoroughly 'other-worldly' philosophy is in fact the psychological support it lends to us in our daily pursuits, struggling to do the best we can for ourselves in intractable circumstances.

A systematic devaluation of the temporal sphere was a central concern of the *City of God*. But Augustine was not intent upon dismissing all involvement with secular affairs as corruptive or irrelevant to one's spiritual life. Indeed Christianity is distinctive among the welter of religious and philosophical ideas which flourished in the later Roman period in its emphasis on the historical disclosure and ultimate triumph of its doctrine in time. Christianity had presented itself as an historical philosophy, with elaborate criteria for appraising the secular world it was confronting. Augustine had thus to combine his critique of pagan worldliness with the rather more subtle task of estimating the significance of successive civilizations.

Rome itself presented him with his most sensitive problem. It was a comparatively straightforward matter to show that Rome had suffered calamities long before Christianity had displaced the pagan gods, thus exonerating Christianity from any direct responsibility for the decline of the empire. In Augustine's account, pagan religious practices had undermined Rome's civic culture from within, condoning sacrilegious and obscene entertainments and failing to sanction a doctrine of right living. And Roman philosophers, gifted though they might have been in technical respects, were not equal to the task of sustaining a flourishing civic and moral culture.

Nor is the failure of the philosophers an incidental consideration. Human weakness is a dominant theme throughout the *City of God*. Our moral and intellectual fallibility is such that reason alone can never serve as the foundation for a way of life. Augustine's strictures against the philosophers should thus be read in the context of his larger case against the autonomy of the secular sphere. The fact remained that Rome had once flourished and had subsequently come to grief. It was crucial, given the context in which he was writing, for Augustine to give some account of this remarkable train of events. Indeed the fortune of Christianity had become so commingled with the history of Rome that he could not effectively address his more narrowly theological concerns without some discussion of its fate. In the event, Rome served him as a paradigm case, illustrating both the significance and the limits of political society. And it was through reflection on the corruption of Rome that he was enabled to counterpoint the transcendent purposes of the Heavenly City.

The corruption of Rome, in fact, presents Augustine with much less of a dilemma than its manifest success at its zenith. An empire that had been seen to be coextensive with civilization itself could not be without some merit or significance. Augustine was not content with the rather facile teleological view which looked beyond Roman institutions to the role of the empire in fostering and sustaining the Church. Instead he attributes Rome's success to the wisdom of her institutions and the austerity of her public and private morals in the early days. Quoting Scipio from Cicero's *De Republica*, he likens 'concord in a community' to 'harmony in music', with 'different classes, high, low and middle', united, 'like the varying sounds of music, to form a harmony of very different parts through the exercise of rational restraint'.[2] The crucial element in this 'harmony' or 'rational restraint' is, of course, a notion of justice. Augustine again draws upon Cicero for his initial definition. A community is seen not simply as 'any and every association of the population, but 'an association united by a common sense of right and a community of interest'.[3] It follows from this 'that a commonwealth only exists where there is a sound and just government', leading inexorably to the conclusion that a tyranny of any kind (whether rule is by one, a few, or the many) is tantamount to the dissolution of the community.[4]

Augustine does not wholeheartedly endorse this contractualist position. Later in his argument he will be at some pains to demonstrate that a true sense of justice presupposes the realization of the ends enshrined in Christian doctrine. But he was equally reluctant to accept a position which would not only deny that Rome was a commonwealth properly so called but would also exclude the very possibility of a just polity being established. Even in a hypothetical Christian polity, a distinction between the elect and the reprobate would persist, leading to division and conflict between groups and individuals and to a need for institutional procedures for the pursuit of purely secular goals. A revised contractualism serves well enough to account for the limited agreements we make in order to further our practical interests. According to these more modest criteria, Augustine could endorse the commonly held view that Rome 'was better ruled by the Romans of antiquity than by their later successors', without thereby compromising his central contention that the political world in general had only a relative significance in relation to the wider ends of human communities.[5]

Accounting for the decline of Rome was a much more straightforward affair. Augustine had no need to revise the standard accounts of Rome's degeneration to be found in Sallust or Cicero. If it was moral probity that had once sustained an empire, it was moral corruption which finally sealed its fate. Instead of glorying in a reputation for public service, Romans began to 'lust for power' for its own sake.[6] The moral restraint which had enabled the country to flourish and secure its liberty gave place to unbridled greed and sensuality. Public office, which had once been regarded as a sacred duty, was now seen as a private perquisite, significant only as a means of satisfying one's appetites. Under pressure of this kind, it was only a matter of time before the empire would collapse. Anxious to ensure that no responsibility for the decline of public spirit should attach to Christianity, Augustine could let the story of Rome's cultural inanition speak for itself. Impeccable Roman authorities were sufficiently vehement in their condemnation of the later empire to serve his purpose. It remained for him simply to augment their accounts with particularly vivid illustrations of the decadence that had been tacitly supported in pagan religious practices, pausing always to highlight the rectitude of Christian doctrine by contrast.

We should be clear, however, that (for Augustine) Rome's decline is not to be explained in terms of a concatenation of contingent circumstances. The moral corruption which had sapped the vitality of her culture could not be reversed simply by men taking stock of their situation and remedying such abuses as came to their notice. Augustine's point is much more far-reaching. His contention is that any moral, religious or political theory which attributes undue significance to worldly felicity will be rendered absurd in the face of the misfortunes that necessarily befall us in the course of our engagements. Some of these problems will appear to be self-inflicted, with ambition, greed and lust for power upsetting the most carefully devised plans; others will be the product of natural disasters that could not (in principle) have been foreseen; but misfortunes of both sorts will always be a feature of the human condition.

Nor can we expect to discern a pattern in the misfortunes that afflict us. Good and bad are equally vulnerable, unable either to understand or guard against life's calamities. Yet Augustine insists that there is an order to events. What might appear to be random or fortuitous is actually 'in accordance with the order of events in history, an order completely hidden from' men, 'but perfectly known to God himself'.[7] Earthly dominion, for example, which is generally counted among life's boons, is given to both good and evil precisely in order that we might be weaned away from ephemeral values. The very fact that Rome had once flourished so mightily thus makes it a perfect example for Augustine of the transience of the things of this world. One has either to accept that human life is wholly unintelligible or have recourse to the larger fideistic framework afforded by the *City of God* for an account which lends a positive significance to our overwhelming sense of bewilderment.

In the last resort, even the strongest polities are rendered ineffectual as events unfold. Rome was compromised (crucially) by its reliance on worldly ambition, 'the hope of glory in the sight of men'.[8] And though there was 'a clear difference between the desire for glory before men and the desire for domination', there was nevertheless a 'slippery slope' which led from 'excessive delight' in the one to 'burning passion' for the other.[9] Once the lust for domination predominates in our deliberations, self-restraint is effectively at an end. We stoop to the 'most barefaced crimes' in order 'to accomplish' our 'heart's desire', becoming 'worse than the beasts' in our cruelty and self-indulgence.[10] The type of rule associated with this disposition is personified in Nero, for whom public office was simply a means of private gratification. A tyranny on Nero's scale nevertheless remains a part of God's order, designed to chastise a wayward people and to encourage the wise to seek their salvation elsewhere.

So much, at least, can be gathered of God's plan for men from an examination of the rise and fall of empire. But Augustine is clear that this is only to scratch the surface. What God's ulterior purpose might be is always beyond human comprehension. Yet the supposition that there is a rational design behind appearances, in the civil no less than in the natural world, serves Augustine as a regulative assumption in his account of the limitations of practical and theoretical endeavour. The postulation of an altogether different manner of association in the Heavenly City functions as a criterion in his explanation of the darker side of human nature. As a political theorist he is concerned with the forces which impel human beings to contend with one another for status and reward – ambition, greed, lust for power – in disregard of the wider ties that bind communities together. In order to understand the specifically political dimension of his thought, however, it is essential to grasp at least the lineaments of the theological views that inform his position.

Two issues, in particular, need to be addressed before we can examine his central political arguments. In the first place, given that Augustine is concerned (among other things) to justify institutional restraint in terms of the deficiencies of human nature, we need to ask ourselves how responsibility for actions is to be understood in a scheme of things based upon the presupposition of an omniscient and omnipotent God. And secondly (and relatedly) we must establish precisely what significance should be attached to the evil that institutions are designed to counter.

On the question of the relationship between God's foreknowledge and man's free will, Augustine found himself trying to steer a middle course between a fatalistic determinism on the one hand and a radical indeterminism on the other. Both positions are incompatible with crucial aspects of Christian doctrine. A universal determinism would equate God's providence with fate or destiny, leaving no scope for the special relationship that sets human beings apart from the rest of God's creation. We are dependent upon God; but we nevertheless have a capacity to share in God's reason, understanding something of the nature and limits of our own conduct. If we feel ourselves to be distant from God in our current predicament, this is no more than a consequence of our sinfulness. By sinning as a species, we have destroyed an original harmony. Henceforth our reason will be swamped by the conflicting demands of the passions, undermining any sense we might have had of our own integrity as individuals and pitting us against our fellows. The crucial point for Christian doctrine is that the pitfalls and calamities of practical life should be construed as self-inflicted wounds. Without this assumption, God would appear to be little more than a perverse and spiteful tyrant. In Augustine's view, however, the misfortunes that God visits upon us are a necessary means of our redemption. Suffering actually fosters self-awareness. It enables us to enjoy God's grace without sacrificing our position as self-conscious agents.

If a providential determinism denying the reality of free will is thus unacceptable to Augustine, it does not follow that he should commit himself to a view that simply acknowledged God's providence while exempting the human will from its sway. Augustine took particular exception to Cicero's treatment of the issue in *De Divinatione* and *De Fato*. Cicero had supposed that granting God's foreknowledge involved acceptance of the view 'that everything happens according to necessity'; but this would leave our understanding of human life in disarray since we would have no grounds for making moral judgements.[11] There would be 'no point in making laws, no purpose in expressing reprimand or approbation, censure or encouragement'; nor, in the sphere of justice, would there be grounds for 'establishing rewards for the good and penalties for the evil'.[12] According to Augustine, however, such a view is based upon a false dichotomy, as if allowing some scope for free will necessarily involves the denial of God's foreknowledge. He argues, on the contrary, that man's free will is actually a part of God's preordained order. There is no need to belittle the significance of our agonizing about how we should behave simply because God happens to know from the outset what the outcome of our deliberations will be. Nor does God's foreknowledge make him a cause of our conduct. As Augustine puts the point succinctly, 'the fact that God foreknew that a man would sin does not make a man sin'.[13] Responsibility, on this view, remains with man; it is the consequence of sin that manifests an inexorable inevitability.

It cannot be claimed that Augustine's attempt to balance the notions of free will and determinism is, in the final analysis, successful. The emphasis in his argument is always on grace rather than desert, relegating the individual to something of the role of a marionette. And, indeed, later workings of an essentially Augustinian doctrine, especially in the forms of Calvinism and Jansenism, were treated with hostility or suspicion by the Catholic hierarchy. Orthodox theologians of the sixteenth and seventeenth centuries were troubled specifically by the implications of the doctrine of predestination for an understanding of man's free will. But the issue had, in fact, surfaced in Augustine's own day, in his controversy with Pelagius. Whether or not Augustine's view is defensible, however, it tells us a great deal about the character of his political thought. His stress on grace rather than human endeavour in the redemption of mankind was predicated upon a profound conception of sin. In this view, we are moulded in Adam's image and tainted by his original folly. Our sinful natures set clear limits to what can (in principle) be achieved in the secular sphere. All that can be expected from social and political institutions is a moderation of the consequences of sin. The realization of our finer possibilities is deferred to another realm.

How, then, is evil to be understood in Augustine's thought? In his earlier days, while still a follower of the Manichaeans, Augustine had conceived of good and evil as two independent principles, locked in cosmic conflict. And it is true to say that certain remnants of Manichaean doctrine continued to inform his mature thought. Indeed the fundamental division in the *City of God* between spiritual and earthly realms can be traced back to Manichaean sources. The dualistic account of good and evil, however, could no longer be accommodated to his conception of God. A God whose attributes included not only goodness but also omnipotence and omniscience could not be portrayed as in any way vulnerable to the force of evil. But this, of course, left Augustine with the task of explaining how such a God could tolerate the existence of evil.

Augustine's response to the dilemma was to deny the reality of evil itself. He contends that everything in nature has been created good. What we call evil is not, in fact, a separate entity or principle but 'merely a name for the privation of good'.[14] It can best be understood by analogy with the harmony of nature, where even the loss of an eyebrow on a human face detracts from the beauty of the whole. In this example, even (apparent) want of harmony should be interpreted in a positive light, fulfilling some aspect of God's design which we have failed to discern.

Augustine conjures up an image of original harmony undermined by human sinfulness. He portrays human beings, like all other natural creatures, as faultless in their original creation. As a species, we once enjoyed a perfect harmony in our faculties and dispositions. All this has been destroyed, however, by an act of will. Augustine focuses on the detail of the biblical account. Adam and Eve (whatever specific misdemeanours they might have committed) chose not to follow God's instructions. They subverted the original harmony of their existence through disobedience, exchanging the effortless enjoyment of God's goods for pain, hardship and death. Thenceforth they would know no tranquility. Their minds would be tossed by incompatible desires, leading to deep anguish as reason and will are set in opposition to one another.

We may recognize the source of our difficulties from the Bible, but we lack the resources to redeem ourselves by taking thought. The corruption of our natures is such that our unaided efforts are likely to deepen our misery. In Augustine's account, human ingenuity has become a slave to the passions that tear us apart; the more we strive to disentangle ourselves from the myriad snares of practical life, the more complete our slavery becomes. The wise man, no less than the fool, is trapped in a vicious circle of sin and degradation. What had occurred at the Fall was wilful, a deliberate 'falling away from the work of God'.[15] Augustine sees the will itself as the root cause of evil, 'the evil tree which bore evil fruit'.[16] Hope for us, in these circumstances, depends upon turning away from ourselves. The choices we make will be genuinely free when our subservience to sin has been eradicated. And this can only be achieved through acknowledging our total dependence upon God's grace.

Here we see the beginnings of Augustine's fundamental distinction in the *City of God*. While we all pursue happiness, we do not necessarily follow the same path to our goal. Some, blissfully unaware of their corruption, will insist on living 'by the standard of men'; while others, acknowledging their weakness and degradation, will accept that they must live 'by the standard of God'.[17] At issue here is a choice between the paths of falsehood and truth, sin and righteousness. To persevere in following men's standards is, in fact, to embrace a contradiction. Since our principal objective is to promote our own welfare, our motive in sinning must be to promote that end. The upshot of sin, however, is always an exacerbation of the internal conflicts that undermine our best endeavours, leaving us wretched and vulnerable even in a moment of (apparent) delight.

What distinguishes the life of the righteous is not a more successful pursuit of earthly happiness but an acceptance that such happiness is simply unattainable. While 'death, deception and distress' disfigure human life, all three consequences of sin, we are denied the enjoyment of the happiness which our natures crave.[18] The righteous, instead, fix their sights upon an image of heavenly bliss. By setting the possibilities of practical life in a proper perspective, they are given peace of mind. But, more important in the context of political theory, they are enabled to see a positive significance in institutions and arrangements that might otherwise seem irksome and unnecessary.

To Augustine, then, the crucial division in the history of social and political life is not between separate territorial units or rulers and ruled but between the righteous and the reprobate. He considered 'the rise, the development and the destined ends of the two cities, the earthly and the heavenly, the cities which we find . . . interwoven, as it were, in this present transitory world, and mingled with one another'.[19] And, significantly, he traces the source of the two cities not to sets of incompatible principles but to 'two kinds of love: the earthly city was created by self-love reaching the point of contempt for God, the Heavenly City by the love of God carried as far as contempt of self'.[20] The one city 'glories in itself', looking 'for glory from men', the other 'glories in the Lord', finding 'its highest glory in God, the witness of a good conscience'.[21] In the earthly city, 'the lust for domination lords it over its princes as over the nations it subjugates'; while in the Heavenly City, 'those put in authority and those subject to them serve one another in love, the rulers by their counsel, the subjects by obedience'.[22] What is at issue is whether we should live according to the transient standards which regulate the affairs of this world or according to the eternal standard enshrined in God's providential order. And though we might not have the intellectual capacity to discern the rationale of God's order, we are nevertheless enjoined to follow his injunctions as an act of faith.

We should be clear, however, precisely what Augustine is claiming for his distinction. He is not suggesting that the earthly city and the Heavenly City correspond with any actual communities or institutions. Though he had drawn his models from his reflections on the Roman Empire and the Church, he never wavers in his contention that good and evil are intermingled in all human institutions. Even the Church, which might have been supposed to be exempt from the limitations imposed on human institutions by the consequences of sin, is seen as a human contrivance. Though inspired by God's will, it is nevertheless made a reality by human endeavour. And, like any other institution, it is open to use and abuse by men whose motivation is purely selfish. Indeed Augustine was in no doubt that Christianity's acceptance as the official religion of the Roman Empire had compounded the difficulties involved in identifying the Church as the expression of God's will. Once status and influence had been accorded to the Church as an institution, it was clear that it could be regarded by the ambitious as a convenient means of self-advancement. Both the elect and the reprobate were thus involved in the life of the Church, swimming 'without separation, enclosed in nets until the shore is reached'.[23] The Church certainly served God's purpose and was a vehicle for the ultimate triumph of the Heavenly City but, as a temporal institution, it suffered from the inevitable distortions and trials associated with human corruption.

Nor was Augustine oblivious to the positive benefits that the earthly city could confer. Even though, earlier in his argument, he had described kingdoms without justice as 'gangs of criminals on a large scale' and criminal gangs as 'petty kingdoms', he did not deny that standards of some sort are employed in the earthly city.[24] A criminal gang itself should be understood in terms of certain principles of association ('a group of men under the command of a leader, bound by a compact of association, in which the plunder is divided according to an agreed convention'). All that distinguished a criminal arrangement from a kingdom was the scale of villainy, 'the title of kingdom' being conferred not as a consequence of the 'renouncing of aggression but by the attainment of impunity'.[25] And, despicable though order secured by such means might appear to be in relation to the natural harmony which had been sacrificed through sin, Augustine is adamant that it has something to contribute to the realization of God's purpose.

It would thus be misleading to interpret Augustine's portrayals of the Heavenly and earthly cities as a stark contrast between the principles of good and evil. Nothing in God's creation could be dismissed as wholly evil. Even the devil, in so far as existence was one of his attributes, enjoyed a semblance of goodness. But the terms in which pagan thinkers had characterized goodness and the good life could not be accepted. What was wanting in their analyses was any recognition of the limitations of human understanding and endeavour. In Stoic thought, for example, reason itself is seen as a sufficient instrument to overcome human foibles. It is not supposed, of course, that we can all be redeemed through reason. There will always be the fool for whom immediate pleasures are far more arresting than the intangible advantages of a settled mind. Yet there is no obstacle, in principle, to the attainment of virtue and happiness.

This was precisely the view that Augustine was concerned to reject. He was nevertheless faced with a problem. He could not identify worldly wisdom with evil (in the manner of the Manichees) without undermining his own view of God's providence. What he had to do, instead, was to highlight the shortcomings of pagan notions of virtue in relation to Christian doctrine, while making clear that pagan social and political order was a necessary requirement for the final triumph of Christianity.

Yet this was a position fraught with difficulty. In attempting to steer a middle course between pagan and Manichaean conceptions of the good life, Augustine left himself exposed to criticism both from Christian thinkers who rejected worldly values altogether and from the perspective of traditional Greek and Roman notions which located the highest good in either the individual or the community. His own view, which might best be described as a theory of degrees of goodness, occupied him throughout book XIX of the *City of God*. In what is his most sustained statement of political doctrine, he defended a view of *de facto* authority, which political theorists have often compared with Hobbes. The affinity in their arguments on the specific question of obedience, however, disguises a wider divergence in their justifications of authority. Where order for Hobbes is justified in utilitarian terms, Augustine values earthly peace as a necessary but not sufficient condition for the emergence of the *summum bonum* in the Heavenly City. Indeed it is axiomatic for Augustine that consideration of value (in whatever sphere) must be in terms of God's providence. Thus any attempt to examine the political ideas of book XIX in disregard of the central theological arguments of the *City of God* is seriously misleading. In the last resort, Augustine's treatment of social and political order is intelligible only as an implication of his conception of sin.

Augustine's theory of political institutions is a direct corollary of his view of sin. What we have sacrificed through sin is a harmonious enjoyment of ourselves and our fellows in which obedience is owed only to God. After the Fall, however, the basic passions (pride, lust, envy, greed, fear) set us apart from one another, making each individual a potential enemy of every other. And because the root cause of our wretchedness is the corruption of our own natures, we cannot look to our own resources for a remedy. We are saved only by God's providential ordering of human affairs. Among our cardinal sins is a lust for domination which aggravates relations between both individuals and communities. But the very fact that we are basely motivated to dominate one another at least ensures that certain sorts of ordered relations emerge in human affairs. Augustine treats slavery, for example, which he regards as a wholly unnatural institution, as a direct consequence of our refusal to accept God's natural order. If we cannot bring ourselves to obey God's natural law, we are obliged to endure the discipline of slavery as a punishment for our transgressions. And though slaves might naturally resent the authority which their masters have taken upon themselves, they should nevertheless accept that order of some kind is a necessary condition for the enjoyment of any way of life.

Nor is slavery unique among social institutions. Order at the most basic level is established through relations of command and obedience. The smooth functioning of a household, for example, will depend (in Augustine's view) upon a hierarchy of command stemming from the husband and extending through the wife to children and servants. The head of the household, of course, should not indulge his 'lust for domination'. Indeed, having accepted the necessity for domestic peace, relations within the family can be construed as an 'ordered harmony about giving and receiving orders among those who live in the same house', with those in authority assuming a 'dutiful concern for the interests' of their dependants.[26] It remains the case, however, that the need to impose order within the family only arises because our natures require discipline and correction.

Coercion, indeed, is (for Augustine) an ineradicable feature of social life. Its exercise is absolutely essential if order is to be sustained in society. And though it would be wrong for a good man to delight in the infliction of punishment for its own sake, it is certainly not a service to an individual or society to allow error and sin to go uncorrected. If peace in the household or city is a desirable end, then coercive measures must be employed to restrain unruly passions.

Nor is it simply that punishment is justified in utilitarian terms. The correction of a wrongdoer is a moral obligation incumbent upon anyone in authority. From the household to the city, a system of ordered relations should prevail. Just as the wise parent should chastise a wayward child, so rulers in the city should strive to impose standards of conduct upon their subjects. Augustine, in fact, sees no qualitative distinction between rule in the city and rule in the family – 'the ordered harmony of those who live together in a house in the matter of giving and obeying orders' contributing 'to the ordered harmony concerning authority and obedience obtaining among the citizens'.[27] And in other writings he was perfectly prepared to use the need to punish sinfulness as a justification for the employment of secular power in defence of religious authority.[28]

An ordered peace is thus the objective of social and political institutions in the earthly city; but it does not follow that the terms on which that peace is established would satisfy the requirements of the Heavenly City. In his account of social order Augustine retains the dualistic conception that pervades the whole of the *City of God*. His crucial distinction is between the elect and the reprobate, with the former able to take advantage of the institutional arrangements that sustain fallen men without losing sight of the limited significance of social and political goals. What is pursued in the 'earthly city' is, in fact, an 'earthly peace', limited to a 'harmonious agreement of citizens concerning the giving and obeying of orders' which establishes 'a kind of compromise between human wills about the things relevant to mortal life'.[29] While the Heavenly City, by contrast, 'which lives on the basis of faith', treats earthly peace as a temporary convenience, essential for the daily management of mortal life but without intrinsic significance.[30] What both cities share, however, is a need to live together; and hence pilgrims should 'not hesitate to obey the laws of the earthly city by which those things which are designed for the support of this mortal life are regulated'.[31] The only exception Augustine allows is in the case of laws prescribing religious practices contrary to the tenets of Christianity. But even in the face of persecution, Christians are enjoined to limit their response to a passive dissent which leaves the secular order intact.

Augustine is still left with a problem in his characterization of justice in the earthly city. Earlier in his argument he had reported Cicero's definition of a commonwealth as 'an association united by a common sense of right and a community of interest'.[32] The implication of Cicero's insistence on 'a common sense of right' as a criterion distinguishing a 'people' from a 'multitude' is 'that a state cannot be maintained without justice'.[33] Yet what sense could there be in describing a commonwealth as just which laboured under a fundamental misconception about the relations between its citizens and God? According to this definition, not only would it have to be denied that the Roman state was just, it could not actually be classed as any sort of community. Indeed, on the strictest interpretation of Cicero's position, justice would be identified with the pilgrimage of the Heavenly City on earth. And though Augustine had no wish to weaken his characterization of true justice, he was nevertheless unhappy with a view that could not discriminate between the different modes of political association within the earthly city.

His solution to the dilemma was to introduce a dual standard of justice. While true justice (and, with it, true virtue) could not be attained without the support of true religion, it remained possible for the more limited objectives of social and political communities to be achieved despite a manifest wrongheadedness on matters of faith and doctrine. Instead of insisting on moral and political rectitude as a constitutive requirement for the existence of a community, Augustine is content to argue that a human gathering may be regarded as a people whenever an 'association of a multitude of rational beings' is 'united by a common agreement on the objects of their love'.[34] Precisely what the 'objects of their love' might be is left unspecified (though Augustine is clear that the quality of a community's 'loves' is the relevant criterion to appeal to in any wider appraisal of its worth). His crucial point, however, is that a community's righteousness is not a necessary condition for the attainment of a minimal standard of social and political order. It is common objectives that make a polity viable, not the quality of those objectives. No matter what form a social consensus might take, it will necessarily involve a degree of harmony and peace. And without peace, social life of any kind becomes problematic.

What emerges from Augustine's account of civic life, then, is an absolute insistence on the need to sustain the established relations of authority within a community. From the family to the highest offices of state, a chain of command and obedience structures the dealings of individuals with one another.[35] Authority, of course, may be abused; and Augustine has rich passages on the misery that the lust for domination has wrought in human history. In the last resort, however, he cannot trust the political judgement of fallen men. Our corrupted inclinations have rendered each one of us potential enemies. And while we continue to turn our backs upon the natural harmony that obedience to God would restore, we must endure coercive institutions as both a punishment for our sins and as the necessary means for the further enjoyment of social life.

The peace of the earthly city is thus a poor thing in itself. Yet it does serve a wider purpose. The final triumph of the Heavenly City depends upon the maintenance of a framework for the pursuit of social and political ends. God's pilgrims, embattled with the evil before them, are bent upon the creation of institutions that are parasitic on a wider legal order. They therefore have an interest in preserving temporal peace, despite reservations about the terms on which that peace is established.

In the final analysis, though, Augustine is concerned with the meagre benefits of civil society only in relation to his larger vision of the perfect peace and tranquility that awaits the elect. The passions that disfigure social life – envy, fear, greed, lust – will no longer prevail in the Heavenly City; and hence coercive institutions will be redundant. The precarious peace of the earthly city will give place to untrammelled enjoyment, leaving individuals wholly at ease with themselves and with one another. But all this is dependent upon absolute obedience to God. We lack the intellectual and emotional resources to create a situation of this kind for ourselves. All we can do is to trust in God's grace, while exploiting the moral criteria implicit in our vision for a richer understanding of the possibilities of human life.

Yet there remains in the *City of God* a theory of *de facto* authority that stands independently of Augustine's theological arguments. It is, to be sure, a more sombre position than the one he actually defends, with no hope for a final transcendence of suffering and strife. The emphasis is upon the endemic problems that give human life the character of a struggle. But it would be wrong to give the impression that we are dealing here with a gloomy argument. Given the plight we find ourselves in, it is something of a miracle to Augustine that communities are able to flourish. And though he is wont to attribute the continuance of social life to God's providence, he is clear that human beings supply the means for their preservation. Despite our mistaken notions, we continue to be ingenious and resourceful creatures. What has led us astray is our inability to understand our own natures. Self-knowledge, for Augustine, is a matter of grasping the limitations of human nature. And nowhere is this limitation more evident than in the political sphere. We can contrive a set of institutional arrangements to satisfy our immediate needs; but tampering with social and political devices will not transform our natures. Redemption is not to be had through politics. In the economy of human culture, the state stands as a significant but limited contrivance, valuable as a means to certain ends but without intrinsic worth.

Augustine's synthesis was to dominate Christian thought down to the twelfth century. It was never unquestioned, but it supplied terms of reference that kept the spheres of faith and reason properly distinguished as far as the Church was concerned. Provided this distinction was accepted, important work (in logic, for example) could proceed without posing any threat to the intellectual and spiritual authority of the Church. In the moral and political realms, however, original thinking was strictly confined. Difficult issues, of course, arose; but care was taken to ensure that they were treated within appropriate parameters.

From a modern perspective, this may sound like a desperate holding operation on the part of the Church. This is a quite misleading assumption. A view of the world that made daily life intelligible to people for 800 years cannot be so lightly dismissed. And, indeed, Augustine's influence has continued into the modern period, though without such consistent institutional support.

The challenge to the Augustinian position came from classical sources that were working their way back into European thought by a circuitous route. Just as Augustine had elaborated his own position by accommodating as much as he could from Plato, Cicero and others, so from the twelfth century theologians would find that newly recovered pagan ideas were threatening fundamental aspects of their received views. This time it was not Plato, but Aristotle and the Roman lawyers who were exciting the most attention. The University of Bologna had established itself as a centre for Roman legal studies, increasing interest in a set of ideas that had always been indirectly influential through canon law. Crucial questions arose, relating to the grounds of the authority of secular rulers and the status of natural law in the appraisal of *de facto* authority. Aristotle's defence of reason as a natural faculty posed an even more sensitive challenge to the prevailing orthodoxy.

Aristotle gained currency in Christian Europe through the work of Averroes (1126–98), an Islamic philosopher working initially in Spain, who focused specifically on the relation between faith and reason. Using the authority of Aristotle, Averroes argued for a categorial distinction between the two spheres, treating reason as an autonomous faculty that operated in terms of rules and procedures that had nothing to do with faith. The implication for Christian theology was clear. Where Augustine had treated reason as the handmaid of faith, followers of Averroes would argue for the radical self-sufficiency of reason. This still left scope for a fideistic separation between faith and reason. Once the decoupling had been effected, however, there was very little that could contain the wilder flights of personal revelation and inspiration. The door was thus open to subjectivist interpretation that could undermine the authority of the Church.[36]

Here was a challenge that had to be taken up. Averroes could be ignored, but not Aristotle. As Aristotle's works began to circulate in new Latin translation, informed by the thorough commentaries for which Averroes was renowned, Christian thinkers clearly had work to do to repair their positions. In one way or another St Thomas Aquinas's life's work may be seen as a response to this challenge. What began as an attempt to rebut a specific doctrinal error finally became a full-scale incorporation of Aristotelianism within Christian thought.

Aquinas's central claim, throughout his career, was that philosophical reflection on human nature can tell us a great deal about possible and sustainable ways of living. In an early commentary on Boethius's *De Trinitate*, written sometime between 1255–9, he sought to reject the categorial separation between faith and reason that Averroes had defended, arguing instead that 'though the rational light of the human mind is inadequate to make known what is revealed by faith, nevertheless what is divinely taught to us by faith cannot be contrary to what we are endowed with by nature'.[37] To suppose otherwise would be to treat an omnipotent and omniscient God as a trickster, endowing us with a capacity for rational reflection but ensuring that our conclusions are always misplaced and inadequate.

Aquinas does not contend that our thinking is unaffected by the fact of our sinfulness. He does not reject Augustine's analysis of sin and its consequences, but stresses rather the intellectual discipline that we must expect of ourselves, given the limitations of our 'fallen' motivations and desires. His position may be summed up in a dictum from his monumental *Summa Theologica* (left unfinished at his death) that 'grace does not destroy nature, but perfects it'.[38] We cannot expect 'human reason . . . to prove faith (for thereby the merit of faith would come to an end)', but it can 'make clear other things that are put forward in this doctrine'.[39] From this perspective, it makes perfect sense to exploit 'the authority of philosophers in those questions in which they were able to know the truth by natural reason'.[40] What is sometimes read as a rejection of the Augustinian synthesis is actually an attempt to save the kernel of Augustine's position from the sceptical implications of a radical separation between faith and reason.

Aquinas's new synthesis nevertheless involved considerable departure from Augustine. His treatment of natural reason, in particular, is much more robust. He uses Aristotelian teleological argument to specify a host of conclusions about proper living which follow from philosophical reflection on human nature. He develops the implications of the Aristotelian view that 'man is naturally a social and political animal'.[41] We do not need revelation in order to recognize that human beings are needy by nature, unable to provide for themselves without elaborate social co-operation. Unlike other creatures, their natural faculties leave them vulnerable unless means can be found of co-ordinating activities in order to satisfy needs that can only be met in common.

Government, in this view, must be regarded as a natural necessity, rather than a punishment for human sinfulness. The good of each individual can only be secured if there is adequate provision for a good that is common to all. Human instincts are not sufficient to disclose this common good. And experience shows us that revelation cannot be relied upon in all communities. What we are left with is human reason, fallible though it may be in specific cases. We can reflect on our needs and propensities as a species. These needs and propensities, it should be noted, are not things we conjure up in our imaginations. They are part of our natural endowment, and can be catered for well or ill by our institutional arrangements. When we think about the good that is common to us all, we can make mistakes. If we organize ourselves badly, our communities will not flourish. Thinking about what we are like thus furnishes us with normative guidelines for the conduct of our private and public lives.

Reflection, then, enables us to specify criteria for the conduct of our lives. Note that (for Aquinas) these criteria are not culturally specific preferences but injunctions we should follow if we want to flourish. They relate to basic truths about us. And, as injunctions, they take the form of laws. Aquinas's most extended discussion of these injunctions can be found in the treatise on law from the *Summa Theologica*.[42] He explores the status of different forms of law (eternal, natural, human and divine), incorporating, in addition to traditional Christian teaching, relevant ideas and arguments drawn from Aristotle and the Roman lawyers. He offers both a normative account of the purpose of law and an analysis of the forms of law in constituted communities.

A law, says Aquinas, 'is nothing else than an ordinance of reason for the common good'.[43] In an ideal sense, we may think of law as a 'dictate of practical reason emanating from the ruler who governs a perfect community'.[44] Such perfection, of course, cannot be expected of human communities, but God's government of the universe through divine reason can be conceived in no other way. In our imperfect condition, using natural reason as best we can, we thus have an idea of perfection which can be applied as a regulative idea in all our dealings. Our reason may not be sufficient to grasp the detail of God's eternal law; but enough is disclosed to (some of) us through revelation to enable us to argue analogically about its implications. If we find Aquinas's theology daunting, we may think of eternal law as an 'ideal type' or model of perfection.

The crucial link in Aquinas's argument concerns the relation between eternal law and natural law. The 'light of natural reason' has inescapable shortcomings, but it is not systematically misleading.[45] As we stand in our natural condition, we have no choice but to depend upon it, despite its necessary imperfections. It enables us to discern the rudiments of 'what is good and what is evil', simply by reflecting on our natures.[46] The knowledge we are able to gather from our own resources can itself be regarded as a gift from God. Aquinas describes it as 'an imprint on us of divine light'.[47] Our rational reflection on what we need in order to flourish is a way of reading God's book of the world without having recourse to revelation. What we gather through reflection, however, is not incompatible with the truths of Christian doctrine. Our efforts on our own behalf yield a body of truth, 'the natural law', which can be seen as 'the rational creature's participation of the eternal law'.[48]

These arguments are not new. We noticed in chapter 3 how the Roman lawyers used a distinction between the *jus naturale* and the *jus gentium* which enabled them to link together the idea of a moral order with the variety of practices that we encounter in ordinary experience. What Aquinas adds is an elaborate discussion of the way natural reason contributes to the maintenance of moral order. Far from distrusting our drives and inclinations, we can use them as data for reflection. Our happiness and fulfilment depend upon a harmonious enjoyment of our natural faculties. In our fallen condition, we may find that our inclinations, taken singly, destroy the harmony which should be our goal. The intensity of sexual pleasure, for example, may tempt us to pursue instant gratification rather than an ordered family life. Aquinas turns the argument around. He treats the intensity of sexual pleasure as an indication of the significance of family life. Procreation is essential to us as a species. Thinking about the point of human practices enables us to see our experience as a whole. Natural reason can thus provide something of a corrective to natural inclinations. It may not have the authority of God's eternal law; but by its means we can grasp (some of) the implications of eternal law in our ordinary experience.

Aquinas's treatment of natural law cannot be simply equated with Roman accounts of *jus gentium*. Where the Roman lawyers set out to embrace and order the variety of institutional structures available to them, Aquinas focuses much more narrowly on the ends human communities should pursue. When he looks at specific practices, it is always in terms of their contribution to the wider purposes of human life. But note that the claim that there are such purposes does not depend upon an acceptance of Aquinas's specific Christian values. The functional interdependence of our practices can be grasped by reason alone, albeit in an inadequate fashion. The point to stress here is that Aquinas can make no sense of human practices outside a normative framework. Practices are designed to fulfil human purposes, which may be well or ill conceived. Neutral description can tell us nothing about their point.

When Aquinas moves on to consider human or civil law, he keeps the normative dimension to the forefront of his attention. Here he departs significantly from the Roman lawyers. For where the *Corpus juris civilis* had contended that the will of the sovereign should have the force of law, Aquinas does not accept the normative autonomy of even properly constituted authorities. A legal injunction is an expression of practical reason. But 'human reason is not, of itself, the rule of things.'[49] It enables us, with effort and in a necessarily fallible fashion, to grasp 'general rules and measures of all things relating to human conduct'.[50] When we exercise practical reason, it should always be in full awareness of these general relations.

Properly used, therefore, practical reason provides a means for the evaluation of the legal pronouncements of political authorities. Civil laws that are incompatible with natural law cease to be authoritative. In the limiting case, Aquinas argues that 'a tyrannical law, through not being according to reason, is not a law, absolutely speaking, but rather a perversion of law'.[51] It does not follow that in these circumstances a specific tyrannical law should necessarily be disobeyed. Stability is essential to the smooth functioning of a society viewed as a scheme of social co-operation. We cannot make life plans (exercise our practical reason) if we are perpetually in doubt about relations between command and obedience within our society. Prudence may thus dictate that we should set aside our reservations about specific laws in order to enjoy the more fundamental benefits of legal order. And there is always the radical uncertainty of the consequences of active disobedience to set us on our guard against precipitate action. The fact remains, however, that when we decide not to disobey a tyrannical law, it is with an eye on the greater good of human communities as specified in natural law.

It should not be supposed that civil laws are simply the institutional embodiment of natural law. On some matters it is important that something should be decided, not what should be decided. In a modern context we accept that it is important that we should drive on one side of the road rather than another, but we also recognize that it is a matter of indifference which side that might be. Aquinas cites with approval the dictum from the *Corpus juris civilis* that 'it is not possible to give the reason for all the legal enactments of the lawgivers'.[52] Where a determinate decision is required, but there are no theoretical grounds for preferring A to B, lawgivers quite rightly follow established practices, customs and conventions. In such circumstances, legal options are not problematic. Natural law is relevant when difficult questions are at stake.

Aquinas explains the point in terms of two modes of deriving civil injunctions from natural law. Some issues are so fundamental that civil laws can be derived from natural law deductively. To use Aquinas's example, 'that one must not kill may be derived as a conclusion from the principle that one should do harm to no man'.[53] But natural law cannot tell us how wrongdoers should be punished. This is a matter for judicial decision in relation to specific cultural circumstances.

Some of the details in Aquinas's *Summa Theologica*, especially regarding family life and the role of women, will strike modern readers as unsympathetic and even harsh. This should neither surprise nor disturb us. The point of reading Aquinas (or any other philosopher) closely is not that we should assume his views on particular matters are authoritative. What we are interested in, rather, is the structure of his thought, the way problematic issues in particular spheres of conduct are related to a wider body of ideas. Our interest is not in the specific positions he finally justifies, but in the arguments he advances in support of his views. Viewed from this perspective, his treatment of natural law is crucially important to us. It focuses on the idea of an objective good for human beings which all communities should strive to attain. It draws a clear distinction between the passing preferences we may have, and the objectives we should properly pursue. In this scheme of things, political philosophy has a vital role, specifying the conditions in which we might expect to flourish as a species.

Practical reason thus plays a crucial role in Aquinas's system. But it does not operate autonomously. Aquinas does not envisage us holding up all our beliefs and values for rational scrutiny. Unlike the Kantian view that has been so influential in modern moral philosophy, Aquinas does not portray reason itself as the foundation of all our moral choices. Divine law always takes precedence over natural law for Aquinas. Through rational enquiry we can find our way around God's created universe. We have been given intelligence by God precisely so that we may assume responsibility for our choices. And those of us who have grown up without the benefit of revelation or Catholic tradition have necessarily to rely upon our natural understanding. In Aquinas's thought, human understanding is fallible but indispensable. When we use our intelligence, we are actually exploiting God's greatest gift. We may be said to be under an obligation to God to think clearly. Through rational enquiry, we can strive to discover things about ourselves and the world. The world itself, however, is fixed and finished, given to us by God. The best we can do is to try to accommodate ourselves to the way things are.

The political implications of Aquinas's position are far reaching, though he barely developed them himself.[54] His most important achievement in political philosophy was to re-iterate from a Christian point of view the intrinsic significance of conducting political affairs in proper fashion. Plato and Aristotle had both seen the *polis* as a means of securing human flourishing. Political life was not seen by them as an ultimate good, but the way it was conducted could nevertheless contribute indispensably to the attainment of human excellence. This point had been lost from sight in the wake of the extreme fideism which Augustine's portrayal of the earthly city had facilitated. In response, Aquinas had argued that though political values may not be the most important in our lives, the rules we set ourselves in political life can nevertheless be measured against standards which link civic values with eternal values on a continuum.

Aquinas's specific political values are not coherently developed. In different parts of his writings, and at different times, we find him defending monarchy as an ideal form of government ('whoever . . . rules a perfect community, be it a city or a province, is rightly called a king'), while acknowledging the value of political community as a good shared in common.[55] Indeed in certain passages we find him defending the idea of a mixed constitution in terms drawn directly from Aristotle, and even embracing the notion that political community involves ruling and being ruled in turn. These positions are not necessarily incompatible, though we must regret that Aquinas did not discuss them systematically himself. What we have, however, is a philosophical foundation for constitutional government, even if the constitutional detail is not presented adequately.

The story of the detailed development of late medieval constitutional theory cannot be told here. It may be noted in passing, however, that constitutional developments which are often associated with the modern state actually had their roots in medieval theory. Two themes, in particular, were prominent in thirteenth and fourteenth century discussions of authority.

The first, building on the Augustinian distinction between spiritual and secular spheres but incorporating Thomist Aristotelianism, sought to specify appropriate domains for state and Church. The most radical figure in this development was Marsilius of Padua (1270/80–1342/3) who was accused of 'Averroism' in his attempt to defend a categorial separation between state and Church. Where Aquinas had argued that eternal law, natural law and civil law were mutually involved in the exercise of authority in political communities, Marsilius, in *Defensor pacis* (1324), argued that the Church itself, as an institution exercising authority in specific spheres, had necessarily to be subject to the jurisdictional authority of (something like) the state.[56] It could preserve its exclusive responsibility for spiritual affairs, provided it recognized that it operated as an institution in a world of other institutions. The prime function of political authorities, as Augustine had argued, was to secure peace. If disputes within the Church could be shown to threaten the peace of the earthly city, it followed that the relevant political authority had a right to intervene in order to secure harmonious conditions for the pursuit of secular interests. On this argument, a special spiritual role for the Church could only be maintained if it dropped the presumption that it could speak with authority in political affairs.

Marsilius had endorsed a purely naturalistic view of the state, effectively challenging Aquinas's attempt to make Aristotle's political philosophy safe for Christian purposes. The *Defensor pacis* was condemned as heretical by the Church in 1327. But Marsilius continued to be influential in Church circles. The Church may be a spiritual institution, but its internal organization involved authoritative relations between groups and individuals. Pressure for constitutional reform within the Church has come to be known as the 'conciliar movement' and gathered pace in the fourteenth and early fifteenth centuries. It is instructive, especially in relation to the secular orientation of later constitutional theory, to note that the building-blocks for many early modern and modern discussions were fashioned in an ecclesiastical context. The details need not concern us here. We should be aware, however, that when we ask ourselves who speaks for the people or the state, we are drawing upon arguments that were originally developed to tackle the vexed question of the authority of a pope to represent the Church. At a time when the Church itself was often deeply divided, it was clear that a great deal could hinge on an analysis of the source of a pope's authority. If the pope was 'authorized' (or a council of the Church) to act as its principal representative in relations with the wider world, then his authority could be said to derive from his 'office'; and his 'office' had been set up to fulfil specific objectives. In this view, a pope should be regarded as answerable to his Church, just as a modern political leader may be said to be answerable to citizens or subjects.

What emerges from these tangled developments in ecclesiastical history is a theory of authority that seeks a measure of distance from the 'inspired' role of the Church. To be sure, the first steps in this direction were tentative, couched in a language that political theorists tend no longer to adopt. Yet these shifts have had explosive implications that have never been resolved satisfactorily. Once the state (or any institutional hierarchy) is separated from normative guidelines that are held to be authoritative, it becomes deeply problematic how questions of value in the secular sphere may be resolved. We may think of the state as a means to attain the common good of a community; yet when we try to develop the detailed implications of that proposition, we are likely to find ourselves overwhelmed by a babble of contending voices. 'Inspiration' can take many directions, not least within the Church itself. In these circumstances, questions of value do not go away. Whether we like it or not, we have to make hard choices. The theological paradigm that had been effective for so long in orientating people's lives now proved to be a part of the problem. Questions of political authority could no longer be handled comfortably within theological terms of reference. Peace as a value had been central to the thinking of Augustine, Aquinas and Marsilius. It became more important than ever in deeply divided times. Focus had now to be on the state as an autonomous institution. This was a defining moment in the history of modern political theory.

5

The State

The modern state as a distinctive political form began to take shape in the early modern period, though its effective and juridical parameters took time to settle. The idea of a centralized political authority, holding sway within the confines of a unique territory and commanding the obedience of subjects without distinction of rank, was a radical innovation in European political thought. The complex networks of personal allegiance that bound barons to their king in a feudal context had to be set aside, as did the exclusive right of the Church to control spiritual and moral affairs.

The conciliar movement had sparked a debate that would in time transform political relations in Europe. Yet much more than the institutional structure of the Church and its specific jurisdiction was now at stake. The very idea of a *respublica christiana* was threatened following Luther's dramatic challenge to the authority of the Church in 1517, leading to religious controversy that threatened the peace of Europe throughout the sixteenth and seventeenth centuries. But more conventional security issues, too, obliged political elites to assume functions and responsibilities that had a massive impact on the internal organization of states.

The provision of security is a primary function of political orders. Indeed it may be seen as a primary determinant of the shape and style of political life. As technology changes the practice of warfare, for example, so we find political orders and economies adapting to the resource and manpower requirements that might make communities minimally safe. This is a task that can never be said to be ultimately accomplished. Conflict and competition for resources are features of all eras and regimes, managed more or less effectively, but never finally successfully, by elites.

This takes us to the heart of what we understand by the concept of political order in any context. Peace is not something that we naturally enjoy. It is created by human artifice and ingenuity, often in the most unlikely circumstances. The paradox, however, is that while we can readily accept that peace is a necessary condition for many of the ordinary things we take for granted in our daily lives, it is sustained by a preparedness to use public violence to counter the myriad threats to an orderly way of life.

Our focus here should be on the idea of public violence. The modern state is characterized by a claim to exercise a monopoly over the legitimate use of violence within a territory. We know that private violence has never been eradicated from communities. Yet the idea that an individual or group might claim the right to monopolize the violent potential of the whole community in order to secure certain public goods was audacious in its time, and continues to be challenged by groups that refuse to acknowledge the legitimacy of a given political order.

How and why this claim was made is the focus of this chapter. It raises difficult questions at a number of levels. We need to establish the circumstances which made the claim plausible in the first place. But once it is accepted that the containment of violence by the exercise of a public monopoly of its use is justifiable, we still need to be clear who should exercise that monopoly and how. The right to use violence, like any other right, can be used and abused. Do we grant our leaders unlimited discretion in the exercise of violence? Or if we insist that the right is conditional, how do we ensure that appropriate limits are not breached without threatening the peace, security and possibly the existence of the state by countervailing violence?

Violence has an internal and external dimension, though they are inextricably linked. Political competition, after all, has always involved strategic alliances with neighbouring powers. If a state is not internally secure, it can expect more or less systematic interference in its domestic affairs. If it is seen as excessively strong in relation to bordering states, it is likely to be confronted by an alliance of states seeking to address collectively a security dilemma they are each too weak to resolve separately.

This is a perennial predicament in political life, as familiar to the Greek city-states of antiquity as they are to us today. Yet for long stretches of European political history they barely received theoretical attention, largely due to long experience of imperial domination. Whenever something like a competitive states system has emerged, however, a balance-of-power logic has always asserted itself. In modern European history it emerged most strikingly in the Italian renaissance in the late fourteenth and fifteenth centuries. The politics of city-states centred on Florence, Venice and Milan, with other cities drawn inexorably (but unpredictably) into their spheres of influence, led to the emergence of a diplomatic system that has continued to be a feature of European political life.

The intense politics of the Italian Renaissance city-states generated a style of theoretical reflection that marks a decisive break with classical normative theory. Questions of how we should ideally live were treated as secondary to the immediate problems of political survival. Whatever we might think of the good life for human beings would be of little avail if we could not guarantee the survival of our political orders in some shape or form. And here what counted was power, not moral rectitude. Short-term considerations came to the forefront of even the most sophisticated political discussion. All active politicians know that they can do nothing without power. That reality now dominated political theory.

Niccolò Machiavelli (1469–1527) has given us the starkest analysis of the political culture of the Renaissance. He served as an important political functionary in the Florentine Republic from 1498 until the return of the Medici family to political prominence in 1512. Personal experience representing Florentine interests in international contexts, especially in France and the papal court, deeply affected his political thinking. He became acutely aware of the political irrelevance of a small republic in the face of the great powers of European politics. He observed at first hand that weak states are reduced to the status of supplicants, waiting for an audience while other players determine the fate of one's country. One could deplore this situation, but only effective use of political power would change it. Machiavelli came to see that domestic political consolidation was a necessary condition for the pursuit of a robust foreign policy. And without a robust foreign policy a state was more or less at the mercy of the great powers of the day.

Machiavelli's career nicely illustrates the theoretical point that dominated his theory. His public career was abruptly cut short, not simply because of sweeping political change in Florence, but because Spanish military incursions in Italy undermined the Florentine Republic. The Medici regime, in this sense, was a direct product of shifts in the European balance of power.

Machiavelli's personal and political misfortune (he was briefly imprisoned and tortured as a prominent opponent of the Medici) has clearly been posterity's gain. Daily involvement in public affairs would scarcely have given Machiavelli the time and space to develop his political ideas. Yet out of office, Machiavelli's obsession with politics remained. Instead of dispatches, we now find him working on texts that are widely regarded as masterpieces of realist political theory. *The Prince* (1513) and the *Discourses* (1513–17) were for Machiavelli a poor consolation for the active career he had lost.[1] Both works, however, are suffused with the experience Machiavelli had gained in his public career. They defend an art of politics that is uniquely focused on the immediate concerns of institutional life. A measure of Machiavelli's success is that his name has become a byword for a particular style of politics.

The thought at the heart of Machiavelli's political theory is beguilingly simple. The circumstances of political life simply make the moralism of classical theory inapplicable in a world that necessarily operates according to quite different standards and criteria. The fragmented politics of the Italian peninsula had clearly focused Machiavelli's mind. Political commentators might pay lip-service to the pious expectations of natural-law theory, but in practice political decisions are based on (more or less effective) calculations of advantage. Machiavelli's theory seeks to dispel political hypocrisy. His concern is to adapt theory to practice, rather than the other way around.

This is certainly a ruthless reading of politics, but it is not necessarily cynical. It makes the world of difference to a community that leaders should be clear and realistic about political goals. Successful states are strong, secure and predictable. Citizens know where they stand and can make their myriad plans accordingly. Foreign powers, too, know what to expect from secure political leaders. Everyone gains from a strong state. But a state cannot sustain its position unless leaders acknowledge the reality of the use and abuse of power.

Machiavelli was aware that his approach marked a radical departure from tradition. He claims in the preface to the *Discourses* that he has set himself 'upon a new way, as yet untrodden by anyone else'.[2] And yet in his two major works of political theory he had self-consciously adopted a traditional literary genre as a vehicle for his ideas. *The Prince*, for example, was cast in the mould of an advice-book for princes. These were commonplace in the Renaissance, urging princes to be fine, upright and God-fearing fellows. All would be well for them politically if they aspired to the highest moral and religious standards. Machiavelli inverted the argument. Princes might very well want to observe the normal rhetorical conventions, but a gulf separates the world of politics from moral and religious discourse. '. . . how men live is so different from how they should live that a ruler who does not do what is generally done, but persists in doing what ought to be done, will undermine his power rather than maintain it'.[3]

This is the crux of the issue for Machiavelli. He insists that he wants his work to be useful. *The Prince* is addressed to elite figures striving for power. Machiavelli accordingly concentrates 'on what really happens rather than on theories and speculations'.[4] He is scornful of theorists who 'have imagined republics and principalities that have never been seen or known to exist'.[5] Rulers should focus, instead, on the way the political world actually works, not on the lofty exhortations of commentators. Machiavelli is emphatic. 'If a ruler who wants to act honourably is surrounded by unscrupulous men his downfall is inevitable.'[6] The lesson, then, unpalatable though it might be to conventional sensibilities, is that 'a ruler who wants to maintain his power must be prepared to act immorally when this becomes necessary'.[7]

Machiavelli pursues the logic of his argument ruthlessly. He lists conventional virtues (generosity, loyalty, mercifulness, affability etc.) and then asks how these qualities would affect a capacity to rule effectively. Generosity, for example, would very soon empty the public treasury, thus limiting a ruler's scope for further action. It would also create expectations that would be impossible to fulfil and hence disappointment. Generosity, in fact, in Machiavelli's estimation is 'self-consuming': 'the more you practise it, the less you will be able to practise it.'⁸ A ruler would be forced to adopt extreme measures in order to replenish public resources, inevitably antagonizing subjects or citizens.

More dramatically still, Machiavelli asks 'whether it is better to be loved or feared'.⁹ Where conventional advice-books for princes encouraged rulers to be almost like father-figures to their peoples, Machiavelli urges distance. If a ruler is loved by his people, he can, of course, profit from a good reputation. Yet men, insists Machiavelli, 'are ungrateful, fickle, feigners and dissemblers, avoiders of danger, eager for gain'.¹⁰ They will be quick to take advantage of a ruler who has made himself loved, but will always be more hesitant in approaching a ruler who is feared. The point here is that 'a wise ruler should rely on what is under his own control'.¹¹ Dependence on other people is fatal to decisive government. Hence it makes sense for a ruler 'to avoid incurring hatred', which might incite opposition, but he can happily profit from the fact that he may be feared.¹² A ruler must remain the master of his own destiny.

Machiavelli leaves no scope for moral constraints on political action. He needs to be read with care, however, because his language is highly instructive. He does not deny that conventional virtues are, in fact, virtues. He leaves us free to do the 'right' thing if the costs are not too high. In a discussion of promise-keeping, for example, he does not question the moral worth of honesty. 'Everyone knows', he says, 'how praiseworthy it is for a ruler to keep his promises, and live uprightly and not by trickery.'¹³ Yet 'experience shows that in our times the rulers who have done great things are those who have set little store by keeping their word'.¹⁴ In the cut-and-thrust of political life, honesty is simply a luxury that a leader cannot afford.

But neither will a ruler be successful if it is assumed that he can never be relied on. Liars are poor players in the game of social co-operation, and even ruthless princes require co-operation from others. Machiavelli is perfectly well aware of this point. He champions the idea of a strong state because he wants to see legality and predictability entrenched in social practices. Indeed he sees government through law as peculiarly 'appropriate for men', but for men who are aware of the overwhelming importance of stability for the pursuit of any other goals in social life.¹⁵ His point is that in anarchic situations exceptional measures are required that would not ordinarily be justified.

The burden on rulers is immense. Their ruthlessness must be of a peculiarly public-spirited kind. They must combine the cunning of a fox with the strength of a lion, but not simply in order to satisfy a frenzied lust for domination. They must do whatever is necessary to create order. Personal ambition may be a means to that end, but it is not an end in itself. Indeed Machiavelli frankly admits that his advice 'would not be sound if all men were upright'.¹⁶ The fact that they are not colours all Machiavelli's political calculations. A prudent ruler must expect the worst from his fellow human beings and act accordingly, no matter what the moral cost.

Machiavelli's greatest fear is that weakness or vacillation will under-mine prospects for success in political situations that are in a state of con-stant flux. Overly scrupulous rulers will find that their principles are impediments to effective action. Shifting circumstances are simply a fact of political life. It follows (this is a bare statement of political logic for Machiavelli) that rulers 'are successful if their methods match the circum-stances and unsuccessful if they do not'.[17] On balance, Machiavelli sug-gests 'that it is better to be impetuous than cautious, because fortune is a woman, and if you want to control her, it is necessary to treat her roughly'.[18] Whatever one might make of Machiavelli's metaphor, his stress on decisive action is clear.

Yet Machiavellian strategy cannot guarantee success. He pictures a world governed by a logic of its own. Fate (or *fortuna*) 'is the arbiter of half our action'.[19] But the prudent ruler still has to read situations, responding to necessity when he must, grasping opportunities as they arise. For Machiavelli this involves close reading of historical situations, without committing inflexibly to an ideal scheme of practices or institutions. In the last resort, success is the only relevant criterion for assessing political actions.

Success, however, is not measured simply in terms of the personal aggrandizement of a ruler. In a telling example, Machiavelli focuses on the tactics of Agathocles, who rose from the status of an ordinary citizen to become King of Syracuse. Here was a political schemer of the first order, apparently unaffected by moral scruples of any kind. He conspired with accomplices to kill potential opponents ('all the senators and the richest men of the city') after calling them to a meeting.[20] And his subsequent use of violence in conflicts with the Carthaginians was similarly ruthless and effective. Agathocles's record, surely, should satisfy Machiavelli's criterion of political success? Yet, significantly, he qualifies his judgement. '. . . it cannot be called virtue', he insists, 'to kill one's fellow-citizens, to betray one's friends, to be treacherous, merciless and irreligious; power may be gained by acting in such ways, but not glory.'[21] That Machiavelli admired Agathocles's audacity is beyond question. But his discussion suggests clearly that instrumental violence can be justified only in appropriate cases.

There is a suggestive contrast in Machiavelli's treatment of the career of Cesare Borgia. Borgia, like Agathocles, used strategic violence to further his interests. Through his father, Pope Alexander VI, he was able to exploit rivalries in the Romagna in order to cultivate a political domain for himself. He cleverly set faction against faction, without becoming depen-dent on his erstwhile allies. Borgia used a merciless intermediary, Remirro de Orco, to quell the resultant disorders. The cruelty of Remirro's methods, however, had created implacable enemies. Peace had been bought at a price that threatened Cesare Borgia's interests. In response he happily pre-sented the dismembered corpse of Remirro to the people, effectively distancing himself from the methods that had been instrumental in creating stability and order in a persistently divided territory.

Cesare Borgia's methods look, on first inspection, every bit as reprehensible as Agathocles's. Yet Machiavelli insists that 'he succeeded in laying very strong foundations for his future power'.[22] His suggestion, though he does not develop the point, is that this was much more than a personal triumph. In securing his own power and interest, Cesare Borgia had 'won over all the inhabitants, for they had begun to enjoy prosperity'.[23] The implication is clear. Violence used to secure appropriate public objectives is always laudable. Personal ambition might drive individuals to seek glory, and they may use the most distasteful methods in the process. A commentator, however, can draw a distinction between worthy and base goals. To be sure, nothing is achieved in politics without dirtying one's hands. But basic political interests trump merely personal ambition, at least in the eyes of posterity.

The Prince is addressed to a very specific dilemma – how a new prince might best establish his rule. The general benefit of political order is a theme that Machiavelli handles only indirectly, focused as he is principally on political strategy. In the *Discourses*, however, he has rather more to say about order as a necessary condition for human flourishing. Like *The Prince*, the *Discourses* are based on a traditional literary genre – in this case, commentary on a classic text. Machiavelli uses Livy's great history of Rome as the loosest of pretexts for the development of his own political and historical theory.

Commentators have always been struck by Machiavelli's declared preference for republican institutions in the *Discourses*, sometimes suggesting that *The Prince* should be read as a narrowly self-interested attempt by Machiavelli to ingratiate himself with the Medici. Indeed there is no doubt, from the tone of the dedicatory letter to Lorenzo de' Medici, that he would very much have welcomed a renewal of his active political career. It would be a mistake, however, to read too much into the dedication. The political theory of both *The Prince* and the *Discourses* is plainly misread if they are set apart from one another. Machiavelli is no less ruthless in his recommendations in the *Discourses*. Violence remains indispensable to political success, and it should be employed decisively. What is different is the range of political circumstances in which agents find themselves.

Machiavelli broadens the scope of his discussion in the *Discourses*. He is no longer concerned with the immediate problem of securing political order at any price. Through reflection on Livy's treatment of Roman history, he can comment on effective tactics in a variety of political contexts. The politics of republican Rome emerges as a clear preference for him, though it does not follow that republican institutions are possible or desirable in all situations. Machiavelli defends a contextual theory of political ethics. He tempers his advice to fit the different phases in an inexorable cycle of political development. Like Plato, Aristotle and Polybius in antiquity, he sees the rise and fall of political orders as a determining factor in the fate and fortune of public life on any specific occasion. No political order will last forever. Effective politics is a matter of seizing an appropriate moment, adapting one's tactics to fit a particular phase in a larger political cycle. Reading fortune's wheel is thus crucially important for political agents in any context.

Forms of order come and go, and any commentator will have specific preferences, yet Machiavelli views stability in any context as a foundational political value. In a revealing passage, for example, he (apparently) sets his republican sympathies on one side in his praise of Sparta. Sparta, he comments, 'observed its laws for more than eight hundred years without corrupting them and without any dangerous disturbance'.[24] If a political order is tyrannical or excessively authoritarian, we might regard its success as a mixed political blessing. Machiavelli, however, is emphatic. 'Happy indeed', he says, 'should we call that state which produces a man so prudent that men can live securely under the laws which he prescribes without having to emend them.'[25] He contrasts this situation with the condition of a community always struggling to create stable institutions and practices. The underlying point is clear. Energy and initiative in a community are not in infinite supply. If too many people are involved in desperate measures to maintain security and order, often frustrating one another in the process, they clearly cannot devote themselves to the very many other pursuits that distinguish a good life. Indeed Machiavelli lays it down as a general rule that a state should be regarded as the more unhappy, 'the more remote' it is 'from order'.[26]

The priority of order is thus a dominant theme in both *The Prince* and the *Discourses*. The *Discourses*, however, add rich detail on the precise implications of that commitment. Machiavelli regards human nature as a constant in his reflections. Yet how human beings comport themselves will vary widely in different institutional contexts. A polity that works with the grain of human nature is likely to be more durable and effective in the long term than one that requires too many *ad hoc* interventions from rulers whose wisdom cannot be guaranteed. In a striking discussion that is remarkably prescient from a modern institutional perspective, Machiavelli highlights the specifically self-correcting qualities of republican institutions. The interests of citizens will clash in any polity. What distinguishes republican institutions is the recourse to public procedures whenever problems and abuses arise. Disputes are managed through legal channels in the ordinary way of things. Conflict cannot be eradicated. But recourse to the laws serves 'to stabilize and strengthen a republic'.[27] There is no need for discretionary executive intervention, which is likely to antagonize losers in a painfully personal way. Legal processes are reinforced, even in the face of antagonism and hostility between citizens.

Machiavelli gears his (conditional) defence of republican institutions to his central theme. If the maintenance of order is a primary political responsibility, citizens must be aware of the many ways it is likely to be undermined. In a republican context, confidence in public order is most likely to be threatened by the adoption of private means for the resolution of disputes. 'Calumnies', as Machiavelli styles them, can arise in any context.[28] They are furthered by gossip and intrigue, effectively undermining trust and massively increasing the costs of social co-operation. The weak need protectors, the strong fear rivals. No one is secure. 'Public indictments', by contrast, make citizens aware that their personal interests are best defended through open procedures.[29] Disparities between the strength and wealth of citizens are mitigated in a context in which public institutions are seen as the first recourse in the pursuit of individual interests. And in an intriguing aside, Machiavelli makes it clear that though his discussion is focused in this passage primarily on republican institutions, the point holds true 'in all other forms of society'.[30]

Machiavelli studiedly avoids recourse to first principles. What we find in his writings, instead, are maxims for the use of political agents in a variety of different contexts. Republican institutions, for example, can only flourish in certain circumstances. Machiavelli accepts that it is 'impossible to maintain a republican form of government in states which have become corrupt'.[31] And if, in fact, one is in the unfortunate position of trying to establish government (the dilemma confronting the 'new prince'), then 'it would be necessary to introduce into it a form of government akin rather to a monarchy than to a democracy'.[32] Machiavelli's defence of republicanism is purely instrumental. At its best, and in the right circumstances, it can manage the passions and ambitions of men as well as any other political form. Once regard for public culture and institutions has been lost, however, other methods will have to be adopted.

The tone of Machiavelli's writing is both dispassionate and urgent. Public order is treated as a fragile achievement on which all else depends. In an emergency, every other consideration must be set aside. Machiavelli asserts categorically that 'one's country should be defended whether it entail ignominy or glory'.[33] As ever with Machiavelli, care must be taken with his language. *The Prince* and the *Discourses* are both focused on necessary tactical means of political success in different contexts, but success is not measured in personal terms. Rulers and active citizens are urged to sacrifice their interests for the common good if need arises. '. . . when the safety of one's country wholly depends on the decision to be taken, no attention should be paid either to justice or injustice, to kindness or cruelty, or to its being praiseworthy or ignominious.'[34] Machiavelli's advice is unconditional. Everything that an individual holds dear might have to be subordinated to the demands of a political crisis. '. . . every other consideration' should be 'set aside', he insists, in order to 'save the life and preserve the freedom of one's country'.[35]

The narrowness of Machiavelli's focus is evident in this passage. As in passages noted earlier from *The Prince*, he inverts a conventional scale of values in order to make a dramatic tactical point. But what does he have to say to readers who may simply not accept the priority he attributes to political values? He gives us ample material to construct an argument, but readers find themselves filling out positions that are sometimes left frustratingly incomplete.

The final chapter of *The Prince* is a perfect illustration of an attentive reader's dilemma. Tactical analysis gives place to a passionate 'exhortation' to anyone who dares 'to liberate Italy from the barbarian yoke'.[36] A natural reading suggests that this is a plea for political self-determination, along lines that later became fashionable in the great nation-building movements of the nineteenth century, despite the fact that the idea of the nation barely existed in early sixteenth-century discourse. It would be idle to suggest a definitive reading of the chapter here. At the very least, however, it is clear that the question of why we should value political order needs to be treated rather differently from the means we might use to maintain it. Machiavelli raises an issue that he cannot effectively address in his own terms, not least because he has such little faith in conventional styles of philosophical justification.

Machiavelli's stress on the reality of political power was a breath of fresh air, even to readers who were scandalized by his contempt for conventional political morality. He threw down a challenge to political theory that remains arresting to this day. His obsession with the instrumental use of power, however, left many questions unanswered. He has very little to say about precisely how political order should be justified to parties that may simply feel that power is being wielded at their expense. States are coercive instruments, and coercion hurts. Coercion can also be exercised in support of good or bad ends, in more or less appropriate contexts. Machiavelli's preoccupation with instrumental political violence is ill-equipped to deal with such issues. Yet justification in wider terms became manifestly necessary as states were consolidated in the early modern period.

Orthodox defences of rule in the period invoked a curious mix of Thomist natural-law theory and neo-Platonism, often in bowdlerized form. Kings claimed to be God's lieutenants on earth, occupying a distinctive place in the great chain of being that justified both the immense power they assumed and their awesome responsibilities. Any inversion of the natural order would invite chaos, directly threatening not only the state as a political entity but the ordinary certainties of social and family life.

Sensitivity about the fragility of political order was heightened by the threat of civil war. In France, for example, consolidated monarchical rule was exposed to challenge from both the sizeable Protestant minority and doctrinaire Catholics who sought to use the state as a direct means of enforcing religious orthodoxy. Both positions assumed without question that political order should be justified in specifically religious terms. In this scheme of things, a monarch's position in a political hierarchy might have to satisfy a direct (and more or less detailed) religious test. And in a context of acute religious controversy, the state itself would be rendered vulnerable to shifting currents in religious culture.

Theories of absolute government were a perfectly intelligible response to deeply dangerous political circumstances. Jean Bodin (1530–96), for example, in his influential *The Six Books of the Commonwealth* (1576) developed a political theory with a doctrine of absolute sovereignty at its heart.[37] As a political order, for Bodin, the state transcends any passing configuration of associated powers, responsibilities and functions. These could come and go as occasion and opportunity arose. The state, however, must embody an 'absolute and perpetual power' if it is to exist at all.[38] Hence it would follow that sovereignty could not be 'limited either in power, or in function, or in length of time'.[39]

Bodin treated the idea of constitutional limits to the powers of a king as a contradiction in terms. Ranging across classical and more recent historical examples, he sought to show that countervailing powers set against the prerogatives of a king would implicitly amount to a condition of civil war, since no organ of government possessed the ultimate right to decide controversial cases. A king may delegate powers at his pleasure, specifying appropriate functions and conditions. And only he can judge whether his pleasure has been served. On Bodin's view, delegated powers can be revoked, even on a passing whim, without exposing a king to constitutional objections.

Bodin's argument is deceptively simple. He is perfectly well aware that capricious kings make bad rulers. He is obsessed, however, with the thought that (contestable) arguments against this or that decision will make stable government impossible. He accepts that kings are not the arbiters of right and wrong. Divine and natural laws apply to 'every prince on earth'.[40] Unlike Machiavelli, Bodin insists that kings should observe 'just and reasonable contracts', along with all their subjects.[41] His point, however, is that kings cannot be compelled to keep their contracts without creating numberless occasions for (potentially ruinous) turmoil and dissent.

Bodin combines recognition of the priority of order with continuing regard for conventional political morality. This is the sanitized version of political realism that has served elites very well in various forms over the centuries. It accepts the necessity of executive discretion, while leaving scope for normative critique couched in anodyne language. In conceptual terms, however, it remains a fudge, juxtaposing positions that can barely be reconciled theoretically. The contrast with Machiavelli is highly instructive. Where Machiavelli had highlighted the inevitable tensions between public and private morality in the new political world of emerging states, Bodin writes as if the conventional order of values remains intact. And, in truth, Bodin's position is much easier to defend in the context of day-today political exchange. If Machiavelli is right, no Machiavellian politician would dare to admit it. Hypocrisy and wishful thinking have a place in political life, assuring political losers that, for all their humiliation, the game is still worth playing.

Concentrations of power in the hands of monarchs, across larger swathes of territory, had clearly created a problem that theorists had yet to respond to effectively. Traditional religious language was stretched to cover unprecedented political situations, lending a semblance of plausibility to the new political order. The image of the king as the father of his people, for example, appeared to justify both the need for executive discretion and the essentially coercive nature of the apparatus of the state. Sir Robert Filmer's *Patriarcha* (first published in 1680 but probably written in the early 1640s) is the canonical statement of this position in the British tradition.[42] For all that Filmer was deeply influenced by Bodin and Aristotle, his text is oddly parochial in tone, reflecting the very specific travails of the English monarchy. The style of writing, too, is assertive, combining biblical exegesis with selective use of historical examples. What is important to notice in this context, however, is the rhetorical power of Filmer's central image.

Filmer asserts in his very first sentence that 'the first kings were fathers of families'.[43] He sees paternal power as the first source of social order and, by analogy, the best possible justification of a public political power that would otherwise appear to be wholly arbitrary. And throughout the text he uses what he regards as a 'natural' theory about the origins of social order to undermine 'the supposed natural equality and freedom of mankind'.[44] For if you grant that human beings are in any sense naturally free, you open the way to the claim that they may have 'liberty to choose what form of government' they please.[45] The consequence, for Filmer, would be the destruction of order at every level of social life.

Filmer's concerns are no doubt fuelled by the imminence or outbreak of the English civil war. The royalist world view was then put to practical test in the most dramatic fashion. In retrospect, of course, Filmer's fear that everything he held dear would be wrecked by endemic disorder looks exaggerated. Two of his central claims, however, are of lasting significance. It is simply the case that we do not choose the social structures that shape our lives. Many later theorists who would have no sympathy whatever for Filmer's royalism could nevertheless endorse his contention that a world of values is in a very real sense given to us. We make judgements from embedded positions in social life. Theorists who accept the priority of social order could share Filmer's scepticism about the political implications of a presumed 'natural liberty', though they need not, of course, find themselves committed to his view that 'it is unnatural for the people to govern or choose governors'.[46]

Filmer's further point, which was to be crucially important in the later development of the British legal tradition, was that 'positive laws do not infringe the natural and fatherly power of kings'.[47] Kings can lay down laws, but they cannot bind themselves. For Filmer, 'kingly power is by the law of God, so it hath no inferior law to limit it'.[48] Indeed kings are beyond legal reproach even when they breach God's law. It is a simple fact of political life for Filmer 'that there were kings long before there were any laws'.[49] Hence the immense advantages of legal order are directly attributable to kings, no matter how far they might abuse their positions in specific instances.

The common theme in absolutist theories is an unprecedented elevation of the prerogatives of rulers. In this scheme of things, subjects might have advantages conferred upon them and can enjoy the benefit of a legal order authorized by a king; but they have precious little scope to seek redress for kingly wrong-doing. King James I captured the issue succinctly in his *The Trew Law of Free Monarchies* (1598).[50] Without kings, James argues, there would be no law at all. Law is an act of the king's will. He makes 'daily statutes and ordinances, enjoining such pains thereto as he thinks meet'.[51] He may take advice from parliament or other bodies, but he does so at his pleasure. And 'it lies in the power of no parliament, to make any kind of law or statute, without his sceptre be to it, for giving it the force of a law'.[52]

A good king will recognize his moral and political duty. He 'will frame all his actions to be according to the law'.[53] But he cannot be bound by a law which depends solely on his act of will. Law prevails at the king's discretion. If he were not 'above the law', there would in fact not be a legal order of any kind, for someone, somewhere, has to be endowed with a power of discretion to give particular decisions a legal status.[54]

James I, like Filmer, was happy to portray a king as a father to his people. Care would be linked to a right to inflict punishment, always at the father's discretion. In a similar commonplace image, he speaks of a king as the 'head of a body composed of divers members', giving force and direction to an organic entity otherwise formless.[55] In the last resort, the king's will alone animates, orientates and controls.

The flaw at the heart of conventional absolutist theories is precisely dependence on the almost talismanic quality of the person of the king. Defence of executive discretion is shrouded in discussion of a king's peculiar place in a (presumed) natural hierarchy. In reality, of course, discretion is exercised by a human being with all the usual foibles. Kings may very well show themselves to be wise, conscientious and humane; they may also be fools, knaves or worse. In practice monarchies devise ways of managing when a king is demonstrably unfit for office, though the mechanisms are likely to be slow, cumbersome and arbitrary. Subjects are likely to find themselves in highly sensitive and vulnerable situations, aware that their interests require a measure of order but not necessarily convinced that order is best conceived in narrowly personal terms.

Thomas Hobbes (1588–1679) produced a more rigorous defence of political order, focusing specifically on the benefits to subjects of stability and peace. Hobbes developed his position through painstaking efforts in a long writing career. A humanist education gave him a remarkable command of classical culture. His 1629 translation of Thucydides's *History of the Peloponnesian War* was his first publication. And he continued translating Greek texts into deep old age. Exposure to developments in modern science, and in particular mathematics and geometric modes of argument, however, enabled him to fashion a style of philosophy that set new standards in clarity and rigour.

He came to political philosophy comparatively late, but in a remarkable productive decade in the 1640s worked out an independent position of his own. His first work in political philosophy, *The Elements of Law*, was completed in 1640 but not published until 1650. In1642, exiled in Paris, Hobbes published a Latin version of central political arguments, *De Cive*, which drew public attention to a distinctively Hobbesian style of analysis. An astonishing decade's work culminated in 1651 with the publication of *Leviathan*, unambiguously his masterpiece.[56]

The three treatises very much form part of a single project. While *Leviathan* is the longest and most complete, it is not necessarily the most systematic. Hobbes continued to work within the structure he had set out in *The Elements of Law*, though extensive material was added, especially on religion, to *Leviathan*. While Hobbes scholars will focus on variations between the texts, it is nevertheless appropriate for political philosophers to treat them as successive statements of a single position. Though Hobbes was to develop some themes further in subsequent writings, the authoritative status of *Leviathan* as a statement of his position was not challenged. That text will accordingly be the focus of the discussion that follows.

Hobbes is often read as an advocate of authoritarian rule. What is distinctive about Hobbes, however, is his close analysis of human nature. He asks himself why strong political structures are necessary for human beings such as ourselves, with all our passions, foibles and erratic predilections and inclinations. He transforms the commonplace assumptions about human beings available in his day, very much informed by orthodox Christian conceptions of sin, into a close analysis of human nature, identical in each and every one of us. He subjects human motivation to minute 'scientific' analysis, within the terms of reference of the most advanced thinking of his day. His central claim is that, given our natures, demonstrated systematically in his book, certain political conclusions are inescapable for any rational observer. It would be idle, for example, to assume that we could all sit down together to devise a mutually acceptable political system. Our reasoning simply does not work like that, driven as it is by unavoidable partiality. We are impelled to pursue our interests, often in self-defeatingly narrow fashion. The upshot is social and political turmoil that potentially threatens everyone. Recognizing these traits, we have to take steps to save ourselves from ineradicable features of our natures. It would be idle to wish that we were more benign or reliably rational. The only hope for peace and stability in the long term is that we confront our natures as they are, and construct a politics accordingly.

This is political philosophy of the most abstract kind, though Hobbes notes that it is 'occasioned by the disorders of the present time'.[57] His thinking is dominated by the catastrophic consequences of civil war in England. He looks at the implacable confrontation between religious and political zealots and asks what we can learn from this experience about the scope for reasonable agreement. Intelligent men were committing themselves to a course of wholesale destruction. This is the paradox at the heart of all Hobbes's political thinking. Purportedly rational conduct led to manifestly irrational practices, for no one could seriously be assumed to want to destroy himself and any prospect for a stable social life. The solution, for Hobbes, is to focus precisely on how we should characterize reason, alerting ourselves to the disasters that might befall if we overreach the natural limits of our capacities.

The detail of Hobbes's analysis of human nature need not detain us unduly. He pictures human beings pursuing pleasure and avoiding pain, each according to their own lights. He treats the objective qualities we attribute to things as mere projections of our fancies. Instead of a world of objective values (such as we find in Platonic, Aristotelian and Thomist ethics), Hobbes portrays individuals making purely subjective judgements about the way the world impinges upon them. Thus 'whatsoever is the object of any mans Appetite or Desire; that is it, which he for his part calleth *Good*: And the object of his Hate, and Aversion, *Evill*;. . .'[58] Note that Hobbes claims that we call things good or evil, not that they are actually good or evil. In Hobbes's view, objective judgements of value in everyday discourse have no standing. We talk as if values are objective, but all the time we are simply giving vent to our personal preferences.

Hobbes follows the implications of this thought relentlessly. Ordinarily we picture ourselves thinking carefully about the options before us. Hobbes insists, instead, that we are actually oscillating between contrasting inclinations. Thus 'in Deliberation, the last Appetite, or Aversion, immediately adhaering to the action, or to the omission thereof, is that wee call the WILL;. . .'[59] The stress is again on what we call an attribute or quality, not on what it actually is.

This is certainly not a flattering view of human conduct. Hobbes takes our ordinary language and shows how deeply misleading it is. Organizing ourselves in terms of our ordinary views of things is, in fact, a recipe for disaster. At each turn, what we claim to know is merely a description, pleasing to us but of no significance whatever. Even the satisfaction of our personal happiness is an illusion. We cannot even specify what is the object of our desires. Hobbes says that we are caught between '*Apparent*, or *Seeming Good*' and '*Apparent*, or *Seeming Evill*'.[60] Hobbes offers us no escape from this vicious circle of illusions within the terms of everyday culture. Even the pursuit of happiness (or 'felicity'), which might be viewed as a settled goal of passionate creatures, is simply a train of satisfactions that are utterly unrelated to each other. We do not know what it means to be happy. Hobbes will only say that *'continuall successe* in obtaining those things which a man from time to time desireth, that is to say, continuall prospering, is that men call FELICITY;. . .'[61] They call it 'felicity', but it does not actually amount to anything at all.

Prospects for individuals in this scheme of things are not promising. We are each driven to seek satisfactions that (quite literally) do not add up to anything. The very idea of lasting satisfaction, for Hobbes, is a contradiction in terms. We can say of a man's power that it is simply 'his present means, to obtain some future apparent Good'.[62] But there can, of course, be no guarantees, because all individuals are driven in similar fashion to try to secure those things that seem good to them.

Hobbes is at pains to stress the depth of this predicament. He certainly wants to disabuse us of any thought that natural intelligence can resolve this dilemma for us. We can enjoy neither rest nor contentment, surrounded as we are by individuals anxious to garner at least some satisfactions in highly vulnerable situations. We are all competitors in a game of survival played at very long odds. Hobbes generalizes the predicament. He says, 'I put for a generall inclination of all mankind, a perpetuall and restlesse desire of Power after power, that ceaseth onely in Death.'[63] We can no more get ourselves out of this fix than we can transcend our own natures. Our insecurity is chronic. Left to ourselves, we cannot even plan reasonable survival strategies. The more power we try to accrue to ourselves, the more likely we are to excite the fear and resentment of others. We certainly cannot trust anybody. Nor can we assume that anyone else will share our personal preferences.

Hobbes's initial account of human nature pays no attention to social and political circumstances. He discounts bonds of affection and the natural social hierarchies that figure so prominently in royalist political theory. He gives us the bare bones of human motivation, as if we are structured to operate within narrow (and inescapable) parameters. His readers, however, familiar with the miseries and uncertainties of civil war, would be very well aware of the political implications of the argument. And Hobbes spells out the implications in vivid passages in chapter thirteen of *Leviathan*.

His first point will surprise readers accustomed to seeing him as a defender of traditional forms of authoritarianism. Experience had taught him that natural hierarchies are no defence against fanaticism. The disorders of government must be traced to a deeper source. His point precisely is that natural inequalities are insufficient as a foundation for stable government. In complete contrast, he maintains that 'nature hath made men so equall, in the faculties of body, and mind; as that though there bee found one man sometimes manifestly stronger in body, or of quicker mind than another; yet when all is reckoned together, the difference between man, and man, is not so considerable, as that one man can thereupon claim to himselfe any benefit, to which another may not pretend, as well as he. For as to the strength of body, the weakest has strength enough to kill the strongest, either by secret machination, or by confederacy with others, that are in the same danger with himselfe.'[64]

This is a starker dilemma than even the most pessimistic royalists had envisaged. Hobbes depicts a desperately competitive situation that seems to make social co-operation all but impossible. Natural equality, coupled with natural vanity, leads each man to construct a universe according to his own lights. Each will assume that his judgement is as good as any other, and that he has an equal right to any of the goods that nature might bestow. He will claim a right to the use of anyone else for his pleasure and convenience. Competition for everything generates suspicion. There can be no lasting alliances in this state of chronic insecurity. Hobbes does not even offer us a prospect in which the fittest will prevail. The strong and adept will sustain their positions only so long as weaker individuals fail to recognize the threat to themselves. But temporary alliances of the weak will shatter as individuals are driven to secure more, in dread fear of losing everything they have.

Hobbes treats human nature as a limiting constraint on any viable politics. He asks his readers to picture, as a thought experiment, what life might be like if people were left to themselves, without the (sometimes irksome) restrictions imposed by government. We may all have our differences about modes of government we might prefer. Yet these differences pale into insignificance if we contrast life under limiting governmental rules (arbitrary though these might be) with natural lawlessness. Hobbes's point would not have been lost on his contemporaries. If we are too precious about the government we are prepared to tolerate, we run the risk of undermining government of any kind. A state of nature, however, far from maximizing our options, actually renders any of our enjoyments precarious.

Hobbes emphasizes the point in dramatic language. He describes 'the time men live without a common Power to keep them all in awe' as a state of war.[65] And in a famous passage he specifies just what that would mean for our daily lives. We would enjoy none of the advantages of industry 'because the fruit thereof is uncertain: and consequently no Culture of the Earth; no Navigation, nor use of the commodities that may be imported by Sea; no commodious Building; no Instruments of moving, and removing such things as require much force; no Knowledge of the face of the Earth; no account of Time; no Arts; no Letters, no Society'.[66] The ordinary things that we take for granted would be impossible. Worse, says Hobbes, we would be haunted by 'continuall feare, and danger of violent death'.[67] Our lives would truly be 'solitary, poore, nasty, brutish, and short'.[68]

Hobbes's argument is purely hypothetical. What he offers is not an empirical description of a state of nature, but a deduction of consequences from his account of human nature. However he asks readers whom he may not have convinced theoretically to examine the evidence of their own conduct. On journeys, he notes that people take precautions (they go armed and seek 'to go well accompanied'); at night they lock their doors and chests, despite the fact that 'there bee Lawes, and publike Officers, armed, to revenge all injuries'.[69] Is this not evidence enough, asks Hobbes, that daily actions condemn 'mankind', quite as much 'as I do by my words'?[70] He treats mutual suspicion as a pervasive sentiment, familiar to each and every one of us, and asks us to read his theory in that light.

This is a bleak account of human nature, but Hobbes is careful not to criticize our natural failings. It makes no more sense to deplore that we are driven by our passions than to regret that we breathe. Our passions are simply what they are, 'till they know a Law that forbids them'.[71] And laws cannot exist until government is instituted. Moral criteria are simply not relevant in a state of nature. Indeed, says Hobbes, 'notions of Right and Wrong, Justice and Injustice have there no place'.[72] Moral criticism is a luxury we can afford only in structured social and political contexts.

There is doubtless some prevarication in Hobbes's use of language here. He wants us to recognize that the state of nature is utterly undesirable, without invoking specifically moral language. His reasoning is clear, even if he finally fails to convince. When we challenge the legitimacy of government (rather than the wisdom of this or that policy), much more than political order is at stake. It is barely possible to conceive a world in which evaluative criteria are not invoked, with some scope for attributing settled meanings to the terms we use. We may assume that the stability of our language reflects our ability to grasp the way things are. But here we deceive ourselves. Hobbes treats political order as a necessary condition for the very many goods we might pursue in social life. It is these tangible enjoyments that he values, not the detail of a specific political regime. Thus when he links public power to law ('where there is no common Power, there is no Law: where no Law, no Injustice') he extends the discussion to include our ordered understanding of the way the world works.[73] Political orders are an artificial imposition on our otherwise disordered natures. Yet they are a necessary condition for the continuance of social practices that in other theories are regarded as natural. Political turmoil thus threatens the manifold activities that make our lives meaningful.

Given the depth of the (hypothetical) predicament Hobbes depicts in his state of nature, we may wonder how (in principle) it would ever be possible to get out of it. Here we must remind ourselves that Hobbes assumes his readers are aware of the benefits of government, though he clearly thinks they have been rash in some of their political experiments. We should also note that he deplores the state of nature, and expects his readers to come round to that view. He is on the verge of urging that we have a moral obligation to leave the state of nature, but holds back, continuing to insist that moral language cannot be appropriately applied in a context dominated by drives and impulses. Some of these natural passions, however, hold out at least a possibility of agreement on minimal conditions for a viable social life. Hobbes assumes that all men recognize the benefits of peace, even if they can have little expectation of securing it in a state of nature. They also fear death, which marks the end of any enjoyment whatever. This is a political theory driven by anxiety. Hobbes's readers know that political stability can be easily upset. They can picture the worst that could happen from their recent experience. Hobbes asks them to pay heed to some of their basic passions, in light of a theory that insists they cannot change their motivational set.

Hobbes changes terminology abruptly in chapter fourteen of *Leviathan*, focused on natural laws and contracts. The pleasure seeking, pain avoiding creatures he had described earlier are now depicted as possessors of a 'right of nature' which 'each man hath, to use his own power, as he will himselfe, for the preservation of his own Nature; that is to say, of his own Life; and consequently, of doing any thing, which in his own Judgement, and Reason, hee shall conceive to be the aptest means thereunto'.[74] The implication here is that instrumental reason has an organizing role to play that was scarcely evident in the earlier account of human beings buffeted by contending passions. This enables Hobbes to move from a bare description of individuals hard-wired to preserve their lives to the expressly moral position which obliges them to sustain themselves by whatever means may be to hand. In effect, Hobbes bridges the gap between facts and values in the space of a couple of sentences, with no suggestion that he has made a startlingly contentious philosophical move.

He formulates the position in a 'law of nature', described as 'a Precept, or generall Rule, found out by Reason, by which a man is forbidden to do, that, which is destructive of his life, or taketh away the means of preserving the same; and to omit, that, by which he thinketh it may be best preserved'.[75] The exercise of this right in a state of nature gives individuals unlimited discretion, where 'every man has a Right to every thing; even to one anothers body'.[76] Prudent reflection, and a glance at chapter thirteen, shows that this is a recipe for mutually assured destruction, not security. Instrumental reason, tutored by Hobbesian analysis, accordingly adds the further principled commitment, styled by Hobbes a 'Fundamentall Law of Nature', that 'every man, ought to endeavour Peace, as farre as he has hope of obtaining it; and when he cannot obtain it, that he may seek, and use, all helps, and advantages of Warre'.[77] Note that where their security is at stake, individuals can still resort to violence, entirely at their own discretion. The trick, for Hobbes, is to create circumstances in which that move would be seen to be manifestly self-defeating.

The crucial move is to introduce a principle of reciprocity. Hobbes's 'second Law of Nature' asserts 'that a man be willing, when others are so too, as farre-forth, as for Peace, and defence of himselfe he shall think it necessary, to lay down this right to all things; and be contented with so much liberty against other men, as he would allow other men against him-selfe'.[78] This is a conditional commitment. No one can be obliged to lay down a right of self-defence unilaterally, nor to put himself in a position of acute vulnerability by trusting the good will of others. Only a fool or a saint would fulfil contractual obligations in a state of nature, where a gullible move may very well be one's last. Yet 'in a civill estate, where there is a Power set up to constrain those that would otherwise violate their faith, that feare is no more reasonable; and for that cause, he which by the Covenant is to perform first, is obliged so to do'.[79] Hobbes strives for a mechanism that will overcome the lack of trust in a state of nature. His solution is the institution of *Leviathan*, a public body vested with over-whelming power, able to coerce doubting souls to fulfil civil obligations that are morally defensible in any case, without putting themselves at a disadvantage in the face of cheats and free-riders.

Hobbes is not interested in the details of the actual institution of gov-ernments. His concern is justification rather than historical explanation, despite the image of (hypothetical) transition from a state of nature that he uses to make his case. The ruthlessness of his logic sometimes alarms modern readers. He focuses narrowly on necessary conditions for a sus-tainable life for creatures such as ourselves. He discounts any prospect of discursive agreement on moral and political principles, effectively side-stepping complex discussions of the good life in the style of Plato and Aristotle. But if we cannot expect to agree with strangers on the way we should live, we can, at least, assume that we can recognize the basic con-ditions that might sustain social co-operation over the long term. This is a theory of justice stripped to bare essentials, consisting, says Hobbes, 'in keeping of valid Covenants'; but covenants cannot be regarded as valid until 'the Constitution of a Civill Power, sufficient to compel men to keep them'.[80] Only then, he continues, can 'propriety' begin, reminding us that it is the daily enjoyments of social life rather than the specific complexion of government that should concern us.

Hobbes describes Leviathan as an 'Artificiall Man', specifically consti-tuted by the (hypothetical) agreement of subjects aware of their dire predicament in a state of nature.[81] Whether actual government is monar-chical or collective is a secondary issue for Hobbes. Indeed, when (hypo-thetical) individuals decide to institute Leviathan they have no control of the form government might take, nor of the range of powers that Leviathan might assume. The contract to institute government, in Hobbes, leaves individuals very much exposed to the vagaries of executive discre-tion in relation to the sovereign. The central issue is not that this or that function should be exercised by government, rather that contentious prob-lems that threaten the security of the state should be matters of executive discretion.

Hobbes is very subtle here. In relation to religion, for example, it is a fine judgement whether theological controversy is likely to threaten the peace of the realm. If it does, in the judgement of Leviathan, then specific guidelines can be promulgated on what should be professed, though Hobbes is perfectly aware that little can be done about people's actual beliefs. Likewise the doctrines taught in universities might be subject to public scrutiny if they are deemed to be dangerous. There is immense scope here for seemingly endless extension of the scope of government, yet Hobbes is relatively sanguine on the matter. It is not in the interest of the sovereign to interfere excessively in the lives of subjects, and certainly not to undermine their livelihoods. Good government will leave individuals to pursue the vast majority of their projects unmolested. Where the law is silent, Hobbes insists that 'men have the Liberty, of doing what their own reasons shall suggest, for the most profitable to themselves'.[82] Yet specific laws remain matters of executive discretion. The crucial point, which would be highly contentious in the later development of liberal theory, is that 'the Soveraign of a Commonwealth, be it an Assembly, or one Man, is not Subject to the Civill Lawes'.[83] To try to constrain the sovereign through constitutional means is to divide sovereignty. And divided sovereignty is a recipe for civil war.

Peace is the overriding concern of government, and in Hobbes's account it remains precarious, no matter what institutional arrangements are in place. Our least bad option might thus be to authorize a group or individual to act in the name of the community, to invite them to make their word law. The reservations we might have about particular laws would pale into insignificance in relation to the prospect of a lawless state of nature. We bestow power on Leviathan so that contrary arguments need not be heard, assuming that discursive agreement (in the last resort) is unattainable. What we gain in return, however, if we are lucky, is a stable order in which we can enjoy our lives in peace.

Leviathan's discretion, though vast, is not unlimited. Hobbes, in a hugely important move, allows that individuals retain a natural right to secure their lives. That is why they (could be presumed to have) authorized the establishment of Leviathan in the first place. If Leviathan should threaten the life of any individual, even legitimately through legal punishment, then Hobbes grants that that individual is free to fend for himself. Indeed he outraged some of his royalist friends when he extended the same argument to cases of civil disobedience. 'The Obligation of Subjects to the Soveraign', he insists, 'is understood to last as long, and no longer, than the power lasteth, by which he is able to protect them.'[84] Personal loyalty to a monarch barely figures in Hobbes's scheme of things. Individuals cannot relinquish the right they 'have by Nature to protect themselves'.[85] Doubtless this is a precarious defence against intrusive government. Yet it shows that there are limits to the authority of the state. Subjects harassed and coerced arbitrarily are, in any case, unlikely to be passive and biddable. Leviathan's best interest is likely to be served by interfering with individuals only where the wider well-being of the state is at stake. Principled agreement on what that well-being might involve is highly unlikely, but political revolt is a possibility lurking behind any ruler's strategic calculation. Though this is not a theory of rights in any strong sense, it does mark recognition that political order must be justified in relation to the demands it imposes on subjects. It opens up conceptual possibilities that have radically transformed our understanding of states and their peoples in the modern world.

6

Rights

Hobbes presented his readers with a stark choice. They could either accept the scheme of political order imposed by a *de facto* sovereign or fend for themselves in a state of nature that resembled a 'war of all against all'. If these were the only options, then rational agents would have no choice but to endorse whatever government they enjoyed. Inadequate or irksome government at least leaves some scope for the pursuit of private interests, while the anarchy of a state of nature leaves everyone a prey to (unpredictable) hostile forces.

What Hobbes had discounted was the prospect of any sort of organized social life outside the realm of government. Yet an earlier tradition of thought, extending from Aristotle, the stoics and later natural-law theorists, had always maintained that human beings are naturally sociable. They might argue about the extent and reliability of that sociability, but they pictured government as a means of rendering the natural delights and advantages of social life more certain.

In the early modern period the position was defended authoritatively in Grotius's hugely influential *On the Law of War and Peace* (1625).[1] Grotius was a prodigy in his day, with an unrivalled mastery of the intellectual resources of the humanist tradition. In his native Netherlands he also held important judicial and diplomatic positions, which led him into complex difficulties as domestic politics became dangerously fraught. Imprisonment and exile, however, allowed Grotius to focus on scholarly pursuits across a range of disciplines, embracing law, theology, biblical exegesis and ecclesiastical history.

On the Law of War and Peace is undoubtedly his crowning achievement. In a period racked by religious strife, Grotius sought to introduce a measure of order. Building on earlier discussions of just war, Grotius focused on rights and obligations created in war and sustained through conflict. International lawyers look back on Grotius's text as the beginning of their discipline in its modern form. His detailed treatment of the rights of combatants, the status of acquisitions in war, the appropriate limits of state violence, the status of contracts and other property rights, was unparalleled in his day. Yet the wider implications immediately captured the attention of philosophers. Even in war, where civil order is manifest in only an attenuated form and obligations to enemies might be discounted, Grotius insists that combatants need to exercise a measure of restraint.

Implications for our understanding of moral rules in political contexts are far reaching. In the absence of civil rules, obligations to strangers persist. They are modified and attenuated, to be sure, in the extreme circumstances of war, but standards of judgement must necessarily be invoked when we dispose of people and their property. Who may be killed with impunity, who should be spared, what is the status of the property and dependants of defeated parties? Grotius's detailed answers to these questions are less important from the perspective of this book than the simple fact that they necessarily arise.

Grotius defends a view of normative judgement as a necessary feature of any conceivable social situation. His specific position is rooted in a conception of sociability, derived ultimately from classic stoic sources, that gives us a very different view of the limits and possibilities of human life from Hobbes. The contrast is telling. Where Hobbes grounds his view of politics in an account of a human nature dominated by egoistic drives and interests, Grotius focuses on ordinary judgements that are evident in all our social relations. Thus, in the classic 'prolegomena' to *On the Law of War and Peace*, he insists that a basic 'characteristic of man is an impelling desire for society', but (crucially) not any and every kind of society.[2] Our natural attributes include a capacity to make discriminating social judgements. Man, he says, will seek a 'peaceful and organized' social life that satisfies 'the measure of his intelligence'.[3] For Grotius this is a foundational and self-evident claim. He treats it as a 'universal truth' that directly challenges the view (which Hobbes would later defend) 'that every animal is impelled by nature to seek only its own good'.[4]

Natural sociability does not commit us to any specific view of the principles or values we might want to endorse. And it is true that throughout the 'prolegomena' Grotius conducts the discussion at a level of abstraction that leaves readers hungry for detailed specification of implications. At the very least, however, he has highlighted a 'faculty of knowing and of acting in accordance with general principles' in all ordinarily competent human beings.[5]

Principles come in many guises. Grotius worries his readers when he rushes directly from the abstract account of principles to specific endorsement of core principles which (he suggests) underpin any viable conception of law. Thus he insists that a system of law ('properly so called') will involve 'abstaining from that which is another's, the restoration to another of anything of his which we may have, together with any gain which we may have received from it; the obligation to fulfil promises, the making good of a loss incurred through our fault, and the inflicting of penalties upon men according to their deserts'.[6] Grotius may be right about these details, but he does not show us how the argument hangs together. We can still argue about the moral and political implications of our natural sociability. He is on much stronger ground when he insists on our formal 'power of discrimination which enables' us 'to decide what things are agreeable or harmful'.[7] His confidence in 'well-tempered judgement' is striking.[8] Indeed he claims categorically that 'whatever is clearly at variance with such judgement is understood also to be contrary to the law of nature, that is, to the nature of man'.[9]

'Well-tempered judgements', of course, will often clash, in instances where partiality and limited knowledge lead us to contrary positions. We can all recognize these limitations, while accepting that our flourishing depends upon effective co-operation across the full range of our activities. Grotius does not pursue the full implications of this thought, but leaves us with highly suggestive remarks that were taken up by his followers and critics. Knowing that individual judgement may fail in given cases is not a ground for mistrusting judgement in all cases. Natural sociability is compatible with individual fallibility. What we cannot do, if we remain true to our social natures, is opt out of social relations altogether. Recognition of individual weakness and fallibility actually leads Grotius to endorse a principle of reasonableness. We cannot flourish alone. The 'Author of nature willed that as individuals we should be weak'.[10] This, in Grotius's view, is an additional incentive 'to cultivate the social life', motivated by a principle of 'mutual consent'.[11]

The building blocks are in place here for a fully-fledged contractual theory of political obligation, though we have no more than hints to work with in the text. A crucial point is that legal obligation cannot be defended in terms of 'expediency alone'.[12] Powerful states or individuals have opportunities to exploit their positions in immediate circumstances. Yet, in the context of international relations, Grotius insists that 'there is no state so powerful that it may not some time need the help of others outside itself'.[13] And the same argument applies even more forcefully to the flourishing of individuals.

Legality as a virtue trumps individual opportunities and advantages. Grotius comments that 'all things are uncertain the moment men depart from law'.[14] At the very least, we have here a distinction between long and short-term considerations that obliges us to look at the different justificatory arguments at work. When we take the longer view, the principle of sociability changes the balance of considerations. Grotius is emphatic on this point. He maintains that 'shameful deeds ought not to be committed even for the sake of one's country'.[15] Machiavellian expediency is put firmly in place.

The temptation to read more into the 'prolegomena' than the text warrants is almost irresistible. Grotius was not writing a treatise of political philosophy in the conventional sense. An argument for rights, however, even in the extreme situation of war, highlights issues that might be glossed over in more orthodox treatments. The point to stress from the perspective of this book is the argument for natural rights. And here, again, it is not the actual rights that are of striking interest, but rather the thought that their validity derives from certain natural facts about human beings. Grotius refers to 'certain fundamental conceptions which are beyond question' as the foundation of the 'law of nature'.[16] These conceptions are described as 'manifest and clear, almost as evident as are those things which we perceive by the external senses'.[17] To ask for justification of principles at this level would be as odd as questioning the reliability of our ordinary sense observations. In Grotius's view it would involve an infinite regress, questioning the reasoning that sought to establish that our reasoning is sound. Yet an air of paradox remains. We are asked to treat as self evident commitments that are in fact controversial. Grotius effectively answers the sceptic by declining to give reasons for his foundational principles.

It would be asking too much to expect Grotius to resolve a conundrum that has continued to bedevil discussions of rights to this day. He offers brief advice on method that is rich in potential but undeveloped in the text. Harking back to discussions in Roman law, he refers to two distinct lines of enquiry, one focused on 'a correct conclusion drawn from the principles of nature', the other from 'common consent'.[18] Adapting the terminology of the *Corpus juris civilis*, he describes the former as a 'law of nature', the latter as a 'law of nations'.[19] In disciplinary terms, he is asking us to combine philosophical and historical enquiry in order to validate universal moral claims. Following David Hume's insistence in *A Treatise of Human Nature* that 'facts' and 'values' should be strictly demarcated, logicians have told us that the conflation of the two kinds of enquiry is fraught with difficulty.[20] The temptation, however, is irresistible, as anyone who has hazarded an example in a moral philosophy seminar will attest.

These difficult formal issues were not effectively addressed by Grotius, or indeed any of the other leading philosophers of the early modern period. What we find, instead, in the detail of the text, is a strong commitment to individuals as a source of rights claims. In an intriguing discussion of contracts, for example, Grotius adopts far-reaching positions simply by focusing on the logic of reciprocal and binding engagements. Thus entering a contract (and we can barely imagine a world in which contracts of some kind did not apply) presupposes that the parties are aware of both mutual advantage and 'mutual obligation'.[21] They may not agree about the presumed weight of obligation and interest. Incentives to make agreements will be generated by all manner of background circumstances. But the fact of agreement generates an equal formal commitment to the terms of their mutual agreement.

Grotius thinks of contracts in the broadest possible terms as 'all acts of benefit to others, except mere acts of kindness'.[22] Parties enter these engagements knowingly and openly. It follows that they should enjoy equal standing. And Grotius insists that that standing is generated by the 'law of nature', irrespective of whether the formal equality of contracting parties is actually recognized in the civil law.

Grotius focuses on the myriad forms of actual contracts and agreements, not the hypothetical agreement that may warrant the discretionary acts of governments in the maintenance of collective goods. He does not compromise the free and equal status of the individuals who put themselves under contractual obligations in the pursuit of their rich and varied practical concerns. We cannot conceive of contracts without committing ourselves to 'freedom of choice', and that recognition in turn is unintelligible without acknowledgement of 'a kind of equality between the contracting parties'.[23]

How far does this thought take us? Grotius himself is much bolder than modern defenders of the free and equal status of citizens. He is at pains to balance the 'natural measure of the value of each thing' in terms of need with the fluctuation of prices in relation to more or less abundance.[24] He also asks himself when, 'according to the law of nature', a sale might be regarded as 'completed'.[25] There is a clear indication here that the 'fictions of the civil law' might not match the strict moral conditions of the law of nature.[26] And similarly with monopolies, Grotius asks how far acquisitions may be allowed to extend in relation to different kinds of goods. These are fascinating questions, though the details do not need to detain us here. What must be stressed, however, is that these are matters that cannot be settled by legislative fiat alone. Legislators of all kinds respond to contingent circumstances. Monopolies may be established by force and fraud and subsequently endorsed by a sovereign authority. Grotius insists that sovereign endorsement does not necessarily make them legitimate, though it does not follow that breach of the law of nature in a specific case justifies disobedience. Wielders of sovereign authority might simply be asked to think again, as would be the case with individuals who find themselves entangled in mutually incompatible contractual obligations.

Grotius's defence of sociability framed by laws of nature gives him a clear set of criteria against which to assess the conventional devices we use to further our interests. Honesty and fairness, for example, far from being conventional virtues that ordered government might promote, are portrayed by Grotius as natural properties of human beings, integral features of any conceivable social life. We have a natural capacity to make moral and social judgements. And while there is immense scope for error and confusion in social relations, we have natural resources to work with as we manage our lives.

The political implications here are far reaching. Human beings so endowed are not in the situation of the poor creatures portrayed in Hobbes's state of nature. They do not have to endorse political order at almost any price. Their natural reason is a supremely effective moral compass. They know that they might have to make concessions to one another in order to render difficult situations more amenable, but their judgements will be informed by awareness of the qualities and potential of organized social life.

The conceptual building blocks are in place for the development of a classic contractual model of political legitimacy. We can grasp both the benefits and burdens of our mutual involvement. We can also see that social co-operation, indispensable to our flourishing, can be secured on better and worse terms. The precise terms may be controversial in any given case. But the thought driving contract theory is that all agreements are limited and conditional.

Social contract theory emerged in a variety of guises, each responding in different ways to the turmoil and insecurity generated by the wars of religion in the seventeenth century. The Treaty of Westphalia (1648), bringing to a close the (so-called) Thirty Years War, sought to settle political and religious controversies that threatened to undermine the state as an effective means of containing the disparate groups of people sharing a given territory. Absolutist theories buttressed by divine right would hardly look persuasive to subjects who disputed the basic religious premise of the argument. Yet arguments which justified resistance in the name of religion came close to denying the right of political authorities to maintain order in the face of deep religious conflict.

At one extreme contract theory ran the risk of making political obedience discretionary. If we deem our obligations to God to be supreme, we may well regard obedience to a heretical ruler as a species of collaboration in sin. Resistance literature had indeed flourished since the Reformation, with representative texts spanning the religious spectrum.[27] The novel contribution of contract theory was to argue in terms of theoretical grounds that can appeal across a range of confessional positions. What we find, in fact, is the beginning of a secular defence of conditional political order, which would develop in later liberal theory as an attempt to specify the limits of a reasonable pluralism. In the mid-seventeenth century, however, the various steps in the argument are much more circumspect. Political and religious controversy is deeply interconnected. Philosophers arguing in contractual terms are exploiting the resources of different theological traditions, with barely a suggestion that the political and religious dimensions of the argument could be radically separated.

The distinctive forms of individualism which have dominated certain currents in Western political thought were very much formed in this highly polemical context. Modern philosophers have probably been too ready to view these debates from the settled perspective of later liberal (and emphatically secular) theory. Reading these texts today, we have to remind ourselves that these were dangerous statements that could have dire consequences for authors. Imprisonment or exile were real possibilities of passages read unsympathetically in powerful quarters. When we seek to distil the philosophical heart of an argument, we undoubtedly change the tone of discussion. Disparate and entrenched religious positions may be treated as examples of deep pluralism, but the description is specifically designed to take the heat out of the argument, to advance a perspective that makes compromise less costly in personal terms. Contract theorists reward attention not least because they were striving to establish the legitimacy of these (highly sensitive) opening strategies in what has proved to be an enduring political controversy.

Samuel Pufendorf (1632–94) is an intriguing case because he fashioned his views through close engagement with both Hobbes and Grotius. He was a polymath, like Grotius, with a comparable European reputation. His publications span philosophy, history, jurisprudence and theology, and though he is much less read today than Hobbes, he was one of the commanding figures of his day. The traumas of the religious wars made a deep impression on him. Indeed he endorsed Hobbes's view of peace as a necessary condition for any of the other enjoyments of social life. Yet he also retained (from his reading of Grotius) a much more expansive conception of the natural social attributes of human beings.

Two of Pufendorf's texts warrant attention in this book. The first, his monumental *On the Law of Nature and Nations* (1672), is a full engagement with the controversies of his day, involving detailed exploration of arguments that modern political philosophers would not normally notice.[28] He followed this, however, with a much more concise statement of his position, *On the Duty of Man and Citizen According to Natural Law* (1673), which is much more accessible for modern readers.[29]

The first thing to notice is the clear rejection of a Hobbesian account of human nature. Pufendorf depicts human beings fully endowed with social understanding, aware of moral norms and able to give considered direction to their lives. In this view, we can discriminate between right and wrong but may not always do it effectively. Confusion and error is a natural corollary of the fact that we are able to think for ourselves. Our ordinary failings are sufficient to show that social co-operation is often difficult. Pufendorf feels no need to invoke a stark and amoral picture of man in a state of nature in order to focus our minds on the overwhelming advantages of ordered government.

This is a complex position, but one that is readily understandable. Pufendorf describes man as 'an animal with an intense concern for his own preservation, needy by himself, incapable of protection without the help of his fellows, and very well fitted for the mutual provision of benefits'.[30] We have the potential for a mutually rewarding social life. Yet, at the same time, Pufendorf notes that man is also 'malicious, aggressive, easily provoked and as willing as he is able to inflict harm on others'.[31] The point to stress is that natural social reason is sufficient to make us aware of these failings. We can see for ourselves that 'in order to be safe', we have to be 'sociable'.[32] We can see what needs to be done, even if we cannot trust ourselves to do it.

The fact that our sociability is a natural trait is crucial to Pufendorf's argument. He describes the laws of 'sociality' as 'natural laws' and sums them up in a 'fundamental natural law': that 'every man ought to do as much as he can to cultivate and preserve sociality'.[33] He treats the precepts of natural law as self-evident, 'borne in upon us by the natural light which is native to man'.[34] Natural social intelligence enables us to diagnose the needs of our condition. We can see both that government is necessary, and that it needs to satisfy specific requirements.

It is important to stress just how far natural social obligations extend. Honesty, for example, far from being a virtue that would require a high degree of security and civil trust in order to be exercised as a matter of course, as in Hobbes's state of nature, is portrayed by Pufendorf as a necessary feature of any conceivable social life. He describes honesty as a 'duty prescribed by natural law' and formulates it in terms that have a strong affinity with a Kantian categorical imperative: 'no man should deceive another by language or by other signs which have been established to express the sense of his mind'.[35]

Pufendorf's precise defence of honesty as a virtue is intriguing. He goes beyond obvious utility to show that intelligibility is analytically tied to consistency in the use of terms. We may quibble with Pufendorf's account of the way linguistic consistency and stability actually emerged. He treats meanings as conventions, established through 'a tacit agreement to be made among users of the same language to denote each thing with one particular word and not another'.[36] Speakers incur obligations to one another. Pufendorf is more flexible than Kant, allowing for perfect and imperfect obligations in speech, extending beyond silence to a right to dissemble (for example, in dealing with children) when it would be unreasonable to expect the 'naked truth' to be intelligible.[37] His list of exceptions to strict truth telling is instructive. He allows that 'dissembling discourse' is appropriate in order to 'protect the innocent, placate the angry, comfort the mourning, give courage to the fearful, encourage the squeamish to take medicines, break the stubbornness of one or subvert the evil design of another, draw a veil, so to speak, of fabricated rumours over secrets of state and policies which must be kept from the knowledge of others and divert misplaced curiosity, or use the stratagem of deceiving with false stories an enemy whom we might openly injure'.[38] This is a homely list, covering very many of the ordinary exceptions we allow ourselves in ordinary discourse. Pufendorf does not want his formal requirements to be too exacting. He is commenting on social life as we understand it, with all the ingenious qualifications we devise to fit the demands of different contexts. Pufendorf can accept, unlike Kant, a distinction between 'logical truth' and 'moral truth'.[39] The point to highlight is that these distinctions and reservations are still covered by natural law and indicate the range and subtlety of our natural social intelligence.

Despite the natural social sophistication of human beings, Pufendorf still sees the point of invoking the idea of a state of nature. In his treatment, however, it is a richly variegated condition, depending upon the analytical perspective from which the argument begins. Religious and moral obligations obtain, as do complex levels of obligation incurred in particular associations gathered together for specific purposes. Pufendorf deploys the analytical fiction of a state of nature alongside quasi-historical or anthropological descriptions of the emergence of groups of extended families engaged in complex social practices. The development of these social practices, however, is stunted by a manifest lack of security. For, 'to put the matter in a few words, in the state of nature each is protected only by his own strength; in the state by the strength of all'.[40] Notwithstanding his distance from Hobbes in the characterization of a state of nature, Pufendorf adopts studiedly Hobbesian language in his account of its shortcomings. 'There no one may be sure of the fruit of his industry; here all may be. There is the reign of the passions, there there is war, fear, poverty, nastiness, solitude, barbarity, ignorance, savagery; here is the reign of reason, here there is peace, security, wealth, splendour, society, taste, knowledge, benevolence.'[41]

Paradoxically, it is very much our social sophistication that commits Pufendorf to endorsing a strong sovereign authority. Our natural obligations and affections are a 'rather weak force among those who live in natural liberty with each other'.[42] Strangers cannot be relied upon. Social incentives of various kinds can overwhelm our capacity for social discrimination. 'Hence in the natural state there is a lively and all but perpetual play of suspicion, distrust, eagerness to subvert the strength of others, and desire to get ahead of them or to augment one's own strength by their ruin.'[43] We have complex skills, but little trust, and yet we recognize that our flourishing depends upon sustained social co-operation. Fortunately for the continuance of the species, our resources and ingenuity are a match for our predicament.

Pufendorf's commitment to individualism is deep rooted. Given the equal moral status of individuals in a state of nature, only express agreement can create a hierarchy of ranks and responsibilities. He pictures a 'union of wills' as the indispensable means of establishing a power sufficient to counter the natural divergences between individuals in a natural state. But, typically, the procedure he recommends is complex. He envisages, initially, a unanimous agreement 'to enter into a single and perpetual union', followed by decrees instituting a specific form of government with designated officers.[44] A state so formed is a 'composite moral person', whose will can henceforth be taken to represent the 'will of all'.[45] Pufendorf treats the particular constitutional form of the state (whether 'the bearer of government is called a monarch, a senate or a free people') as a secondary issue.[46]

The specific functions of the state are dictated by its overall purpose – to ensure that 'by mutual cooperation and assistance, men may be safe from the losses and injuries which they may and often do inflict on each other'.[47] Anything that threatens dissension and conflict in the state can (in principle) be controlled. Here, again, Pufendorf moves much closer to Hobbes than his account of the state of nature would suggest, though he shows decidedly more patience with aristocracy and democracy as possible forms of government than his illustrious predecessor. What matters to him in the last resort is the unity of the state, with powers and functions appropriately co-ordinated to guard against internal and external points of conflict. In Pufendorf's case, a personal preference for monarchy does not rule out the viability of other forms of government, though he clearly supposes that aristocracy and democracy multiply occasions for controversy.

The distinction between state and government had fateful consequences in the later development of political thought. Pufendorf himself was very cautious in exploring the detailed implications of a crucial distinction in his theory. His preoccupation with the security of the state led him to circumscribe occasions for political opposition much more narrowly than would seem appropriate to later thinkers in more settled political contexts. The maintenance of supreme sovereign power was so important to him that he was prepared to countenance an authority that is in some sense 'unaccountable', superior to 'human and civil laws as such, and thus not directly bound by them'.[48] All this, it must be remembered, in a theory based on the capacity of individuals to devise appropriate means for the maintenance of their political security and interests.

At the heart of Pufendorf's theory is thus a dilemma that is far from adequately resolved. What he had highlighted, however, perhaps inadvertently, is a tension between the rights of individuals and the authority of established rules that may finally be irresolvable theoretically. Individuals exercising their rights will draw lines in different places. The unanimity condition in Pufendorf's first agreement to form a state is thus deeply revealing. We are left with a requirement that could not possibly be satisfied as a prerequisite for the limitations on individual discretion that would otherwise be rendered illegitimate. Social contract theory has continued to operate within these (highly controversial) terms of reference to this day.

Not all contract theories were focused on the abstract consent of unadorned individuals. Johannes Althusius (1557–1638), the prolific Calvinist theorist, presented in his influential *Politics* (1603) a complex picture of organized societies instituting a quasi-federal centre of government to act on their behalf in appropriate (and limited) spheres.[49] Althusius accepts, with orthodox contract theory, that individuals, naturally 'naked and defenceless', are utterly dependent on one another for sustenance, let alone the finer things that social life might offer.[50] But instead of beginning his account with needy individuals in a hypothetical state of nature, he stresses the role of actual communities of various kinds contributing to the provision of basic goods and services that constitute a sustainable way of life.

Althusius treats contract literally as a decision to provide collectively goods that could not be provided individually. His theory focuses on association at the very many different levels we are all familiar with in our daily lives. His discussion begins with the family as a 'special covenant', designed to bring together and 'hold in common a particular interest'.[51] He calls covenanters 'symbiotes', a term he applies across the range of human associations. What distinguishes them is a special kind of communication appropriate for the given range of activities they have agreed to pursue together. Thus in the family the 'symbiotes' are united 'by a certain bond' that institutes a 'structure and good order for communicating' mutual needs on a consensual basis.[52]

The family is a natural organization, yet its particular organization is established through agreement. Broader associations are structured in similar fashion 'to serve a common utility and necessity in human life'.[53] Althusius conceives of 'association' in the widest possible terms. Thus when 'three or more men of the same trade, training, or profession are united for the purpose of holding in common such things they jointly profess as duty, way of life, or craft', they are said to constitute a 'collegium, or as it were, a gathering, society, federation, sodality, synagogue, convention, or synod'.[54] In all these spheres of activity, 'a plan of life' is 'set forth in covenanted agreements'.[55] The terms of reference may be more or less extensive, depending upon the kinds of activities undertaken by the collegium. But the authority of the rules and conventions derives from the collective agreement of the 'symbiotes'.

Strictly political authority is generated by precisely the same logic. Althusius's key contention, however, is that the agreement to form wider political orders stems from the private associations themselves, grouped together in wider provincial associations, recognizing their mutual needs and devising appropriate measures. Althusius describes political authority at the level of city or province as 'an association formed by fixed laws and composed of many families and collegia living in the same place'.[56] What is created when such groups band together is a 'representational person' which specifically 'represents men collectively, not individually'.[57] The terms of association are specified by a 'public symbiotic right' that designates roles and responsibilities.[58] This is not a creation of 'right' out of a 'rightless' state of nature, but a refinement of the ways and means established in private associations to manage collective needs. Political sovereignty so conceived is very strictly limited, answerable to the constituent groups that constitute this level of authority. As with other modes of social authority, political authority is the product of 'a tacit or expressed promise to communicate things, mutual services, aid, counsel, and the same common laws to the extent that the utility and necessity of universal social life in a realm shall require'.[59] Althusius is careful in his form of words.

Political authority exists to manage interests. It extends no further than the multifaceted needs of the complex communities it represents. Political authority is created by agreement, and agreement is necessarily limited and conditional.

What is distinctive about Althusius's conception of political authority is his view of each sector of social life as a discrete sphere of activity, extending from family, through collegium, to city and province, until we reach the level of the state itself, which enjoys a universal jurisdiction within a given territory but for limited purposes. Rights, roles and responsibilities are designated according to functional effectiveness, with associates exercising their discretion about appropriate means in each case.

Associates, however, do not operate in a moral vacuum. Althusius treats the *Decalogue* as the authoritative source of the ground rules of social practices. Associates at various levels can establish all number of consensual practices among themselves, but they cannot breach basic rules guaranteeing mutual respect. The laws of the *Decalogue* function much like precepts of natural law in other theories, prescribing the 'duties vouchsafed to our neighbour'.[60] As associates, we work within fixed moral parameters. It is not open to us to suspend the requirements of justice. When we render justice to our neighbour, Althusius insists that we do to him 'what we wish to be done to ourselves'.[61] And he is happy to follow the spirit of the *Decalogue* in his treatment of specific practices, in relation to property rights, sexual morality, personal injury and so on. But he is careful to distinguish the universal principles at work in the *Decalogue* from the specific precepts that Moses will have devised to fit the circumstances of the 'Jewish commonwealth'.[62] Universal rules always need to be interpreted. And that burden necessarily falls on associates discharging the detailed responsibilities of their spheres of activity.

Althusius's detailed discussion of modes of administration need not detain us here. What needs to be noticed, however, is his attempt to adapt a politics of principle to the contingent circumstances that communities find themselves in. The focus is on judgement in a variety of social contexts, carrying with it a burden of shared responsibility that will vary with different kinds of engagement. Althusius's covenanters are thus fully formed social creatures, able to bring rich understanding to the business of deciding what to do next in difficult circumstances. As discriminating individuals with social responsibilities, they will be guarded in their commitments. The social orders and practices they create will have specific purposes. They will also be revocable. Circumstances will change, involving new provision in areas that could not have been foreseen. And agents in positions of responsibility may abuse the trust that has been placed in them. In these circumstances, associates will have to think again about the specific structures of authority they have ordained, though they will be cautious in the measures they adopt to remedy a breach of social trust. Althusius's specific recommendations for managing political crisis will strike modern readers as odd (an ephorate as a kind of supreme court of judgement). The point, however, is that tyranny comes in many forms, some of then endurable for the sake of the wider benefits of an ordered social life. But agents capable of making considered social judgements will not put their trust unconditionally in any specific authority figures or structures. Put simply, social and political discrimination cannot be suspended.

As theorists of social contract, both Althusius and Pufendorf treated the radical implications of the doctrine with caution. Both sought to devise institutional means of distinguishing between radical opposition to government and rejection of a regime. Yet critical cutting edge remains. Unconditional authority is a contradiction in terms. Authorization involves terms of reference. And breach of those terms of reference undermines authority. The appropriate political response to such a situation is a matter of judgement. Hobbes's residual commitment to a natural right to life has thus been fleshed out to embrace the range of social competences that individuals naturally possess. The crucial point to focus on here is that socially competent individuals and groups could not reasonably be expected to authorize a government with absolute powers to hold sway over them. Government exists to fulfil a purpose. When the purpose is not fulfilled, other measures must be sought.

John Locke's *Two Treatises of Government* (1689) is the classic statement of the doctrine of conditional political authority.[63] A text that was once regarded as a celebration of the Glorious Revolution of 1688, which removed James II from the crown of England is now thought to have been initially drafted some ten years earlier.[64] Clearly this dating makes the book a much more radical political statement. Locke's personal involvement in attempts in 1682–3 to exclude James from the throne because of his presumed Catholicism and sympathy for absolutism exposed him to acute risks. He was closely identified with the Whig political elite of his day. His political patron, the Earl of Shaftesbury, fled to Holland in 1682. Locke followed in 1683, hoping to avoid the fate of Algernon Sidney, who was executed. Locke only felt safe enough to return to England after the satisfactory conclusion of the Glorious Revolution, with the new political regime of William and Mary in place. He was thus fully aware of the radical implications of his treatise and the consequences that might have befallen him had it been published earlier. In the event, Locke still preferred to publish anonymously in 1689, though his identity as the author was widely known.

What we are confronted with is thus a complex text, formulated in response to two distinct contexts that reflect different concerns. The *First Treatise*, for example, much neglected by modern political theorists and students, is preoccupied with the issue of patriarchalism in the version defended by Filmer. Filmer, we must remind ourselves, was regarded as an authoritative figure in royalist circles in the late 1670s and early 1680s.

His *Patriarcha* was in fact published for the first time in 1680, long after the author's death, as a contribution very specifically to the contemporary debate about the prerogatives of the crown.

Locke accordingly set himself the task of rebutting the most authoritative defence of absolutism available in the early 1680s. He encapsulated Filmer's position in two propositions: 'that all government is absolute monarchy' and 'that no man is born free'.[65] He then proceeded to attack Filmer on his own ground, marshalling detailed biblical argument to make his case. It must be said that the wider thrust of Locke's argument gets lost in the painstaking critical assault. Where Filmer had conflated 'paternal and regal power', Locke insists on strict separation.[66] The larger point, of course, is to challenge the relevance of the image of God the father, creating a universe out of nothing, to an account of the authority of a king as the father of his people, creating order out of what would otherwise be chaos.

In Locke's view, Filmer has confused the question of how (paternal and regal) authority is acquired with the quite different question of the justification of the authority individuals might have to exercise power in different contexts. Thus the relevant question is 'not whether there be power in the world, nor whence it came, but who should have it'.[67] The clear implication here is that authority depends upon the appropriate exercise of power. Filmer's argument, so Locke claims, fails on its own terms. Biblical support for the unconditional patriarchal model is not forthcoming, nor can it be conceptually defended.

Locke develops his own positive proposals in the much more widely read *Second Treatise*. Essentially a text of its time, contributing to the tortured debate about the proper roles of parliament and executive in the aftermath of the Glorious Revolution, Locke also managed to mount a philosophical defence of limited government that has continued to be an inspiration to liberal theory and practice to this day. It would be very difficult indeed to understand contemporary liberalism without taking Locke's ideas on board. Yet we must also remind ourselves that he was writing for a very narrow intellectual and political elite that had little interest in, or awareness of, the social and economic circumstances of a wider citizenry. A text that is seen as a basic building block for liberal democratic theory was not itself defending liberalism or democracy in the modern sense. The implications of Locke's ideas, however, continue to resonate, in ways that would certainly have surprised him.

The contemporary relevance of Locke's politics is the more surprising in light of the traditional form of his argument. He uses the conventional devices that we have noticed in Hobbes, Pufendorf and Althusius – a state of nature, social contract, and wider conception of natural law – yet gives these notions a decidedly radical twist. The contrast is most readily evident in his initial account of a state of nature. He writes categorically that 'to understand political power right, and derive it from its original, we must consider what state all men are naturally in, and that is, a state of perfect freedom to order their actions, and dispose of their possessions, and persons as they think fit, within the bounds of the law of nature, without asking leave, or depending upon the will of any other man'.[68] All the ingredients of a reasonable social life seem to be available here, including property and the idea of a natural legal framework.

He goes on to assert that this state of nature is also 'a state . . . of equality, wherein all the power and jurisdiction is reciprocal, no one having more than another'.[69] He simply denies that natural distinctions between human beings (so central to Filmer's argument) have any moral relevance at all. Notice that he does not feel the need to introduce arguments in support of these claims. He is not giving us empirical descriptions that might be challenged if other evidence were available. He is telling us what might be said to be implicit in the way we behave and think, though that simple truth is disguised in false theory (like Filmer's) focused on narrow and partial interests.

Not only do we enjoy free and equal status in a state of nature, we also have a fully developed capacity to regulate our own conduct and to assume responsibility for broader breaches of the law of nature. Thus though a state of nature may lack executive and judicial institutions, we are nevertheless not at liberty to do as we please. The 'state of liberty' (in a state of nature) should not be construed as a 'state of licence'.[70] Locke is emphatic on this point. The area of our personal discretion is vast, yet we are bound by natural moral constraints. 'The state of nature' (Locke insists) 'has a law of nature to govern it, which obliges every one: and reason, which is that law, teaches all mankind, who will but consult it, that being all equal and independent, no one ought to harm another in his life, health, liberty, or possessions.'[71] These are far reaching obligations. In stark contrast with Hobbes's account of a state of nature, then, where amoral survival precepts hold sway, Locke gives us a picture of fully rounded individuals, aware of responsibilities to one another, sharing both natural rationality and a natural moral code.

Locke's rich account of the rights and responsibilities of a state of nature is deeply revealing. Indeed he goes beyond depicting natural social capacities to give us the rudiments of social regulation without the state. Legal punishment, for example, which might be regarded as a quintessential function of the state, is portrayed as a feature of a state of nature, albeit in an undeveloped form. Locke argues that if the rights enjoyed in a state of nature are to have any substantive status, then means must be in place to restrain us 'from doing hurt to one another'.[72] He accepts that a law without a means of execution would be merely a pious moral exhortation. Yet social organization in his state of nature is much more robust than that. In the absence of formal governmental structures, 'the execution of the law of nature is in that state, put into every mans hands, whereby every one has a right to punish the transgressors of that law to such a degree, as may hinder its violation'.[73] Hobbes had claimed that law without coercive means to enforce it is a contradiction in terms. Locke accepts the point but stresses the natural capacity and responsibility we each share to ensure that the law of nature is observed.

Locke's position is based upon hugely optimistic assumptions about human nature. Where Hobbes was haunted by the endless possibilities for disagreement, Locke discounts the challenge of moral and political scepticism altogether. He regards the exercise of practical reason as a perfectly straightforward affair. What we should do, he insists, is 'so plain' that it is 'writ in the hearts of all mankind'.[74] Hobbes saw no prospects for natural social co-operation because he assumed that moral and political reasoning is a matter of finding pretexts for the pursuit of interests, and interests are always likely to clash. The massive discretion Hobbes allows Leviathan stems directly from the inevitable failure of practical reason to overcome natural partiality. Locke, by contrast, maintains that 'truth and keeping of faith belongs to men, as men, and not as members of society'.[75] Conditions for consensual co-operation exist in a state of nature. The state of nature is not a state of chronic insecurity, nor is it a state of war. Indeed Locke insists, in a passage which calls Hobbes to mind, though he is not cited, that 'the plain difference between the state of nature, and the state of war, which however some men have confounded, are as far distant, as a state of peace, good will, mutual assistance, and preservation, and a state of enmity, malice, violence, and mutual destruction are from one another'.[76] If this is our natural condition, then we will think long and hard before surrendering our natural discretion to anyone.

What we would certainly not do is put ourselves in a position of absolute vulnerability. Locke reminds us that though the 'inconveniences of the state of nature' may be considerable, 'where men may be judges in their own case', that would scarcely justify us in authorizing anyone, least of all 'absolute monarchs', who 'are but men', to exercise unlimited discretion in deciding our fate.[77] The restrictions we are prepared to endure under government will reflect the gravity of the 'inconveniences' of the state of nature. Locke is at pains to portray a relatively benign situation, such that the natural rights and responsibilities we enjoy can serve as the measure of the benefits government should provide.

Locke's initial account of the state of nature is indeed so positive that we get barely an indication of the incentives that might incline us to leave it. The 'inconveniences' he hints at are not developed in any detail. Reading between the lines of other sections of the text, however, we can put together an account that ties Locke's thinking on this issue much more closely to certain prevailing economic assumptions of his day. In a chapter on property he advances (what later thinkers have construed as) a labour theory of value that, in modified form, paves the way for capital accumulation and significant economic inequalities.[78]

It is important to Locke that he sets a right to property on a solid, pre-political foundation. Property ownership is among our natural rights. And respect for that right, in particular, significantly limits the scope for governmental interference in the private affairs of citizens. Indeed later liberal insistence on a distinction between public and private spheres can be traced back to Locke, though he defends his position by recourse to theological arguments that modern liberals would find decidedly odd. Locke proclaims that God has given the earth to 'mankind in common' for mutual sustenance, though he later qualifies that as a gift to the 'industrious and rational', rather than to the 'fancy or covetousness of the quarrelsome and contentious'.[79] Yet we do not continue to hold the earth in common. We develop a specific title through our labour, exercising the exclusive 'property' we enjoy in our 'own person'.[80] The language here is strained, and barely intelligible outside a very specific theological context, but Locke harnesses it to make a formidable political point that continues to be invoked in contemporary political theory.[81] He treats work as a primary source of value and entitlement. Thus whenever we remove a resource 'out of the state that nature hath provided, and left it in', we have mixed our 'labour with, and joyned to it something that is' (very specifically) our 'own'.[82] Through our work we create an entitlement 'that excludes the common right of other men', though with the proviso that we leave 'enough, and as good . . . in common for others' to enjoy.[83] This is a specific and complex commitment, yet Locke insists it should be honoured in a state of nature, 'without any express compact of all the commoners'.[84]

Entitlement to property through labour is limited by Locke's insistence that nature's bounty is strictly available for use and consumption. We can appropriate 'as much as any one can make use of to any advantage of life before it spoils'.[85] Locke pictures natural resources being enjoyed 'within the bounds, set by reason of what might serve for . . . use'.[86] Natural abundance, coupled with limited consumption, creates rough equilibrium. Balance is destroyed, however, by 'the invention of money' which, through 'tacit agreement', allows unlimited accumulation by serving as an imperishable measure of value.[87]

Locke has no reservations about the ethics of accumulation in these new conditions. He contends that a money economy so expands productive capacity that God's natural provision is being multiplied. We then have a distributional problem to address, though Locke gives us few clues about how this might be handled. Whatever measures might be devised, however, would clearly have to respect the status of property rights as natural rights. What is certain is that emerging inequalities, perfectly justifiable following the introduction of money, will exacerbate the original 'inconveniences' of the state of nature. Conflict and crime, we must assume, will become urgent issues in a social world which sees the 'industrious and rational' compounding their initial competitive advantage. Gainers from the money economy will have deep suspicions about the motives of the 'quarrelsome and contentious'. The incentive to introduce a regular coercive apparatus might in these circumstances be compelling.

Locke's state of nature functions as much more than a hypothetical device highlighting the problems we could anticipate outside political orders. Instead he gives us a detailed account of the dynamics of social co-operation in two contrasting situations (before and after the introduction of money). The details are important. The state of nature is not simply a hypothetical problem to resolve. Locke shows how natural sociability within a state of nature can radically change terms of social co-operation. If, in the light of dilemmas that emerge as new conventions and practices are established, we feel impelled to introduce radical changes, these are very much matters of degree. The transition to political society from a state of nature is portrayed as falling comfortably within the natural competence of human beings left to their own devices. They know what they can do and what they enjoy. They can perfectly well envisage taking instrumental steps to enhance the natural satisfactions of their lives. But they would not do anything to make the tangible benefits of social life more precarious.

Locke highlights two key implications that follow directly from his account of a state of nature. While the 'inconveniences' of a state of nature make moves towards civil society rational, the commitment would have to be conceived consensually and conditionally. Locke is categorical in his defence of both points. He asserts without qualification that 'men being, as has been said, by nature, all free, equal and independent, no one can be put out of this estate, and subjected to the political power of another, without his own consent'.[88] In this particular passage he barely stops to ask what might actually be involved in giving consent, and indeed throughout the text the issue is addressed only in the loosest terms. Significantly, however, he stresses the concrete advantages of civil order. We agree 'with other men to joyn and unite into a community, for' our 'comfortable, safe, and peaceable living one amongst another, in a secure enjoyment of' our 'properties, and a greater security against any that are not of it'.[89] Our moral status remains as it was in a state of nature. And it is assumed that we have a capacity to judge whether or not the anticipated benefits of civil order have actually been attained.

Our incentive to establish political society is thus very specific indeed. We 'unite for the mutual preservation of' our 'lives, liberties and estates', which Locke calls 'by the general name, property'.[90] Locke's use of property as a summary term is revealing. It should not be read necessarily as an indication of the narrowness of his (class-based?) concern, but as a studied means of achieving specific objectives. We need 'an establish'd, settled, known law, received and allowed by common consent to be the standard of right and wrong' in order to facilitate our dealings with one another.[91] And this requires 'a known and indifferent judge' to issue authoritative rulings, backed by a power sufficient to 'support the sentence when right, and to give it due execution'.[92] Essentially we are transferring our natural discretion to do as we think appropriate to preserve ourselves and others 'within the permission of the law of nature' and our natural 'power to punish the crimes committed against that law' to a public body authorized to act on our behalf.[93] This is a very particular brief to pursue 'no other end, but the peace, safety, and publick good of the people'.[94]

Government so conceived is a trust, and trusts may be well or ill fulfilled. It follows that whatever institutional structures are adopted, they would necessarily have to be revocable if government were not meeting its purpose. Locke accepts that legitimate government can assume different forms. Absolute monarchy, however, is ruled out as a matter of course, as indeed would be the case with any other form of absolute government, because wielders of power are not answerable to a wider citizenry. One would as well assume, remarks Locke, 'that men are so foolish that they take care to avoid what mischiefs may be done them by pole-cats, or foxes, but are content, nay think it safety, to be devoured by lions'.[95] Locke has his own preferences about forms of government, but he allows that democracy, oligarchy and monarchy (hereditary or elective) may all be legitimate provided they are regarded as provisional means of sustaining the public good. In institutional terms Locke thus moves from an initial commitment to majority rule, when men first resolve 'to make one community', to more flexible means of delivering government.[96] The point to stress, however, is that legislative power in limited hands is nevertheless answerable to the people at large.

Locke's specific constitutional proposals need not detain us unduly. His insistence on a separation between legislative and executive powers has had a profound impact on the subsequent development of liberal constitutional theory, though he shows little awareness of the significance of specific constitutional safeguards to the independence of the judiciary. Instead he adds a 'federative' power to the legislative and executive spheres which concerns the international relations of the commonwealth. And though he remarks that the 'executive and federative' powers should be 'really distinct in themselves', he accepts that in practice executive and federative functions will be in the same hands.[97] Locke's tripartite division thus anticipates later liberal insistence on separation of constitutional powers, though in confused terms and with a notable omission.

His discussion of the supremacy of the legislative power, however, is revealing. He reiterates the view of government as a trust, set within 'bounds' specified by the 'law of God and nature'.[98] As we are all God's creatures, so law will apply indifferently to each and every one of us. There will be 'one rule for rich and poor, for the favourite at court, and the country man at plough'.[99] Further, 'laws ought to be designed for no other end ultimately but the good of the people'.[100] And, more specifically, laws which 'raise taxes on the property of the people, without the consent of the people' cannot be regarded as legitimate.[101] Nor can the legislature 'transfer the power of making laws to any body else, or place it any where but where the people have'.[102] These are demanding criteria, ranging across formal and substantive matters. The supreme organ of government is thus strictly limited in its procedures and goals. When a legislature exceeds its brief, it breaches the trust of the people and ceases to be legitimate. Here, at a moment of crisis, and with the Glorious Revolution in his reader's minds, we would expect Locke to be at his most precise and careful. Yet he hedges his bets, leaving dark areas where we cannot be sure where lines of resistance should be drawn and by whom.

Locke discusses the vexed issues of opposition and disobedience in a chapter on the 'dissolution of government' that is far from satisfactory.[103] If he is to sustain his claim that legitimate government is necessarily limited, it follows that remedies should be in place if people are 'expos'd to the boundless will of tyranny' or rulers 'grow exorbitant in the use of their power'.[104] But, as with any theory of resistance, a line has to be drawn between the irritations of specific government measures and systematic abuse of office sufficient to justify a change of regime. Here Locke's distinction between the 'dissolution of government' and the 'dissolution of society' comes into play.[105] We should note, however, that the very idea of a 'dissolution of society' takes him much closer to a Hobbesian world view than would be warranted from an orthodox reading of his account of a state of nature. Locke's defence of limited government presupposes a view of the state of nature as a social world. Within his terms of reference, 'dissolution of society' at that level is inconceivable.

What clearly worries him is that the dissolution of the legislative body, which was initially 'established by the majority', would make subsequent co-ordinated activity deeply problematic.[106] If the people, at a time of revolutionary crisis, become 'a confused multitude', who is authorized to represent the genuine interests of that multitude?[107] Locke is clear that a society can never lose the 'native and original right it has to preserve it self'; but once trust in government is lost, it is by no means obvious how it might best be redeemed.[108]

In the ordinary way of things, Locke assumes that people have the wit and ingenuity to prevent problems from getting out of hand. Yet he also acknowledges that dire circumstances take us beyond theory. Revolutions challenge structures of authority. When government is dissolved, we cannot answer the question, 'who shall be judge?', because 'there is no judge at all'.[109] For all that he had earlier wanted to play down the stark Hobbesian contrast between a state of nature and civil society, he now accepts that 'where there is no judicature on earth, to decide controversies, amongst men, God in Heaven is judge'.[110] And doubtless all protagonists will claim that they have God on their side.

Little can be done to save Locke from the difficulties of his final chapter. He was publishing his book from the perspective of a successful revolution accomplished by an aristocratic elite. He clearly assumes that natural leaders of this kind will emerge to fill the gap left by organized government. Indeed his account of a state of nature is compatible with a leading role for a property-owning elite. Yet there is an obvious tension between his commitment to the free and equal status of individuals in a state of nature and the distinction between politically active and passive classes that informs his view of opposition.

Nor is this incidental to his theory. In his earlier discussion of consent, he had made a distinction between 'express consent' and 'tacit consent' that has always troubled his commentators.[111] 'Express consent' involves 'a sufficient declaration of a mans consent, to make him subject to the laws of any government'.[112] In Locke's day, among an aristocratic elite, this might have been achieved through an oath of allegiance that would mark someone out as 'a perfect member of that society'.[113] This is clearly beyond the experience and expectations of a wider population. Ordinary citizens, Locke assumes, will give their 'tacit consent' simply through enjoying the benefits of government. Thus, whether 'enjoyment' might amount to 'possession' of land, 'or a lodging only for a week', or 'barely travelling freely on the highway', Locke suggests that it can be construed as tacit endorsement of the government of the day.[114] This obviously stretches the meaning of 'consent' beyond the normal range of the term. He had been at pains in earlier sections of the text to portray 'consent' as a voluntary commitment that could (in principle) be withheld. But 'tacit consent' cannot be withheld while remaining within the confines of a territory. The majority of the population, for whom travel abroad is not a realistic option, are thus left endorsing government no matter what might happen to them.

Doubtless Locke's allusions to status divisions in his citizen body tell us a great deal about the entrenched political assumptions of his day. They should not be allowed to distract, however, from the radical implications of his theory. His insistence that human beings with natural rights and powers, including a natural right to property, will think long and hard before investing authority in anyone contributed signally to a new understanding of the proper relationship between the state and the individual. Individuals will view the state as a means of advancing their interests and nothing more. They will recognize a politically lawless condition as inconvenient rather than insupportable. And they will take for granted that they are each endowed with a natural sense of responsibility to act in defence of the basic rights that everyone should enjoy. It makes perfect sense in this context to institute government as an effective means of fulfilling responsibilities that could fall to anyone, at any time. But, crucially, government so conceived is held in trust. And systematic abuse of that trust renders void any earlier concession of a right to rule.

The modern doctrine of limited government is very much built on Lockean foundations. The conduct of a limited politics, however, is a deeply complex affair, as Locke's difficulties with the notion of consent surely reveal. The fact that an elite will dominate decision making in a state does not undermine the equal standing of citizens, though it stretches our understanding of what it is we share as citizens in ways that Locke barely recognizes. What we have is a critical criterion which legitimate government has to satisfy. To be sure, this position leaves a great deal to be resolved. How in practice government could be exercised effectively without concentrating threatening powers in too few hands is a matter that political cultures have had to address in the light of their own experience. Pufendorf was anxious not to confer a right of resistance to rulers that might be too readily invoked, while Locke hedges a proclaimed right of resistance with conditions that make it very much a matter of last (and desperate) resort. Yet both could insist that legitimate government had necessarily to be limited. The principle of constitutional government had been established, even if detailed constitutional proposals might look quaint or naïve.

7

Enlightenment

Natural rights argument put immense stress on the idea of consent, willing agreement to or hypothetical authorization of practices and institutions. Much less attention was given to the frail and fallible individuals who are presumed to be giving their consent. A theory of human nature had always underpinned conceptions of natural rights, but detailed examination of human nature itself might lead to significant modification of theories of rights.

The prodigious advance of the natural sciences in the seventeenth and eighteenth centuries provided the context for the emergence of a science of human nature. Treating the physical universe as a material system, open to empirical enquiry, had demonstrably enhanced human capacity for technological innovation. There was no reason, in principle, why similar assumptions should not be employed in relation to human culture and conduct. Once innate ideas and occult qualities had been dismissed to the realm of superstition, untold possibilities emerge for understanding and control of the human world. Knowledge (in whatever sphere) assumes the guise of a configuration of sense-impressions on a mind originally bereft of concepts and categories. Our conceptions of moral and physical harm can then be derived from a common source – experience of the painful consequences of particular occurrences. Conceptual possibilities here are tantalizing. There may be no qualitative difference between a 'bad conscience' and a 'burnt hand'. Human conduct (quite as much as physical phenomena) may be regarded as governed by laws of motion in the form of attraction and aversion. The word 'good' may be little more than a description of the things we happen to desire. Once human conduct is rendered in these terms, old-fashioned metaphysical discourse on (for example) the essential nature of the 'will' become obsolete. The clear implication is that methods of enquiry that have proved their worth in disclosing the mysteries of the natural world could transform our understanding of what it is to be a human being, ushering in prospects for social, political and economic improvement that seemed limitless to their most optimistic advocates.

Seeing human beings as natural objects in a world of natural facts was a first move in a long series of tortuous developments. The philosophical ground was prepared by Spinoza in his *Ethics*, published posthumously in 1677, where human beings are portrayed as natural creatures in a causally determined universe.[1] What distinguishes human beings, in this scheme of things, is not a capacity to choose or will freely but a broader (if only implicit) awareness of their place in a system of nature.

Spinoza was both a follower and critic of Descartes and developed his argument in strict geometrical form. This poses immense difficulties for modern readers accustomed to discursive styles of argument, but there is a limpid quality to Spinoza's thought, once grasped, that has powerfully influenced thinkers down to our own times from a range of philosophical and political traditions. The *Ethics* cannot be casually consulted. It makes sense as a system or not at all, and resists simple summary. At the heart of the system, however, is a celebration of a relationship between knowledge and freedom. We do ourselves no favours if we wallow in received under-standings of things, comforting though familiar ideas may be as we stumble through our lives. Supposing that we are free to think or do or believe anything, for example, undermines our efforts to understand our-selves. But nor does it help to treat ourselves as puppets in the hands of a personal God, orchestrating our lives in mysterious ways. Understanding enriches our lives and may change the way we respond to specific occur-rences. Spinoza supposes that we are free when we rid ourselves of error, not when we stand salivating in front of a tray of delights. We simply are natural phenomena. We express our freedom, for Spinoza, when we con-sciously accept natural necessity, setting aside traditional moral or reli-gious notions to see ourselves as products of complex networks of natural forces.

Spinoza's key distinction is between 'adequate' and 'inadequate' ideas.[2] The latter comprise our ordinary notions and preferences, accumulated in the course of experience. What we actually experience in our lives is, of course, an entirely contingent matter. And our judgement in specific instances may be distorted by fear, anger, passion, vanity and so forth. We may think of 'inadequate' ideas as opinions. All we can say about them is that they are our own. The intensity of our convictions may guide our actions, but we have no warrant for concluding that our convictions are true. Awareness of the subjectivity of our convictions, however, opens up an entirely new perspective. Understanding why we think what we think enables us to make causal claims about the genesis of ideas. These would hold for anyone, anywhere. Spinoza insists that knowledge should be demonstrable, though his specific version of the way that demonstration might work is highly contentious.

We cannot form 'adequate' ideas, of ourselves or the natural world, unless we treat nature as an integrated system. Spinoza identifies nature as a whole with God, though in a metaphysical rather than personal sense.

He has in his mind a picture of theoretical perfection which he uses as a criterion to assess our experience. We may use the idea of God as a shorthand for this notion of perfection. Thus 'all ideas, in so far as they have reference to God, are true'.[3] God is here equated with anything we can conceive of, viewed as a whole. As individual things, of course, we are 'contingent and corruptible'.[4] We can grasp the theoretical idea of a complete system of knowledge, without supposing the collection of our ideas adequately reflects the world as a whole. What we have, though, is the beginnings of a critical criterion that enables us to assess the adequacy of our actual ideas.

Spinoza's 'geometrical' demonstration of his view of the world in the *Ethics* did not focus on specific political prescriptions, though his discussion of human motivation and freedom has political implications which have attracted the attention of a host of later philosophers. He accepts, with Hobbes, whom he had studied closely, that we are naturally buffeted by emotions that seriously distort our understanding of the workings of our minds and bodies. Thus all our emotions 'have reference to pleasure, pain, or desire'.[5] If we remain at that passive level, however, we will have little understanding of what an emotion actually is. We have to grasp that human beings, like all other natural phenomena, strive to maintain themselves in activity. This simple thought enables us to distinguish between the bewildering array of passions and emotions that confront us throughout our lives. Some, like anger or fear, may so torment us that we cannot pursue a steady course of conduct. If I am haunted by the thought that I may die at any moment, I am unlikely to be able to give considered attention to any project. But what do I actually fear when I contemplate the end of my life? The phantoms of popular religion may terrify us but, for Spinoza, death is simply the absence of activity. And absence of activity is, literally, nothing. Could a wise man fear death, knowing that death is nothing at all? Spinoza is categorical on the issue. 'A free man,' he insists, 'thinks of nothing less than of death, and his wisdom is a meditation not of death but of life.'[6] Recognizing how things are dispels illusions. Knowing the truth frees us from superstitious attachments. But, more important, from the fallible perspective of human understanding, we are presented with an attitude of mind that helps us to analyse sources of error.

Spinoza's view of human flourishing has strong affinities with classic stoic ideas. He defends the relationship between freedom and necessity as forcefully as any modern writer. A free man would not be moved by passion and emotion. Understanding the world and himself, he would always act appropriately. The distinction between good and evil would simply not exist for him, because he would never have to ask himself how he should behave. Spinoza declares emphatically that a free man would always have 'adequate ideas' and would accordingly have 'no conception of evil'.[7]

The key theme here is the link between evil and ignorance. A free man, blessed with hypothetically perfect knowledge, cannot knowingly pursue evil. Perfect knowledge, for Spinoza (as, later, for Kant), functions as a regulative ideal. We experience life as a struggle because we are fallible and imperfect creatures. Spinoza's point, however, is that we can conceive an idea of perfection. That changes things for us. We remain natural entities, subject to the vagaries of health and luck, but we do not allow our view of ourselves to be dictated by the accidents of everyday life. We know what it is to be a human being (and not simply this particular bundle of sensations and emotions). This is a celebration of enlightenment in a literal sense. We see things clearly.

Spinoza does not tell us in the *Ethics* what an enlightened politics would commit us to in practical and institutional terms. In other writings, however, specifically the *Tractatus Theologico-Politicus* (1670) and the *Tractatus Politicus* (left unfinished at Spinoza's death in 1677), he develops the political implications of his views using traditional interpretative methods.[8]

The *Tractatus Theologico-Politicus* is especially revealing in relation to Spinoza's intellectual development. Educated in the Jewish tradition, he was nevertheless excommunicated in 1656 because of his heterodox ideas. Yet he remained a formidable Hebrew scholar. The *Tractatus Theologico-Politicus* is, in form, a work of biblical exegesis. Spinoza sought to extend to the Bible the naturalistic principles that informed his philosophy. He treated the speculative figments that dominated theological controversy as pathological consequences of a credulity born of ignorance of the natural order. Instead of regarding the Bible as a repository of esoteric truths, Spinoza treated it as a *mélange* of popular history and fable that demanded interpretation. He focused narrowly on the meaning of the text, not on the truth of specific passages.[9] His mastery of Jewish history and culture is evident throughout, yet that did not prevent the book from being condemned in orthodox religious circles.

The *Tractatus Theologico-Politicus* demands attention here, however, because of Spinoza's penetrating discussion of sovereignty and natural rights in chapter sixteen.[10] In brief span, we are presented with a summary of what we may regard as a basically Hobbesian position, with a proviso that makes Spinoza's position particularly arresting for modern readers. Spinoza uses the distinction between a state of nature and civil society in conventional fashion. He shares Hobbes's pessimism about the capacity of passionate human beings, dominated by 'inadequate' ideas, to pursue their long-term interest consistently. We each require stability and security in order to co-operate on any sustained basis, yet we are unlikely to agree to appropriate terms of co-operation, nor to have sufficient confidence that agreements will be honoured in good faith. Knowing what we do about ourselves and others, it is simply unreasonable to trust strangers in a state of nature. We are, insists Spinoza, natural creatures, programmed to pursue our interest as we see it. But we may not see that interest clearly.

There is no scope in Spinoza's theory for a conception of natural co-operation, even as an ideal. We have to start from the thought that human beings, like any other natural entities, are causally determined to maintain themselves. They have a natural right to anything within their powers. That is a limiting condition for any scheme of social and political order. It is a 'supreme law of nature . . . that everything does its utmost to preserve its own condition'.[11] This is not something to regret or deplore. It is a fact of natural life (and, therefore, of social and political life).

Human beings blessed with a natural right to anything and imperfect knowledge are difficult companions. Because their conduct is not solely 'determined by sound reason', they are unpredictable.[12] Nature, says Spinoza, 'forbids nothing save what nobody desires and nobody can do'.[13] Since social co-operation is a necessary condition for our flourishing, we each have an overwhelming interest in establishing terms of mutual engagement. These terms are matters of human contrivance. Spinoza treats them as contractual commitments ('firmly resolved' and actually undertaken) to place limits on our appetites, desires and inclinations.[14] These agreements are based on nothing more than perceived interest, though Spinoza assumes they will be far-reaching. In a disarmingly casual passage he suggests that we will accept that 'anything harmful to another' should be forbidden, that nobody should inflict on another 'what he would not wish done to himself', and that we should defend a 'neighbour's right as if it were' our 'own'.[15] These guiding principles simply give expression to interests that we can all (in principle) recognize. Indeed Spinoza insists that 'a contract can have no binding force but utility'.[16] Agreements that cease to serve interests are null and void. Yet we can all see (at least in principle) that a capricious perception of interest could undermine any prospect of social co-operation. The state comes into the picture as a guarantor of good faith among individuals who can never be presumed to be 'guided by reason alone'.[17] There is no suggestion that authoritative political decisions are always reasonable, rather that chronic uncertainty is a greater evil than frustration of the (purely hypothetical) presumption of always getting one's way.

So far, we might think, so Hobbesian. But Spinoza surprises us. Instead of invoking a mighty Leviathan to maintain order, Spinoza takes seriously the thought that natural rights (equated with powers) are imprescriptible. A key to the formation of a viable polity is that 'everyone transfers all his power to the society'.[18] In a move that would later be echoed by Rousseau, Spinoza envisages a situation in which a 'sovereign power' is constituted by universal transfer of rights.[19] What is constituted is not a body over and above the citizens in a society, but a collective public entity that embraces them all. Spinoza describes such a society as a 'democracy'.[20] And while the (democratic) sovereign enjoys the unlimited powers of Leviathan ('bound by no law', enjoying 'in its corporate capacity the supreme right to do everything it can'), it specifically represents the rational interest of each and every citizen.[21]

Spinoza gives very little institutional detail in the *Tractatus Theologico-Politicus*. He is clear, however, that democracy is 'the most natural form of state' because it comes 'nearest to preserving the freedom which nature allows the individual'.[22] Natural right and prudence are effectively balanced because 'no one transfers his natural right to another so completely that he is never consulted again, but each transfers it to a majority of the whole community of which he is a member'.[23] Natural equality is preserved, while the enlarged scope of public discussion filters out capricious and arbitrary arguments. A sovereign, no matter how constituted, must be assumed to be self-interested. The crucial safeguard in a democracy is that the interest of the sovereign is identical with the community.

Spinoza provides institutional detail in the *Tractatus Politicus*, especially in relation to monarchy and aristocracy, but regrettably had barely begun the promised section on democracy at his death. Yet he confirms his view of democracy as a 'completely absolute state'.[24] All citizens of a democracy can 'claim the right to vote' and are eligible 'to undertake offices of state'.[25] The democratic state is thus all-embracing, though Spinoza (in common with the conventional wisdom of his day) continued to exclude women from public life.

Yet while the *Tractatus Politicus* moots themes that would only be fully developed in the twentieth century, when experience of mass-based politics gave a new dimension to the idea of an absolute politics, the text also recalls the discursive style of classical and early-modern political theory. Aristotle, Tacitus and Machiavelli are prominent sources of detail. And Spinoza insists that a political theory that strays too far from experience is likely to be deeply unsatisfactory. The fact that human beings are passionate creatures, which Spinoza feels he has amply demonstrated in his *Ethics*, tells us very little about the way they should be practically managed. Here we have no choice but to rely on experience. It is no accident, says Spinoza, 'that statesmen have written more successfully about politics than philosophers'.[26]

What the *Tractatus Politicus* illustrates, above all, is Spinoza's unwavering commitment to knowledge as the driving force of human improvement. Spinoza has no time for moral and political philosophers who simply deplore human failings and vices. Utopias of any kind, whether projected into an ideal future or a supposed bygone golden age, are rejected as 'obvious fantasies'.[27] Nothing is achieved if we 'sing the praises of a human nature nowhere to be found', and 'rail at the sort which actually exists'.[28] Spinoza treats 'human passions like love, hate, anger, envy, pride, pity, and the other feelings that agitate the mind, not as vices of human nature, but as properties which belong to it in the same way as heat, cold, storm, thunder and the like belong to the nature of the atmosphere'.[29] His is a clarion call for a science of human nature. Scientific method generates theories and concepts that enable us to dispel the errors and confusions of received wisdom. We have to treat ourselves as objects of enquiry, accepting ourselves as we are. By working with the grain of our natures, we can radically improve the management of our affairs.

Spinoza formed his view of philosophy and method through close study of Descartes. Other currents in natural philosophy and science followed more closely the empirical method advocated by Bacon.[30] Experimentation in the natural sciences, and exhaustive empirical enquiry in the humanities, were seen as vital components in the advancement of knowledge. Implications for a science of human nature are clear. Experience, in the widest sense, began to assume the central role that Hobbes (for example) had assigned to introspection. Observation (direct or indirect) of human conduct was treated as the necessary foundation for a science of human nature. What we see in this period is very much the beginnings of modern social science, practised along lines that are still recognizable to us today.

Received moral, political and religious ideas began to look highly vulnerable. The sheer diversity of human experience can be marshalled to highlight the flimsy basis of our most cherished beliefs. The critical potential of this explosion of empirical and historical awareness quickly became evident. Pierre Bayle, for example, exposed the absurdity of the many superstitions that buttressed conventional wisdom through simple description. His *Historical and Critical Dictionary* (1697) became a focal point for a generation of scholars.[31] Bayle attacked received opinion by juxtaposing irreconcilable testimonies purporting to describe the same state of affairs. There is an apparent disregard of systematic criteria in the arrangement of the work. Bayle simply proceeds, in alphabetical order, to demolish the traditional notions prevalent about a random selection of individuals. The subject of a particular entry may be a figure of some importance in the history of philosophy (such as Spinoza, Zeno of Elea or Pyrrho) and criticism may focus on a philosophical examination of views. Or Bayle may simply mention Caniceus, for example, of whom he can discover nothing further to Agrippa's claim that he was the author of some love letters. The importance of the topic is not central for him. His concern is to expose misconceptions (in whatever field) irrespective of the intrinsic interest of the topic.

Bayle studiedly avoids bringing discussions to a conclusion. He raises the question of whether the followers of Pyrrho and Sextus Empiricus could possibly attain salvation only to leave the reader with a description of the conflicting views of La Mothe le Vayer, Calvin and Jean la Placette. And he describes the contradictory details to be found in the biblical account of the life of David, remarking that 'if a narration like this were found in Thucydides or Titus Livy, all the critics would unanimously conclude that the copyists had transposed the pages, forgotten something in one place, repeated something in another, or inserted additional passages into the author's work. But it is necessary to be careful not to have such suspicions when it is a question of the Bible.'[32] Bayle makes no attempt, after the initial critical enterprise, to explain the paradoxes he has discovered. He simply indulges his learning in painstaking detail, embarking on laborious footnotes to illustrate matters which might seem to be little connected with his main text. It was left to a subsequent generation to use his ironical erudition in a more confident assault on tradition and superstition.

Important political lessons were nonetheless clear to all readers. Bayle's political ideas, as a Huguenot, were dominated by the impact of religious intolerance and superstition. His sceptical compendium of diverse perspectives highlighted the contingency of any particular point of view. Recognizing diversity as a simple fact of human experience, it was but a small step to defend tolerance as a matter of principle. Bayle does not in fact make the principled argument in the *Dictionary*, though it informs everything he writes. He urges us not to take our convictions too seriously. If our circumstances had been different, we would assuredly see the world in a radically different way. A clear implication is that convictions are necessarily personal. And what is personal cannot, in principle, be assumed to be shared. It makes little sense to exhort one another to share convictions, though we may very well exchange arguments and might change our minds. Arguments, however, cannot be forced. A decent polity has to take diversity seriously, no matter what constitutional form it might take.

Context and circumstance were thus recognized as essential dimensions in a properly balanced discussion of moral and political ideas. Theories of justice, for example, could not be construed in purely abstract terms, because effective management of affairs depended upon harmony between culture, natural constraints and opportunities, extent of territory and population, and a host of factors that could only be properly addressed after painstaking empirical enquiry.

This is a massive project that has continued to inform work in the social sciences to this day. At its heart is a highly contentious claim that prescriptions about how human beings should live, to have any sense at all, must be constrained by regard for social and natural facts. Empirical and normative theory, however, can be brought together in many different ways, each involving acute logical difficulties. The text that dominated discussion in the eighteenth century was Montesquieu's monumental *The Spirit of the Laws* (1748).[33] It was one thing to proclaim that the methods of the natural sciences held the key to the remedy of political, social and legal abuses, and quite another to show in any detail what this involved. Montesquieu had spent the best part of his working life collecting details of the customs and practices of a bewildering variety of times and climes from all manner of sources. He had an intimate knowledge of the legal scholarship that had flourished in France since the sixteenth century; a command of classical history, literature and philosophy; a deep respect for the close observation of natural phenomena associated with the Royal

Society of London (of which he was a member) and the Academy of his own Bordeaux; and an insatiable curiosity that led him to pursue even the most incidental reports of strange customs. But it was only when he had established his method that he felt able to deploy this wealth of learning to advantage.

He announces boldly in the preface: 'I began by examining men, and I believed that, amidst the infinite diversity of laws and mores, they were not led by their fancies alone. I have set down the principles, and I have seen particular cases conform to them as if by themselves, the histories of all nations being but their consequences, and each particular law connecting with another law or dependent on a more general one.'[34] Following Aristotle, Montesquieu forms a catalogue of types of society, documenting the dispositions, practices and constitutional arrangements that are generally found together; but he broadens the enquiry to include a causal explanation of the emergence of institutions. Instead of describing different legal systems, he seeks an analysis in terms of the general characteristics that distinguish one system from another. In this view, it is the 'spirit', rather than the letter, of the laws that enables a legislator to understand how the different facets of a way of life cohere and find expression in constitutional form.

Montesquieu's crucial distinction is between the 'nature' and 'principle' of government. 'There is this difference between the nature of the government and its principle: its nature is that which makes it what it is, and its principle, that which makes it act. The one is its particular structure, and the other is the human passions that set it in motion.'[35] Democracy, aristocracy and monarchy, for example, the legitimate forms of polity appropriate in different contexts, are informed by the principles of virtue, moderation and honour; and each risks degenerating (upon an imbalance between constitution and customs) into despotism, where the only guiding principle is fear. These principles subsequently inform all aspects of the life of a society, from education and family life to civil law and commerce.

These 'principles' of government are subject to physical influences. Montesquieu argues that the various human dispositions flourish well or ill in different climates, a temperate climate favouring political virtue and moderation, excessive heat encouraging a lethargy that would ultimately be motivated to action only by fear. Extent of territory, similarly, is an important determinant of the kind of polity likely to prosper. The vast expanses of Asia encourage despotism as surely as the natural divisions and moderate extent of European states help to preserve the rule of law. The fertility of the soil, the manner of subsistence it supports, the importance of trade for the survival of the society, each influence the manners and customs of a polity. A legislator has to balance all these factors. He cannot disregard physical circumstances, but nor should he passively submit if the natural inclination of such circumstances seems deleterious to the principle of his government. Where nature has been niggardly, it falls to education to encourage the attitudes and attributes essential to a government. But there are limits to what can be achieved by legislation; 'moral' and physical causes are involved in such a complex interrelationship that a legislator can only arrange his policies to preserve a natural harmony. Once the balance of society has been irrevocably disturbed, and the principle of government corrupted, there only remains the hideous equality of fear to bind a polity together.

The scope of Montesquieu's science of society is without parallel in the eighteenth century. But critics have found it much more difficult to discern the logical structure of his method. The principles that epitomize the different types of society appear sometimes in the guise of inductive generalizations gleaned after a painstaking survey of the evidence; while on other occasions it is clear that Montesquieu is deducing consequences from them. In terms of eighteenth-century conceptions of science, these two operations need not necessarily be incompatible. Montesquieu himself never repudiates the Cartesian heritage; and he nowhere speaks of a conflict between seventeenth-century rationalism and Baconian or Newtonian empiricism. The variety of his sources in *The Spirit of the Laws*, the wealth of incidental details and digressions, would ill become a rigorous Cartesian; but there can be no doubt from Montesquieu's explicit statements about method that he regards his work to be in the spirit of Descartes. The method (on reflection) lacks constancy and manifests the same eclectic tendencies as the sources from which he works.

But it is not as a systematic treatise that *The Spirit of the Laws* warrants our attention. Montesquieu is at his best in his treatment of details. It is the way these are deployed to support his political views that most effectively illustrates the characteristic concerns of an empirically-minded political theorist. In an age when the bounds of reason seemed limitless and the permanent enjoyment of the fruits of peace and prosperity appeared to require only a final effort of technological and administrative rationalization, Montesquieu urges moderation. People can improve the minutiae of their lives in countless ways but they cannot radically alter their condition. If they are to preserve their freedom (and without this all other satisfactions are illusory) they have to maintain a balance between nature, culture and constitutional arrangements. And given that the possibility of human folly can never be excluded, it is essential that the precise powers of any individual should be tempered by the privileges inherited by the various groups within society.

In the France of Montesquieu's day, the political rationalists largely supported advocates of enlightened despotism. The so-called *thèse royale* had its own conception of French history. Only the recalcitrance of the nobility (it was contended) prevented a prince blessed with sufficient power and intelligence from maximizing the happiness of his subjects. The thesis had been vigorously argued by Dubos in his *Critical History of the Establishment of the French Monarchy* (1734). The privileges of the aristocracy in the feudal period, in this view, were usurped from monarchs whose rightful authority had been enshrined in Roman law. Hence any such privileges which continued into the eighteenth century were without a legitimate historical foundation. It was an old argument (refurbished and buttressed by considerable erudition) that had been consistently attacked by opponents of the crown since the sixteenth century.

The case for the nobility had been more recently stated by Boulainvilliers in his *History of the Ancient Government of France* (1727). Here the liberties currently enjoyed by Frenchmen were seen as vestiges of the authority the nobility had exercised in the middle ages. Only the *parlements* now stood between Frenchmen and an abject subjection to the whim of a monarch. The most pressing constitutional debate of the day was being conducted on the basis of an interpretation of an obscure period of French history. Montesquieu entered the fray, thoroughly versed in antiquarian studies but with a broader case to argue. He endorsed the specific positions of neither of the leading protagonists. But between the *thèse royale* and the *thèse nobiliaire*, his sympathies were clearly with the latter. In the most sustained piece of historical analysis in *The Spirit of the Laws* Montesquieu develops his own view of the independence of the nobility from a close criticism of Dubos and Boulainvilliers. His political philosophy of moderation is supported by a scholarly appraisal of the evidence, setting the fruits of erudition in the broader context of a conception of the harmony of feudal culture.

The constitutional issues Montesquieu had raised would surface again in the charged atmosphere of the late 1780s. And indeed a drastically revised version of the *thèse nobiliaire* would later serve Tocqueville in his vigorous defence of liberal constitutionalism. The point to stress here is that the force of Montesquieu's constitutional arguments depends entirely on an elaborate theory of groups in civil society. This debate would gather renewed momentum in the early nineteenth century, involving advocates across the political spectrum. At the more narrowly constitutional level, however, Montesquieu's arguments had an immediate impact. He put immense stress on a separation of constitutional powers as a necessary constraint on the temptation of wielders of *de facto* power to over-reach themselves. Here, again, Montesquieu's method is revealing. He does not offer formal analysis of separation of powers as a principle, but rather defends the idea in the course of an extended (and misleadingly idealized) discussion of the English constitution.[36] The interdependence of constitutional and social theory could not be more vividly illustrated.

Montesquieu's fusion of advocacy and description was typical of mainstream Enlightenment thought. How the synthesis might be logically defended, however, was never made clear. It was simply assumed that an empirical science of human nature was a key to the betterment of humankind. Yet one of the foremost advocates of the project, David Hume, early highlighted logical difficulties that have continued to bedevil theories of moral and political progress to this day. In his ground-breaking *A Treatise of Human Nature* (1739–40), Hume distinguishes the status of analytical, empirical and moral propositions in such a way that conventional approaches to moral and political philosophy, both classical and modern, appear to be consequences of casual confusion of categorially distinct notions.[37] In a disarmingly simple passage, Hume comments that 'in every system of morality, which I have hitherto met with, I have always remark'd, that the author proceeds for some time in the ordinary way of reasoning, and establishes the being of a God, or makes observations concerning human affairs; when of a sudden I am surpriz'd to find, that instead of the usual copulations of propositions, *is*, and *is not*, I meet with no proposition that is not connected with an *ought*, or an *ought not*'.[38] Hume is clear that this is something we all do in our daily discussions. But why should we assume that the casual juxtaposition of different sorts of statements has any logical force? Hume cuts the ground from under such arguments altogether. 'For as this *ought*, or *ought not*, expresses some new relation or affirmation, 'tis necessary that it shou'd be observ'd and explain'd; and at the same time that a reason should be given, for what seems altogether inconceivable, how this new relation can be a deduction from others, which are entirely different from it.'[39]

The implications for moral and political philosophy are radical. Hume contends that rigorous application of his distinction between *is* and *ought*, description and prescription, would 'subvert all the vulgar systems of morality' at a stroke.[40] Whatever we might say about the 'distinction of vice and virtue', we should not assume that our principles are 'founded merely on the relations of objects, nor' are 'perceiv'd by reason'.[41] They may simply be statements of preferences. And preferences have no authoritative status whatever.

Hume's position is deeply instructive. He has shown how persuasion is largely a matter of special pleading, developing assumptions about human motivation that had already been advanced by Hobbes, Locke and Spinoza. Where he is more radical than his predecessors, at least with regard to philosophical method, is in extending the same thought to political philosophy as an intellectual engagement. Within Hume's terms of reference, the philosopher is as guilty of rationalizing his own interest as anyone else. Reflection begins with impressions of experience. A disciplined philosopher can describe the emergence of particular moral sentiments in relation to the agreeable or useful consequences that stem from their adoption; but he cannot prescribe, from a basis of philosophical reflection, the specific moral principles which ought to prevail. 'Reason is, and ought only to be the slave of the passions, and can never pretend to any other office than to serve and obey them.'[42] For rational discourse to aspire to larger ambitions would amount to a denial of the empirical method that Hume sought to apply to moral and political matters.

It would be misleading, however, to suggest that Hume managed to avoid normative prescription entirely in his writings. His distinction between 'facts' and 'values' alerted him to an obvious source of logical confusion. Yet certain 'facts' about human life are too universal in scope to be set aside. It is simply the case that we have to make decisions in conditions of uncertainty, unaware of the wider ramifications of our conduct. And we have to co-operate with other people whose interests, values and commitments will always remain to some extent obscure to us. Co-operation with strangers is a difficult business; but without it we simply cannot flourish at all.

Whatever practices or institutions we might devise to help us manage our practical affairs have to respect these 'facts' if they are to be of any use to us. In the revised statement of his view in the *Enquiries Concerning the Human Understanding and Concerning the Principles of Morals* (1748–51) Hume addresses the issue directly. '. . . the rules of equity or justice', he says, 'depend entirely on the particular state and condition in which men are placed, and owe their origin and existence to that utility, which results to the public from their strict and regular observance.'[43] Note that we cannot say on *a priori* grounds which rules would be most suitable. That would depend entirely on circumstances. Hume assumes that rules of justice are appropriate when societies enjoy neither absolute scarcity nor absolute abundance. Absolute scarcity would commit us to a desperate struggle for survival that would make even Hobbes's 'war of all against all' look benign. If my survival is necessarily at your expense, it would be unreasonable of me to expect you to hold back if my food fell within your grasp. And, by the same token, in conditions of absolute abundance none of us could possibly care what anyone else possessed since there would always be more of the same available for our delight. Whatever else might matter to us in that happy situation, we can assume that personal ownership would have a very low priority.

Though we can envisage notional extremes of scarcity and abundance, our normal concerns are very different. Having more or less (goods, benefits, conveniences) matters to us in relative terms. We recognize that our own interests cannot be achieved without the involvement of others who may well be completely indifferent to our fate and fortune. We need general rules to secure the 'conveniences and necessities of mankind'.[44] And in circumstances in which resources are relatively distributed, questions of more or less are paramount. We strive to maximize our interest precisely because it makes sense to accrue more of the goods that social life might offer. Yet because we recognize that we cannot flourish alone, our perception of practical opportunities must minimally embrace the interest of others.

Hume captures this issue in his discussion of property. No matter how property might be distributed in any actual society, Hume argues that rules of justice will have to respect 'three fundamental laws of nature, that of the stability of possession, of its transference by consent, and of the performance of promises'.[45] These 'fundamental laws' can be pictured as minimum conditions of social co-operation among strangers. If our social and physical circumstances were different, they would scarcely apply at all. If, let us say, we were physically invulnerable and blessed with perfect foresight, what we now think of as practical reasoning would take a very different form. For creatures constituted the way we are, however, with many and varied interests, capacities, abilities and weaknesses, something like Hume's 'fundamental laws' are indispensable. They can be adapted to suit changing contexts and circumstances. The distribution of property may be more or less equal, transference of property may be more or less formal, and different conventions may surround the performance of promises. But without some notion of entitlement, backed up by stable rules and expectations, very little could be achieved in practical terms.

Hume paints an entirely plausible picture of people muddling through in the ordinary business of their lives. He does not expect too much of us. He sees us as partial creatures, attached to familiar ways of doing things. But our self-interest does not preclude a genuine identification with the interests of our families and friends. We are capable of benevolence, though our focus is likely to be confined to a narrow circle. In Hume's view, we combine strong personal attachments with an indifference to strangers that is likely to be familiar to us all.

Our political ideas build upon these natural sentiments. We can recognize the need for social co-operation, without embracing it with the enthusiasm and generosity we bestow on our loved ones. But we can happily endorse practices, customs and institutions that have proved their worth in our myriad practical dealings with one another. Experience enables us to refine our conceptions of interest. We develop a wider sense of allegiance as our sphere of activities expands. Our practical and political thinking is driven by the (more or less successful) pursuit of our interests. We muddle ourselves, suggests Hume, if we confuse interests with principles. It makes sense to be determined (but not zealous) in the pursuit of interests. In light of Hume's discussion of the social genesis of ideas, fanaticism of any kind looks faintly absurd.

The direct political implications of Hume's position cannot be easily drawn. If reason is the slave of the passions, as Hume asserts, it is by no means clear how a critical philosophy can do more than debunk conventional views. This can set us free from indefensible views of our attachments and commitments, though we might very well have to resign ourselves to carrying on practically in more or less the same way. We gain detachment rather than direction, with no better understanding of what we ought to do.

Negative critique, however, proved to be a powerfully destructive political tool. Voltaire, for example, in a widely read series of critical essays, histories, cultural commentaries and satires, focused his formidable polemical skills on exposing the nonsense (as he saw it) at the heart of Christian doctrine.[46] In light of this barrage of criticism and ridicule, it is simply not possible complacently to follow conventional wisdom. Indeed conventional wisdom is precisely the problem – it is a repository of prejudice and superstition masquerading as the intellectual stock of ages. Christianity, in Voltaire's view, is vivid testimony to the gullibility, ignorance and vulnerability of simple folk. One would be no more justified in punishing someone for absurd beliefs than in according extraordinary authority and respect to an individual who claimed to be God's anointed representative on earth.

It was an article of faith among leading Enlightenment figures that knowledge (in any sphere) should be valued as a means of improving the human condition. Nothing could be taken on trust. Received wisdom had to be critically scrutinized. Social and natural science became part of a concerted effort to better the world, while history was treated as both a repository of information for subsequent reflection and generalization and as a weapon in a war against entrenched attitudes and opinions.

Thinkers were engaged in a practical progressive crusade. The intellectual confidence and ambition displayed in the period is remarkable. Diderot and d'Alembert, for example, in an unprecedented feat of intellectual collaboration, invited leading philosophers, scientists and theorists to take stock of the current state of knowledge in their monumental *Encyclopaedia*, such that future enquiry need not be distracted by the accumulated folly of the past.[47] Science, so it was assumed, could help us to address our prejudices, leaving us free to embark on projects properly attuned to our natures and circumstances.

Neither Voltaire nor Diderot worked out a systematic political philosophy. Both responded to the moral imperative to improve the human condition with the critical weapons at their disposal. They thought in terms of actual improvements, rather than ideal regimes. And it is no accident that both felt comfortable, at least for a time, in basking in the patronage of 'enlightened' monarchs who had the power to put practical proposals into effect. Voltaire's association with Frederick the Great of Prussia was short-lived, as was Diderot's with Catherine the Great of Russia. That they could embrace (so-called) 'enlightened despotism' at all highlights the conceptual distance that separated them from Montesquieu and Hume. What they all shared, however, was a genuine commitment to practical improvement.

The key commitment in these (significantly different) positions is to knowledge as a key to human well-being. And knowledge cannot be advanced unless we are free to pursue any line of enquiry, no matter how shocking to contemporary sensibilities. Kant summed the matter up in his essay of 1784, 'What is Enlightenment?', in terms of the responsibility we each have to decide questions for ourselves.[48] The stress is on human judgement and will, rather than received bodies of knowledge. We all bear responsibility, no matter who or where we are, for the way the world goes, at least in some small degree. Not even a successful political revolution, or the inauguration of what we might see as an ideal constitution, can absolve us of the fundamental responsibility to exercise critical discretion in our dealings with each other. 'A revolution may well bring about a falling off of personal despotism and of avaricious or tyrannical oppression, but never a true reform in one's way of thinking.'[49] Yet, without that reform, 'new principles will serve just as well as old ones to harness the great unthinking masses'.[50] The crucial issue, for Kant, is that a commitment to 'freedom to make public use of one's reason in all matters' should be assured.[51] Though our reasoning on any specific occasion may be flawed, we cannot renounce the use of our reason as various contingencies present themselves. It may be more comfortable for us as individuals to follow designated authorities. But that, says Kant, is the path of 'laziness and cowardice'.[52] We owe it to ourselves and others to think hard as problems arise. We cannot allow custom or dogma to do our thinking for us. And this opens the way to a critical philosophy focused on methods and procedures instead of substantive knowledge claims.

Kant drew these themes together in the three great volumes of his systematic philosophy – the *Critique of Pure Reason* (1781), the *Critique of Practical Reason* (1788) and *The Critique of Judgement* (1790) – which together mark a decisive turning point in the development of philosophy as a discipline, focusing on the criteria human beings use in their active engagement with the world and one another.[53] All these texts make fundamental contributions to the way in which we see ourselves and our minds, though they have little to say directly regarding classic questions in political theory. Yet it was clear to Kant himself and his contemporaries that his approach left no area of philosophy untouched. He proclaimed that he had launched a 'Copernican revolution' in philosophy; and for once an author's confidence is not misplaced.[54]

Kant's working assumption is that people see the world through structural criteria (forms of intuition and categories) which impose a pattern on experience that would otherwise be unintelligible. These criteria are not arbitrary. For minds constituted such as ours, it is simply the case that we use notions of time and space to order experience. We cannot say what the world would look like if we did not invoke such terms. But we cannot conclude from the way we happen to perceive the world that the world in fact is so structured. In Kant's view, we cannot jump out of our minds to make a judgement from a perspective that is not shaped by the way we order our experience. He thus insists on a distinction between the way in which the world appears to us and the way the world is in itself.

This is not an argument for radical scepticism. Kant presupposes in the *Critique of Pure Reason* that natural science has produced a body of reliable knowledge. Yet, since we cannot understand the world intuitively, it remains a philosophical puzzle how knowledge is attained, and why we should be reasonably confident about (at least some of) the claims we make.

In the moral sphere, matters are significantly different. Here we do not make judgements about a world given in experience that we are trying to grasp. We make judgements which dispose us to behave in certain ways rather than others towards people. The fact that we make these judgements is not in question. Yet we do not regard all the judgements people make as authoritative. People can deceive themselves, act partially towards friends and family, and use extraordinary ingenuity to justify themselves in the pursuit of their interests. We recognize this in our ordinary practical experience. Kant asks himself what we may be presupposing about ourselves to make these judgements at all. We carry on trying to distinguish sense from nonsense, right from wrong, despite the evidence before us that people are very often deeply mistaken. We have no choice but to think hard when we are not sure what we should do next. As a philosopher, Kant asks what precisely may be said to be going on in such cases.

These issues may appear to take us a long way from political theory. But if we think about what we implicitly assume people are capable of when they make moral judgements, we are led to question the kind of politics that would be appropriate for beings with these capacities. Kant's treatment of these matters is highly technical, and it is not possible to pursue the finer points of his moral theory here. Yet close attention to the form of moral judgements committed Kant to strong normative views in politics and ethics. Moral judgement involves reflection. In our ordinary moral language we urge people not to do things for reasons we assume they can grasp. We are also sometimes categorical in urging them to respond in particular ways in given situations. We might say that everyone should tell the truth, simply because it is the right thing to do. For the moment we need to focus on the form of the imperative. It applies to everyone, equally. We presuppose that all normally functioning people are able to make moral judgements. We know that they may not always do the right thing, but we assume that they can. They are free to do the right thing if they are so minded. (It would make very little sense to urge them not to do what they are biologically determined to do in any case. I could not be taken seriously if I instructed someone to stop breathing.) Simply by focusing on our ordinary moral language, we are thus led to a view of people as free and equal, at least in certain respects.

Kant advanced these arguments initially in the *Groundwork of the Metaphysics of Morals* (1785), a preliminary version of the *Critique of Practical Reason* that continues to command the attention of moral philosophers to this day.[55] The text, though short, is very demanding. For the purposes of political theory, however, it is possible to distil arguments that Kant deployed in his political writings towards the end of his career.

The first (and crucial) point is that if human beings are creatures who can do things for good reasons, then they must be treated as autonomous agents. We implicitly value our own autonomy when we wonder seriously what we should do. It follows that we should also respect the autonomy of others. Kant formulates the point categorically. He insists that 'all rational beings stand under the law that each of them is to treat himself and all others never merely as means but always at the same time as ends in themselves'.[56] The implications are profound, and cannot be pursued fully here. We may take it as a fact about human conduct that we can give ourselves goals. Kant asks us to reflect on a logic that could claim this capacity for ourselves but withhold it from others. We would be involved in an internal contradiction. Where Grotius or Locke (for example) would argue that we are the possessors of natural rights, Kant contends that we are logically committed to endorsing a principle of reciprocity in our dealings with people. Kant expresses the commitment as a 'single categorical imperative': 'act only in accordance with that maxim through which you can at the same time will that it become a universal law'.[57] Kant's various iterations of this principle in the text need not detain us. The point to stress is that a specific moral law is implicit in our conduct as rational agents. It follows that we should apply it to any conceivable rational agent.

Universality is a key dimension of Kant's 'categorical imperative'. It applies to all human beings, everywhere, no matter what values they may have. He specifically contrasts rational freedom under universal law with what he calls 'heteronomy', a condition in which motivation is dominated by specific interests or passions.[58] In the latter case, we adopt an instrumental style of reasoning. If we happen to want A, we should pursue B. But if we do not want A at all, the imperative would have no force for us. In such a situation the imperative to act would always be conditional upon the end to be pursued. (Read Kant carefully if you want to be a philosopher; practise the guitar if you want to be a rock star.) What makes Kant's position distinctive, though, is his claim that conditional imperatives would make no sense unless at least some imperatives were categorical or unconditional. Kant sees this as a logical point, not a comment on our ordinary experience of human motivation. Yet recognizing its force changes the way we may view moral and political questions.

Kant says very little about specifically political issues in the *Groundwork*, though there are startling implications. He insists, for example, that we should all regard ourselves as legislators 'in a kingdom of ends'.[59] The phrase is used metaphorically in the text, but we must assume that Kant intended us to take the political connotations seriously. In a later text, *Toward Perpetual Peace: A Philosophical Project* (1795), he shows how the universal scope of moral reasoning obliges us to take a global view of political affairs.[60] His central point is that the conventional distinction between politics and morality is untenable, just as he had argued in the *Groundwork* that conditional imperatives depend upon the possibility of unconditional (or categorical) imperatives.

Toward Perpetual Peace is especially revealing because it was written in the aftermath of the French Revolution. Kant was an enthusiast for French and American revolutionary ideas, though he denies that revolution is a legitimate means to attain them. His reasoning here, though contentious, is not obscure. If we are to treat 'autonomy of the will as the supreme principle of morality', as he insists in the *Groundwork*, we must accept that we cannot use violent or manipulative means to achieve our ends. Radicals have never been entirely happy with the passivity of Kant's stance. But it clearly follows from his moral theory.

Kant views the French Revolution as both opportunity and warning. The emergence of republican states had opened up prospects for more stable and peaceful international relations, since governments answerable to their peoples would not be in a position to pursue reckless policies that threaten the basic interests of citizens. Yet the French revolutionary wars had also shown that modern warfare could be desperately destructive and difficult to contain. Kant thus sees political prudence and moral principle tending in the same direction. Peace and stability are desirable in themselves as a background condition for autonomous agents to pursue their many goals. Citizens can also see that the risks attached to warfare far outweigh any possible speculative benefits.

Kant is much less happy with French revolutionary experiments with democracy. He maintains that 'democracy in the strict sense of the word is necessarily a despotism', because there are no constraints on what an executive may do in claiming to represent the democratic will of a people.[61] Typically, democratic legitimacy will stem from a majority vote. But if democratic authorization is sufficient warrant for anything a government may decide to do, prospects for minorities look decidedly precarious. Kant's preference, instead, is for a republican constitution, embodying commitments to 'the freedom of the members of society (as individuals) . . . the dependence of all upon a single common legislation (as subjects), and . . . their equality (as citizens of a state)'.[62] Only these three commitments taken together are compatible with 'the idea of the original contract', which would guarantee that all citizens are treated as ends in themselves, and not simply as means to the (supposed) greater good of the community.[63]

In the text Kant uses the idea of a social contract to justify both the original emergence of civil society and the commitment which republican states should make to ensure that international relations are as law-like as possible. Kant argues for a loose federation of 'free states' rather than a global state, since he regards the diversity of cultures as a limiting condition for the formation of a narrowly political order.[64] To reduce a variety of cultures to a single state would inevitably distort the 'natural' development of some cultures. The concentration of power that such a political order would require could not be justified in terms of the requirements of a republican constitution. Yet citizens and leaders of all republican states could appreciate the benefit of making international relations more law-like rather than less, just as individuals can recognize the advantage to be gained from the hypothetical sacrifice of natural freedom for civil freedom under a republican constitution.

Toward Perpetual Peace barely gets beyond the idea of a republican state in terms of constitutional and institutional detail. Kant has much more to say on the matter in *The Metaphysics of Morals* (1797), which is among his final publications.[65] Here again, as with the case of revolution, radicals have often been disappointed with the strictly rule-based model of the state that Kant defends. He accepts that political orders are coercive, but wants to limit the legitimate use of coercion to occasions that all rational agents could accept. Kant adapts the formulation he had developed in the *Groundwork*. 'Any action is right if it can coexist with everyone's freedom in accordance with a universal law, or if on its maxim the freedom of choice of each can coexist with everyone's freedom in accordance with a universal law.'[66] Kant's derivation of institutional consequences from this maxim is not as rigorous as we might expect, often reflecting the preferences and prejudices of the period. But we should note that the scope for positive legal action is always limited by the 'innate' and 'original right belonging to each man by virtue of his humanity' to have his freedom and autonomy respected.[67] The will of a legislator is, of course, in one sense arbitrary. Hence, whenever we urge a legislative remedy for any dilemma, we have to ensure that the freedom and independence of individuals is not 'being constrained by another's choice'.[68] Whether this requirement can be strictly met in any actual polity is a much disputed issue. The point to stress, though, is that procedural rules can be much more readily justified than substantive goals.

A specific politics cannot be deduced from Kant's moral theory. Controversial issues remain that cannot be decided by appeal to foundational principles or maxims. What we find in Kant, however, is open recognition that human beings, viewed as free and equal, require a certain kind of consideration. We cannot guarantee that we are 'right' in our politics. But we can at least offer reasons to fellow agents who find themselves involved with us in the pursuit of their various projects. In the last resort, it is not policy or institutional detail that is vital for Kant, but respect for the autonomy and dignity of fellow human beings. For Kant this is an unconditional commitment. It does not follow that we should all be fellow citizens, subject to identical laws and professing the same values and beliefs. The point is that we should give due consideration to each other, knowing that our best efforts will not always be satisfactory. We can recognize the need for specific laws, without necessarily agreeing what those laws should be. We can acknowledge the force of laws we would not have chosen, provided those laws are framed in such a way that our freedom and autonomy are respected.

Kant's philosophy is often portrayed as the purest expression of the world view of the Enlightenment, yet aspects of his thought already point beyond the assumptions of Voltaire, Diderot and the other *philosophes*. Enlightenment theory stresses expertise, and expertise need not be widely shared. In Kant, however, each of us must bear responsibility for our actions, no matter what the consequences might be. He simply assumes that all normally functioning adults are blessed with a sufficient command of practical reason to distinguish right from wrong. Expertise has no place in the moral sphere. Doing the right thing is not a technical matter. Science may help us to understand our natures, minds and dispositions in all sorts of ways, but it cannot tell us how we should behave towards other people. When we act, we act alone. There can be no question of deferring to the authority of scientists, priests or charismatic political leaders.

The moral and political implications of Kant's position are radically egalitarian. Indeed, for all that Kant was recognized immediately to be a startlingly original moral theorist, his modern followers (rightly or wrongly) have generally regretted his political caution. The radical implications of the position are sharply portrayed, however, in Rousseau's *The Social Contract* (1762), a text that had deeply influenced the development of Kant's ethical theory.[69] Rousseau announces boldly in his opening chapter: 'Man was born free, and he is everywhere in chains.'[70] He has his own views about the way these chains emerged, expressed most fully in his earlier *A Discourse on the Origins of Inequality* (1755).[71] In that text he asserts categorically that 'the first man who, having enclosed a piece of ground, bethought himself of saying 'This is mine', and found people simple enough to believe him, was the real founder of civil society'.[72] Civil society is portrayed as a work of moral and political deception, destroying an earlier innocence that at least enabled human beings to recognize one another as naturally equal creatures.

Innocence, however, cannot be restored. Rousseau asks himself in *The Social Contract* how, from where we stand, we might envisage a form of social co-operation that represents our equal moral status. His concern in *The Social Contract* is purely theoretical. He asks whether we can picture a legitimate polity, not whether we (hopelessly corrupted creatures of civil society) can actually create one. Yet the thought experiment highlights practical implications that troubled Rousseau's contemporaries, and have continued to trouble political theorists to this day.

Rousseau takes it as axiomatic that 'no man has any natural authority over his fellows'.[73] He is also clear, however, that we cannot flourish alone. Social co-operation is essential to us throughout our lives. Yet the form it generally takes in civil society is distorted by obvious discrepancies in wealth, power and status. A political order that replicated the personal (and humiliating) dependencies of civil society could not be regarded as legitimate. Agreement would be dictated by power relations. And 'force', insists Rousseau, 'alone bestows no right'.[74] Rousseau is adamant that 'all legitimate authority among men must be based on covenants', but the covenants cannot follow the pattern we are all familiar with in civil society, where the poor man may be obliged to accept a demeaning job from his rich neighbour.

Strict reciprocity is a necessary condition for binding political commitment. This requirement sets Rousseau's position apart from versions of social contract theory influenced by Hobbes and Locke. He is at pains in the opening book of *The Social Contract* to specify what such an agreement would look like, utterly untroubled by the thought that it is too demanding to be a realistic proposal. He highlights 'articles of association' which, 'rightly understood, are reducible to a single one, namely the total alienation by each associate of himself and all his rights to the whole community'.[75] The crucial point is that 'as every individual gives himself absolutely, the conditions are the same for all, and precisely because they are the same for all, it is in no one's interest to make the conditions onerous for others'.[76] Strict equality, Rousseau argues, makes despotism inconceivable, since no one would choose to impose tyrannical restrictions upon himself.

Rousseau's founding commitment to form a polity is thus no ordinary agreement. It is certainly not motivated by narrow self-interest or social survival. Indeed, in a revealing passage, Rousseau presents the actual decision to leave a state of nature as an almost incidental development. He notes almost in passing: 'I assume that men reach a point where the obstacles to their preservation in a state of nature prove greater than the strength that each man has to preserve himself in that state.'[77] Far from being driven by dire necessity, the inhabitants of Rousseau's state of nature are simply faced with a situation in which practical problems prevent the full enjoyment of their natural liberty. They are motivated to improve their condition, but not at the expense of liberty. What they do, instead, is exchange natural freedom, where actions are determined by instinct and inclination, for moral freedom, with 'the voice of duty' taking 'the place of physical impulse'.[78]

New possibilities are opened up. Human beings can now act on principle. Possession, which in a state of 'natural liberty' is 'based only on force or 'the right of the first occupant', rests in a civil state on 'legal title'.[79] Above all, what human beings gain is 'moral freedom, which alone makes man the master of himself; for to be governed by appetite alone is slavery, while obedience to a law one prescribes to oneself is freedom'.[80]

Rousseau's defence of a notion of personal autonomy is thus quite as forceful as Kant's, though expressed in a rhetorically looser fashion. Indeed Rousseau's language, in this passage as elsewhere, is beguiling. Having initially sought to play down the significance of the transition from a state of nature to civil society, he nevertheless commits himself to what amounts to a moral transformation of human nature. The stakes here are very high. Rousseau is not always clear what this would amount to in terms of government, though we should note that the language of virtue invites more intrusive intervention than Hobbes had envisaged. Hobbes, we should remind ourselves, always assumed that human nature was fixed and needed to be managed. Rousseau defends the prospect of a qualitatively better mode of existence as a moral goal.

Rousseau's radical innovation is in his conception of what it means to pursue goals. He makes a distinction between the 'private will' we each have as individuals with a host of particular interests, which clearly sets us apart from one another, and the 'general will' we share as citizens.[81] He notes that we may all have a 'natural' tendency to put our private interests first, to free-ride on the public commitment of our associates. But this 'would bring about the ruin of the body politic'.[82] More importantly, it would also undermine the moral point of opting for civil society in the first place. Rousseau insists, in a passage that has become notorious, on the moral, and not merely prudential, priority of public over private commitments. He says: 'Hence, in order that the social pact shall not be an empty formula, it is tacitly implied in that commitment – which alone can give force to all others – that whoever refuses to obey the general will shall be constrained to do so by the whole body, which means nothing other than that he shall be forced to be free;. . .'[83] This commitment is the condition of our enjoyment of autonomy, for otherwise we would continue to be at the mercy of discrepancies in wealth, status and power. Contractual agreements in any other contexts 'would be absurd, tyrannical and liable to the grossest abuse'.[84] If we will the end, Rousseau suggests, we had better will the means. In the process he had highlighted a dilemma at the heart of all transformational politics.

Rousseau's specific claims for the 'general will' are startling. He asserts, for example, 'that the general will is always rightful and always tends to the public good; but it does not follow that the decisions of the people are always equally right'.[85] Thus while it would be absurd to suggest that we could be wrong about our narrow preferences, it is perfectly possible that our assessment of the common interest is mistaken. Indeed the term 'general will' gives a misleading impression. The crucial question is not what we, the people, actually decide, but whether our institutions and practices embody the objective interest of the community. Our concern is to identify a common good that all right-thinking people would recognize. We are certainly not asked to express anything as trifling as an opinion or preference. As Rousseau puts the point, 'we always want what is advantageous but we do not always discern it'.[86] The 'general will' is Rousseau's term for what he takes to be a fact of life, that there is an objective public interest in any community. It is certainly not simply a prevalent opinion.

The distinction between the 'general will' and the 'will of all' gives Rousseau's theory a radical edge that is lacking in mainstream Enlightenment theory.[87] The 'general will' trumps ordinary opinion, yet it must be grasped through the ordinary exercise of practical reason. It is also important for Rousseau that something is judged to be right for the community that depends on will and nothing else. He does not appeal to a doctrine of basic human needs in distinguishing between what we should and should not do. Yet immense problems remain. How the 'general will' should be discerned, and who might be said to embody it, are vital to political legitimacy and stability. But Rousseau does not provide us with a clear criterion to help us when we are genuinely puzzled.

Rousseau is clearly aware that the 'general will' might be construed as a licence for authoritarianism, and specifically counters hypothetical objections in a number of passages. He insists, for example, that 'the general will, to be truly what it is, must be general in its purpose as well as in its nature; that it should spring from all and apply to all; and that it loses its natural rectitude when it is directed towards any particular and circumscribed object – for in judging what is foreign to us, we have no sound principle of equity to guide us'.[88] The 'general will' represents the sovereign will of the people. It is not a recipe for government. Rousseau regards the execution of policy and the articulation of policy as quite distinct spheres of activity. The 'general will' is best identified with what a later (sympathetic) reader of Rousseau, John Rawls, would describe as the 'basic structure of society'.[89] Rousseau himself uses the image of a legal order. And laws, of course, are general injunctions applicable to all citizens without distinction.

In the democratic context Rousseau envisages, authoritarianism looks inconceivable at first glance. If the 'general will' does not 'go beyond the limits of the general covenants', and citizens have genuinely 'exchanged an uncertain and precarious life for a better and more secure one', then it is difficult to see how citizens could reasonably complain about the imposition of measures that are a necessary condition for their enjoyment of the benefits of civil society.[90]

Rousseau clearly values the predictability and stability that stems from legal order. Indeed we may regard predictability and stability as indispensable for effective social co-operation among strangers. The language Rousseau uses to defend legal order, however, goes beyond the idea of a procedural framework. He has in mind a specific set of rules, rather than merely formally stable rules. In the end, it is his strong commitment to equality and autonomy that informs his particular prescriptions. He wants a civil order in which virtue can flourish, not one which simply enables us to muddle through more or less effectively.

Rousseau's ambivalence on the issue is once again evident in his language. Despite using the idea of will as a criterion of political legitimacy, he nevertheless contends that 'what is good and in conformity with order is such by the very nature of things and independently of human agreements'.[91] What is to count as the 'general will' thus has to satisfy requirements that go beyond the simple fact of agreement. Again, in an adjacent passage, he says that 'there is undoubtedly a universal justice which springs from reason alone'.[92] These are the conditions that the 'general will' must fulfil if it is to have authority.

Reasoning, of course, is what human beings do, but not all their reasoning is to count. Rousseau specifies some procedural safeguards that must be met. He insists that if 'justice is to be admitted among men it must be reciprocal'.[93] And because 'when the people as a whole makes rules for the people as a whole, it is dealing only with itself', we must assume that this mystical entity, 'the people', could not systematically exercise a tyranny over itself.[94] All this may be very well in an ideal situation. Rousseau is clear, however, that fallible individuals make judgements. Wanting what is good for a polity as a whole is not the same as recognizing it. As Rousseau expresses the point in his usual paradoxical style, 'individuals see the good and reject it; the public desires the good but does not see it'.[95] He notes bluntly, 'both equally need guidance'.[96]

The conundrum of political leadership could not be more sharply specified. We are all in a fix and do not know what to do. Rousseau tells us that there is a solution to our basic question (can there be 'any legitimate and sure principle of government, taking men as they are and laws as they might be'?).[97] But from where we stand, enmeshed in complex social, economic, cultural and personal relations, how could we be sure that we had come up with a defensible response? A simple majority would not be sufficient, for it may represent nothing more than the 'will of all'. One among us, or a select group, may have grasped the 'general will', but how would we know? Having taken us to the very brink of an ideal democratic polity, Rousseau appears to turn round and tell us that it could not possibly work.

Rousseau's solution highlights the enormity of the dilemma. He says: 'To discover the rules of society that are best suited to nations, there would need to exist a superior intelligence, who could understand the passions of men without feeling any of them, who had no affinity with our nature but knew it to the full, whose happiness was independent of ours, but who would nevertheless make our happiness his concern, who would be content to wait in the fullness of time for a distant glory, and to labour in one age to enjoy the fruits in another. Gods would be needed to give men laws.'[98] What he pictures is a mythical lawgiver in the classical fashion, blessed with superhuman powers but wholly lacking mundane interests and passions. He takes for granted that 'nations, like men, are teachable only in their youth; with age they become incorrigible'.[99] A lawgiver charged with establishing an ideal polity would have to be prepared 'to change human nature, to transform each individual, who by himself is entirely complete and solitary, into a part of a much greater whole, from which the same individual will then receive, in a sense, his life and his being'.[100]

This is an audacious undertaking, going well beyond the opening thought of *The Social Contract*, which promised to take 'men as they are'.[101] Indeed Rousseau suggests that 'the founder of nations must weaken the structure of man in order to fortify it, to replace the physical and independent existence we have all received from nature with a moral and communal existence'.[102] When Rousseau focuses on the strategic demands of polity building, the tone of the text changes markedly. Machiavelli is very much a guiding presence. Rousseau is now content to stress the gulf which separates the political world we all know, and the ideal that could have been ours but for the heavy burden of habit and custom. He presents the binary opposition of options in the manner of Machiavelli. Thus 'the nearer men's natural powers are to extinction or annihilation, and the stronger and more lasting their acquired powers, the stronger and more perfect is the social institution'.[103] The language encourages a political ruthlessness that is worlds removed from Rousseau's opening concern with political rights.

We should not assume that Rousseau regarded *The Social Contract* as a programme to be put into effect. What he presents, instead, is a withering critique of the political world of eighteenth-century France, with Enlightenment culture furnishing a veneer that distracted attention from a more fundamental moral and political malaise. He insists: 'For a newly formed people to understand wise principles of politics and to follow the basic rules of statecraft, the effect would have to become the cause; the social spirit which must be the product of social institutions would have to preside over the setting up of those institutions; men would have to have already become before the advent of law that which they become as a result of law.'[104]

Rousseau's contemporary readers, however, were not so cautious. And there are practical proposals in the text that look like standard political advice. He has discussions of constitutional forms that echo Montesquieu, and indeed frank recognition 'that all forms of government do not suit all countries'.[105] All this looks like matter for practical political reflection. Yet what catches the eye is his preoccupation with culture rather than constitutional or institutional forms. Thus: 'When we see among the happiest people in the world bands of peasants regulating the affairs of state under an oak tree. And always acting wisely, can we help feeling a certain contempt for the refinements of other nations, which employ so much skill and mystery to make themselves at once illustrious and wretched?'[106] Enlightenment sophisticates can hardly have been flattered by Rousseau's picture.

The link between political change and fundamental moral renewal sets Rousseau apart from even the most radical of his contemporaries. He is blithely unaware of the scale of the modern state and the huge impact it would very soon have on every aspect of a way of life. Yet the far-reaching (and almost intimate) proposals he calls for create space for deeply intrusive government. He accepts, for example, that a 'censorial tribunal' will be necessary as an 'arbiter of the people's opinion'.[107] He has little interest in (what would later become) the standard liberal insistence on a distinction between public and private affairs. He asserts categorically that 'it is useless to separate the morals of a nation from the objects of its esteem'.[108]

Anyone seriously interested in moral and political transformation thus has necessarily to endorse strategic measures that will shake citizens out of their complacency. 'Reform the opinions of men,' says Rousseau, 'and their morals will be purified of themselves.'[109] In Rousseau's view, it would be sheer hypocrisy to endorse an end without appropriate means. And though he gives only a sketch of possible institutions for his ideal polity, they extend beyond the scope of the traditional political sphere.

Modern readers will be troubled by Rousseau's proposal for a 'civil religion'.[110] And though he tries to limit its scope to principles of sociability, the language hints at a secular confession of faith that would be deeply divisive in the context of a pluralist society. Rousseau, we must remember, supposed he was defending small-scale, face-to-face politics, where conformity to basic principles could be taken for granted. His readers, however, exhilarated by his vision, wanted to transform France. As they adapted Rousseau's teaching to the demands of large-scale societies, so the sinister elements in his theory became more prominent. Yet these would only become evident after experience of revolutionary turmoil. The French Revolution of 1789 stretched the political imaginations of supporters and opponents alike in the most trying circumstances. *The Social Contract* became a text for the interpretation of an event that Rousseau could not possibly have envisaged. In the process, deep lessons were learnt about the limits of political possibility.

8

Revolution

The simple thought that political practices, procedures and institutions should be rationally defensible had radical implications for any extant polity. Nothing, in principle, could be taken on trust. The received language of justification (in terms of tradition, the sanctity of order or whatever) had to meet the more demanding requirements of the practical reason of citizens. The idea that citizens should be free to pursue their interests and happiness, each in their own way, is beguilingly attractive, yet difficult to deploy as a narrow criterion of political legitimacy. The rhetorical power of these ideas, however, proved to be devastating in the crises that engulfed Britain's north American colonies and the French monarchy in the 1770s and 1780s.

The American and French revolutions mark a watershed in the development of modern political thought. Ideas that had been nurtured over the past two hundred years gained a wider (and politically more destructive) currency in political conflicts that mobilized populations on an unprecedented scale. Freedom and rights were demanded as a natural inheritance. How these demands could be matched with the traditional need for governments to secure stability and order in their territories was initially treated as a secondary consideration. The political tone had changed abruptly. Political philosophy had been translated into political propaganda, with fateful consequences for the later development of public discourse.

1789 is thus a momentous year in modern political history. The outbreak of revolution in France and the inauguration of the federal constitution in the United States symbolically mark the beginning of an epoch in which human beings in the round (regarded as citizens) sought to wrest control of their political lives out of the hands of hereditary or imperial elites. Documents and propaganda from both countries reflect an optimism about possibilities for political improvement that may strike us today as utopian or even naïve. Yet they ushered on to the political stage normative and constitutional criteria that continue to serve as points of reference in our political discussions.

The tone is captured in the first of *The Federalist Papers* (1788), a series of newspaper articles written by Alexander Hamilton, James Madison and John Jay in defence of the ratification of the federal constitution under the pseudonym 'Publius'. Hamilton remarked in the opening paragraph: 'it seems to have been reserved to the people of this country, by their conduct and example, to decide the important question, whether societies of men are really capable or not, of establishing good government from reflection and choice, or whether they are forever destined to depend, for their political constitutions, on accident and force.'[1]

The challenge is dramatic and remains unfulfilled in our own age. What it highlights, however, is the simple thought that political arrangements are the concern of each and every one of us, though we may differ profoundly among ourselves about how these responsibilities may best be fulfilled. We cannot shrug our shoulders in resignation and assume that fate, chance, or a dominant elite will shape things no matter what we think. To be sure, none of us can dictate the pattern of events or institutions. Yet the fact remains that institutions are man-made conventions designed to meet the demands of circumstances and the need to establish terms of co-operation for our engagements. This is true even if we choose to acquiesce in the entrenched customs and conventions of our day. To choose to carry on as we have in the past is a daily endorsement of a co-operative scheme. And if things go wrong for us, or those in authority make unreasonable or odious demands on our time and resources, in the last resort we have a responsibility to raise our voices. These responsibilities have become ingrained in our public consciousness in democratic polities, even if they are honoured merely passively. But it was not always so. The rhetoric of the revolutionary period threw down a challenge that continues to haunt us, no matter where we stand on the political spectrum.

The two revolutions championed broadly the same Enlightenment ideals, yet their political trajectories soon diverged markedly. The rights of man could clearly be realized in manifestly different ways. Commitments that Enlightenment thinkers had regarded as self-evident for all decent people yielded political and constitutional outcomes that were scarcely reconcilable. The (so-called) Enlightenment project disguised a plethora of currents and contradictions.

The American and French revolutions are thus deeply revealing as crucibles for the development of contrasting styles of political thought and practice. Vastly different contexts dictated strategies that coloured the later emergence of institutions and practices. Instructively from the perspective of political thought, some of these differences are evident in the theory and propaganda from the outset.

The *Declaration of the Rights of Man and of Citizens* (1789) presented natural rights argument at its most optimistic. Proclaimed in Paris as representatives sought to establish themselves as a National Assembly, it served as a clarion call to the political world. In the *Declaration* matters that

were previously assumed to be ordinary misfortunes are treated as consequences of human contrivance and neglect. The political world was turned
upside-down. Whereas monarchy and aristocracy had been regarded as
guardians of order and civilization, they are now seen as the perpetuators
of the 'ignorance, neglect, or contempt of human rights' that are 'the sole
causes of public misfortunes and corruptions of government'.[2] The clear
implication is that human lives over centuries have been blighted by the
wanton denial of conditions that could (and should) be made available to
everyone. These conditions are 'natural, imprescriptible, and inalienable
rights'.[3] There is nothing obscure about them. They are based on 'simple
and incontestable principles'; yet they have almost everywhere been
denied to people.[4] The only obstacle to their enjoyment is the ill will and
malice of those in authority. Hence governments everywhere must be held
responsible for the baleful consequences of their neglect.

Rights apply universally. Thus it is asserted that 'men are born, and
always continue, free and equal in respect of their rights'.[5] Any 'civil distinctions' introduced into a citizen body should 'be founded only on public
utility'.[6] The point of government is simply 'the preservation of the natural
and imprescriptible rights of man'.[7] And 'the source of all sovereignty' is
said to reside in the nation collectively, acting on behalf of the people as a
whole.[8] As things stood in 1789, no political authority would meet the
stringent requirements of the *Declaration*. Hereditary monarchy would be
ruled out as a matter of course, but so too would any representative system
based on the prerogatives of particular classes or estates. There is no hint
in the text that these claims may be controversial, or that their political
implementation might generate intractable difficulties.

Yet it was unclear at the time, and became less clear as the French
Revolution progressively unfolded, precisely how these principles might
be translated into viable political institutions. And because the principles
were held to be self-evident, it could be concluded that dispute on points
of detail was in bad faith. To contest the meaning or justification of a self-
evident principle might be to declare oneself a political enemy. The text
proclaims that 'no man ought to be molested on account of his opinions',
yet by 1793 reservations about the latest incarnation of revolutionary principles could lead a sceptic to the guillotine.[9] Freedom and equality (so it
seemed) were compatible with extreme political intolerance.

Within the terms of the *Declaration*, what can we say if men of good faith
disagree? The nation may be the collective expression of the people's will,
yet various interpreters of that will might have radically different views.
If people are all born with rights, when do they acquire the right to represent their interests? And if individuals cannot speak for themselves, who
should be authorized to speak for them? We should not expect a revolutionary proclamation to resolve these difficulties. But there remains a
strong implication in the text that new principles will inaugurate a style of
politics quite unlike anything that has preceded it. Power and interest will

be replaced by equity and rights. Like so many brave new beginnings, the politics of the French Revolution very soon exposed the shortcomings of pure theory.

The *Declaration*, however, is not a treatise of political theory. It provides a series of rallying cries, rather than closely argued political and constitutional proposals. Yet its basic implications were clear to the established princes of Europe. No state could be regarded as legitimate in light of these criteria. Positions hardened after 1792, as France found herself at war, striving to fend off counter-revolution at home aided and abetted by interested powers. The formal overthrow of the monarchy on 10 August 1792 polarized views throughout Europe. And with the execution of Louis XVI on 21 January 1793, an ideological line was drawn in European politics that left little room for compromise.

A new phenomenon was unleashed in 1793. The *levée en masse* declared on 23 August saw the whole of France set on a war footing. This was a first taste of 'total' war, with all the ideological mobilization and centralized control that later became typical features of European states at war. Indeed, nothing so terrified the elites of *ancien régime* Europe as the spectre of French revolutionary armies demanding 'liberty, equality and fraternity' for all men, everywhere. Such ideological motivation was difficult for established elites to counter, generating enthusiasm and fervour comparable only with earlier wars of religion. It cut across traditional territorial and dynastic claims, leading to a redrawing of the political map of Europe according to new and uncertain standards.

Revolution had been 'internationalized'. The progress of French armies would be met by uprisings of 'patriots', anxious to see the principles of the Revolution established in their own countries. Republics were declared in Milan in 1797 and Naples in 1799, though they lasted no longer than the military hegemony of France. It was clear to all, nevertheless, that peace and stability in Europe would henceforth be decided at continental level. For better or worse, the involvement of the masses was a factor in politics, even if they were exposed to hideous exploitation by elites.

Revolutionary principles thus had dramatic intuitive appeal. Yet, for all that they were presented as self-evident truths, they were always contentious and divisive. The *Declaration of the Rights of Man and of Citizens*, in particular, presupposes elaborate theoretical arguments that are taken for granted in the text. It is best considered a brilliant feat of synthesis. How the grounding principles should be interpreted, however, remains deeply problematic.

We can go some way towards unpacking the colossal burden of the text by looking at contemporary defences of some of its leading themes. Defences of revolutionary principles, of course, were far from dispassionate. They were conceived as contributions to dramatic political events, written in haste, and sometimes placed their authors in acute personal danger. But a common pattern of argument emerges. Universal claims are advanced for an understanding of the proper relationship between political institutions and the citizens they are designed to serve. Arguments which had been introduced into political debate by Locke and Rousseau were given a democratic twist that made immediate demands on political institutions. Indeed it remains a moot point whether any actual institutions could possibly sustain these normative expectations. At any rate, theory and rhetoric were mixed together in an explosive political cocktail. Theory had become subversive as never before.

In terms of immediate impact, Emmanuel Sieyes's *What is the Third Estate?* (1789) was a resounding success.[10] The text is a response to a very specific political crisis. Problems for the French monarchy gathered pace in the 1780s, threatening the capacity of the king and his ministers to perform basic political functions. The crown had become virtually bankrupt, unable to raise credit on financial markets, hemmed in ideologically by radical intellectuals on the one side and a disaffected aristocracy on the other, anxious to maintain fiscal and other privileges. Reform of the monarchy had thus become imperative if it were to survive. A consensus emerged for convening the Estates-General, which had not met since 1614, in order to consider far-reaching financial and institutional reform. In its previous incarnation the Estates-General had been grouped into blocks, representing the 'first estate' (clergy), 'second estate' (nobility) and 'third estate' (representatives of the wider population). As voting had been in blocks, it was easy for the first and second estates to combine to counter radical proposals from the third estate. If the Estates-General were to convene again, even in an advisory capacity, it thus made a huge difference how the estates would be represented, whether they would meet in combination, and who should be authorized to speak for the nation as a whole.

Sieyes addressed the issue directly. Previously the third estate, effectively the working population on whom all functions depended, had been excluded from decision making. In institutional terms it was virtually invisible. And yet all 'private activities and public services' were provided by the third estate.[11] It was a 'complete nation'.[12] The clergy and nobility, by contrast, were entirely parasitic. Sieyes's argument is stark and simple. The political fate of France should be in the hands of the working population of France. He put the point succinctly: 'Nothing will go well without the Third Estate; everything would go considerably better without the two others.'[13]

In terms of basic principles that should underpin any legitimate polity, Sieyes appeals to a version of social contract theory. He simply assumes that 'every nation ought to be free', and that its freedom is made manifest in a form of voluntary association.[14] He pictures a 'fairly considerable number of isolated individuals who wish to unite'.[15] This is sufficient in itself to form a nation. Once associated together, however, the collective actions of individuals constitute a 'common will'.[16] What individuals lack in isolation is the power and resources to achieve their objectives. Crucially, they form a nation precisely because they recognize the necessity of a social union. It would be absurd to identify a set of ends and objectives without the requisite means. Hence individuals must be assumed to authorize the 'common will' that makes a community effective. Sieyes thus sees power as a social product, indispensable for attaining anything like a reasonable life. But wielders of power must remain answerable to the community as a whole.

How this should be achieved is a matter of detailed constitutional design that cannot detain us here. Sieyes (we must remember) was contributing to an urgent debate about constitutional reform. What needs to be stressed for the purposes of this book is the normative argument that warrants particular constitutional schemes. Sieyes accepts that the complexity of social co-operation commits us to 'government by proxy'.[17] An institutional body will act on behalf of the community, but cannot replace the will of the nation or community. That will, insists Sieyes, 'is inalienable'.[18] Functions can be delegated, but not the will. Agents of government enjoy powers conferred on them by the nation; and those powers may always be withdrawn and placed in other hands.

These are rhetorically powerful arguments, but they gloss over problems that haunted revolutionary France and continued to occupy political theorists and commentators throughout the nineteenth century. Sieyes asserts that 'the nation is prior to everything. It is the source of everything. Its will is always legal; indeed it is the law itself.'[19] But having delegated powers to agents of government, the 'nation' is in an ambiguous position. Pronouncements of government are made in the name of the nation, and the authority of the nation is said to be unconditional. How, then, do the people hold governors to account? 'Prior to and above the nation', says Sieyes, 'there is only natural law.'[20] Yet natural law may be interpreted in a variety of ways. Sieyes insists that government cannot change constitutional terms of reference, but is unable to address effectively problems of mundane accountability.

Throughout his career Sieyes remained fascinated by the intricacy of constitutional theory, shifting position later to support Napoleon's exercise of power. Yet he never managed to resolve the basic conundrum facing all constitutional theory. Constitutional rules apply in normal political conditions. We can recognize their desirability when they are lacking. But political crises create pressures that cannot always be resolved by constitutional means. Normative theory then has to switch to justify extraordinary actions in exceptional circumstances. The best we can hope for in these circumstances is broad normative guidelines. It should not surprise us that outcomes in revolutionary contexts are deeply uncertain.

Sieyes highlights the contrasting themes of individualism and collectivism in French revolutionary theory. For, while the nation is constituted by the association of individual wills, it cannot be constrained in turn by constitutional (or other) rules that assembled representatives might devise. 'A nation must not and cannot identify itself with constitutional forms.'[21] This point, for Sieyes, follows from the simple observation that political divisions should not be construed as divisions within the nation. The nation remains a conceptual whole, though it exists only as a form of association. On extraordinary occasions, such as the convening of the Estates-General to address a crisis for the French nation, it is the nation itself that must be supreme, not any preconceived notions about the way in which the nation is represented. Hence the proposed divisions within the Estates-General are conceptually flawed. 'A political society', Sieyes insists, 'cannot be anything but the whole body of associates.'[22] And the associates gathered as a nation cannot bind themselves in perpetuity to fixed rules and procedures. The nation specifies appropriate rules, and remains the judge of performance of functions under those rules. The fact that 'the sole elements of the common will are individual wills' does little to mitigate the collective authority of the nation.[23]

Attempts to realize the freedom proclaimed in the *Declaration of the Rights of Man and of Citizens* is thus compatible with significant constraints on the discretion of individuals in the name of nation or state. What later liberals saw as a paradox at the heart of democratic theory had yet to be clearly expressed, but contemporaries were nevertheless well aware that the pursuit of liberty in radically unequal societies could generate an oppressive and intrusive governmental apparatus.

The democratic theory advanced in the early revolutionary period barely hinted at problems that lay ahead. Thomas Paine, for example, whose defence of both American and French revolutions made him an international celebrity, based his argument on a doctrine of natural sociability that advocated the lightest touch from government compatible with co-operative efficiency. He is adamant in *Common Sense* (1776) that while 'society in every state is a blessing . . . government even in its best state is but a necessary evil'.[24] He describes government as the 'badge of lost innocence', evoking the possibility of decisions made after due deliberation among people motivated by a clear conscience.[25] It is sufficient that such circumstances are conceivable for us to deplore the heavy hand of actual government.

When Paine turned to the French Revolution in the *Rights of Man* (1791–2), he continued to extol limited government. 'The more perfect civilization is', he urges, 'the less occasion has it for government, because the more does it regulate its own affairs, and govern itself.'[26] Ordinary transactions among human beings who recognize their mutual dependence and vulnerability served as his model of good government, not the inherited privileges and arcane practices of a landed elite. In the text he castigates Burke's refusal even to consider the possibility that political affairs could be different. Burke had portrayed precedent and custom as institutionally enshrined wisdom.[27] For Paine it is simply avoidance of clear thinking on

the part of interested groups who had a great deal to gain from the per-
petuation of manifestly unfair practices. The mystery and ritual of established government, far from lending authority to political decisions, is a
massive exercise in obfuscation. A principal task of theory, in Paine's eyes,
is to dispel that confusion and open institutions and practices to the
scrutiny of untutored common sense.

The course of the Revolution did little to justify Paine's optimism.
Indeed, as events unfolded, the idea that reasonable social co-operation
could be readily attained sharpened reactions to the ordinary disagreements and compromises that are a feature of any political process. Lofty
expectations led to disappointment and recriminations. Political conflict
was at its most bloody in 1793–4, as Robespierre and his Jacobin colleagues
sought to establish a regime of republican 'virtue'.

It is not easy to interpret the theory implicit in revolutionary propaganda, especially in the frenetic atmosphere of Paris in 1793–4. What is
clear, however, is that political ambition had attained a new scale.
Robespierre's central role on the Committee of Public Safety makes him a
pivotal figure.[28] While he should in no sense be regarded as a political theorist, he nevertheless exploited theory to rally support for his faction in a
style that would be echoed by later populist leaders. In a remarkable
speech of 5 February 1794 he sketched principles of political morality in
the loftiest terms. He pictures a utopia in which all the good things in life
would be realized – 'peaceable enjoyment of liberty and equality', a reign
of 'eternal justice' replacing tyranny, a culture in which 'all souls are
enlarged by the constant communication of republican sentiments and by
the need to earn the esteem of a great people'.[29]

Yet at the same time, revolutionary crisis imposed its own demands.
While Robespierre extols 'popular government in time of peace' as a
'virtue', in a revolutionary context 'virtue' must be linked with 'terror'.[30]
'Terror', he insists, 'is nothing other than justice, prompt, severe, inflexible.'[31] He sees it as an 'emanation of virtue', a direct 'consequence of the
general principle of democracy applied to the most pressing needs of our
country'.[32] National emergency, in other words, warranted the suspen-
sion of the idyllic standards that Robespierre undoubtedly championed.
And indeed he presented himself as the unique spokesman for the purity
that might be lost in a complacent nation. In desperately dangerous
times, he allowed his personal paranoia to guide political decisions,
interpreting opposition to him personally as opposition to the republic.
He used the guillotine almost as a personal political weapon. No one
could feel safe, and indeed Robespierre clearly expected his favoured
weapon to be turned against him in due course. In the event, repeated
denunciations galvanized opponents. Robespierre was executed, along
with a small group of close associates, including Saint-Just, on 28 July
1794, effectively bringing the most tumultuous phase of the revolution to
a close.

The limits of 'normal' politics are vividly exposed. In the chaotic conditions of 1793–4, it was not sufficient that reasonable people should establish acceptable terms of social co-operation in order to facilitate their various projects; they were exhorted to identify with the republican nation as the embodiment of their better selves. A distinction between public and private spheres could be maintained in this scheme of things only if the priority of the public sphere were always acknowledged. Pretexts for the vilification of political opponents multiplied. Stability and predictability, necessary conditions for social co-operation among strangers, were undermined by infighting among revolutionary factions. The revolution threatened to destroy its tangible achievement as the pursuit of 'liberty, equality and fraternity' brought France to the verge of anarchy. This was not an auspicious beginning for mass-based democratic politics. Finally the revolution had to be brought to an end. A more conventional style of authoritarian politics was introduced, first under the Directory in 1795, then under Napoleon as First Consul in 1795 and as Emperor in 1804.

The American Revolution, though inspired by the same principles as the French, followed a significantly different path. The detailed story of events cannot be told here. But in *The Federalist Papers* we have a remarkable set of articles revealing the thinking behind the federal constitution. The absence of a hereditary aristocracy, and the fact that American independence had been declared after a successful war against Britain, doubtless helped to make democratic procedures and principles more broadly acceptable than was the case in France. We must remember, however, that the United States under the Articles of Confederation (1781–9) was regarded as a failure by its citizens. The confederal union had not provided stable government. The powers of the constituent states, which were technically regarded as sovereign units under the constitution, left the confederal centre too weak to raise taxes on a consistent basis to pay for debts incurred in the War of Independence. The confederal union was dependent on the good will of the constituent states for the provision of military forces. It could not control a national political agenda effectively, nor sustain a framework for pursuit of a consistent foreign policy, leaving the constituent states a prey to interested powers (Britain, France and Spain) which might be tempted to pursue their rivalries on the American continent. Electoral and legal systems varied in the constituent states. Those that endorsed annual elections were regarded as too 'democratic' to sustain stable government. Legislatures were generally seen as too strong, the state and national executives as too weak, to dispatch the ordinary business of states and union.

In 1787, when a congress to revise the Articles of Confederation was convened in Philadelphia, it was by no means clear that the union would be retained in its current form. Disaggregation into constituent units was a possibility, as was a division into two or three broad groupings. And there were even voices that harked back nostalgically to British imperial rule. Democratic politics itself was cast into question, not least because received wisdom from classical Greek and Roman history equated democracy with instability and factional strife. Debates in Philadelphia thus touched on themes that would be vital to a form of political order that had yet to establish itself as a viable proposition in a mass-based polity. Had American revolutionary politics followed the pattern of France, we must assume that prospects for democratic politics in the nineteenth and twentieth centuries would have been significantly different.

We note from the outset in *The Federalist Papers* a very different tone from Sieyes and Paine. If the spirit of Rousseau haunted the French Revolution, Montesquieu was a moderating influence in America. Hamilton, Madison and Jay by no means saw matters alike. Hamilton, the organizational driving force behind the project, was anxious to see a consolidated national government in the United States, while Madison placed greater emphasis on the need for constitutional checks and balances to contain the exercise of power. All three were clear, however, that national government had to be strengthened in light of the experience of political life under the Articles of Confederation.

The real question was whether democracy is compatible with good government. We should be wary of attributing a common position to the authors of *The Federalist Papers*. Yet they each discounted a form of politics that reduced government to the whims of fleeting majorities. Democracy thus had to be contained, whatever its wider merits might be. Unlike in French revolutionary rhetoric, there is no suggestion that constitutional change can somehow transform the human condition. The approach of *The Federalist Papers* is pragmatic, not utopian. A strong commitment to rights is evident, but balanced by recognition of the intractability of individuals driven to pursue their interests and happiness in various ways. *The Federalist Papers* do not assume that competition and co-operation between equal citizens will always be benign, but rather set out to fashion institutional structures that make a virtue out of competitive human traits. Constitutional devices are treated as limited measures to channel the ambition of each and every citizen, such that the clashing interests of individuals might serve as means to guard against abuses of power.

Madison goes to the heart of the issue in Paper 10.[33] He focuses directly on the problem of factions and instability. But instead of striving to remove the causes of factions, as Robespierre urged in his quest for republican virtue, Madison accepts that factional disputes are an inescapable feature of any polity that takes liberty seriously. The choice he set before citizens is clear. If Americans value freedom, they must find means to live with the consequences of faction. And since 'the latent causes of faction are . . . sown in the nature of man' (in the variety of opinions, abilities and circumstances that shape human conduct), any attempt to eradicate faction would require a draconian and intrusive politics.[34] The remedy would be worse than the disease. The benefits of liberty were obvious to Madison and his contemporaries. Human beings are free to pursue a variety of interests, to associate together as and how they please, to resolve private controversies through formal and informal channels that seem reasonable in particular circumstances, without seeking permission from a distant (and ill-informed) authority. If one faction or another were to dominate in a polity, however, the consequence for other groups and factions could be disastrous. The solution, for Madison, was to ensure that representation of citizens was sufficiently broad that no faction could expect to dominate permanently.

Madison accepted that fallible human beings might always abuse power. The problem would not disappear with the emergence of a democratic politics that professed to respect the rights of citizens. Disputes would arise; interested parties would manoeuvre for position; efforts would be made to keep certain issues off the agenda. Power and its temptations remain a factor in any polity. But if power were dispersed, the worst consequences for marginal groups would be less likely to materialize. And if the exercise of power required agreements across (shifting) factions, all political agents would have to moderate their ambitions in order to assure themselves sufficient support to pursue (at least some of) their projects.

Majorities are, in any case, fickle and unreliable. To give a passing majority the right to speak for (and bind) a whole community is a recipe for authoritarianism. If we take rights seriously, we necessarily have to contain the options available to governments, in a democratic polity as in any other. Thus democracy in itself should not be treated as a solution to the various ills of bad government. Democracy may be desirable for any number of reasons, but it is not a panacea.

Madison specifically defends a representative system against 'pure democracy'.[35] He conceives of democracy operating within the confines of a small-scale society, involving direct citizen participation in government. In a system of this kind, he says, there can be 'no cure for the mischiefs of faction'.[36] Passions will be raised; a majority will speak for the whole of society, with no safeguards in place 'to check the inducements to sacrifice the weaker party, or an obnoxious individual' on the part of government.[37]

In an extended republic, by contrast, direct citizen involvement in government is impossible. The interests of citizens are in the hands of representatives (who, of course, are electorally accountable to the citizen body). Passions are mediated through institutional channels. Representatives will take a detached view, dependent as they are for electoral support on a variety of factions and interests. Intense citizen identification with the nation is anathema to Madison, who values instead the plethora of interests that effectively check each other as they contend for power and influence. In an extended republic, though 'factious leaders may kindle a flame within their particular states', they will hardly be in a position 'to spread a general conflagration through the other states'.[38] Madison pictures 'a variety of sects dispersed over the entire face' of the union.[39] Nothing will change the partiality and limited vision and understanding of the ordinary run of citizens. But with an appropriate constitutional and institutional structure, 'a republican remedy' can be applied to 'the diseases most incident to republican government'.[40]

Madison gives further detail on how this might be achieved in Paper 51. In a characteristic article, combining foundational argument with detailed constitutional and institutional proposals, Madison defends a principle of separation of powers in both public and private spheres. Where division of functions is possible, he urges that it should be pursued. But in order to make such a system work, we need more than constitutional rules. People in any sphere of authority require 'the necessary constitutional means, and personal motives, to resist encroachments' of other sectors.[41] 'Ambition must be made to counteract ambition.'[42] Should we deplore this concession to selfishness and partiality? Madison argues that we should not. No good purpose is served by presuming that human beings are other than they are. 'If men were angels, no government would be necessary.'[43] Madison is adamant that we must take men as we find them, as we do in pursuit of our private interests. If we expect too much of our fellow human beings, disappointment and frustration may encourage draconian forms of persuasion and enforcement.

We are all aware in our private and business dealings of the need to balance 'opposite and rival interests'.[44] Madison suggests that we extend the same caution to our management of public affairs. The United States is thus presented with a unique opportunity. The confederal union had shown that government within the separate states was likely to be unstable, inconsistent, riven by faction. The extended republic, however, could use the combination of confined perspectives for its own purposes. In addition to formal separation between legislative, executive and judicial branches of government, the United States could exploit a 'natural' division between regional and national levels of government. Madison could conclude from experience that 'oppressive combinations of a majority will be facilitated' in more narrowly 'circumscribed confederacies or states'.[45] But instead of rejecting democracy as a principle of government, he argues that it can be contained by its very vices in the wider context of an extended republic. The key is that concentrations of power should be avoided, if possible, at all levels of society. Since we would require massive concentrations of power to counter the partiality of citizens in local politics, we should instead use local rivalry and competition to prevent excessive concentration across the continent as a whole. In this way, we can combine the merits of local democracy with the wider benefits of stability and predictability on a continental scale.

Among the authors of *The Federalist Papers*, Madison is the most anxious to constrain the exercise of power through constitutional procedures. But all three are aware of the limitations of any conceivable political system.

Hamilton, in particular, is so concerned about the weakness of a politics dominated by a strong legislature that he adopts an almost Hobbesian tone in his discussions of the necessary conditions for peace and stability. He insists (in Paper 9) that 'a firm union will be of the utmost moment to the peace and liberty of the states as a barrier against domestic faction and insurrection'.[46] He has no faith in mini-democracies effectively managing their own affairs in the absence of a sufficiently strong central power to guarantee their subordination. Where Madison sees power as a matter of containment, Hamilton focuses rather on the need to wield it effectively if peace is to be secured. 'The hope of impunity', he says in Paper 27, 'is a strong incitement to sedition'; and he happily draws the corollary that power must be adequate to foster a 'dread of punishment'.[47] Whatever their differences on power, Hamilton and Madison share a pessimistic view of human capacity for naturally enlightened judgement. Though they champion natural rights, they have no faith in natural sociability. What we are presented with is a novelty for the times – a robust defence of democratic politics built on deeply sceptical assumptions about human nature.

The intriguing dimension here is that commitments to freedom and equality, prominent in both American and French revolutionary rhetoric, should generate such strikingly different politics. The political trajectories in each case, of course, were products of much more than theory. Detailed analysis of why the revolutions diverged so markedly cannot detain us here. We need to focus, however, on the foundational assumptions that began to enjoy widespread political currency. Henceforth claims that human beings (in some sense) are free and equal could not be ignored, though they might well be disputed. The destructive course of the one revolution could not be attributed solely to ideas that had proved to be remarkably benign in the other. Yet we might wonder what commitments to freedom and equality really amount to in the light of contrasting political experience. This raises deeper philosophical questions than the revolutionary texts of the period ever address.

Each revolution pursued (what would later be claimed to be) distinctively liberal themes, though in sharply contrasting style. Where theory, rhetoric and propaganda in America drew heavily on Locke and Montesquieu, French revolutionaries (Robespierre, Saint-Just, Sieyes to a more limited extent) gave a radical twist to Rousseau's conception of the 'general will'. It cannot be said that revolutionary theory in either context attained the standard of the formative texts. Yet we do have striking examples of polemical writing addressed to a new and wider audience that set a style for later ideological argument.

In this respect, Sieyes's *What is the Third Estate?* is a classic of its kind. Rights are presupposed rather than defended, and then deployed with remarkable effect in a particular polemical context. Simply by championing the rights of the producing classes, Sieyes manages to turn the institutional order of *ancien régime* France upside down. A political order designed to secure the interests of parasites could no longer be justified.

The language of rights functioned similarly in constitutional debates in America, presupposed as a grounding assumption but scarcely defended. A right to be represented cannot settle the vexed question of where that representation should be focused. Advocates of a strong and effective federal centre can use the language of rights as freely as defenders of the prerogatives of constituent states in a union. The debate between federalists and anti-federalists is thus deeply instructive, highlighting the indeterminacy of arguments drawn from common foundational principles.[48] And, of course, the later use of states-rights argument in the civil war (1861–5) lent support to a decidedly illiberal political cause.

Divided though they were by priorities and methods, American and French revolutionaries were nevertheless adamant that the political world can indeed be fashioned anew to satisfy the common sense of citizens. The stress is on removing the arbitrary constraints that prevent common sense from prevailing. If we are to persist with traditional practices and principles, it must be because we endorse them daily in our reflective practice, not because they are hallowed features of an order that we dare not amend. This is a demanding politics for citizens, but one that presupposes no more than disinterested concern for the public good. Whether citizens can rise to the challenge, of course, is quite another matter. The French example suggested to close observers that thinking constructively about politics requires much more than a (notionally) open mind. Traditionalists (like Burke) countered that we have to take some things for granted in order to focus our thinking effectively on particular abuses.[49] Crucially, however, that was an argument that now had to be made in the cut and thrust of political debate. The simple fact that a practice existed could not be taken as a warrant for its continuance.

What was challenged beyond question was any thought that we could go back to an unreflective politics that required no justification. Critics of revolution had to defend their case in front of the very same citizen audience that had been the target of revolutionary theory and propaganda. Stability and order had to be justified theoretically, as indeed a theoretical case had to be made by traditionalists for established practices that are assumed to be handed down to us in social contexts. Anti-theory had to use theoretical weapons. Doubtless this is deeply paradoxical and unsatisfactory. But it is part and parcel of the world of political ideologies.

9

The Age of Ideologies

The style and temper of political theory changed significantly in the post-revolutionary period. Theory had become a major political weapon. The political world now embraced all groups and classes potentially, though not all would play active roles. Political leadership and legitimacy were hotly disputed. Ideas had to be projected in order to secure interests. Political success or failure often hinged on effective mobilization of previously quiescent groups. Stakes were high. And theory had to be tailored to meet the demands of complex circumstances.

The traumas of the French revolutionary period were not finally resolved until the defeat of Napoleonic France in 1815. Yet attempts to draw a line under the upheaval, instability and turmoil of the revolutionary and Napoleonic years remained deeply problematic. Conservative and reactionary advocates of a return to the dynastic politics of the *ancien régime* had to take account of profound changes that had transformed the economic and political life of Europe since 1789.

Two factors, in particular, imposed limits upon the style and character of any viable state. In the first place, there was a need to seek justification for the state beyond the accident of family inheritance. Monarchies which had once been successfully challenged could not simply fall back upon a tacit assumption that hereditary rule was a part of a natural or divinely ordained scheme of things. Order itself, as well as reform or revolution, had to be defended at a theoretical level. The second factor concerned the scale and organization of the state. Technological and economic developments required dynamic management of society at large. What this involved at the practical level was a mobilization of populations on a larger scale than had been the case before 1789. Such mobilization need not, of course, take overt political form. It was not simply a question of extending the franchise or involving wider groups in decision making. Most people's contact with the state would be through local or national bureaucracies. The point to stress, however, is that the state, in responding to changing circumstances, was impinging on a wider range of interests.

And explaining and justifying its procedures would necessarily involve recourse to broad principles. To speak of 'popular' politics in the early nineteenth century would be anachronistic. Yet we can see the beginnings of a process that has continued to this day, with ideological argument becoming a crucial factor in practical political debate.

The most detailed philosophical specification of the emerging form of the modern state is to be found in Hegel's *Philosophy of Right* (1821).[1] Hegel had already worked out a complex account of the relationship between ideas, cultures and institutions in his seminal *Phenomenology of Spirit* (1807), which treats the development of consciousness as a key to historical change.[2] The details of this extraordinary odyssey cannot detain us here. What needs to be stressed here is Hegel's insistence on the significance of culture for an understanding of all human activity. Individuals are rooted in a social world. Each culture is regarded as the consummation of all its predecessors. The discipline of philosophy itself is seen as a historically specific product. A philosopher tackling the most minute contemporary issue is thus implicitly making a judgement about a whole tradition of enquiry. It follows that philosophical transparency requires the adoption of an essentially historical point of view, not as an optional extra but as an integral dimension of philosophical thought.

When Hegel came to give a definitive form to his political philosophy, he thus had behind him an elaborate and comprehensive system. In the *Philosophy of Right* his central concern is to grasp the character and significance of the modern state, considered as the culmination of a long tradition of practice and reflection. The approach exemplifies the fusion of logical and historical analysis. He divides the state into its logical constituents, examining legal entitlement ('abstract right'), the domain of individual judgement ('morality') and the claims of the community ('ethical life'). But these spheres ('moments'), far from being purely logical constructs, are in fact mutually dependent dimensions of the modern state. They can be isolated for purposes of analysis, but are interwoven in daily life in a fashion that distinguishes the modern state from its precursors. Each of these subordinate 'moments' has, moreover, been intimated in the course of political history as the characteristic feature of a dominant polity. What marks the modern state, though, is its capacity to overcome the one-sided currents which sustain it, furnishing an institutional framework sufficiently flexible to absorb the aspects of historic polities that are of permanent value. Thus the naïve unity of the Greek polity (where individuals hardly have an identity outside the community), the formal rule of law in the Roman Empire, the right of individual conscience stressed by Christianity, the abrasive pursuit of self-interest in the modern economy, are each preserved as logical 'moments' that contribute to the fulfilment of the individual in the state.

Hegel saw the state, then, as a product of its history, properly intelligible only as a repository of practical wisdom. This gave his political philosophy a distinctively interpretative thrust. In a polemical preface, in which he comments in uncharacteristically harsh fashion upon various political developments in his own day, he is at pains to distinguish his own approach from currently accepted views of the relationship between philosophy and politics, theory and practice. What he objected to was the conception of political philosophy as a projection of a preferred scheme of things, a recipe for a more or less far-reaching reconstruction of the state. We can all give vent to our frustrations and disappointments by imagining a world in which things are ordered differently. But we would not ordinarily mistake our day-dreaming for philosophy. This, according to Hegel, is precisely what had happened in a Europe which had yet to settle down after the traumas of the French revolutionary and Napoleonic upheavals.

Hegel was adamant that political philosophy should not 'attempt to construct a state as it ought to be'; its task, rather, was to 'show how the state, the ethical universe, is to be understood'.[3] Nor is this limitation specific to political philosophy. Philosophy as a discipline is bent upon exploring the immanent logic of whatever form of experience has been disclosed in the course of historical development. 'To comprehend what is, this is the task of philosophy, because what is, is reason.'[4] To attempt to conjure up merely possible worlds, whether political or natural, is idle fancy. Even when philosophers appear to be depicting an ideal state, Hegel insists that they are in fact giving expression to fundamental assumptions which inform their own cultures. Like every other pursuit, philosophy is a product of its past. 'Whatever happens, every individual is a child of his time; so philosophy too is its own time apprehended in thoughts.'[5]

Hegel's concern with changing patterns of thought and practice in the past should not be confused with the orthodox historian's insistence upon an exact portrayal of events. As a philosopher, he had little interest in what was haphazard or contingent, the unique form which ideas or institutions might assume in response to particular circumstances. He was intent, rather, on grasping the essential form, or identity, of an idea or practice. Thus in the *Philosophy of Right* his focus is on the character of the modern state, and not the particular characteristics of the Prussian, French or British states. One could not, of course, make sense of the modern state as a phenomenon without studying specific states. But Hegel's point is that one should not lose the conceptual identity of the state in the motley array of practices and procedures which might have emerged to meet the demands of ephemeral exigencies.

In the last resort, Hegel held that the idea, or conceptual identity, of the state is more solidly based in reality than its transitory manifestations in empirical guise. 'What is rational is actual and what is actual is rational' might be a dark and potentially misleading saying; but the thought behind it is neither obscure nor paradoxical.[6] When we think about the modern state (rather than this particular state), we call to mind certain universal attributes and functions – a potentially all-embracing and reciprocal

relationship between government and governed, a publicly acknowledged legal system applied without discrimination to all ranks and classes
in society, administrative provision relating to all matters of public
concern. In any specific state these functions will be performed in all
manner of ways. The distinction between public and private spheres will
differ; law will be variously formulated and enforced; public administration will be more or less extensive. What matters to the philosopher is not
how particular functions are performed, but that the community as a
whole should be organized into a complex of institutions that reflect a
shared responsibility for the public good.

Public responsibilities can, of course, be indifferently or deplorably fulfilled. When Hegel equates 'rationality' with 'actuality', he is not suggesting that whatever institutions happen to exist should be adjudged to be
rational and therefore defensible. His point is that the modern state should
be identified with a certain general (and, in his day, novel) conception of
public life, involving an elaborate series of relationships, rights and duties.
Our understanding of ourselves as both individuals and members of communities hinges upon a proper specification of this overall conception, as
indeed does our capacity to make intelligent criticisms of the conduct of
business in public life. But a political philosophy is not a blueprint for
policy; nor can it aspire to more than a provisional understanding of how
we happen to see ourselves and our past for the moment.

Hegel makes it clear throughout his argument that he is presupposing
the complex institutional adaptations and refinements that have made the
modern state what it is. But he fixes his attention on the 'proper immanent
development of the thing itself', the rational core which is the truly significant dimension in the long history of political organization.[7] And though
the various conceptual stages can often be equated with specific historical
innovations, the argument is cast in strictly deductive form. Hegel generates the idea of the modern state, which happens to have emerged historically, from first principles, thus supplying a rational justification for what
might otherwise be regarded as merely fortuitous. What he seeks is the
logical presupposition of institutional life as we know it. And, significantly
in the light of his reputation in some quarters as an apologist for the authoritarian state, he finds this logical presupposition in the human will.

Hegel sees the whole panoply of institutions, laws, social procedures,
practices and relationships as an expression of the human will. He does
not mean, of course, that we have each chosen to live in certain ways or
have formally endorsed the political and social arrangements of our communities. His point is more fundamental. If we try to think of ourselves as
individuals, we find that we cannot but think in terms of social relationships, obligations and duties. Though the specific institutions and relationships we encounter daily may be analytically separable from our
identities (we could, after all, have grown up in other cultures), we cannot
think of ourselves outside some sort of social framework.

But this is only the beginning of the story. Acknowledging the necessity of some sort of social framework, Hegel invites us to ask ourselves whether we can actually think of our identities other than in terms of (something like) the culture and institutions we have grown up in. His contention is that we should see our political and social institutions as a 'world of mind brought forth out of itself like a second nature', an expression, in other words, of our identities rather than an arbitrary restriction upon our options and possibilities.[8]

Nor does Hegel see his defence of (something like) the prevailing world of institutions as a denial of human freedom. He specifically identifies the will with freedom, not in the sense that we are blessed with an arbitrary capacity to choose the other thing, but because of our nature as thinking beings. Thinking involves evaluating more or less adequate concepts of things, refining our views in certain ways, or embroiling ourselves in error. In each of its operations there is thus an active assertion of ourselves against an initially alien or impenetrable world. Thinking is something we do, not something that simply happens to us. In the light of this active dimension, says Hegel, it is no more possible to conceive of thought without freedom than to imagine bodies without weight.[9]

Hegel's account of freedom of the will, though distinctive, is not controversial. Where he leaves his readers uneasy is in his claim that social and political institutions are in fact 'the realm of freedom made actual'.[10] Here we must remind ourselves that he is referring not to institutions which simply happen to exist, but rather to those that reflect the modern state and its potential for the sustenance of human well-being and fulfilment. The crucial point to focus upon is the role of institutions in enabling us to develop our capacities and form conceptions of ourselves. Whether or not we care to admit it, argues Hegel, this is the function that institutions fulfil. We can live and enjoy ourselves in ignorance of this truth; but we would be living a stunted life, oblivious of our natures and tangling our best endeavours in a web of conceptual error.

Will and personality are thus crucial to Hegel's wider account of politics and the state. In the *Philosophy of Right*, however, his discussion of these matters is condensed into a tightly argued introduction. He presupposes that his readers are familiar with the more developed statement of his philosophy of mind in the *Encyclopaedia of the Philosophical Sciences* (1817), and makes few concessions to a more narrowly circumscribed interest.[11] Yet attentive reading provides a sure foundation for later sections of the text dealing with more straightforward ethical and political issues.

Paragraphs 5–7, for example, should be savoured, both for their substantive content and as an illustration of Hegel's characteristic mode of argument. In paragraph 5 he asks us to envisage a perfectly free will, bound by neither external constraints nor physical, social and psychological needs. This he calls 'the pure thought of oneself'.[12] But what exactly do we call to mind? Stripping ourselves of our particular characteristics, roles, obligations, etc., involves setting aside precisely the features that serve to identify us as individuals. We can assume any role in principle; but an actual role cuts us off from the endless options that alone seem to be commensurate with our freedom.

The practical implication of this 'unrestricted possibility of abstraction from every determinate state of mind' is a 'flight from every content as from a restriction'.[13] In political terms it amounts to a restless dissatisfaction with whatever arrangements happen to prevail. Hegel sees the process at work in the French Revolution, where institutional innovations would always be found wanting when compared with the purity of an ideal, leading revolutionaries to destroy 'once more the institutions which they had made themselves'.[14] The gulf between an abstract idea of perfection and its realization in practice is so wide that 'giving effect to this idea can only be the fury of destruction'.[15]

The instability of negative freedom is evident even as we try to characterize it. We might think of ourselves as free to be or do anything; but as soon as we focus upon who we actually are, we find that we have to have recourse to descriptions that seem to commit us to a particular identity and no other. Hegel calls this the 'finitude or particularization of the ego'.[16] It might be regarded as the antithesis of the limitless potential he had portrayed in paragraph 5; yet we cannot avoid limiting descriptions when we speak of willing something.

Paragraphs 5 and 6 each present one-sided pictures of the will. Hegel shows how reflection on the will leads us to see ourselves as both free and bound by circumstances. The apparent contradiction between the two positions is overcome if we modify our views of both freedom and circumstantial constraints. We should see the will, in fact, as 'the unity of both these moments'.[17] When we decide or act we certainly exclude alternative courses of thought or action. But we should think of these commitments not as constraints but as expressions of our identities. Our style of life (career, interests, indulgencies, etc.) is not accidentally appended to us, but an embodiment of our individuality. Our friends can say on particular occasions that we have behaved in (or out of) character. In being 'restricted and determinate', we retain our 'self-identity and universality'.[18] We are still free (in principle) to do the other thing, express ourselves in different ways. In pursuing a particular course of conduct, however, we are not denying our freedom, but making a reality of it.

The conception of personal identity advanced in paragraph 7 is purely formal. In arguing that we have necessarily to express our freedom in determinate ways, Hegel has not given grounds for preferring any particular attitudes or patterns of conduct to any other. What he needs in order to sustain his view of the state, though, is precisely a demonstration of the necessity of the institutional framework in which our conceptions of ourselves develop. In other words, he wants us to see the familiar institutions and conventions of our society as no more separable from us than our personal characteristics.

The crucial point, for Hegel, is that institutions should be derivable from the formal properties of the will. He is interested in institutions not as more or less efficient means of advancing human interests (peace, security, well-being or whatever), but as an essential dimension of our identities. We might put the point somewhat differently by asking ourselves what makes individuality possible? To see ourselves as individuals presupposes that we exist in a world of other individuals. At the very least, we must see ourselves as 'persons' – that is, as potential bearers of rights. This is the sphere of what Hegel calls 'abstract right'.[19] It is a sphere characterized by legal or social recognition, rather than developed relationships. Hegel sums up the 'imperative of right' as: 'Be a person and respect others as persons.'[20] We remain mutually indifferent, but cannot do without one another if we are to have any conception of ourselves at all.

But it is not enough to be simply potential bearers of rights. As Hegel puts the point, 'a person must translate his freedom into an external sphere in order to exist as Idea'.[21] This 'external sphere' is the realm of private property. What we gain through property, however, is not simply the use and enjoyment of things, but an 'embodiment of personality'.[22] The things I own are useful to me; but in a wider sense they give other people some indication of the person I am.

Yet I cannot identify my personality unconditionally with the things I happen to own. Ownership, as an expression of will, presupposes a capacity to sell or transfer possession of a thing when that thing no longer reflects the identity of its owner. Divesting ourselves of things thus involves us in relationships with others. In contracting to buy or sell, for example, we necessarily recognize others as 'persons and property owners'.[23] Hegel describes 'this relation of will to will' as 'the true and proper ground in which freedom is existent'.[24] In place of the straightforward relation between ourselves and the things we use and enjoy, we now have a complex relationship between agents who have chosen to 'embody' their personalities in particular ways.

With contractual relationships comes the possibility of deception and wrongdoing. Sometimes this will be inadvertent, or 'non-malicious', as when individuals contend over the legitimacy of a title of ownership.[25] In these cases there is no dispute about the right of ownership, only about the possession of that right. Matters are complicated when one party to a transaction knowingly presents a false claim in the guise of an honest one. Even in cases of fraud, however, the 'principle of rightness' is respected, though the intention is clearly to mislead.[26] Rightness itself is directly challenged in the case of coercion and crime, where an individual seeks to impose his capricious will without regard for propriety. The challenge must be met, since it threatens to undermine the conventional framework that makes the expression of our individuality possible.[27]

Punishment is justified precisely because it is a reassertion of a necessary condition for the continued flourishing of a community of individuals with various interests, dispositions, weaknesses and foibles.[28] A criminal, in trying to impose himself upon others, is implicitly asserting the unconditional right of a particular will to impose itself in whatever way it sees fit. If his conduct were adopted as a universal principle, however, we would be unable either to estimate the consequences of our actions or to anticipate the likely responses of others to our initiatives. Willing of any kind would be problematical. Since the criminal has been asserting the claims of a particular will, his conduct can be regarded as not only wrong but contradictory. His punishment can thus be regarded as a correction in both the legal and conceptual senses, restoring the conditions in which it might be meaningful to deliberate, resolve and act.

Non-malicious wrong, fraud and crime each highlight in their different ways a dilemma that cannot be resolved within the conceptual world of abstract right. Abstract right is best equated in modern terms with formal legal entitlement. The application of that entitlement is largely a procedural matter, ambiguous perhaps in marginal cases (such as minors), but seldom involving a reappraisal of basic principles. But where legal entitlement is wrongly denied, a new situation arises, demanding a response in a particular case that will be unlike any other in detail. What we are concerned with, in the first instance, is a specific crime, not crime as such or even a given class of crimes. A particular problematic situation faces us that *ought* to be remedied. And this 'ought' implies that we have acknowledged the significance of a principle and made it a ground for our own actions. We reassert the value of right in the face of its denial by wrongdoing.[29]

The crucial dimension that emerges here is self-consciousness. We begin to see ourselves not simply as bearers of rights (and by definition identical with all other bearers of rights) but as subjects with a distinctive identity. In recognizing that a wrong needs to be addressed we have specifically identified ourselves with a principle, adopted a particular course of conduct that fits our view of ourselves. Hegel describes this assumption of responsibility for our characters and actions as the sphere of 'morality'.[30] It involves a differentiation of ourselves from one another, but, at the same time, a recognition of wider obligations and duties which both facilitate our mutual dealings and enable us to recognize ourselves as individuals.

How can wider responsibilities be generated from reflection upon will and agency? In the first place, we cannot but accept responsibility for our immediate purpose in performing an action without rendering the idea of an action unintelligible. (I am throwing a ball, not simply waving my arms around or enduring involuntary spasms.) But our responsibility initially extends no further than the consequences we actually envisage.[31] Actions, however, have an external dimension. What we do might spark off a concatenation of reactions that we could reasonably be expected to have anticipated.[32] (It would make little sense to say that I did not intend to break anything if I were throwing a ball in a china shop.)

Nor would it be realistic to isolate particular actions. We might class various actions together as means towards more general goals ('welfare or happiness').[33] And this clearly involves taking stock of our lives and acting with a view to the satisfaction of a certain conception of ourselves. In forming a general view of our fulfilment, however, we necessarily find ourselves taking account of the fulfilment of others, initially as components of our own satisfaction, but later as ends in themselves.[34] We are thus led to see our actions in ever more complex interrelationship with others, culminating not in a pursuit of particular satisfactions but in an overarching idea of goodness.[35]

Hegel describes the idea of the good as 'the unity of the concept of the will with the particular will'.[36] The will has now become thoroughly self-determining, choosing to pursue specific goals precisely because they accord with a universal ideal.[37] But nothing yet has been said about the character of these ideals. Our conception of the good remains formal and self-imposed. We recognize that we should fulfil our duty, but are not told what that duty entails. Indeed, we regard it as essential to our status as free and responsible agents that we should be answerable only to ourselves in the specification of our duties. Duty 'should be done for duty's sake', with appeal neither to tradition nor to authority.[38]

Hegel identifies the formal conception of duty with Kant's moral philosophy. Kant's achievement, according to Hegel, is 'to give prominence to the pure unconditional self-determination of the will as the root of duty'.[39] But his insistence that duty in particular problematic situations could be determined by universalizing moral judgements ('act only in accordance with that maxim through which you can at the same time will that it become a universal law') is vacuous according to Hegel.[40] If the criterion of good conduct is said to be 'absence of contradiction', then 'no transition is possible to the specification of particular duties'.[41] Without recourse to a 'fixed principle' of some sort, Kant's moral philosophy amounts to an 'empty formalism', opening the way to the justification of any and every 'line of conduct'.[42] A philosophy expressly designed to secure moral judgements against contingent considerations has actually made them vulnerable to special pleading.

What makes the Kantian position untenable, in Hegel's view, is its reliance on individual judgement. In the absence of a binding logical resolution of moral disputes, we are left with only conscience to guide us.[43] But we have no guarantee that our most sincere convictions correspond with a viable system of principles and duties.[44] We can give or withhold consent to any moral practice.[45] And our dissatisfaction with some actual practices can readily extend to a rejection of all. With a little ingenuity, we can present our private predilections in the guise of the good, elevating evil itself to the status of a universal principle.[46] If private conviction is our only criterion, there is nothing to prevent us from defending evil as an end in itself.[47]

Hegel's analysis highlights a crucial limitation in the 'moral' point of view. That we should act in accordance with principles which fit our conceptions of right conduct is essential to our status as free and responsible agents; but without reference to an actual way of life, our moral reflection can easily prove to be counter-productive, enabling us to distance ourselves from any practices that we might find irksome or restrictive. The dilemma is resolved if we set our moral reflection in proper perspective. Self-conscious deliberation on how we ought to behave necessarily involves abstraction from how we actually behave. Yet it does not follow that we should isolate the moral point of view as (arguably) Kant had done. The things we value are rooted in the complex interrelationships that make up a way of life. Reflection can enable us to find a way around that life, and recognize both its richness and its limitations. But principles alone cannot serve as an adequate foundation for the manifold practices and attitudes that happen to distinguish our conduct of social and political life.

Hegel's point is that our ability to think in principled terms derives from an established moral and institutional framework. He conceives of that framework in the broadest terms, extending from the family, through the various organs of civil society, to the state and the international arena. What institutions supply is precisely the objective point of reference that is so conspicuously lacking in the moral sphere. But they should not be regarded merely as external constraints upon our subjective opinions and caprices. We certainly need institutions in order to function in social and political life; yet at the same time they directly embody our needs, aspirations and awareness of ourselves. We are 'linked to the ethical order by a relation which is more like an identity than even the relation of faith or trust'.[48] When Hegel speaks of institutions being necessary, he has in mind the stronger logical, rather than instrumental, sense.

Nor is the institutional framework which nurtures us morally neutral. Hegel sees institutions as the embodiment of value, furnishing us with a sense of direction and significance which we could not attain through purely conceptual analysis. To identify with our institutional order, whether through 'simple conformity', 'habit' or active endorsement, lends substance to our otherwise ephemeral pursuits, enhancing both our personal identity and our understanding of the wider importance of familiar patterns of conduct.[49]

Hegel refers to the established institutional framework generally as 'ethical life'.[50] It is something we encounter in the very first moments of our lives, and from which we can never finally detach ourselves. We grow to an initial awareness of ourselves, indeed, not as individuals but as members of a family, where bonds are based upon natural affection rather than reflection.[51] As lovers, we renounce our individual personalities in union with our partners; as parents or children, we acquire duties and rights that have not been specifically chosen; but we also learn to confront an indifferent or potentially hostile world where affection holds no sway.[52]

The limitations of the family are both natural and necessary to the development of personality. As children, our identification with the family is unconditional, both in our own eyes and in wider social and legal terms. With adulthood, however, comes an assumption of roles and responsibilities of a quite different order, involving relations with others based simply on the reciprocal satisfaction of needs and appetites.[53] This interrelated 'system of needs' is essentially the world of work and consumption.[54] Hegel understands it broadly in the terms of the classical economists (Smith, Say and Ricardo), though he is more interested in the sociological impact of patterns of work than in mechanisms of production and exchange.[55] He stresses, for example, the varieties of outlook and attitude that are generated as work is divided into narrow specialisms, leaving only a small class of civil servants (the 'universal class') to focus on the general interests of the community.[56] The crucial factor at this stage, though, is that through the system of production and exchange we are mutually dependent upon one another, whether we recognize it or not.

A complex economy, though it might be an integrated system, is not self-regulating. It requires an extensive and comprehensible legal framework to serve as a point of reference for the decisions of individual agents.[57] And where wrongdoing does occur, individuals must be familiar with the procedures to follow if their particular interests (and, by implication, the interests of the whole community) are to be safeguarded.[58] What we see in the legal field is explicit recognition of our interdependence in civil society. We become aware, even if only formally, that the pursuit of private satisfactions cannot be isolated from the larger concerns of the community.

Hegel describes the political and legal apparatus characteristic of civil society as 'the external state, the state based on need, the state as the Understanding envisages it'.[59] It is a contrivance for fulfilling limited ends, a more or less useful mechanism enabling us to pursue our private interests, but neither an object of affection nor a dimension in our understanding of ourselves. In theoretical terms, it has become familiar through Hobbes, Locke, Hume, Constant, Humboldt and others, and has enjoyed something of a renaissance in recent times with the resurrection of the 'night-watchman' state in the works of Hayek and Nozick.

For Hegel, however, it is an arrested political form. The exigencies of civil society demand intervention in social and economic life on a scale that makes certain theories of the state obsolete. Civil society is morally significant precisely because it fosters a multiplicity of talents and lifestyles; but with variety comes discordance. Interests clash, fortunes are won and lost through chance or misfortune, while at the bottom of the social hierarchy a 'penurious rabble' is created that has neither a stake in society nor any expectation of tangible improvement in its lot.[60] Anticipating Marx, Hegel sees that 'despite an excess of wealth civil society is not rich enough' to cater for the needs of the poor.[61] Yet what Marx would see as an incentive for revolution is, for Hegel, an impulse propelling civil society 'beyond its own limits' towards more extensive management of resources, both domestically and internationally.[62]

Nor is social and economic management invariably imposed from above. Within the business class, entrepreneurs begin to accept that their interdependence demands an assumption of responsibility for a whole sector of the economy, and not simply for particular enterprises. Corporations emerge which concern themselves with welfare, education and planning within sectors.[63] But the affairs of sectors cannot be isolated from the wider interests of society.[64] Work for the specific interest of a corporation inexorably broadens intellectual horizons, transforming the interdependence that was originally a crude fact of economic life into a guiding principle of policy.[65]

The organs of civil society never afford more than a partial understanding of the complex relationships that constitute the life of a society. We aspire to an inclusive perspective through the state, where subordinate, and often apparently contradictory, aspects of our lives are set in a wider institutional frame of reference. The conceptions of human nature implicit in family and economic life, for example, might seem at first glance to be irreconcilable. Yet, viewed in a different light, we can accept emotional identification with others and the need for self-assertion as equally necessary to our development. What the state provides is precisely a conceptual and practical focus for our endeavours, enabling us to recognize the larger significance of pursuits that might otherwise seem restrictive and belittling.

Hegel describes the state as 'the actuality of the ethical idea'.[66] His point is not simply that the state embraces the gamut of our moral and practical affairs, but that through the state we are led to identify ourselves with the community which has nurtured and framed our lives. In a purely empirical sense, we might be regarded as the products of long-entrenched customs, practices and habits that are simply handed down from generation to generation. Reflection on the state, however, ensures that we go about our ordinary business with a deeper awareness of social bonds and reciprocal obligations. We may not act differently, but we gain in clear-sightedness.

The point may be clarified in relation to Hegel's concept of freedom. In his view, we are always implicitly free. We cannot conceive of ourselves as agents without invoking notions like deliberation and choice, which presuppose a capacity to do the other thing. But what that freedom amounts to in practice is obscure to us until we gain a proper understanding of the relation between the individual and the community. In the state our rights and duties are embodied in institutions. We wonder what to do not in abstract terms, but in determinate circumstances. Freedom so structured Hegel describes as 'concrete', in contrast to the purely hypothetical capacity to do anything whatever.[67] What the state recognizes is not simply our right under the law to pursue a course of conduct, but our identities and interests as these have emerged in the family and civil society. Our pursuit of private interests becomes, indeed, a contribution to the 'universal end' of the state, cementing bonds within the community and enlarging our social and political understanding.[68]

There is no need to dwell here on the details of Hegel's legal and constitutional proposals. It is important to note, however, that traditionalist though he was in certain respects, Hegel opposed unthinking adherence to customary practice. He did not share the misgivings of Savigny and the historical school of jurisprudence about the formulation of a systematic legal code. The codification of a system of law in a rational constitution is not, for Hegel, a distortion of a tradition. His contention, rather, is that the ideals which inform a tradition have to be given the status of coherent legal principles before people can profit from the educational experience of being members of a political community.[69]

The constitution that Hegel recommends is an articulated reflection of the functional interdependence of significant sectors of the community. It is essentially a constitutional monarchy, with a monarch at the head as a symbol of unity and focus of ultimate authority, supported by an executive, in which a dispassionate class of civil servants serves as guardian of the higher interests of the state, and a bicameral Assembly of Estates, representing the particular concerns and dispositions of agricultural and business classes.[70] We may quibble with Hegel about the proper distribution of roles and responsibilities. The point to stress, however, is that he sees a constitution not simply as a means of channelling the exercise of power, but (more importantly) as a public expression of the character and identity of the community.

Hegel presents political life very much as a voyage of discovery, leading us to a proper appreciation of our relations with the community and the state. The harsh tone of his dismissal of the abstract individualism so characteristic of seventeenth- and eighteenth-century political theory has often alarmed readers accustomed to seeing the state portrayed as a vehicle to serve the interests of individuals. He attributes to the state, for example, a 'supreme right against the individual, whose duty is to be a member of the state'.[71] And in the international arena, where conflicts between states can sometimes be resolved only by war, he sees the sacrifice of the individual for the good of the state as a 'universal duty'.[72] But we should be clear that, though the state encompasses our lives, it nevertheless preserves ample scope for the expression of our personal interests. We identify with the state as the public embodiment of our culture; but the state does not assume the detailed direction of all our affairs.

We have come a long way from Hegel's initial characterization of will and agency. He sought to explain the structure of modern political institutions as a corollary of properties of the human will, linking our inner life inextricably with a wider social and political context. It was an audacious undertaking. Whether his argument is ultimately successful remains a hotly contested issue. Few philosophers today would follow the form of his argument, presenting as it does a variety of more or less plausible transitions in deductive guise. Nor is the metaphysical view that underpins his system widely held to be compelling. More narrowly conceived, however, his political philosophy advances an analysis of the modern state as penetrating as any that has come down to us. He has shown how modern political and economic life demands at once ample freedom for the pursuit of private interests and intense identification with the community. Precisely how the institutional balance between these conflicting demands should be struck is still a vexed question. In one sense, of course, this is a perennial dilemma, going back to Plato and beyond. Hegel's *Philosophy of Right* is a sustained philosophical analysis of the issue as it emerged in the aftermath of the French Revolution. Much has changed in our day to make the state both more pervasive and more alarming. But Hegel's terms of reference continue to be indispensable for an understanding of the philosophical significance of institutions, focusing our pursuit of self-knowledge on the mutual involvement of public and private worlds.

Mobilizing opinion in this new political context involved a wide range of theoretical and rhetorical skills. The comfortable world of old-style political elites had been decisively shaken. Henceforth fresh and abrasive voices demanded to be heard. Broad coalitions of interests had to be put together in conditions that scarcely had precedents in the *ancien régime*. Traditional political issues, regarding rights, obligations and duties continued to demand attention, but the interests of previously excluded groups and classes could not be easily discounted. The tone and rhetorical range of argument broadened accordingly as the nineteenth century progressed, often involving blatant manipulation of received symbols, values and ideas. High theory had to adapt to changing political conditions. Political rhetoric became genuinely mass-based long before the advent of democratic politics as we understand it. In the process theory became a political weapon of a distinctively novel kind. Rhetorical effectiveness was as significant in political debate as truth or consistency. Ideological politics had come of age.

Liberalism

The French Revolution was a crucial point of reference for all European ideologies in the nineteenth century. The commitment to natural rights in the *Declaration of the Rights of Man and of Citizens* was sustained in subsequent liberal theory, though often defended in radically different ways. It was an article of faith in liberal theory that the legitimacy of a state should be judged according to its capacity to facilitate the ends and ambitions of individuals. The position had to be modified in the light of the strictures of conservative and reactionary critics of the revolution, which often focused on rampant individualism as a root cause of insecurity and terror. Liberals, however, had the resources to accommodate these objections. They could draw on established constitutional theory, stemming from Locke and Montesquieu, to counter abuses of power of whatever kind. It is a central tenet of liberal theory that all power is likely to be abused, and not just the arbitrary power of hereditary monarchs and tyrants. What we see is a subtle synthesis of diverse traditions, culminating in vigorous defence of limited government.

Benjamin Constant was a seminal figure in the reorientation of liberal thought. He was anxious to disavow any connection between liberal ideals and the principles of 1793. His particular reading of the French Revolution led him to associate popular government with tyranny, despite the lofty ambitions of radicals and reformers. In a seminal lecture of 1819, Constant specifically contrasted ancient liberty, which stressed direct popular involvement in government, with modern liberty, focused on the idea of the rule of law and representative institutions.[73] He saw the civic republican ideal as peculiarly suited to the small-scale states of antiquity, where a sizeable proportion of the citizen body might plausibly meet to resolve issues in public forums. Citizens had the advantage of a slave class to spare them the burden of maintaining themselves and could be presumed to share strong substantive values.

What Rousseau (and more especially his Jacobin followers) had done, according to Constant, was to lift the ancient view of citizenship out of context, inspired as he was by the vision of collective responsibility being assumed for the burdens of public life. In attempting to apply ancient participatory ideals to the modern world, modern republicans, argues Constant, had failed to recognize the practical difficulties that made the modern state a different political species from the ancient *polis*. The scale of the modern state, and the diversity of interests it represents, dictates a modification in political and constitutional principles. A cult of virtue, for example, of the kind associated with Robespierre or Saint-Just, might very well be a fitting reflection of the cultural homogeneity of an ancient republic. In a state the size of France in the nineteenth century, however, an insistence on moral or political uniformity would necessarily involve the suppression of a plethora of interests and points of view. Modern citizens, according to Constant, prize individual liberty above all else. They glory in the rich mosaic of their private interests and attachments. They are content for the political authorities to 'confine themselves to being just'; they are perfectly prepared to 'assume the responsibility of being happy' for themselves.[74]

The crucial point at issue in Constant's contrast between ancient and modern liberty is the characterization of the proper relations between individual and state. Rousseau and the Jacobins had insisted that each individual had a right to participate in government or at least to authorize the actions of a government. What this means in practice is that a government claiming to derive its authority from the people would be blessed with unlimited theoretical powers. An isolated individual opposed to specific policies would place himself in the position of opposing the collective will of the community. In effect, this would mean that opposition could be construed as an assertion of narrow self-interest. Moreover, since the collective will of the community would simply be a partial interest that had succeeded in presenting itself in the guise of the collective interest, there would be ample scope for a determined minority to dominate the many interests of the different groups within the community.

Constant views this as a clear recipe for tyranny. His solution to the dilemma is to treat the state not as an instrument for the realization of liberty in any abstract sense but rather as a guarantor or protector of the very many liberties that might be enshrined in a way of life. In any civilized society people enjoy a variety of rights (to be subject to the law rather than the whim of individuals, to be free to express opinions, to pursue a profession, to associate with others, to be foolish or frivolous in the quiet of their homes). The principal role of the state in this scheme of things is to preserve a system of constitutional guarantees that would enable individuals to go about their business in their own ways. Vested interests, which had been viewed by the Jacobins as a series of obstacles to the inculcation of public virtue, would have to be respected as a tangible means of containing the state within proper bounds, much as they had been for Madison in *The Federalist Papers*. In general, private life would be regarded as the principal focus of an individual's endeavour and ambition. Political devices serve merely to facilitate the private realm, ensuring sufficient stability and security for the pursuit of a multitude of individual ends.[75]

Privacy and pluralism became central themes in the liberal defence of the individual against the creeping encroachment of the potentially tyrannical state. Liberals were less certain about the value of popular participation in political life. Though Constant denied that political participation was an end in itself, he saw a measure of participation as a necessary means of securing the state in its rightful role. But this was far from the standard liberal position. Constant's liberal peers were haunted by the thought that an unholy alliance of radical intellectuals and the Paris mob had lead a movement of political reform to degenerate into revolution and terror. What they feared above all was that political liberty would not survive attempts to put the state at the head of a radical programme of social and economic transformation. They certainly had little sympathy with egalitarian political projects. The limits of their political ambitions were very much set by a concern to preserve the prevailing balance in society.

The over-mighty state was an obvious menace to liberty by the 1830s. Subtler forces were also at work in economy and society which, by degrees, threatened to undermine an individualist culture at its source. Liberals feared that the adaptation of industry and commerce to the demands of an emerging mass society would lead to a levelling of standards, stifling energy and initiative and encouraging a dull, bureaucratic mentality. Constitutional guarantees had clearly only limited value in dealing with dilemmas of this order. Part of the problem was that people had begun to look to the state for a solution to all their difficulties. Yet it was precisely reliance on the state and its cumbersome apparatus that seemed to many to compromise political liberty in the longer term.

The prognosis for liberalism was far from encouraging. Alexis de Tocqueville, for example, surveying the course of recent history in his seminal *Democracy in America* (1835–40), saw an inexorable advance of the principle of equality at the expense of liberty.[76] Political liberty in the past, in his view, had been secured by a balance of power within society, with vested interests (aristocracy, church, municipalities, etc.) constituting bulwarks against the encroachments of central authority. Doubtless Tocqueville had an excessively sanguine view of the actual power relationships at work in modern societies. He pictures the 'power of a few subjects' erecting 'insurmountable barriers against the tyranny of the king', while kings themselves, 'endowed with an almost divine character in the eyes of the populace', felt so secure in status and authority that they felt no temptation 'to abuse power'.[77] However matters may once have stood, Tocqueville was clear that in modern times a whole series of factors had served to erode hierarchy, rank and privilege. In the wider European context, the Protestant Reformation had given a religious sanction to egalitarianism. And the transformation of industry and trade since the late eighteenth century had made the egalitarian ethos of the bourgeoisie the dominant influence in society.

Tocqueville's view of these developments was always ambivalent. As the product of an aristocratic family, he felt acutely the erosion of respect and security that had shattered a comfortable and complacent social world. Yet he had no sympathy for attempts to restore the institutions, practices and values of the *ancien régime*. He regarded egalitarianism as an irresistible social and cultural force in modern conditions. He describes 'the gradual unfurling of equality in social conditions' as 'a providential fact', destined to be 'universal' in scope and beyond any possibility of 'human interference'.[78] What disturbed him was not so much egalitarian values as the political implications of those values. A democratic revolution in France in 1789 had swept away institutions which, while no doubt open to abuse, had nevertheless managed to contain central authority to some degree. Once the equal right of all citizens had been proclaimed, however, what moral, political or constitutional principle could counter the collective force of a majority? If the people collectively are regarded as a sovereign body, how could they be effectively opposed? If the people collectively possess the power of both decision and implementation, there is nothing to check the vagaries of popular enthusiasm. This is precisely the issue that had so disturbed Hegel in the *Philosophy of Right*.[79] Tocqueville describes it as democracy 'abandoned to its primitive instincts', like children who 'are left to fend for themselves in the streets of our towns and who come to learn only the vices and wretchedness of our society'.[80] This, in effect, amounts to 'democracy minus anything to lessen its defects or to promote its natural advantages'.[81] The reactionary response to this dilemma is simply to reject the democratic revolution, as if the modern world could somehow be effectively opposed. Tocqueville's stance is much more sophisticated. In his view, theorists and the emerging political class had to learn the lessons of experience, tempering the impact of democratic politics without undermining democratic principles. In short, 'a new political science' is required 'for a totally new world'.[82]

Tocqueville's *Democracy in America*, though it has attained classic status, is unlike most of the texts in the canon of political philosophy. It eschews formal political argument, developing instead through close political, social and cultural observation. Indeed, hasty abstraction or generalization is presented throughout the text as a temptation to avoid at all costs. Yet it is driven by a political agenda. If a levelling of social conditions is inevitable, how are European cultures to sustain their commitment to political liberty in the face of the administrative and political centralization that had been such a marked feature of the political forms that had emerged in the aftermath of the French Revolution? Tocqueville is interested in the United States precisely because its revolution has given rise to a regime that enables both liberty and equality to flourish. How had the United States managed to reconcile political values that European liberals had come to regard as mutually incompatible? Tocqueville is clear that theory alone will not resolve the conundrum. Democracy in practice has to be observed at close hand before any sensible political conclusions can be drawn.

Tocqueville used an official visit to the United States to study the prison system in 1831–2 as an occasion to chart the detailed vagaries and development of a democratic culture that had manifestly succeeded where European political cultures had failed. Nothing, in Tocqueville's view, could stop the social revolution that was everywhere tending towards acceptance of the principle of equality. Europeans, therefore, had to ask themselves how its benefits could be attained without the political tyranny that had disfigured democratic experiments in Europe. Tocqueville is clear that Europeans cannot simply borrow from American political experience. The impact of political ideas and innovations is framed and shaped by cultures in complex ways that only detailed observation can discern. Europeans would not be able to avoid the democratic revolution that awaited them. But they could at least understand how democracy works effectively in the particular circumstances of the United States. Tocqueville has no faith in the 'absolute perfection' of any actual 'system of laws'.[83] If Europeans are to save themselves from a future oscillating between 'democratic' tyranny and blatant authoritarianism, and Tocqueville himself is deeply pessimistic about what could be achieved practically, then they must at least grasp the complex interdependence of customs, laws and circumstances in a flourishing democracy. What they make of that knowledge in political terms will depend upon the resources of their own political cultures. A necessary condition of any constructive reflection is thus an appreciation of the possibilities of a different political perspective.

Tocqueville's concerns are deep-rooted. His stress on background political culture rules out the possibility of short-term solutions to endemic problems. Yet he is also clear that it would be futile for liberals to deplore the modern world and all its works. He set himself the task of distilling the political lessons of American experience, despite his scepticism about the direct applicability of institutional and policy initiatives from one context to another. Some of the cardinal assumptions of liberals of his generation had been challenged by the obvious political success of the United States. It could no longer be assumed that a commitment to equality would necessarily involve the sacrifice of liberty. The citizens of the United States had clearly contrived an egalitarian society without the slightest trace of political tyranny. At the very least, this is food for thought. Tocqueville explains much of this success by reference to the origins of the United States. Distant colonial status had obliged settlers to rely on their own resources in the day-to-day management of their affairs. Without an established class structure or 'natural' aristocracy, they had to fashion schemes of social co-operation among strangers if they were to survive at all. In these circumstances, necessity really does prove to be the mother of invention – grass-roots democracy is perfectly adapted to survival and flourishing in a new world.

The Puritan origins of settlers also fostered a culture of self-reliance tempered by reciprocity. Tocqueville is especially struck by the culture of the New England townships, where it was assumed that 'each man is the best judge of his own interests and best able to provide for his own private needs'.[84] Administration is thus massively decentralized; but the corollary is that a vast majority of citizens recognize that such decentralized procedures work effectively only if there is scrupulous respect for the rule of law. A culture of legality is thus not only seen to be desirable, but is vigorously endorsed in everyday dealings among citizens.

Appreciating the strength of the political culture of the United States involves much more than formal political analysis. Tocqueville has a wonderful eye for detail, highlighting (among many other things) the moral and intellectual equality of women as a basic building block for a 'true concept of democratic progress', a respect for work as an 'honourable necessity for the human race', and a pragmatic approach to matters of judgement that amounts to an 'American philosophic method'.[85] Ready amendment of matters of this order is clearly beyond even the most ambitious legislation.

But, in Tocqueville's analysis, there remain lessons from which Europeans can profit. His portrayal of the federal constitution, in particular, gave his contemporaries an unprecedented insight into the workings of the political institutions of the United States.[86] At a time when Europeans were beginning to question the appropriate political form of newly emerging states, they now had before them for the first time a detailed account of federal theory in practice. Where European liberals still tended to be suspicious of popular involvement in government, Tocqueville insists that broad-based participation at national, state and local levels gives political life a massive solidity that keeps extremist adventurers at bay. Administration itself is so thoroughly decentralized that there is little risk of a single focus of power and influence emerging. And the establishment of clear distinctions between legislative, executive and judicial roles obliges citizens to pursue consensual means of co-operation in (necessarily) complex circumstances.

Tocqueville recognizes that it would not be possible to resuscitate European liberalism simply by selectively applying the best features of American political culture in the vastly different situation that prevailed in Europe. Necessity had taught European states to regard each other as potential enemies. War (or the threat of war) had typically driven political and administrative agendas, irrespective of the ideology or values of particular states. In these precarious circumstances, efficiency demands that power be centralized, and that executive authorities be granted broad authority to respond to crises. And resistance to centralization had been signally weakened by the emergence of the doctrine of natural rights, stressing the equality of all and the irrelevance of inherited status or prerogative. If the people as a whole regard themselves as the collective embodiment of the sovereignty of the state, it is very difficult to orchestrate opposition to political demands on any other basis. Citizens could argue about the appropriate expression of the will of the people, but not about its normative warrant. In practice, argues Tocqueville, 'this naturally gives men of democratic times a very elevated opinion of society's privileges and a very low opinion of an individual's rights'.[87] To oppose the pronouncements of 'democratic' governments could easily be construed as opposition to the principle of democracy itself. Individual rights could be rendered very fragile indeed, precisely because they are notionally shared by all citizens indifferently.

For all his fears, Tocqueville could see no alternative to the final triumph of democracy. Europe had endured its worst excesses in the turmoil of the French Revolution. Europeans accordingly had to learn either to temper democracy or to live with the consequences. Exposure to the political culture of the United States had persuaded Tocqueville that liberty and equality are not incompatible conceptually, but there is little chance of enjoying them together in a polity that is driven by circumstances to focus the exercise of power in a few central hands. Europeans can take heart that all is not lost, despite the deep intractability of their circumstances. At the very least, they have to recognize that the demands of democratic politics require a hugely sophisticated citizenry.

Tocqueville is emphatic on the point. 'The first of the duties currently imposed upon the rulers of our society is to educate democracy, to reawaken, if possible, its beliefs, to purify its morals, to control its actions, gradually to substitute statecraft for its inexperience and awareness of its true interests for its blind instincts, to adapt its government to times and places, and to mould it according to circumstances and people.'[88] This, to be sure, is a very tall order indeed. Citizens are being asked to acquire the sophistication and self-restraint that are essential to a flourishing democracy without being exposed to the rigours of democracy in practice. Europeans had also experienced how devastating the political consequences of democratic failure could be. Tocqueville has no illusions about the enormity of the challenge. Yet he is also aware that a failure of political nerve would be catastrophic. It is important simply to recognize the possibility of a mundane politics, where individuals 'would realize that, in order to benefit from the advantages of society, they would have to bow to its requirements'.[89] Nothing can guarantee success. Citizens associating freely together have only their wits to rely upon. It is certain, however, that if they fail to recognize the fragility of the liberties they enjoy, they will condemn themselves to the torment of political tyranny.

There was little in Tocqueville's analysis to encourage optimism. To the traditional liberal suspicion of the state had been added the more insidious threat of a tyranny of the majority. While practical exigencies gave every opportunity for further centralization, liberals found themselves unable to reverse the trend. From Wilhelm von Humboldt to John Stuart Mill and beyond, freedom was treated as a precious commodity, more likely to be lost through inadvertence than to be brought down by direct political action. Tocqueville himself, in the face of the revolutions of 1848, was filled with foreboding. A shift was evident in people's attitudes and expectations. Where once the defence of political liberty had been the first concern of the articulate classes, attention was now given to substantive social and economic questions. It became clear to him that the principles of classical liberalism had begun to appear quaintly old-fashioned. If the choice were between basic freedoms and a redistribution of property, too many people (so he feared) would have little hesitation in opting for the latter.

What was at stake in these discussions was not simply the kind of state that might be deemed compatible with political freedom, but the character of the individuals who might emerge under its tutelage. Individuals making choices, bearing responsibility, representing themselves in the various arenas of social life, had always been central to liberal claims about the appropriate limits of political power and authority. To picture, by contrast, 'individuals' being shaped, nurtured and moulded by an all-encompassing state, assuming broad economic, social and cultural functions, was to conjure up a very different prospect. Political authorities would be in a position to fashion the 'individuals' they regarded as most effective or desirable, with education and other public goods being considered as instrumental means to the attainment of human 'products'.

Yet a strand in liberal thought had always accorded priority to substantive interests rather than formal moral, constitutional or legal entitlements. Jeremy Bentham famously argued in 1789 that basic human desires could be the only legitimate criteria in the justification of coercive measures by the state. In his view, we have no choice but to pursue pleasure and avoid pain. 'Nature has placed mankind under the governance of two sovereign masters, *pain* and *pleasure*.'[90] For Bentham this is a simple statement of fact, but it has far-reaching implications for the way we should regard moral and political questions. Bentham's concern was to expose the illusions at the heart of traditional debates about values, rights, obligations and so forth. He treated the perennial issues in moral and political philosophy as mere verbiage, a misleading gloss on the real sources of human motivation. In Bentham's view, standard discussions of what we ought to do are simply misplaced. We are programmed to assess our actions in terms of pleasure and pain, 'fastened', as he puts it, to the 'chain of causes and effects'.[91] It is no more possible for us to urge ourselves not to pursue pleasure than to stop breathing.

It is axiomatic for Bentham that we pursue pleasure, no matter what justification we may put to ourselves for our actions. Given that this is the case, it follows (for Bentham) that policy should be assessed in terms of its aggregate impact on the happiness of the community. In his celebrated formulation, 'the greatest happiness of the greatest number' should be 'the measure of right and wrong'.[92] A utilitarian calculation of consequences should replace the qualitative evaluation of moral and political issues. How happiness should be conceived and measured, who should make authoritative judgements about its pursuit, how long- and short-term considerations should be balanced, are, for Bentham and his utilitarian followers, technical issues that can (in principle) be resolved. The crucial point is that traditional questions in political philosophy (What is the ideal form of polity? Do we have any natural rights?) obscure what is really going on when we make judgements. Elaborate moral and political principles disguise the beguilingly simple fact of human motivation. Human beings pursue pleasure and avoid pain. They may describe their pleasures and pains in complex ways, but the responsibility of legislators is to cut through false distinctions and ensure that everyone's pleasure and pain is counted in policy deliberations.

Counting each individual as one, and none as more than one, as Bentham insists, does a great deal to change the character and scope of government policy. Governments can no longer distinguish between the 'higher' and 'lower' interests of citizens. Elite preferences enjoy no special standing. If people gain more pleasure from football than from opera, then it follows that governments should promote the former rather than the latter. But it also remains possible that after a calculation of costs and benefits, governments might decide to promote neither. Individuals might be left to their own devices to wallow in whatever fancies grabbed their attention. Individuals would simply do what they are programmed to do – maximize marginal utility. Governments, by contrast, have to look to the aggregate utility of the society as a whole, viewed as the sum of the satisfaction of individuals. If it can be shown that the sum of the marginal improvement in the welfare of the vast majority greatly exceeds the pain that might follow from a marginal increase in taxation for the rich, then Benthamite theory insists that governments should pursue redistributive policies.

Utility as an objective criterion always remained more an aspiration than a tangible achievement. It is one thing to identify hypothetical units of 'pleasure', and quite another to compare either the 'pleasure' or marginal importance of different activities. Health and education may both be regarded as public goods, requiring support from the state. Yet, despite the apparent objectivity of Bentham's theory, it is quite impossible to avoid invoking qualitative criteria when considering the allocation of scarce resources to various projects. John Stuart Mill addressed this issue directly, though not entirely satisfactorily, in *Utilitarianism* (1861). Despite an early indoctrination in Benthamite ideas, Mill recognized the force of the objection to the essential comparability of all pleasures. He insists that 'it is quite compatible with the principle of utility to recognize the fact, that some *kinds* of pleasure are more desirable and more valuable than others'.[93] What he has in mind is not intensity of pleasure, but a qualitative distinction between 'higher' and 'lower' pleasures, pleasures of the mind contrasted with pleasures of the body, pleasures that contribute to the long-term good of human beings rather than ephemeral satisfactions. That we actually make distinctions of this kind when we prioritize our preferences is clear. Whether what we are doing can be characterized in utilitarian terms, however, is quite another matter.

Mill's defence of the 'higher faculties' is categorical.[94] He simply could not equate the satisfaction derived from resolving a difficult problem with the pleasure of drinking oneself into a stupor. In his view, 'it is better to be a human being dissatisfied than a pig satisfied; better to be Socrates dissatisfied than a fool satisfied.'[95] And if this distinction could make sense only from the perspective of Socrates, so much the worse for the fool. In the text he distinguishes between the 'moral attributes' and 'consequences' of actions, without explaining precisely how these different considerations should be brought together in any particular decision.[96] Nor does he stress, though he is perfectly aware of, the damage done to the crude Benthamite version of utilitarianism by his move.

Mill's innovation effectively undermines the determinist dimension in Bentham's theory. Far from treating pleasure and pain as 'sovereign masters' over individual actions, Mill denies that 'the agent's own greatest happiness' should be the relevant standard in the appraisal of actions.[97] What matters is not that an individual should maximize her happiness, but rather that policy should strive to attain 'the greatest amount of happiness altogether'.[98] Indeed, Mill rejects a narrow hedonistic criterion at the level of policy. Individuals prepared to devote themselves (say) to the provision of sanitary living conditions in industrial cities are in an obvious sense denying themselves the opportunity of playing golf every afternoon. Yet it is perfectly clear to Mill that their discipline and self-denial contribute massively to public welfare. Far from maximizing the general welfare of a community, Bentham's criterion as a rule of thumb for individual conduct would detract significantly from the provision of public goods. Mill argues, instead, that utilitarianism 'could only attain its end by the general cultivation of nobleness of character', effectively encouraging individuals to put the public good before their private satisfactions.[99] In this scheme of things, utilitarianism becomes an optional theory available to assess the merits of various policy proposals, but clearly cannot claim definitive status as a 'scientific' solution to the problem of explaining and justifying actions. It takes its place along with a range of contending theories in the public domain, open to various interpretations, applicable to certain spheres of activity more obviously than others, one feature in a complex background of argument and discussion.

Utilitarianism, in fact, contributed signally to the emergence of a reformist ethos in Europe in the mid-nineteenth century, especially in Britain. This was not so much a matter of putting theory into practice (policy implications were much too contentious for that) as a recognition that the interests of a whole population had to be taken into account. No clear guidelines, however, could be drawn from utilitarianism on the vexed question of the role of the state in driving a reformist agenda. This was the burning issue for Tocqueville in his agonizing assessment of prospects for liberalism in an industrial future. And John Stuart Mill, who had been deeply influenced by Tocqueville, sought to address the issue directly. He recognized (with Tocqueville) that pragmatic adjustment to co-ordination problems as they arose would lead to a structural shift towards centralization of powers and responsibilities. If freedom were to be defended as a value, it had to be restated in relation to dramatically changed circumstances. People had to be persuaded that their long-term interests and potential would not be fulfilled if they sought solutions from government for all the ills that might beset them. It could not be assumed that the prerogatives and values of an earlier political order would be sufficient to contain government in a broadly representative political context. A new principle was required to focus the thinking of government and governed alike.

This was precisely the task that Mill set himself in *On Liberty*. First published in 1859, the text has often been regarded as a defence of a libertarian style of government. Yet this is a significant misreading of a deceptively complex text. Mill's point is not that government intervention cannot be justified, but rather that intervention is intrinsically problematic. If there is a standing temptation for governments to do more rather than less, then it follows that all concerned should be clear about the proper role of government. In *On Liberty* Mill defends what he describes as a 'very simple principle', designed to clarify the complex relationships between government, governed and wider society.[100] He contends that 'the sole end for which mankind are warranted, individually or collectively, in interfering with the liberty of action of any of their number, is self-protection'.[101] In this scheme of things, it can be no business of either government or public opinion what individuals do in pursuit of their private interests. They may be misguided, foolhardy or absurd in their conduct, threatening their personal chances of happiness according to any reasonable criterion. They may shock or alarm family, friends, colleagues and associates. And, of course, witnesses to their folly may feel inclined to offer all manner of well-intended advice. If they are adults of sound mind, however, able to bear responsibility for their actions, no one may use or threaten compulsion (either legal or moral) in order to save them from the consequences of their own actions. Compulsion may be used, according to Mill, only if an individual's conduct can be shown 'to produce evil to some one else'.[102] He insists that 'the only part of the conduct of any one, for which he is amenable to society, is that which concerns others'.[103] Legislation or 'moral' intervention of any kind would have to satisfy this requirement before it could be countenanced. Rules of thumb that had governed conduct in the past would have to be examined afresh in the light of this criterion, as would any remedy for any conceivable difficulty that might confront us in the future. We would all know where we stood and what (in principle) we could expect of one another.

Or would we? Mill's 'simple' principle, on closer inspection, is far from clear in its implications. Early critics pointed out that the distinction between 'self-regarding' and 'other-regarding' actions is difficult to maintain, even in theory. We are social creatures, confronting the options available to us from a background of received understandings and complex involvement with other people. Even our most trivial actions may have implications for others that affect their well-being and interests. Conduct that might once have been regarded as entirely private (such as the domain of personal hygiene) may later be seen as an important matter affecting public health. Mill is clear that his principle will not enable him to distinguish precisely between public and private spheres. Our conceptions of what is public or private will shift over time in response to changing perceptions of risk. But conceptions of the person will also change, along with what it might mean to engage in any activity whatever.

Mill's 'simple' principle, then, is inherently contentious, but may still be a useful means of distinguishing between spheres of responsibility. Mill needs to show, in addition, that something like his principle is actually in the wider interest of the members of a society, all things considered. Here he produces powerful arguments for 'liberty of thought and discussion' that have remained influential to this day.[104] If we assume from the outset that certain courses of action are better than others, but are unsure which option to pursue, we will ordinarily try things out, ask around and in general endeavour to learn directly or indirectly from experience. Dogmatic views about what should be done in any context will inevitably narrow the range of possible courses of conduct available to us. Certain things would simply be ruled out, irrespective of any assessment of their consequences. Mill's view is that if we want to do the best we can for ourselves, then we have to retain an open mind. And we should extend the same thought to anyone we may encounter in our society.

Mill explores the implications of this idea in relation to both science and morality. As scientists, we may all have an interest in the truth, though we cannot be sure that the theories we currently favour should be regarded as definitive. In these circumstances, we have to insist that enquiry remains open, even if only to increase confidence in the positions we currently hold. To suppress absurdity, rather than to expose it, actually weakens our ability to pursue the truth. Similar considerations apply in the moral sphere. Our conviction that we should do the right thing is not strengthened by a refusal even to imagine other possible values. We are all aware, of course, that moral arguments are notoriously difficult to resolve, even among groups that share fundamental ideas. Christians may disagree about the practical implications of their interpretations of the Bible. Differences of view will always arise. Our primary consideration must be that we pursue the course of conduct that is likely to make our lives go better; and they are unlikely to go better if we deny ourselves the possibility of thinking hard and imaginatively about the choices we have to make. We have to keep the scope for discussion as broad as possible, all other things remaining equal. None of us can be entirely sure of our own rectitude, either in science or in morality. An eccentric question may mark the tentative early stages of an important discovery. We will not help ourselves if we suppress views that we regard as inconvenient or disagreeable.

Mill's argument hinges on an assessment of the likely benefits that may accrue to individuals and the wider society from a clear conception of appropriate limits to the role of government. He is developing a utilitarian line of argument that had become familiar to his contemporaries from his father (James Mill) and Bentham. Yet he does not endorse utilitarianism in the narrow terms to which he had been exposed in the course of a very unusual education.[105] While he continues to treat arguments drawn from abstract or natural right with suspicion, his view of utility is much broader than Bentham's. Instead of a sum of benefits and costs ('pleasures' and 'pains') aggregated across society as a whole, Mill insists that qualitative criteria have necessarily to be invoked. Unlike Bentham, Mill accepts a conventional distinction between higher and lower pleasures. He continues to view 'utility as the ultimate appeal on all ethical questions', but seeks to assess the impact on policy in relation to 'the permanent interests of man as a progressive being'.[106] This is 'utility in the largest sense', and its precise connotation has confounded critics and commentators alike.[107] The original attraction of utilitarianism was precisely that it avoided contentious (and potentially futile) arguments about values. Human beings are treated simply as pleasure-seekers and pain-avoiders. Nothing could be gained (so Bentham contended) from trying to assess the relative merits of different kinds of pleasure. Long before 1859, through his reading of Tocqueville, Coleridge and Humboldt, Mill had become deeply dissatisfied with the crass egalitarianism that underpins Bentham's view. What emerges, however, looks perilously like a juxtaposition of arguments, rather than a constructive synthesis.

The 'higher' interests that Mill champions revolve around broadening the scope for individuality to flourish. We can envisage any number of possible goods for human beings, but (in Mill's view) they can be discounted if they do not enhance the capacity of individuals to respond to an unpredictable future. He has no regard for soporific satisfactions or idle contentment. He sees human beings as actors in an uncertain world, making choices for themselves, bearing responsibility, revising their views in the light of failure or disappointment. Goods may be various, but they must all enhance the human capacity for action, discrimination and choice. The distinctively human faculties, he says, 'perception, judgement, discriminative feeling, mental activity, and even moral preference, are exercised only in making a choice'.[108] There is no scope for an idea of an intrinsic good in his scheme of things. Indeed, to be presented with life's delights on a plate would run the risk of undermining practical talents that can be nurtured only in active engagement. An 'enlightened' government that sought to care for the interests of citizens from the cradle to the grave would thus be contributing to their corruption and decline. Mill urges government to encourage 'experiments of living', even if these experiments shock and offend conventional opinion.[109] And, of course, in the nature of an experiment, success cannot be guaranteed. Individuals will try things out and sometimes fail abysmally. Provided they are risking only their own interests, however, Mill sees no grounds for intervention. Freedom to fail is a necessary condition for the development of energy and initiative. Such conditions will foster better individuals. They will also maximize prospects for what Mill loosely describes as 'social progress'.[110] Mill is emphatic on this point. 'Mankind are greater gainers', he insists, 'by suffering each other to live as seems good to themselves, than by compelling each to live as seems good to the rest.'[111]

Mill's central contention has remained at the heart of liberal political cultures throughout the modern period. Yet, for all the sophistication he brought to its discussion, application of the principle to concrete cases has proved to be deeply complex. The prevention of harm to others as a criterion for political intervention looks relatively straightforward. On closer inspection, though, it is by no means evident what should count as 'harm'. Mill is clear that offence or outrage to opinion is not a sufficient warrant. But even if we narrow the notion of 'harm' to focus on fundamental interests, there remains a measure of ambiguity about how those interests should be characterized. In some policy areas it is actually essential that some people's interests should be harmed for a policy to be effective. Mill cites the case of competition for jobs in an 'overcrowded profession'.[112] We cannot both appoint the best person for a job and protect the interests of all the applicants. They all want the job, and may indeed be reasonably qualified to do it. Yet there is only one job available. Mill simply assumes (quite reasonably) that it is 'better for the general interest of mankind' to select the best candidate, no matter how devastating the disappointment may be to the life chances of the other applicants.[113] In this context, harm to others cannot readily be avoided.

Similar considerations apply in relation to competitive markets. Consumers and producers have contrasting interests, just as the success of one producer may be ruinous to another. To use legislation to ameliorate the impact of economic failure may remove incentives to produce quality goods efficiently. Mill accepts this principle in general terms. But he is also aware that 'public control is admissible for the prevention of fraud by adulteration' or 'to protect workpeople employed in dangerous occupations'.[114] In these cases judgements have to be made, balancing costs to efficiency against harm to individuals. We can assume that people may be prepared to take some risks for economic gain, though they may not be in a position to assess risks adequately. We cannot specify what should count as a reasonable risk in abstract terms. In working contexts, we rely on received understandings, values, etc. and modify our practices only when we encounter glaring anomalies. Mill is aware that this is how things work in practice, yet he is reluctant to appeal to anything as imprecise as conventional wisdom. In difficult cases, however, there is little else available. Mill's discussion of these issues highlights how inherently problematic it is to put theory into practice.

Mill's suspicion of conventional wisdom is well founded. Where he is on shakier ground is in his insistence that a theoretical criterion will always help us to balance competing considerations. Mill's efforts to apply his principle are actually sensitive to context, sometimes at the expense of theoretical consistency. What emerges from his discussion is a strong commitment to personal autonomy and measures that might be construed as agency enhancing. His treatment of alcohol, drugs and idleness, for example, is far from permissive. While he admits that drunkenness is not ordinarily 'a fit subject for legislative interference', he is nevertheless prepared to place legal restraints on the conduct of individuals who may be suspected of constituting a possible threat to public order.[115] And though idleness may be supposed to be open to legal remedy only in the most tyrannical of states, Mill does not hesitate to recommend legal punishment if 'a man fails to perform his legal duties to others'.[116] Parents who fail to support their children, in Mill's view, might reasonably be expected to undertake 'compulsory labour'.[117]

Mill's views on parenthood more broadly will surprise readers expecting to encounter a social libertarian. Sexual relations are normally considered to be among the most private matters, even in states that are authoritarian in other respects. Yet Mill describes the choice that adults make about having children as a public concern. He sees 'the fact itself, of causing the existence of a human being' as 'among the most responsible actions in the range of human life'.[118] What most of us regard as a matter of personal discretion, Mill contends is an onerous public responsibility. Indeed, he treats the birth of a child that cannot expect 'at least the ordinary chances of a desirable existence' as 'a crime against that being' on the part of parents.[119] And it is not only the child's interest that is threatened, according to Mill. Any increase in population is likely to put downward pressure on wages, thus constituting 'a serious offence against all who live by the remuneration of their labour'.[120] This will strike modern readers as a disturbing and surprising view in a professed liberal, though Malthusian conceptions of over-population were widely shared in mid-nineteenth-century Britain. The point to stress here is that the only consideration that prevents Mill from advancing more draconian measures is the misplaced public outcry that he anticipates would follow. Mill is adamant that restrictions on the right to procreate 'are not objectionable as violations of liberty' in themselves.[121] Public opinion, in this as in other domains, is a poor guide for policy-makers.

Mill's argument in *On Liberty* thus cannot be regarded as entirely satisfactory. He demonstrates through his treatment of examples, however, that tendencies for the state to expand its activities in industrial societies are not easily resisted. The pragmatist will tend to drift towards incremental extensions of state power, running the risk of transforming the relationship between state and citizens through inadvertence as much as design. Mill's concern in the text is to offer a test that must be satisfied before any extension of powers can be justified, rather than a definitive list of powers and responsibilities. His fear is that without a theoretical statement of some kind, centralization would be an irresistible temptation for citizens and government alike.

Yet the 'simple principle' is not self-evident. In its defence Mill slips from utilitarian argument (the truth would not emerge without free discussion, the individual is the best judge of her interests) to support of individualism and diversity as goods in themselves. What finally emerges is a preference for the state to do less rather than more, with due allowance made for the overwhelmingly complex co-ordination problems that beset any mass-based industrial society. Mill presumes, for example, that a thing 'is likely to be better done by individuals than by the government', without ruling out cases in which only government intervention will be effective.[122] He also assumes that even in cases where individuals do not act effectively, much is to be gained in educational terms from leaving them to assume wide areas of responsibility for themselves. It is hugely important to him that an active citizenry should emerge, rather than a passive but contented populace. These were articles of faith for advocates of limited government in mid-nineteenth-century Britain that could be defended in a variety of ways. Mill helped himself from a range of plausible theories, without quite achieving the theoretical synthesis he sought. In political terms, however, he had effectively challenged the assumption that the state knows best.

Mill's defence of individual liberty was vigorous. In the economic sphere it reinforced the strong tendency in mid-century capitalism to see the choices of individuals as the basic source of energy and initiative throughout the system. In the classical view of *laissez-faire* economics, it was held that prosperity would be maximized if trade were freed from political, moral and social constraints. Non-economic considerations were treated as external costs which distorted the decision making of individuals striving to maximize their marginal utility. And of the many 'external' impediments to economic growth, political interference (in the form of taxation and regulation) was held to be the most serious and the easiest to mitigate through legislation.

We should be clear here. No one supposed that everyone would benefit equally from an unfettered capitalism. But it was held that the society as a whole would be better off in absolute terms. It is the kind of doctrine that can look very impressive at times of significant economic growth. Any interruption of that growth, however, can lead to questioning of the basis of distribution within a society. Questions of 'justice' and 'fairness' begin to seem more pressing than productivity and growth.

Britain in the second half of the nineteenth century was very much a test case for the impact of industrialization on a liberal political order. What we see, in fact, is a loss of faith in some of the more facile assumptions that had informed the development of social and economic life. In broad terms, governments had to deal with vast shifts of population. The agricultural labourers who flocked to the new industrial towns can be construed as exercising their freedom of choice. Yet they were hardly in the position of the classic characters depicted in liberal theory, rationally plotting a course of life for themselves after examining the various alternatives. In a literal sense, they could not be said to know what they were letting themselves in for. Their haphazard entry into the emerging industrial towns in hordes created unprecedented social and health problems. Issues on this scale had not been envisaged in the pure theory of capitalism. To many observers, it seemed as if the unfettered market, left to itself, would simply exacerbate the problem.

Liberals, then, were faced with a dilemma. By inclination, they were in favour of leaving matters to be resolved by individual initiative. But they were perplexed as to how to respond if the upshot of individuals pursuing their own ends was a deterioration of a situation in which individual interests and well-being were already adversely affected.

There were more direct theoretical and political concerns. The rise of socialism and the trade union movement gave a new currency to demands for political participation and reform. What many people wanted was control over their own lives. Liberalism had set them free in a legal sense; but that freedom would be rendered worthless if the conditions of their lives made them absolutely dependent upon an employer or a landlord.

How could liberals respond to problems of this order? It became clear to many that their traditional concern for the individual had to be extended from the purely formal legal sphere to include substantive questions of individual well-being. John Stuart Mill had already taken significant steps in this direction. The conception of individuality he championed presupposed certain moral, cultural and political values. When he argued that we should all be free to do as we like in areas where our conduct does not adversely affect the interests of others, it was not so that we could creep back to our homes each evening to idle our time away. He was hostile to political and social controls because he feared that they might lead to the emergence of a stagnant, apathetic society. He defended a very specific conception of vigorous individuality. And he was aware that in certain circumstances the state should intervene in order to encourage (perhaps even to compel) individuals to pursue a progressive course. He had no reservations whatever about obliging children to attend school.

What we see emerging among liberals in the 1870s and 1880s is a much more positive conception of the role of the state. The position of T. H. Green, the Oxford philosopher, is typical. In his *Lectures on the Principles of Political Obligation*, he distanced himself specifically from the atomistic individualism of Locke, Bentham and Mill.[123] Drawing extensively from the political philosophies of Kant and Hegel, he was fiercely critical of both the language of natural right and utilitarianism. But though he objected to the way in which Mill had defended his case, he nevertheless continued to stress a positive view of the individual. Green emphasized the need for individuals to find positive fulfilment in life and work. And he was clear that this could only be achieved if a society were sufficiently attuned to their needs. It would not do, according to Green, for the state simply to provide benefits for individuals. He shared Mill's fears about the emergence of a passive and dependent population. Yet, in his view, there was ample scope for positive action from the state to facilitate the participation of individuals in social, economic and political life.

State intervention could take a variety of forms without undermining individual initiative and freedom. Consider the case of freedom of contract. The classical liberal view pictured society as an aggregation of individuals, each free under the law to make binding agreements among themselves – to buy and sell various items, to render services to one another in return for payment. At first glance this might sound like a fair arrangement, until we consider that a contract drawn up between (say) an individual employer and a hundred individual workers would leave each of the workers (as individuals) vulnerable to the economic power of the employer. A proper balance between the two sides might be struck if the law recognized the collective legal identity of a workforce. Individuals could join together (in a trade union or other such association) in order to press for certain minimal conditions (level of wages, conditions of service or whatever). The point of the amendment to the law of contract is not that the state should confer benefits directly on workers, but rather that the legal framework could be adjusted in order to enable workers to organize in defence of their own interests.

Other liberal thinkers active towards the end of the nineteenth century and beyond were much more directly influenced by socialism than Green. L. T. Hobhouse, for example, sought to distance himself from the German idealist philosophy that had informed the work of Green, Bosanquet and others in the British idealist school. Hobhouse shared the British idealist rejection of narrow individualism, but was deeply suspicious of any suggestion that the state could have any interest distinct from the concrete concerns of citizens.[124] Unlike earlier liberals such as Tocqueville, he saw no necessary opposition between liberalism and socialism. It may be that socialists expressed their political demands in a rather different idiom. But reformist socialists, according to Hobhouse, were essentially intent on extending the advantages of the liberal state to broader sections of the population. Hobhouse, in his widely read *Liberalism* (1911), openly defended what he styled as a liberal socialism, championing democratic involvement in decision making, redistribution of income through taxation, and close control of the right to own property. Arguments such as these provided the inspiration for the great wave of liberal welfare legislation in Britain in the years immediately preceding the First World War. The theoretical building blocks were in place for the later liberal endorsement of the idea of a welfare state.

An uneasy consensus thus emerged supporting a broader role for government, though policy implications were deeply contentious. Liberals found themselves polarized on opposite sides of a series of vital debates. It was accepted that government could intervene to enlarge options for individuals, without necessarily directing individuals in the choice of personal goals. But there was a fine line between leaving individuals to decide their fate and actively encouraging a certain kind of individual, able to bear personal responsibility in a challenging world.

Universal provision of education, for example, presupposed sensitive decisions about what should be taught and to whom. Education directed by the state to the poor might have a very different content from that which the rich could buy for their children. Different kinds of education fashioned citizens for different public and private roles. Questions of active and passive citizenship were raised here that liberal theory was barely able to address. Class attitudes, which had once been seen simply as a natural corollary of a functional division of society, were now being reinforced by state policies. Citizens who had benefited from a rudimentary education were quick to recognize the anomalies of liberal theory. Pressing social and economic problems began to make the principles of classical liberalism appear quaintly old-fashioned. And as new groups began to assert claims to political involvement, the political agenda shifted decisively towards substantive welfare issues. In the course of the twentieth century, especially after the Second World War, liberals would feel able to make common cause with socialists across a whole range of issues, arguing that public provision of basic welfare and educational requirements was a necessary condition for individual fulfilment and contentment. Purists might argue that liberalism had strayed a long way from its roots. What had not changed, however, was its central preoccupation with the individual.

Conservatism

Conservatism as an ideology was very much fashioned in the crucible of the French Revolution and its aftermath. Political expectations were so high in 1789 that frustration and disappointment were inevitable. Intractable problems of co-ordination and control persist, no matter what style of political management is adopted. Initial attempts to introduce a modest measure of constitutional reform in France gave place to the more ambitious pursuit of a democratic regime based upon respect for natural rights. But what emerged instead was a reign of terror in 1793–4 in France and the disruption of war on a continental scale. Quite why the revolutionary project should have gone so badly wrong was much disputed at the time, and continues to excite academic and political controversy.[125] It soon became clear that some of the basic requirements of any political regime, stability and order, had been sacrificed in the quest for more ephemeral political goals. Natural rights could hardly be enjoyed if stability and order were not maintained in the first place. The very thought that natural rights were somehow a natural birthright was brought into question, along with the idea of fashioning a political order anew from first principles.

In the eyes of some critics it was not simply the case that the revolutionaries had made political mistakes and found themselves embroiled in factional struggles that wiser counsel might have avoided. Root and branch transformation was rejected. Significantly, the reaction against revolution focused almost exclusively on France. The manifest success of the American Revolution was discounted, along with affinities between American and French revolutionary ideals.

Edmund Burke is perhaps the most celebrated critic of revolutionary politics. His *Reflections on the Revolution in France* (1790) set a style in theoretical and ideological argument that continues to influence modern conservatives.[126] Long before the Revolution had skirted with terror, Burke had predicted that contempt for established institutions and practices would generate a cycle of violence that could only be terminated by the imposition of authoritarian rule. The fatal flaw at the heart of the revolutionary project, in his view, was the presumption that political institutions could be devised to meet the requirements of a purely theoretical model. It is not a question of theory being more or less adequate. Theoretical models simplify the political world to the point of distortion. Burke objected to (what was later described as) 'rationalism in politics' in any of its guises.[127] No matter how much we assume we know about politics, Burke contends that our theorizing could never be rich enough to grasp the complex interdependence of institutions and practices.

In Burke's analysis, more is at stake than the straightforward folly of the revolutionaries. He is perfectly aware that institutions require reform and amendment in the light of changing circumstances. When we confront abuses and anomalies, however, it should be in relation to settled habits of conduct and practice. We are able to take stock of the shortcomings of some of our institutions and policies in the context of other aspects of our political experience that are serving us reasonably well. For Burke, effective politics is a matter of managing (unavoidable) change in piecemeal fashion. But if we presume to put (abstract) theory into practice, we will confound our problems. Innovations will lead to unforeseen complications that might well be worse than the original dilemmas that demanded attention. As our predicament deepens, so we will have recourse to further theoretical remedies, thus exacerbating a spiral of confusion and disorder.

Burke is deeply sceptical. Yet, before the French Revolution he was widely regarded as a progressive thinker. He had been particularly vociferous in defence of the cause of the American colonists, arguing that the attempt by British governments to exploit America for economic advantage contravened standing assumptions about good government.[128] That Burke should have been so hostile to the French Revolution from the outset surprised his contemporaries. What he deplored in British policy in America, however, was precisely the transgression of deeply entrenched conventions about the appropriate relationship between rulers and ruled that had become a distinguishing trait of British political culture. Burke thus endorses not the abstract slogans of the American revolutionaries ('no taxation without representation'), but the reaction of the colonists to Britain's arbitrary departure from established practices.

Burke distinguishes sharply between the American and French revolutions in his own mind. He is also anxious to disavow any connection between the French Revolution and the English Revolution of 1688. Radicals in Britain (such as Richard Price, whom Burke seeks to counter specifically in the *Reflections*) interpreted 1789 as the French version of the 'Glorious Revolution' that established the broad terms of limited and constitutional government in Britain. Burke rejects the link categorically. He describes the English Revolution as 'a small and a temporary deviation from the strict order of a regular and hereditary succession'.[129] Doubtless this is rhetorical understatement. No one could say in 1688 just how radical the constitutional changes would prove to be. Certainly, in themselves, they were not vastly different from initial French moves to transform an absolute into a constitutional monarchy. But, despite his distortion, it is fruitful to pay careful attention to Burke's language. He treats 'the statute called the Declaration of Right' as a means of 'declaring the rights and liberties of the subject, and for settling the succession of the crown'.[130] He rejects any suggestion that this should be construed as the initiation of an elective monarchy. Indeed, he insists that, 'so far is it from being true, that we acquired a right by the Revolution to elect our kings, that if we had possessed it before, the English nation did at that time most solemnly renounce and abdicate it, for themselves, and for all their posterity for ever'.[131] He stresses concrete rights already embedded in constitutional practice. And if he perceives reform to be necessary in 1688, it is in terms of established conventions and with a view to creating more stability rather than less.

It is important to stress that Burke recognizes the necessity of change. He has no sympathy for theorists who dream of a supposed golden age which they seek to restore. States are complex bodies, dependent on a whole series of factors that defy complete theoretical elaboration. If they are unable to adapt to shifting circumstances, they will not flourish. 'A state without the means of some change', he insists, 'is without the means of its conservation.'[132] Everything depends on the way change is managed. Leading themes for Burke are 'conservation and correction', recognizing the force and utility of established practices, while amending them to meet the demands of new situations.[133] Thus, 'when England found itself without a king', efforts were made to preserve the principle of hereditary succession by modifying the line of descent as little as possible, yet ensuring a protestant succession to the throne.[134] Principles that clash in the person of one king are restored to harmony in the person of another. This, argues Burke, is wisdom at work. He is strangely silent about the events of 1649, when England decapitated a king.

At the heart of Burke's argument is a categorical dismissal of the idea of natural rights. Here, as ever with Burke, his language repays close attention. He is a master of rhetorical presentation, capturing whatever of sense his opponents may have to say while ridiculing the form of their arguments. In rejecting natural rights, for example, Burke holds that he is defending and advancing 'the real rights of men'.[135] He pictures civil society as a complex network of conventions, all devised to facilitate human engagements, but without anything like a preconceived plan. We enjoy the benefits of civil society, and 'all the advantages for which it is made become' our 'right'.[136] What might rights so conceived amount to? Burke focuses on the ordinary things we do every day of our lives. We 'have a right to the fruits of' our 'industry', a right to 'instruction in life, and to consolation in death', a 'right to the acquisitions of' our 'parents', a right to associate together in manifold ways to pursue our interests and advantage, provided we are not thereby 'trespassing upon others'.[137] He sees society as a partnership in which we all 'have equal rights, but not to equal things'.[138] There is no naturally just way of organizing these various and bewilderingly complex engagements. All our practices are entwined in a rich social fabric. The details, he says, must 'be settled by convention'.[139]

Civil society thus supplies the standards against which actions must be judged. We cannot assess the adequacy of these criteria against a notional natural standard, for no such standard exists. What we gain in civil society are regular procedures for managing affairs. Among other things, we acknowledge 'that no man should be judge in his own cause'.[140] We cannot both endorse the value of civil society and refuse to be judged by its standards. That, according to Burke, would amount to claiming 'the rights of an uncivil and of a civil state together'.[141] We accept that judgements will not always go our way. Expecting more from civil and political life would actually deliver a good deal less. In our ordinary affairs, we do not delude ourselves with images of perfection. If we see the force of not being judges in our own case, it follows that we could not claim to be judges of our own polity. Civil society enables us to 'secure some liberty', on condition that we make 'a surrender in trust of the whole of it' to the authoritative institutions of our society.[142] It is the best that we can reasonably expect.

In human affairs, the notion of 'abstract perfection' ceases to be helpful, even as an ideal.[143] Institutions and practices are matters of compromise, trading off certain benefits and advantages against others. Burke describes government as 'a contrivance of human wisdom to provide for human wants'.[144] There is no avoiding the messiness here because we cannot always be sure what we do want. And we may be sure that human beings gathered together with limited understanding and limited benevolence are likely to clash in a world of limited resources. We accept restraints as a means of gaining concrete satisfactions. Burke (again exploiting the language of his opponents) argues that 'the restraints on men, as well as their liberties, are to be reckoned among their rights'.[145] But because liberties and restrictions will 'vary with circumstances, and admit of infinite modifications', we cannot specify the appropriate institutions and practices that should be respected in all times and places.[146] An 'abstract rule' is neither possible nor desirable.[147]

There can be no short cuts to good government. Political judgement depends upon experience, more indeed than any individual can accumulate in a lifetime. No matter how well prepared we may suppose ourselves to be, our wisdom is no match for the variety of circumstances. We have to proceed cautiously. A measure that may initially appear to be 'prejudicial may be excellent in its remoter operation'.[148] And the reverse may also be true, as 'very plausible schemes, with very pleasing commencements' may often have 'shameful and lamentable conclusions'.[149] Theory will never be sufficiently flexible to grasp the 'obscure and almost latent causes' that determine a pattern of events.[150] We have no choice, of course, but to apply our minds to practical problems. We cannot simply carry on exactly as we have in the past. We have to appeal to 'models and patterns of approved utility'.[151] Experience may be fallible; but it cannot be remedied by recourse to abstract theory.

Implicit in Burke's beguilingly effective rhetoric is a powerfully sceptical argument regarding the strict limits of pure theory. We are ingenious creatures. We can contrive metaphysical theories that doubtless capture some aspect of what it might mean to lead a human life. But what we have to deal with in politics is 'the gross and complicated mass of human passions and concerns'.[152] If we try to picture these concerns through the prism of our pet theories, we are bound to deceive ourselves about genuine possibilities for improvement. 'The nature of man', says Burke, 'is intricate; the objects of society are of the greatest possible complexity; and therefore no simple disposition or direction of power can be suitable either to man's nature, or to the quality of his affairs.'[153] These are limiting conditions for any possible political theory. Simplicity may be a merit in pure theory; in government it is quite the reverse, encouraging us to be fanciful where caution is appropriate, distorting our perceptions of the very real difficulties which we may well be able to do something about were we not tempted by the theoretical prospect of resolving all our political problems in one revolutionary sweep.

The implications of Burke's position are far-reaching. Paine and Sieyes had both sought to question the legitimacy of absolute government as a matter of principle. For Burke the question makes no sense. He insists that 'the speculative line of demarcation, where obedience ought to end, and resistance must begin, is faint, obscure, and not easily definable'.[154] We cannot even begin to frame the dilemma to ourselves in these terms. Everyone knows that governments sometimes act badly, that there are instances of corruption and abuse of power in any regime. But we confront these cases as they arise, in the context of a host of attendant circumstances. We cannot focus on a 'single act, or a single event' to determine the limits of our obligation to the state.[155] Burke has no doubt that (on rare occasions) governments implode catastrophically, undermining the very possibility of an ordered civil life. His point, however, is that precise theoretical lines cannot be drawn. In extreme circumstances, subjects and citizens may be compelled to fend for themselves. This, for Burke, is the real connotation of a state of nature. Government has broken down, leaving us no choice but to devise alternative means of social co-operation. It is not that government has abused the trust placed in it in any conceptual sense. The conduct of political affairs may degenerate to a 'lamentable condition'; but in that dire situation, 'the nature of the disease is to indicate the remedy to those whom nature has qualified to administer in extremities this critical, ambiguous, bitter potion to a distempered state'.[156] We are driven into revolution. We cannot reasonably choose it as a means to pursue our interests.

Allegiance to the state is simply not a theoretical issue for Burke. He assumes that people develop attachments and dispositions in the course of their lives that serve as tangible points of reference for their activities and pursuits. Theory will not help us to understand these attachments. We acquire loyalty to people and places, along with the ordinary habits that get us through from day to day. As a matter of principle, Burke takes human beings as he finds them. He turns Paine's argument in *Common Sense* upside-down. Where Paine had stressed natural reasonableness, Burke highlights the quirks and idiosyncrasies that distinguish individuals and peoples. We delight in our own ways of doing things, not because they are rational, reasonable or exemplary, but because they serve us in socially embedded circumstances. Instead of stressing reason, Burke delights in the prejudices that are characteristically our own. When we wonder what to do next in difficult situations, it is in terms of the 'latent wisdom' implicit in our habits and customs.[157] Our sense of what we should do, for Burke, is more reliable than our metaphysical speculations; and it also motivates us in social dealings. 'Prejudice is of ready application in the emergency; it previously engages the mind in a steady course of wisdom and virtue, and does not leave the man hesitating in the moment of decision, sceptical, puzzled, and unresolved.'[158] Reflection of the right kind can help us to discriminate among the various habits that constitute our identities. Thinking about what we should do is not qualitatively distinct from our ordinary dispositions and prejudices. 'Prejudice renders a man's virtue his habit', says Burke, 'and not a series of unconnected acts.'[159] And in a delightfully paradoxical phrase, he insists that 'through just prejudice', our 'duty becomes a part of' our 'nature'.[160]

Burke's politics is thus deeply passive. He presupposes a natural hierarchy in a society, with power and influence shared between landed elite and crown. He can envisage adjustments to patterns of land holding and decision making, but not according to the specification of an ideal theory of justice. If this natural order is disrupted by foolish speculation and political enthusiasm, Burke assumes that the ordinary enjoyments of social, economic and civil life will be rendered precarious. He paints a dire picture of the consequences of trying to reduce complex management of practical affairs to rational order. 'This was unnatural. The rest is order.

They have found their punishment in their success. Laws overturned; tribunals subverted; industry without vigour; commerce expiring; the revenue unpaid, yet the people impoverished; a church pillaged, and a state not relieved; civil and military anarchy made the constitution of the kingdom.'[161] A meddling politics threatens the everyday expectations on which human beings depend. And since human foresight is not sufficient to grasp the complex interdependence of institutions and practices, efforts to remedy the consequences of folly are as likely to produce further difficulties as tangible improvements.

Burks's tone is dramatic. His comments (we must remember) are addressed to his contemporaries in England, rather than the citizens of France striving to reduce the chaos of revolution to institutional order. His picture of France is, in any case, deeply distorted, especially as things stood in 1790. He treats order as a seamless web, despite his recognition of the minute adjustments we make to our affairs on a daily basis. Over time, minute adjustments might lead to a qualitatively different regime. But the process will be long, slow and barely perceptible to agents attending to their concrete concerns.

There is clearly a desperate edge to Burke's writing. As an expert in British constitutional history, he is fully aware of the political significance of the Glorious Revolution of 1688. He also knows that the achievement was couched in terms of a natural rights argument drawn from Locke. There are very real affinities between Locke and Paine, as between Locke and the American revolutionaries. Burke sees all this, but doubts the sophistication and self-restraint of his contemporaries. Endorsing the Glorious Revolution with the benefit of a century of hindsight is very different from advocating a radical shift in succession to the crown in the fevered atmosphere of 1688. The implication of Burke's position in the *Reflections* is that Britain had been fortunate not to reap the revolutionary consequences that beset France in the 1790s. He sounds a warning, quite as much as an argument.

There are two quite distinct dimensions to Burke's political theory. On the one side, he endorses a cautious, sceptical approach to politics that should not be identified with any specific regime. On the other side, we have a spirited defence of a balance of institutions in *ancien régime* Europe, focusing on a complex interrelationship between crown, nobility, church and broader landed interests. As the French Revolution progressed, we see a marked polarization of positions. Prospects for any political accommodation between revolutionaries and reactionaries looked especially bleak after the execution of Louis XVI in 1793. Crown, church and nobility were then implacably opposed to regicides. What they deplored was not the theoretical folly of revolutionaries who had failed to grasp the complexity of government, but a wilful and wicked assault on a way of life.

The most formidable theoretical statement of a sharpened royalist position is Joseph de Maistre's *Considerations on France* (1797).[162] Maistre's politics is avowedly theological. He opens the book with a powerful contrast between the perfection of God's order and the obvious imperfections of anything human beings have created. 'In the works of man, everything is as wretched as their author; views are restricted, means rigid, motives inflexible, movements painful, and results monstrous.'[163] The French revolutionaries had inverted the natural relationship between divine and human achievement. If men make themselves the measure of all things, they open themselves to a torrent of abuses. Revolution is not simply a political mistake, but a sin against human nature itself.

Maistre takes the doctrine of original sin very seriously indeed. He sees Christian doctrine as an appropriate response to the prevalence of evil in the world. It constrains us doctrinally, reinforcing the established (yet apparently arbitrary) power of monarchs. Left to ourselves, we would be ruinously self-destructive. Maistre regards war as the 'habitual state of mankind'.[164] Striving to set ourselves free politically would only unleash heightened levels of violence. The only hope for us is to embrace political constraints. Yet the intellectual optimism of the Enlightenment had extolled our powers of reasoning and our hopes for radical political improvement. What Maistre sees, instead, is a world in which 'evil has tainted everything, and in a very real sense, all is evil, since nothing is in its place'.[165]

In more narrowly political terms Maistre highlights the novelty of the Revolution as a sure indication of its absurdity. He asks rhetorically, 'Can the French Republic last?', clearly suggesting that a political arrangement so unprecedented could not be expected to survive.[166] Having dismantled the institutional structure of *ancien régime* France, all the revolutionaries are left with is a principle of representation that is designed to bind the people together, while somehow preserving their collective status as a sovereign authority. Yet all this could amount to, according to Maistre, is a system of republican representation based in Paris dominating the country as a whole. He takes Rousseau as the theorist of republican representation and glosses over American and British experience of indirect representation. In his rather jaundiced view, this leaves France with a scheme of representation that might see each man 'exercise his turn at national sovereignty once in every sixteen thousand years'.[167] We need not dwell on the detail of Maistre's discussion of representative government. The point to stress is his contention that a republic on this scale would necessarily be a despotism, reducing the people to 'the most deplorable slavery'.[168]

Maistre finds no mitigating features in the Revolution. While Burke had conceded that there could be a case for reform in France, Maistre castigates the Revolution as 'an event unique in history' in 'that it is radically bad'.[169] He contrasts republican talk of virtue with a collapse of morals in both public and private spheres. The French manifestly do not love their revolution, yet they fear the consequences of a restoration. How, in these circumstances, can they hope to escape from the nightmare of revolution?

Maistre urges a rather bleak patience. We can no more expect to plan a counter-revolution than a revolution. But, in time, revolution will devour its own children. No parties or groups are exempt from the orgy of destruction initiated by revolution. 'In the French revolution the people have continually been enslaved, outraged, ruined, and mutilated by all parties, and the parties in their turn, working one against the other, have continually drifted, despite all their efforts, toward break-up at length on the rocks awaiting them.'[170] Providence, in Maistre's account, can be guaranteed to lead France back to monarchy through republican anarchy. The best that right-minded thinkers can do is maintain faith in the proper order of things.

In the last resort, it is France's departure from God's order that has upset her affairs so calamitously. Maistre recognizes that people have grown tired of convulsions and fear the consequences of any renewed constitutional conflict. Restitution of property cannot be achieved without disturbing a range of interests. Families, too, may have scores to settle in any new political order. Counter-revolution thus cannot be undertaken without some consideration of likely consequences. Maistre objects, however, to the 'cowardly optimists' who had initially embraced revolution, now recognize their folly, yet lack the courage to 'bring the king back to his throne and restore order in France'.[171] Attempts to terrify people into permanent acquiescence in a regime that they plainly see is intolerable are contemptible in Maistre's eyes. Yet, fundamentally, argues Maistre, 'it is a great error to imagine that the people have something to lose in the restoration of the monarchy'.[172] Kings work through people and institutions. People's real interests are served when institutions function effectively. And it cannot be in the interest of a king (or within his power if he were so minded) to undermine the smooth functioning of institutions of state that are his vital concern.

For Maistre, in any case, counter-revolution is 'not a contrary revolution, but the contrary of revolution'.[173] It is an attempt to exploit the chaos of revolution in order to restore a natural balance to the workings of institutions and practices. 'The return to order will not be painful, because it will be natural and because it will be favoured by a secret force whose action is wholly creative.'[174] No lasting achievements can follow from persistent contempt for the grain of human nature. Institutions that respect ordinary human failings are actually indispensable to genuine human flourishing. Revolutionary rhetoric had pandered to human vanity, promising heaven on earth, but delivering turmoil. Events disabuse people. Genuine philosophy can restore faith in institutional certainties, even in a political world rocked by 'enlightened' excesses.

The scope for a discursive politics is deeply limited in Maistre's view of the world. Elite co-operation constrains the practical options of monarchs to a certain extent, but constitutional boundaries cannot be drawn around spheres of activity. As with Burke, we have a powerful critique of political rationalism, but with even less prospect of the emergence of a moderate consensus. Maistre's terms of reference encourage oscillation between revolutionary and reactionary extremes.

Both Burke and Maistre, in their different ways, defend political order as a supreme value, easily missed if we allow ourselves to be distracted by images of perfection. Key themes from their work were developed in later conservative and reactionary theory, stressing the priority of practice and community. At the heart of these positions is a deep political scepticism, urging us to accept that our most effective thinking is done piecemeal. Among later philosophers endorsing a broadly conservative view of the world, Oakeshott is arguably the most penetrating in his analysis of the presuppositions of human activity of any kind. He presents political activity as an engagement like any other, dependent upon a host of assumptions that simply have to be taken for granted. He specifically challenges the dominant reformist presumption that all would be well if we only thought hard enough about our problems. To sceptical conservatives, thinking too hard is precisely the root of our problems. Abstract theory is simply too cavalier. This is a cautious, ameliorative politics that is prepared to adjust to a flow of events. In this view, an excessively principled position is a recipe for dogmatism.

Oakeshott's political theory first gained widespread influence with the publication of *Rationalism in Politics and other Essays* (1962), a collection of ten essays written between 1947 and 1961, each concerned in various ways (as he put it in the preface) with 'understanding and explaining' human conduct.[175] He takes practical life in its many and varied forms, each a product of traditions of conduct, standards and institutions that constitute a way of life. He does not focus on one practice as the ideal form for all others, or one society as the ideal model to be followed, but asks, rather, what it means to engage in activities of any kind. He insists, in particular, on a distinction between philosophical and practical approaches to politics, aware that political philosophers in the classic tradition have often shifted in the course of argument from one perspective to the other.[176] Order, liberty, equality or whatever value might be variously stressed as keys to human well-being and fulfilment. Philosophers advancing arguments in this style would often see themselves as contributors to practical political debates. Oakeshott is more circumspect. He treats normative arguments very much as parochial preferences, urging philosophers to focus on the basic presuppositions of normative engagements rather than the substantive goals that theorists might seek to advance.[177]

Oakeshott is particularly concerned with the tendency of political theory to overreach itself. We are tempted to present what is good for ourselves as good for others. The need to secure the co-operation of others if we are to attain our own ends encourages us to present the things we happen to want as somehow objectively desirable. For the most part, we are entirely innocent when we deceive ourselves in these ways.

Philosophers themselves have sometimes succumbed to the false allure of their own pet projects, defending their idiosyncratic conceptions of fulfilment as necessary conditions for human well-being. It may be, indeed, that the temptation to political and moral overstatement is irresistible to us. But it remains a philosophical error. The challenge of political philosophy, for Oakeshott, is precisely to disentangle the confusion of idioms which we have habitually employed in considering our practical affairs. If a principal task of philosophy is to establish appropriate criteria of intelligibility in the various modes of experience, as Oakeshott argues, the practical mode has consistently proved to be the most difficult to contain within its designated sphere. History, science and the arts have often been misleadingly justified in practical terms. More fundamentally still, Oakeshott contends, the way we live and regard ourselves has been distorted by a failure to recognize the conceptual limits of practical life.

Oakeshott invites us to consider, for example, our understanding of 'rational conduct'.[178] To act rationally, we might assume, would be to set aside habit, custom or prejudice and to regulate our conduct solely in terms of the goals we have determined for ourselves. A basic presupposition of rationality, in this scheme of things, is that our goals can be separated analytically from the activities we happen to be engaged in. But when we begin to reflect intelligently on our various pursuits, it is with a mind already informed by the practices and procedures that constitute those pursuits. We cannot think 'rationally' about cricket, cooking, carpentry, politics and so on unless we already know something about them. We may be casually inducted into these pursuits in the first instance. Yet it would be unwise to ask our advice until we have gained some 'knowhow'. To treat a condition of pure innocence, where all acquired knowledge is discounted, as a paradigm case of rational reflection is pure folly.

Lurking behind the error, in this case, is a widely held but wholly misleading conception of mind. The mind is not an entity that subsequently acquires 'beliefs, knowledge, prejudices'.[179] The mind is what it does. It is inseparable from the judgements we make in the course of our thinking and doing. It is not 'an apparatus for thinking' but thought itself.[180] It follows that we cannot step outside our thought to check its rationality. Whatever we think and do is informed by specific assumptions. These can be reviewed as we develop a more sophisticated awareness of what we are doing. But it makes no sense to seek an independent rational standard for conduct as such. We may be said to act rationally when our conduct 'exhibits the sort of intelligence appropriate to the idiom of activity concerned'.[181]

The implications of this position for our understanding of political and moral discourse are far-reaching and radically subversive. Oakeshott suggests that, at least since the Renaissance, respect for practical judgement has tended to be undermined by an obsession with technique. Practical judgement in fact is refined in the course of our experience of various arts, crafts and pursuits. It may be passed on in some measure by a master to his apprentice, or by a supervisor to her research student. But it 'cannot be formulated in rules' or committed in preceptive form to a textbook.[182] We cannot learn to cook from a cookery book, or to drive from close study of the Highway Code. Books of this kind may be useful to us once we know something about cooking and driving. But we need to be shown how to do these things in the first instance, and subsequently improve upon our initial incompetence only with practice.

Why should practical knowledge have been so undervalued in modern times? Oakeshott offers no more than a tantalizing abridgement of a highly contentious view. He argues that Western culture in the last 400 years has become afflicted with a kind of collective impatience. We crave to better ourselves, and to better ourselves in a hurry. We no longer have the time to devote to the acquisition of specialized skills, and instead seek short cuts in technical manuals of one kind or another. Above all, we need to be assured that forced instruction will fit us for our tasks once and for all. What cannot be learned quickly is dismissed as an irrelevance. If judgement is set aside, all we have left to rely upon is technical certainty.

Politics in this rationalist idiom is always 'a matter of solving problems', of applying 'reason' to politics in much the same way as an engineer tackles the business of construction and repair.[183] Just as the technical skills of the engineer are held to be universal in scope and application, so too the 'politician' who knows his business will be able to apply his instrumental criteria in any circumstance or situation. He will not rely upon received political wisdom ('prejudice'), but upon the most up-to-date technical manual ('science'). On closer inspection, however, it will be evident that the rationalist politician understands neither politics nor science. His basic conception of what it means to engage in any sort of practice is so wide of the mark that anything that has been accomplished is bound to appear unsatisfactory to him. He cannot accept accommodation and compromise because what he seeks is perfection. Yet even to envisage perfection in his terms is to conceive of human life as completely other than it could possibly be.

The rationalist analysis of politics, in Oakeshott's view, is thus untenable in theory and unrealizable in practice. Yet its hold on modern discourse is almost complete. It is manifested most obviously in the predilection for abstract formulations of political doctrines and programmes. A political party or movement without its ideology is now considered to be lamentably ill-equipped for the cut and thrust of argument and debate on a public stage. The 'politics of the book' has replaced the kind of practical understanding and discrimination that was once entrenched in an older (and narrower) political class.[184]

What the 'book' offers in a modern context is clear. New classes have risen to power and influence without the benefit of a traditional political education, addressing an enlarged citizenry whose ignorance is even more complete. In these circumstances both rulers and citizens desperately need 'a crib, a political doctrine, to take the place of a habit of political behaviour'.[185] Some of the best political 'cribs' have been written by thinkers of genuine distinction (Machiavelli, Locke, Mill, Marx), who have managed to abridge complex traditions of political conduct in pocket-size form. But the flexibility of a living tradition is lost in the very best abridgements; and in the worst, political argument gives place to the raucous exchange of slogans.

In Oakeshott's view, then, the intrusion of a rationalist frame of mind has seriously corrupted political thought and practice. Yet the damage wrought by rationalism extends far beyond the conduct of public affairs. What we are dealing with is 'an identifiable error, a misconception with regard to the nature of human knowledge, which amounts to a corruption of the mind'.[186] And because it is the mind itself that has been corrupted, it is difficult to see how we might best take stock of our situation and remedy our shortcomings. Following rationalist precepts in all walks of life ('living by the book') leads 'not only to specific mistakes, but . . . also dries up the mind itself', generating an 'intellectual dishonesty' which renders intellectual effort to improve affairs more dangerous than the malaise itself.[187] The rationalist is a liability not only because his projects are ill-advised, but because he fails to recognize what he is doing. He cannot accept that all practices are rooted in traditional modes of conduct. If he sees a problem, he seeks always to wipe the slate clean and start again. Yet the supposition that we can simply 'start again' is the root of our difficulties.

Oakeshott insists that all conduct is in an important sense tradition-bound. This does not mean that we must simply accept the patterns of conduct we happen to have inherited. Traditions are not static; and even a veneration of the past contains within it intimations of how we should respond to the vagaries of circumstance. A tradition 'is neither fixed nor finished; it has no changeless centre to which understanding can anchor itself; there is no sovereign purpose to be perceived or invariable direction to be detected; there is no model to be copied, idea to be realized, or rule to be followed'.[188] But there is 'a principle of continuity', with authority 'diffused between past, present, and future; between the old, the new, and what is to come'.[189] Even as we strive to chart new directions, we are enmeshed in a complex web of practices and attitudes which both constrain and facilitate our dealings with each other.

Underpinning Oakeshott's conception of political thought and practice is a deep theoretical scepticism. We rely on traditions of conduct, not because they are the best we can conceive of, but because they serve (at least some of) our purposes. There can be no theoretical resolution of the many conflicting ends we may happen to desire. In these circumstances, the best that we can hope for is that our way of life might enable us to make (essentially contestable) choices for ourselves. We should not expect governments to devise practical 'solutions' to problems that cannot (in principle) be resolved. Oakeshott focuses, instead, on conditions that would have to be satisfied for any of our (necessarily co-operative) activities to be (at least minimally) effective. He stresses throughout his writings the idea of the rule of law and stable expectations.

In a later work, *On Human Conduct* (1975), he systematized his reflections on agency and practice, distinguishing between 'civil association' and 'enterprise association'.[190] A civil relationship, in Oakeshott's terms, is not directed to the attainment of substantive goals. It is, he says, human relationship viewed 'in terms of the (formal) considerations which compose a practice', the rules (implicit and explicit) that enable us to assess appropriate means in complex social engagements.[191] 'Enterprise association', by contrast, is 'concerned with the satisfaction of chosen wants'.[192] We may (or may not) join private associations for the pursuit of specific goals. We seek certain kinds of employment and join social clubs where we might expect to meet like-minded people. The point to stress, for Oakeshott, is that we can always leave such associations if we become indifferent or hostile to their goals. It is open to us to resign from specific employment or to refuse to renew our subscriptions. The goals of enterprise associations will not be shared by a whole community. But, crucially, nobody should be obliged to join them.

The position is quite otherwise with the state. None of us chooses to be born under the jurisdiction of specific political authorities. We have to abide by (political) laws and rules irrespective of our particular preferences and predilections. To be forced to pursue substantive goals that are contestable will strike many of us as intrusion on our liberty and discretion. Yet we can perfectly well recognize that some co-operative rules and procedures must be in place if we are to flourish. Oakeshott highlights the contrast between formal rules and substantive goals, the former indispensable to social life, the latter optional among citizens who may have very different priorities. In Oakeshott's view, the authority of the state in the long term depends upon a recognition of conditions that are vital to all citizens, and not simply to those who happen to share the same interests.

Oakeshott's political scepticism thus operates on two levels. He defends a strictly limited role for the state, and a similarly limited role for political philosophy. We simply lack the theoretical resources to transform the human condition. Instead, theory can expose the myriad sources of conceptual confusion that set elites and citizens in pursuit of unrealizable objectives. Oakeshott warns of political folly, but offers no panaceas. He urges us to focus on the real satisfactions of varied lives rather than the illusory promise of heaven on earth.

Oakeshott's politics is conservative by implication, though it remains open-ended. In arguing that conceptions of practice are implicit within traditions, he is not committed to the view that acceptance of any tradition can confer authority upon a practice. We cannot understand our practical lives outside traditions of conduct; but it does not follow that all traditions of conduct are equally valid. Oakeshott's starting point is not necessarily the arbitrary traditions we happen to have grown up with. He recognizes (with modern anti-foundationalists) that our practical judgements cannot be supported by an abstract deontological criterion.[193] Traditions, however, are not incommensurable. They contain within themselves different possibilities for conduct and achievement.

In seeking to provide definitive answers to practical dilemmas, some traditions will irredeemably stunt prospects for human well-being and fulfilment. Oakeshott, like so many of his contemporaries, was haunted by the impact of the various versions of collectivist politics that dominated the twentieth century. Yet he could not rest content with a straightforward reassertion of the priority of the individual over the community. He sees individuality as a specifically social product. But it will not flourish in any and every community. In focusing on human beings as the creators of meanings and values, he is clear that he is validating certain sorts of communities and not others. At the heart of any defensible view is a politics of self-restraint. Elites and citizens ignore that necessary limitation at their peril.

Burke, Maistre and Oakeshott have been selected here as representative thinkers, illustrating the persistence of clear themes in conservative thinking. In a broader sense, of course, 'conservative' ideas have a much longer history, extending back to Plato and Augustine in particular, but with unmistakable echoes in Hobbes and Hume. Conservative political thinking, in fact, is compatible with the most radical attitudes in other spheres of activity. In all these writers, there is an evident recognition of stability and order as essential requirements for human flourishing in any of its diverse forms, plus deep suspicion of human reason as an instrument of radical change. The fragility of precarious interdependence is a recurring *motif*. Thinkers will appear more or less authoritarian, largely in response to their interpretations of the significance of various threats to order. In the aftermath of the French Revolution, mobilized political movements became the chief source of anxiety. Conservatives had to respond in kind, formulating an ideological defence of order, despite their principled reservations about ideological mobilization as a political tool. The persistence of recurring themes in conservative thinking is a testimony to their resourcefulness.

Nationalism

Like liberalism and conservatism, nationalism emerged on the European political scene with the French Revolution, though it is deeply difficult to place in relation to other movements and ideas. Though it was very closely associated with the newly emerging professional and business classes, nationalism as an ideology was never simply a political guise for their social and economic interests. Nationalists could defend a seemingly endless range of (often contradictory) constitutional and policy positions. Indeed we find nationalists aligned on both sides in the revolutionary struggles and wars of 1789–1815. But no matter what constitutional form nationalists might favour, they occupy common ground in their insistence that the identity of the nation confers value upon the state. In terms of its capacity to mobilize populations, nationalism is clearly the most effective of our modern ideologies. Taking the longer view of modern European history, it may be that the spectre of the French nation at arms will loom larger in significance than the specific goals the revolutionary armies were pursuing.

The roots of nationalism, however, should be sought beyond the sphere of politics. It had initially emerged in the eighteenth century as a reaction against the predominance of French culture in the literary world. In the minds of most Enlightenment intellectuals, France had been identified as the acme of civilization and refinement. Yet to critics such as Herder, especially in his early writings (1769–74), French cultural supremacy was viewed as intellectually and morally ruinous. Herder contended that Enlightenment thinkers had tended to adopt an abstract, generalizing vocabulary, blind to the subtle distinctions and nuances embedded in local cultural traditions. What made matters worse was that German or Italian or Czech writers were being encouraged to couch their work in an idiom and style which derived essentially from France. Peoples were being alienated from their roots.

The only way to halt the decline, in Herder's view, was to foster local cultures. Herder himself spent a great deal of time seeking to restore national traditions through collections of folktales and songs. He loathed the 'good taste' and 'decorum' of high (French) culture, and admired instead the 'natural' products of unsophisticated cultures. In his travel diary of 1769 he gives a bitter account of the artificial education he and his contemporaries had been subjected to, an education calculated to stifle any spontaneity or original thought. 'O you great masters of all time, you Moses and Homers! You sang from inspiration! You planted what you sang in eternal metre, in which it was held fast; and thus it could be sung again as long as men wanted to sing it. We in our dull, uncertain prose, at the mercy of ourselves and of every passing moment, repeat ourselves and drone prosaically on until at last we say nothing any more.'[194] Herder's is a panegyric to the creative possibilities of primitive cultures, rather than the measured rationalism of the French Enlightenment.

Herder's distance from the Enlightenment is best gauged from a consideration of *Yet Another Philosophy of History* (1774). The aim of this work is openly polemical. It is a response to the uniformity that is a direct product of a rationalist view of the world. Herder rejects attempts to classify cultural phenomena as types of occurrence, particular examples of universal laws. He considers comparison of things essentially unique to be blindness to a realm of experience. 'In order to feel the whole nature of the soul which reigns in everything, which models after itself all other tendencies and all other spiritual faculties, and colours even the most trivial actions, do not limit your response to a word, but penetrate deeply into this century, this region, this entire history, plunge yourself into it all and feel it all within yourself – then only will you be in a position to understand; then only will you give up the idea of comparing everything, in general or in particular, with yourself.'[195] The only way to make sense of history or culture, on this view, is to immerse yourself in it; impose an alien classification, and you are lost before you have begun.

The comparative method, moreover, according to Herder, is based on a misunderstanding of the nature of society. He sees life as an intimate relationship of struggle between nature and tradition. A particular climate and natural environment encourages particular occupations; a tradition emerges which is the heritage of a particular struggle, the acquired wisdom (in the style of Burke) that enables decisions to be made without recourse to the drawing board; a language sums up the spirit of a society in its unique struggle for existence. The criteria by which we judge a particular society should not be the (purportedly) universal maxims of the philosopher; they emerge in a particular situation and are only valid in that situation. 'Each form of human perfection', Herder argues, 'is, in a sense, national and time-bound and, considered most specifically, individual'.[196] For Montesquieu, on this question of the comparative method, Herder reserves the full force of his sardonic pen. 'Words torn from their context and heaped up in three or four market-places under the banner of three wretched generalizations – mere words, empty, useless, imprecise and all-confusing words, however spirited. The work is a frenzy of all times, nations and languages like the Tower of Babel, so that everyone hangs his goods and chattels on three weak nails. The history of all times and peoples, whose succession forms the great, living work of God, is reduced to ruins divided neatly into three heaps, to a mere collection even though it does not lack noble and worthy material. O, Montesquieu!'[197]

Herder's specific focus is on the value of particularity. Not only is he antagonistic to the tendency to reduce history to order under the head of certain arbitrary generalizations, he is also opposed to the habit, dominant in the Enlightenment, of judging historical periods from the standpoint of the present. He refuses to dismiss the ignorance and superstition of the medieval period, the so-called dark ages; rather, his concern is to understand each period or culture on its own terms, as a unique contribution of the human spirit. He stresses empathy as a necessary condition of cultural understanding, enabling observers to grasp the organic nature of societies. 'All the books of our Voltaires, Humes, Robertsons and Iselins are, to the delight of their contemporaries, full of beautiful accounts of how enlightenment and improvement of the world, philosophy and order, emerged from the bleaker epochs of theism and spiritual despotism. All this is both true and untrue. It is true if, like a child, one holds one colour against another, if one wishes to contrive a bright, contrasty little picture – there is, alas, so much light in our century! It is untrue, if one considers the earlier epoch according to its intrinsic nature and aims, its pastimes and mores, and especially as the instrument of the historical process.'[198] Herder considers all periods and cultures to be intrinsically valuable. 'I cannot persuade myself that anything in the kingdom of God is only a means – everything is both a means and an end simultaneously, now no less than in the centuries of the past.'[199]

On this view, the unique perspective of each culture should always be accorded normative priority. Above all, for Herder, it is language that distinguishes natural cultural units. Individuals identify with their language at the most basic level. They acquire not only a means of communication, but also a broader perspective that makes the world intelligible to them. A view of culture that countenances neglect of so much that is important to people runs the risk of moral and intellectual atrophy.

A concern with roots and identity became a leading theme in later nationalist writings. So, too, did Herder's rejection of the idea of progress. Where Enlightenment thinkers had tended to see the past as a succession of types of society culminating in the present, Herder, instead, sees a society as a unique focus of a particular way of life. His nationalism, indeed, is deeply apolitical. He thinks in terms of cultural diversity, language, shared myths and traditions, rather than in specifically political categories. He has a profound suspicion of the modern state as a vast bureaucratic machine that tends either to ignore or to trample upon the distinctive customs of local communities.

What transformed nationalism into a political movement was the reaction against the attempt to return to a system of dynastic politics in 1815 following the defeat of Napoleon. Peoples had grown accustomed to new styles of political thought and practice, and new loyalties had emerged. Problems were most acute in the sprawling Austrian Empire. Educated Slavs, Hungarians or Italians simply could not identify with rule from Vienna. Within these suppressed nations (for that is how they began to regard themselves) movements arose with a very clear political objective – to rid the nation of foreign rule. The ideal of national self-determination was thrust to the forefront of political debate, with the question of the kind of constitutional arrangement that might be appropriate for a community being treated as a secondary issue.

The most striking representative of this new style of nationalism was Giuseppe Mazzini (1805–72). His bent was much more for propaganda than systematic social or political theory. In 1831 he created the organization *Young Italy*, geared to the formation of a united Italian republic through popular insurrections. And indeed, throughout his career, much of it spent in exile in England after 1837, he was indefatigable in keeping the idea of a united Italy before the educated public in a stream of impassioned publications. Despite a deep personal commitment to republican principles, he always stressed that he would support any movement devoted to the liberation of Italy from foreign rule. He insisted, however, that liberation should be the work of Italians themselves, and not the product of a fortunate concatenation of diplomatic circumstances. The manner in which Italian unity was finally achieved in 1861 thus deeply disappointed him.[200] And he remained a bitter and isolated man until his death in 1872.

Mazzini's nationalism had a specifically political focus. Yet he shared many of the assumptions that had informed Herder's view. He rejected, for example, abstract 'scientific' analysis of history and society, focusing instead on identification with the non-reflective attitudes and dispositions that he saw as the foundation of a way of life. He also opposed the narrow individualism that the Enlightenment had bequeathed (in his view) to liberal thought. What matters to him is not so much that individuals should be enabled to pursue their particular interests, but that they should be aware of the ties which bind them to their communities. Harmony and co-operation are his watchwords. The stress on competition and conflict in contemporary liberal and socialist doctrines is for him a principal obstacle to the well-being of communities. Instead, he contends that individuals will grow in moral stature only by co-operating in a common enterprise. Hence it is crucial for him that a people's sense of identity (formed through the medium of language, education, cultural traditions and so forth) should be reflected in their political institutions.

Developments towards national unification in Italy, in Mazzini's view, were but an aspect of a wider process underway throughout Europe. Everywhere the trend is away from the radical individualism that had been characteristic of the Enlightenment and the French Revolution, and towards a deeper awareness of the ties that bind communities together. These sentiments are more basic than a straightforward recognition of mutual interests, embracing unspoken assumptions embedded in a way of life. A national literature is perhaps uniquely fitted to give expression to a bedrock of shared feeling.[201] But Mazzini insists that a vigorous national literature should be neither narrow nor insular. Awareness of national identity necessarily involves recognition of the identity and autonomy of other nations. Nationalism, in Mazzini's formulation, can thus be seen as a European phenomenon that reinforces the bonds between separate peoples. The lesson for Italy is clear: 'the specific history of nations is ending; European history is beginning; and Italy cannot allow herself to be isolated in the midst of a common movement.'[202]

A great future thus beckons both Italy and Europe. But it will come to fruition only if the separate nations are able to establish themselves on a proper foundation. They require both 'political independence and moral unity', not in order to assert claims against each other, but rather as a means of making their distinctive contributions to an evolving European culture.[203] Mazzini had yet to work out the detailed political dimension of his argument in these early essays. But he had a developed view of the dynamics of historical change and institutional interaction that would serve as the basis for the elaboration of more narrowly political strategies in the 1830s.

Mazzini sought to devise a broadly-based revolutionary strategy for the national movement, obsessed as he was with the futility of the insurrectionary activities of the various clandestine political sects. To this end, while exiled in Marseilles in 1831, he focused his energy on the mobilization of a new movement, *Young Italy*, which would combine the dual aims of educating the people politically and organizing popular insurrections. He set immediate political goals in the widest ideological context, seeking to encourage groups previously untouched by sectarian activity to flock to the standard of a free, independent and united Italy. 'The truth', he announces in his 'Manifesto of *Young Italy*' (1831), 'is indivisible', and for the most part already received.[204] The point of the movement is to explore the implications of this central moral insight in such a way that each and every individual will be in a position to further the Italian cause. The tone is thus didactic and exhortatory. Mazzini had grasped the significance of ideology as a political weapon. He is aware that a political message has to be projected and reiterated incessantly in a readily assimilable form. His initial statement of the principles of *Young Italy* can be taken as a model of ideological propaganda. Italians are brought together by geography and language, but political commitment gives them identity. 'The nation', he declares, 'is the universality of Italians, united by agreement and living under a common law.'[205] Nature can provide only the circumstances in which nations might arise. It is for people to embrace that possibility for themselves, growing in moral stature as they strive to bring their political identity to fulfilment.

Mazzini is intent upon rallying Italians to the national cause. But he is adamant that the cause will not be advanced simply by appealing to a lowest common denominator of political support. 'The strength of an association', he insists, 'is to be found not in the numbers' of its followers so much as in the 'homogeneity' and 'harmony' of its support.[206] Given the urgency of the political task, it is thus essential that ideological goals be formulated with crystal clarity. Members of *Young Italy* should be in no doubt about the political complexion of the Italy they are struggling to attain. The movement 'is republican and unitary'.[207] Mazzini's more narrowly political thought is built around these two principles. He can envisage temporary tactical alliances with monarchical groups in particular circumstances, but he will not countenance any deviation from the commitment to a unitary state.

Throughout his career Mazzini was haunted by the prospect of a sectional interest usurping the position of the nation as a whole. But his discussions of precisely how the national interest might be expressed are far from clear. Following Rousseau, he holds that sovereignty is indivisible and is derived not from a set of authoritative procedures but from a substantive moral truth. In *On the Duties of Man*, for example, written in 1859, he identifies the moral law with God's providential design. But he is no more successful than Rousseau in pinning down the moral law to any specific authoritative pronouncements. It will be revealed to men, he claims, through the 'inspiration of men of genius and the tendencies of humanity in the diverse epochs' of its history.[208] He denies, crucially, that sovereignty can ever reside in either the individual or society 'except insofar as the one and the other are in line with that design, with that law, and direct themselves to its end'.[209] He distinguishes legitimate government from tyranny only in terms of adherence to the moral law. His dismissal of constitutional mechanisms is scathing. 'The straightforward vote of a majority does not constitute sovereignty if it evidently contravenes the supreme moral law or deliberately obstructs the path to future progress. Social good, liberty, progress: outside of these three terms sovereignty cannot exist.'[210] Moderate constitutionalists who look askance at Mazzini certainly know their man.

It would be misleading to suggest that Mazzini was original either in his portrayal of the state or in his wider nationalism. He shared many of the assumptions of earlier 'cultural' nationalists. His conception of a nation's unique mission is very much in accord with the views expressed in Herder's early writings, where universal criteria of judgement are rejected in favour of a panoply of perspectives, each uniquely valuable in itself. To be sure, Mazzini did not match Herder's breadth of sympathy. In fact, his preoccupation with the larger sweep of historical development tended to leave smaller nations out of account. In his view, the French had fulfilled their mission by bringing the age of individualism to a close with the Revolution; the Italians were destined to inaugurate a new age of national harmony; while smaller nations could well find themselves swallowed up in wider regional groupings. Writing in 1857, Mazzini could find no place on the political map of Europe for Austria, the various Slav nations, Holland, Belgium or Ireland.[211] But, of course, such narrowness of vision was not uncommon among nationalists. Even Michelet, whose radical credentials were impeccable, sought to mobilize the French people around a very specific image of their civilizing mission.[212] Mazzini differed from Michelet only over which nation's hour had struck.

Mazzini had absorbed, too, the communitarian assumptions that were a common property in Romantic historical and political thought.[213] Thinkers across the political spectrum had come to regard Enlightenment individualism as narrow and restrictive, reducing human beings to calculators of material advantage. Mazzini's language, indeed, with its stress on duty to the community, self-sacrifice, harmony and co-operation, might well, in other circumstances, have marked him out as a man of conservative inclinations. What makes him a radical is his insistence that community values cannot flourish if artificial constraints are placed upon development. He complains insistently that foreign rule or dominance has distorted the natural pattern of institutional relationships throughout Italy, leading to the emergence of local elites whose positions of authority depend upon foreign political patronage, setting groups and individuals against each other within regions, and region against region in the wider national context. Mazzini's ambition was to restore the functional harmony which should have obtained naturally, enabling Italians to perform particular roles in full awareness of their obligations to, and dependence upon, their fellow citizens. Not only would future economic, social and cultural progress thereby be guaranteed, but consciousness of national identity would be sharpened by being brought into political focus.

Mazzini's practical achievements were limited. Insurrections planned for Savoy and Naples were abortive; and various uprisings in the Kingdom of Naples after 1837, culminating in the failure of the Bandiera brothers in 1844, were easily suppressed.[214] To many sceptical observers it seemed that Mazzini had simply encouraged idealistic young men to embark upon foolhardy expeditions that would almost certainly cost them their lives. But even failure has propaganda value. Mazzini became the *bête noire* of the authorities. Though the insurrections he inspired might look pathetic in retrospect, they could not be disregarded. Governments were momentarily overturned in Milan and Naples in 1820–1, and no government could be sure that a local spark would not ignite a wider conflagration. Matters came to a head in the colossal events of 1848, when civil order was threatened throughout Europe. More important from a long-term political point of view, though, Mazzini forced Italian activists to think in terms of national political categories. Traditional loyalties to city or region began to seem anachronistic in the brave new world he evoked. Mazzini's tactics might have done little to shake the *status quo*. His propaganda, however, made a lasting impression across the political spectrum.

Mazzini was far from creating an ideological consensus. Even in radical circles, there was widespread disquiet about his aims and methods. What most isolated him from colleagues who shared his contempt for imperialism was his conception of political independence for Italy as an end in itself. Where federalists and moderate constitutionalists saw ridding Italy of foreign rule as a means of securing other values (liberty, justice, economic and cultural regeneration), Mazzini focused on the achievement of an Italian state as the decisive factor in a process of renewal that left a host of issues unresolved. He said little in detail about the generation of economic growth, or about the vexed question of the relationship between local, regional and national power. Mazzini proposed a purely political 'solution' to Italy's problems, with little or no awareness of the difficulties that might be encountered if a unitary scheme is imposed upon variegated economic, social and cultural practices. The point to stress, though, is that radicals who shared Mazzini's suspicions of the limited class interests of moderate constitutionalists nevertheless saw national independence as a problematic means which had to be assessed in relation to wider economic and social considerations. Just how far national independence might constitute an advance for Italians would depend upon the terms on which it was attained. Mazzini's democratic credentials are not in doubt. What is in question is his assumption that power exercised through the people need not be treated with suspicion. It may be less likely that power will be abused in a democracy, but it would surely be over-sanguine to assume that it could not be abused. Human flourishing is not guaranteed by the removal of specific (imperial) constraints; nor is its continued enjoyment in any context exempt from intractable difficulties that might finally have to be resolved by force. The crucial issue is the appropriate exercise of power. There is no substitute for constitutional procedure.

The ambivalence at the heart of Mazzini's political thought highlights a dilemma in the theory of nationalism. When national self-determination is defended, it is generally with a view to consequences of one kind or another that might be expected to follow. Very many nineteenth-century liberals saw imperialism as a principal obstacle to the realization of rights. When they argue against imperial government, it is because they take rights seriously. A liberal can hardly argue that self-determination is an end in itself, no matter what the community might desire. But this is precisely the dilemma that Mazzini evades in his writings. Far from defending a liberal nationalism, Mazzini simply assumes that a democratic nation would not overreach itself. The sorry history of twentieth-century political populism illustrates how dangerous that assumption might prove to be.

Nationalism had assumed the guise of a liberation movement in response to the challenge of imperial rule. As a political movement, however, it embraced a variety of positions, ranging from radical claims for direct democracy to defence of the most extreme forms of authoritarianism. This flexibility, of course, is essential to the appeal of the movement. Nationalists can set their ideological or constitutional differences aside in a common commitment to the contention that communities with a sense of their own linguistic or cultural identity should have a political voice. There are tantalizing possibilities here for established authorities. Through identification with the state as a symbol of the nation, a sense of political participation can be attained without any real extension of popular involvement in government. Nationalism could thus generate from within its own resources a remarkable transfiguration from an ideology of liberation to the official doctrine of a repressive state.

There had, indeed, always been a darker side to the history of nationalism. Fichte, for example, writing at the very beginning of the nineteenth century, saw the nation in such exclusive terms that a national state would be justified in pressing its claims not only against other states but against its own people. The bond between people who speak a common language, in this view, is seen to be so crucial to their fulfilment that nothing can be allowed to distract them from their common purpose. In *The Closed Commercial State* (1800) Fichte argued that an individual's noblest qualities would flourish only in a state that controlled all aspects of a way of life, while in his *Addresses to the German Nation* (1807–8) he fiercely rejected any accommodation of one language-based community to another.[215] With the leaven of social Darwinism later in the nineteenth century, these ideas would warrant the most aggressive policies. Nations could be pictured maximizing their moral and political energies in competition with one another, with individuals subordinating their interests, and sometimes their lives, to the pursuit of a common good. Once the interests of the state have been identified with the needs of the nation, it is but a small step from a view of a world of diverse nations, each finding a political outlet for its energies, to that of a world in which a nation is justified in asserting itself against other nations. What Mazzini had conceived as a recipe for international harmony and co-operation could be transformed into a pretext for imperial adventures and war.

Nationalism continued to be a dark undercurrent throughout the twentieth century, despite the assumption of both liberals and socialists that it would fade away as a relic of a more atavistic past. In truth, the facile thought that moral and political 'progress' is somehow written into the script of history cannot easily survive close scrutiny of the barbarism of the twentieth century. Indeed, after the Cold War and the collapse of the Soviet empire in 1989–91, nationalism resurfaced in virulent form in much of eastern Europe. As had been evident in the build-up to the First World War, nationalism could very readily fill the political vacuum left by a declining political order.

The fortune of democracy has proved to be inseparable from nationalism. A self-governing polity, after all, must distinguish itself in some terms or other from its neighbours. Linguistic, cultural and (regrettably) racial criteria readily make sense to people, especially in troubled times. Attempts in modern literature to distinguish 'ethnic' from 'civic' nationalism can clearly be traced back to the very beginning of nationalism as an ideology. We must assume that while people value democracy, they will have to learn to accommodate nationalism in its various forms.

Socialism

Socialism as a political movement was very much a response to the consequences of industrialization. Liberalism and capitalism emerged in socialist argument as Janus-faced villains, defending a conception of political and economic freedom that effectively perpetuated the subordination of the working classes. Socialists might not agree about precisely what was wrong with the *status quo*; nor could they necessarily agree on a common programme for the future. But there was a general consensus in socialist circles that the ideals of the French Revolution – liberty, equality, fraternity – could not be attained in a political system built upon an individualist foundation.

Industrialization in the nineteenth century created both new possibilities for ordinary people and massive difficulties. Industrial workers could see themselves as essential to capitalism, yet felt excluded from the manifest productive benefits of industry. Before they could assert themselves politically, however, workers needed a political language that reflected their circumstances and aspirations. It was obvious to many that the rich promise of liberal theory was illusory. Political freedom left them constrained by the logic of capitalism. Advancement on all fronts – economic, social, cultural, political – required close analysis of the workings of capitalism from the perspective of groups most exposed to systemic exploitation.

It was widely held that complex problems of integration and control in the economy could not be left to individual initiative. In the early decades of the century, arguments were being mooted urging a high degree of central control in economic planning. Robert Owen and Saint-Simon, for example, contended that scientific and technical progress had created alternatives to capitalist production that were both more efficient and more humane.[216] Problems that in the past had been treated as the 'natural' concomitants of human life – poverty, exploitation, crime – are, on this view, attributable to an outmoded social and economic system. Owen, in particular, saw the 'moral' shortcomings of workers as a direct consequence of the brutal and insecure conditions they would have experienced in factories. Replace anarchic competition with rational planning, coercion in the factory with co-operation, and not only would productive capacity increase, but there would be no further need for the state to assume a repressive role.

Owen tried to put his ideas into practice in the factory he operated in New Lanark (1800–25). His workers were provided with education, good living conditions and co-operative working practices, in the expectation that their personal potential and sense of responsibility would be enhanced, equipping them for wider social and political roles. While Saint-Simon urged that an elite corps of social scientists should directly manage matters of production, distribution and exchange, thus freeing economic life from the vagaries of market conditions. Here, at least, were proposals that might make the fruits of industrial society available to wider sections of the population, with the tantalizing possibility that a new technology might mark a decisive break with previous modes of political co-ordination and control.

Ideas of this kind were growing in popularity in the 1840s, especially among educated workers in London and Paris. They constituted a frame of reference in which substantive political, social and economic demands could be advanced – for universal male suffrage and annual parliaments among the Chartists of Britain, for radical redistribution of property

The Age of Ideologies

among the Paris workers. But, far-reaching though the practical implications of these demands might be, they were thoroughly reformist in tone.
They would not change the basic structure of society. The contention was
that by amending specific institutions and practices, wholesale benefits
would accrue to working people.

What transformed socialism into a deadly threat to the liberal order was
the supposition that meaningful change could not be achieved within the
confines of a capitalist system. Tinkering with this or that abuse might,
indeed, strengthen the *status quo* by distracting working people from their
revolutionary opportunities. Where reformists had sought to convince a
ruling elite of the justice of their cause, revolutionary socialists vested their
hopes for the future in the dawning political awareness of the working
class. In this view, capitalism had created, along with unparalleled wealth,
an impoverished and brutalized proletariat. As the logic of their class position became clear, so it was argued, the proletariat would undergo a meta-
morphosis. The passive victims of capitalist exploitation would assume
the direction of a new era.

Karl Marx was the principal architect of a class-based socialism. In his
early writing he targeted his criticism on the view, central to liberal theory,
that moral and political principles have universal scope and validity. The
conception of rights embodied in the *Declaration of the Rights of Man and the
Citizen* of 1789, for example, which purports to be a statement of the necessary conditions for the rounded political and social development of
human beings everywhere, is seen by Marx as a defence of the sorts of conventions that might best advance the interests of the emergent bourgeoisie.
Champions of the *Declaration* would not, of course, recognize the narrowness of their perspective. In arguing for certain rights, they mean what
they say. What they have not grasped, however, is that the view which
individuals form of their predicament (expressed in moral, political, philosophical, religious, aesthetic or whatever terms) is a product of their place
in a complex of social and economic roles.

Marx developed his position through painstaking analysis of Hegel's
philosophy.[217] He came to see that it was not enough to apply a Hegelian
method to various aspects of the ideology of modern society. The method
itself had to be exposed as yet another example of ideological mystifica-
tion. Thus where Hegel had portrayed the state as the concrete expression
of the universal good of the community, Marx treats it as the protector of
the economic and social interests of a dominant class. Faced with any statement of formal principles, Marx would always look to the class interest
that had generated it. He views the whole of the ideological realm as a
reflection of more fundamental conflicts in economy and society.

Marx's shift of perspective involves a quite different conception of argument. The ingenuity which past philosophers have devoted to the justification of abstract principles is clearly misplaced. What is required is
not a titanic confrontation of concepts – divine right against natural right,

liberty against equality – but an explanation of the economic factors that sustain particular ways of speaking about political life. Marx's focus is on the way material conditions impinge on people in the course of their efforts to manage their lives. He stresses the predicament of 'real individuals, their activity and the material conditions of their life, both those which they find already existing and those produced by their activity'.[218] The focus throughout is on the logic of subsistence and survival. People must work to satisfy their needs; and by doing so they transform the conditions of human life itself. Work is necessarily a social engagement, but the social relationships people form in the course of their economic activity will not simply reflect their economic needs. The struggle for subsistence against nature is conducted by means of a technology that demands a certain division of labour. And, since 'the various stages of development in the division of labour are just so many different forms of property', the advantages that accrue to particular groups within a society will depend upon their access to and control of 'the material, instrument and product of labour'.[219] The characteristic features of the successive types of society – tribal, ancient urban, feudal, capitalist – are political reflections of the relationships of domination and subordination that arise from the distribution of property in each.

The state, though purporting to represent the general interest of society, is (in Marx's analysis) an instrument of oppression designed to secure the economic interest of the ruling class. In earlier epochs this economic dominance is tempered by lingering natural obligations engendered by personal relationships within the family, tribe or manor; but with the development of capitalism, bonds of personal dependence give place to a notional freedom that allows unbridled accumulation of property. The practical corollary (according to Marx) is a progressive concentration of property in ever fewer hands, coupled with the creation of a proletariat utterly dependent on the vagaries of the labour market. Henceforth all relationships are seen in terms of the cash nexus; and (paradoxically) the preconditions are established for the emergence of a theory that, by focusing on the economic basis of society, at the same time offers the prospect of a future in which technological advance might mark the end of such economic dependence.

Nor is the dominance of the ruling class limited to the maintenance of the rule of law and existing economic arrangements. The class that wields economic power within a society is also able to 'regulate the production and distribution of the ideas of their age'; and hence 'the ideas of the ruling class are in every epoch the ruling ideas'.[220] This is not a deliberate ploy, but an illusion generally shared by rulers and ruled alike. The coherence of an age, which German historians in particular tended to attribute to the prevailing current of ideas, should in fact be explained as the product of predominant economic interests. A historical theory that 'takes every epoch at its word and believes that everything it says and imagines about itself is true' merely perpetuates a myth of the autonomy of ideas which had first arisen with the fateful distinction between mental and material labour.[221] Conflicts in the realm of ideas should be explained in terms of the conditions of production and the conflict of classes. Marx thus rejects the treatment of the French Revolution as a clash between honour and equality. The real battle, in Marx's view, is between an aristocracy clinging to the remnants of feudal society and a bourgeoisie seeking legal and political recognition for economic powers that are fast being entrenched.

Marx, writing in collaboration with Friedrich Engels, drew these ideas together in a pamphlet, *The Communist Manifesto*, that became a model for a new style of political argument.[222] Conceived as a contribution to the turmoil of 1848, as revolutionary uprisings swept through Europe, the *Manifesto* sought to raise the consciousness of the industrial proletariat by explaining the economic basis of their new-found political strength. Marx's initial premise is that all conflicts in society can be traced back to class divisions. 'The history of all hitherto existing society', he asserts without qualification, 'is the history of class struggles.'[223] These divisions could be complex in pre-capitalist societies, with subtle distinctions of status and rank changing slowly in relation to the distribution of economic power. With the advent of mature capitalism, however, a new phenomenon occurs. The interrelationships of earlier societies tend to be replaced by a basic division into two broad classes, the bourgeoisie and the proletariat, with implacably opposed interests. The bourgeoisie, as owners of the means of production, are intent upon maximizing their profits in order to survive the rigours of competition. The proletariat, on the other hand, who are propertyless, are forced to sell their labour for subsistence wages. Since, according to Marx, the exploitation of the workers is the only source of profit in a capitalist system, it follows that the inexorable logic of competition compels the bourgeoisie to squeeze ever more production out of workers in return for the lowest possible wages.

But here we can see problems looming. Economies of scale dictate that production be concentrated in ever larger factories. Yet the discipline of factory life accustoms the proletariat to working together as a body. And it is but a small step from recognition of the interdependence of the system of production to recognition of the proletariat's collective interest as a class. As competition among producers becomes more intense, so extra pressure will be put upon the workers. The workers would be forced by their poverty to resist that pressure, first in the factory and subsequently (as political awareness grows) at national and international levels. Capitalists, in their restless pursuit of profit, would effectively have created the conditions for their own undoing.

Marx's crucial point is that these problems are systemic rather than matters of policy. It is not open to enlightened entrepreneurs to modify their management practices in the light of Marx's analysis. Capitalists and workers alike are locked in structural conflict. Their actions can affect the timing of events, but not the long-term course of development. The revolutionary possibilities Marx highlights in *The Communist Manifesto* depend upon the fullest development of capitalism. Marx is deeply suspicious of efforts by so-called 'utopian socialists' (such as Owen and Saint-Simon) to ameliorate the prospects of workers under industrial capitalism.[224] He treats reform as prevarication, a failure to recognize that political development is actually driven by structural economic crises. He is haunted by the thought that, through manipulation of propaganda, it might be possible to persuade workers for a time that in the long term they could expect to enjoy a reasonable share of the fruits of capitalism. In Marx's view, however, these promises are illusory. Capitalists are involved in deadly competition with one another, and this commits them to ruthless exploitation of workers. The bourgeoisie are thus driven by necessity to create their own 'grave-diggers', a class (the proletariat) that is indispensable to the success of capitalism yet incompatible with its future survival.[225]

Marx's theory is avowedly determinist. Yet running alongside his predictions for the inevitable triumph of the proletariat are 'moral' arguments that cannot always be reconciled with his theory. He values a form of association 'in which the free development of each is the condition for the free development of all'.[226] The implication is that this state of affairs is desirable, not simply that it will inevitably come to pass in due course. And for all that he defends capitalism as a necessary phase in the development of an ideal communist society, his language regarding the exploitation and degradation of workers under capitalism is highly charged. What does freedom amount to 'under the present bourgeois conditions of production' but 'free trade, free selling and buying'?[227] In this situation individuals are free to sell themselves, but not to develop their rounded talents and personalities. Marx's response to the charge that communism involves the abolition of the family is scathing. Family life, he insists, is a disguised system of 'public prostitution', with women treated as 'mere instruments of production'.[228] The position of children is no better. Economic desperation drives poor families to maximize the productivity of their children, exposing them to danger, disease and a generally brutalizing culture. Moralizing will not change this situation. Poor parents cannot enjoy the luxury of treating children as ends in themselves. The abolition of the family, in Marx's view, is a necessary condition for preventing 'the exploitation of children by their parents'.[229] If this is regarded as a crime, Marx is happy to 'plead guilty'.[230]

The *Manifesto* gives no more than a schematic account of the economic context in which modern political battles are being fought out. Marx focuses on the need for the proletariat to base its political strategies on a realistic appraisal of the shifting balance of economic power. Capitalism had created a technology with vast economic potential; but that potential could not be fulfilled within the established legal and political order. The task of the revolutionary intellectual, and the specific point of the

Manifesto, is to bolster the proletariat by showing precisely why capitalism will collapse under its own weight.

Marx's treatment of the detailed mechanics of revolutionary transformation is highly complex. His most succinct statement of the process of systemic change is in the preface to *A Contribution to the Critique of Political Economy* (1859). Here the mainspring of social and political change is located in the uneven development of the 'forces of production' and 'relations of production'. While 'relations of production' correspond to 'material productive forces', they do not adapt automatically to technological innovations. 'At a certain stage of their development, the material productive forces of society come in conflict with the existing relations of production, or – what is but a legal expression for the same thing – with the property relations within which they have been at work hitherto.'[231] Thus, though the definition of property rights will be tied to a particular phase in the development of the forces of production, the forces of production will change in ways incompatible with the established relations of production as these are embodied in legal and moral assumptions. Property rights that had fostered the advance of a particular technology (the unlimited accumulation of the bourgeois epoch was a necessary condition for the development of large-scale industry) finally ossify and are unable to meet the requirements of a new situation (the pursuit of profit, necessary for survival in a market economy, exacerbates the crises of overproduction that are said to plague the later stages of capitalism). 'From forms of development of the productive forces these relations turn into their fetters. Then begins an epoch of social revolution. With the change of the economic foundation the entire immense superstructure is more or less rapidly transformed.'[232]

The relationship between economic base and ideological superstructure has always been a vexed issue in Marxian studies. The tone of the 1859 preface suggests a strong determinism that contrasts sharply with the emphasis on 'praxis' in Marx's early writings. Even in Marx's later writings, however, in which he self-consciously cast his work in the style of a science of society, a commitment to facilitate revolutionary transformation is always evident. His point is simply that the complexity of the social world obliges anyone who takes change seriously to focus in detail on the structures, practices and institutions that shape a political order. Marx rejects the method of the utopian socialists, but not necessarily their goals. From the outset he had taken Hegel's dictum to heart. Philosophy should certainly be construed as 'its own time apprehended in thoughts'.[233] It is just that, for Marx, philosophy cannot be conceived as an independent and autonomous activity. Conceptual clarity can help to change the world, but only if the burden of the world is taken into account.

The only economic system that Marx studied in detail, both because statistics were more readily available and because urgent political questions hinge upon economic analysis, was capitalism. The trajectory of the English economy during the industrial revolution and after serves as his model of capitalism as a system. The point of his enquiries is to show, not that certain economic arrangements are undesirable or reprehensible, but that an economic system has emerged from its predecessor and will succumb to its successor despite (rather than because of) the choices of individuals. Individuals (to be sure) can hasten the demise of an economic system; but in the last resort the direction of change is determined by the forces of production.

In the first volume of *Capital* (1867) – volumes 2 and 3 only appeared after Marx's death, thanks to devoted editorial work by Engels – Marx demonstrates how the logic of capitalist production creates the conditions for the emergence of a new order.[234] A bald summary can barely do justice to the subtlety of the argument. In Marx's account, profit accrues to the capitalist because the subsistence wages he pays to his employees fail to match the value of the goods they produce. This is the so-called theory of surplus value.[235] With the advance of technology and the threat of competition, however, only large-scale, highly capital-intensive enterprises will flourish. This makes production more efficient, but only by increasing the ratio of fixed to variable costs. Yet fixed costs (investments in land, plant and technology) do not themselves generate profits, at least in Marx's view. As the proportion of variable capital diminished, so too will the source of the capitalist's profit in the surplus value produced by his employees. This is the root of the vicious circle that creates the periodic crises of capitalism. Each crisis obliges the capitalist to squeeze ever more profit out of workers; and at the same time competition leads to the extension of automated machinery that puts ever more workers (the only source of profit) out of work. A paradox arises: technology creates unprecedented material plenty, but the situation of the worker is such that he can neither enjoy a reasonable share in those riches nor provide a market that will ensure their continuance.

In *Capital* Marx fleshes out in detail the schematic account of revolution he had presented in the *Manifesto*. He shows through minute analysis of capital accumulation and factory organization how the logic of capitalist production engenders implacable hostility between the bourgeoisie and the proletariat. Yet modes of social organization dictated by class conflict will finally resolve the crisis. The discipline and structure of the modern factory will lead workers to recognize that they have interests in common as a class.[236] The discipline of the factory will be a preparation for the political struggle that the workers will wage against the bourgeoisie, while the degradation and uncertainty of factory life will remind them of how little they have to lose. Capitalism, devoted to the production of 'exchange value', will collapse, because it can no longer satisfy economic needs.[237] The poverty of the proletariat will ruin the home market; imperialist adventures in search of markets and resources overseas will offer only a temporary palliative; and developing technology will undermine the traditional source of profit by reducing the man-hours involved in a particular productive process. As economic conditions deteriorate and class conflict intensifies, workers will focus more precisely on crucial political goals. The property relations associated with capitalism will be recognized as obstacles to the satisfaction of needs that technological development has brought within reach.

In Marx's view, the social organization of the factory should find its proper complement in public ownership of the economy. With the abolition of private property, production for 'exchange value' will give place to production for 'use value'. Capitalist technology is thus a necessary condition for the achievement of socialism. But once material need has been abolished, the necessity for antagonistic relations of production (and hence the state as a means of maintaining order) will be a thing of the past.

Marx develops his argument with a wealth of economic detail, which it is scarcely necessary to reproduce here. Nor are the niceties of his economic theory of primary concern. The point to stress is that he sees the development of the productive forces of capitalism as the root cause determining secondary changes in the political and legal superstructure, and treats the ideological conflict between bourgeoisie and proletariat as but a reflection of the more fundamental contradiction between the forces of production and the relations of production.

Marx is much less precise on what a communist future would look like. His treatment of the state as a coercive apparatus in the hands of a ruling class to contain class conflict has profound implications for a prospective future in which the fundamental causes of conflict have been removed. Co-ordination problems would remain in any conceivable future. But Marx sees these as essentially technical matters. Efficient administrative decisions need not involve the panoply of instruments of coercion and control presupposed in state-centred theory. Indeed, there are passages in Marx's early writings in which he waxes lyrical about prospects for personal fulfilment in a purely consensual social order. In *The German Ideology* (1846) he pictures a scheme of social organization based upon individual disposition and choice, rather than the division of labour. We would no longer be confined to 'one exclusive sphere of activity', but would each be able 'to hunt in the morning, fish in the afternoon, rear cattle in the evening, criticise after dinner, just as' we 'have a mind, without ever becoming hunter, fisherman, shepherd or critic'.[238] But in the same text he also accepts that the proletariat would initially have to 'conquer political power in order to represent its interest in turn as the general interest'.[239] And this, of course, could not be accomplished without the systematic use of force. How long force would be required would depend on the tenacity and resilience of the displaced orders of society, striving desperately to maintain their privileges.

Marx is far from mechanistic in the application of his theory to concrete cases. The theory emphasizes factors that mistaken philosophical assumptions had formerly concealed from political analysts whose judgement had been overwhelmed by details. Indeed, Marx is adept at amending the theory of historical materialism to explain political events. His most instructive essays in this vein are *The Class Struggles in France: 1848–1850* (1850) and *The Eighteenth Brumaire of Louis Bonaparte* (1852).[240] In both, Marx is concerned to account for the apparent failure of the European revolutions of 1848 in terms of an alignment of classes that made revolutionary expectations premature. The polarization of classes announced in *The Communist Manifesto* had failed to materialize. But the fragmentation of classes, the principal obstacle to the revolution in France, can be explained by recourse to the same materialist assumptions that had informed the *Manifesto*. The political divisions in the French ruling class before 1848, in Marx's view, reflect fundamental divisions in the economy. The lack of common interest between landowners, the financial aristocracy and the industrial bourgeoisie is evident in the political sphere in the conflict between Legitimists and Orleanists. Only in the face of a threat from the democratic socialists would such disparate interests find common ground in the need for order to secure their property. Hence (paradoxically) the most appropriate political form for contending royalist aspirations is a bourgeois republic sustained by nothing more substantial than fear of the Paris proletariat.

The mass of the French people do not come into these political calculations. The peasants remain outside the range of class interests represented by the bourgeois republic. For though the peasants 'form a class' in the sense that they 'live under economic conditions of existence that separate their mode of life, their interests and their cultural formation from those of the other classes and bring them into conflict with those classes', yet because they 'are merely connected on a local basis, and the identity of their interests fails to produce a feeling of community, national links, or a political organization, they do not form a class'.[241] Unaware of their common interests and unable to represent themselves, the peasants nevertheless constitute a vast latent force that could be exploited by a demagogue. In Marx's interpretation, this is the basis of Louis Bonaparte's *coup d'état* of 1851. Despite the opposition of both Legitimists and Orleanists, Bonaparte is finally able to count on the support of the bourgeoisie simply because he seems to promise an end to the political chaos and uncertainty that threatens the economy. In the last resort (so Marx contends) only a class analysis can explain the rise of such a mediocrity.

Nor is Marx's faith in the inevitability of proletarian revolution shaken by the evident success of the reaction. Revolutionary failure is itself an educational experience which helps to dispel the myths and illusions that have informed political conduct in the past. Bonaparte's success results in a simplification of class relationships. Henceforth it will be clear that differences within the party of order disguise a common class interest. Faced with 'a powerful and united counter-revolution', the peasants and the petty bourgeoisie will fall in behind the proletariat to form 'a real party of revolution'.[242]

Marx is thus able to refine the schematic account of class consciousness drawn from his theoretical writings in his interpretations of contemporary events in France. He treats historical materialism not as an a priori theory of social change, but as an interpretative device that enables the fundamental factors of a complex situation to be distinguished. Marx does not question the determining role of the forces of production in these essays; yet he is clear that their ideological reflection in political struggles will be dependent upon circumstances. The gap between a model of capitalism and its development in practice can be filled only by empirical enquiry.

Marx's writings have always been notoriously contentious, not least because he addressed a variety of audiences in the course of a prolific career. Theoretical treatises, political pamphlets and newspaper articles could not be expected to share a common form. And once a text becomes an authoritative source in political debate, it is likely to be used and abused for any number of strategic reasons. Considered in the round, however, Marx's writings reveal a striking degree of consistency. His specific predictions, of course, were not to be realized. The revolution which he had confidently expected in 1848 receded in his later writings to a more distant prospect.

Nor can it be said that the states which proclaimed themselves to be 'Marxist' in the twentieth century emerged in quite the way Marx had anticipated. But the fact remains that Marxism has signally enriched political debate. As an analytical tool, it has enabled historians and political theorists to set the conventional terms of political discourse in a novel and perhaps more critical context. More important, at the practical level, it has furnished a theoretical framework that lends political significance to ordinary events in the lives of working people. Grinding experience of home and work had never been more than a background condition in liberal theory, an incentive to individuals to try to better themselves, but without positive value. In a broader context, however, the lessons of life's daily round could assume a national or international relevance, extending the horizons of the working class without detaching them from their immediate concerns. By the 1860s the impact of an organized labour movement was beginning to be felt. Groups which liberalism had largely disregarded were now demanding both a concrete improvement in their working conditions and a more active role in political life. And while there is nothing in liberal doctrine that denies the validity of the widest possible participation in politics, the substantive claims being advanced by working-class organizations were scarcely translatable into the formal language of classical liberal theory.

The success of Marxism is best measured in terms of the breadth of its impact. Groups which would not describe themselves as Marxist could profit from the new emphasis on the politics of labour. Nor was Marx's legacy uniformly revolutionary. Soon after his death in 1883, leading intellectuals (Labriola and Croce in Italy, Sorel in France, Bernstein in Germany) were debating the practical implications of Marx's theories. Bernstein's

Evolutionary Socialism (1899), for example, defends the compatibility of socialist goals with the constitutional framework of a liberal state.[243] In his view, social legislation could transform the position of the working class, opening up possibilities for political involvement without necessarily changing the structure of the state. Legislation could ease the passage from capitalism to socialism, without the unpredictable trauma of revolutionary violence. Skilled workers, in particular, are offered much to encourage them in Bernstein's vision of the future. They are already far removed from the plight of the proletariat depicted in *The Communist Manifesto*, with 'nothing to lose but their chains'.[244] Labriola and Croce, by contrast, focus on the claims of Marxism to be regarded as a science.[245] Sorel stresses the role of Marxism as a political myth, effective as a means of mobilizing the working classes but self-defeating as a predictive theory.[246]

Marxism clearly could not be regarded as an orthodoxy, even when it is taken seriously. Marx himself had shown some awareness of these difficulties, though he always felt torn between the demands of theoretical controversy and effective political propaganda. It becomes evident, though, when due attention is given to particular political contexts, that Marxism can be used to justify an evolutionary as well as a revolutionary road to socialism. What had originally been presented as the doctrine of a small revolutionary sect could by the 1890s function as the theoretical foundation for a broad-based ideology, embracing a multitude of diverse groups and associations.

Positions within the socialist tradition thus split in a bewildering variety of ways. What they all share, however, is a preoccupation with the substantive welfare of the working and excluded masses. In time, parliamentary democracies recognized that they would not be regarded as legitimate if they failed to provide for the basic needs of their peoples. An effective political response to Marxism had accordingly to be practical as well as theoretical. In the early decades of the twentieth century, however, it remained to be seen whether liberal constitutional principles would be retained as states sought to maximize their effective capacities.

A plethora of socialisms emerged in the twentieth century, some of them directly repudiating the Marxist heritage. Indeed the classic divide between communists and social democrats often sets socialists in opposed political camps. A common theme throughout socialist thought, however, is a rejection of a narrowly political view of freedom. The eradication of wider economic and social constraints is seen as a necessary condition for human fulfilment and well-being.

Communism

Communism in its modern form is generally regarded as an off-shoot from socialism. Yet communist ideas, stressing the complete dependence of individuals upon the community and the abolition of private property, can be traced back to early Greek and Christian thought. What transformed communist theory in modern times is its relation to a wider analysis of society and politics. Communal living, which in the monastic ideal was an optional alternative to the depravity of civil society, became a necessary means for the eradication of injustice and inequality.

Gracchus Babeuf is often portrayed as the symbolic inspiration for modern communism, especially as an insurrectionary movement. A devoted follower of Robespierre in the French Revolution, he was bitterly disappointed when Robespierre was betrayed and executed. In 1796, in hideously unlikely circumstances, he organized a 'Conspiracy of Equals', immortalized in Philippe Buonarotti's *La Conspiration de Babeuf* (1828).[247] The conspiracy was ill fated from the outset. Babeuf detested the governing Directory's obsessive concern to maintain the economic *status quo* in France, and sought to mobilize radical opinion around Robespierre's ideals, pressing for restoration of the constitution of 1793.

Babeuf was not a subtle theorist, but he struck a chord with certain radical groups that continues to have significant appeal. He traces all the ills of society to the personal dependence of individuals upon one another. That dependence, he argues, will only end with the abolition of private property. In Babeuf's scheme of things, it is an article of faith that individuals have the same needs. It follows, accordingly, that they should necessarily enjoy the same facilities and benefits from society. In his disarmingly simple analysis, inequality and oppression are identified. And he champions a virtuous dictatorship, in the style of Robespierre, as the only conceivable remedy.

In truth, the Directory had little to fear from Babeuf's shambolic conspiracy. Information was leaked to the authorities, and the uprising was suppressed before it had effectively begun. Babeuf himself was executed in 1797. But his example inspired conspirators throughout the nineteenth century, whether or not they shared the crude economic analysis at the heart of his thinking.

Marx gave communist theory the decisive economic arguments that have made it a force in the modern world. He dismissed out of hand the idea that radical equality could be attained through the insurrectionary activities of a virtuous elite. Everything depends, in Marx, on analysis of structural opportunities, dictated by identifiable phases of economic development. He insists that communism is not a more or less adequate scheme of social and political organization, but an inevitable outcome of the historical process. He continues to argue that private property and the division of labour stunt the prospects of individuals. What is novel in his argument, however, is the contention that such institutions and practices constitute obstacles to further material progress. Particular modes of social organization ultimately fracture as developing technologies engender new opportunities and imperatives. Marx sees collective ownership and direction, a staple in communist theory, as a fitting reflection of the complex interrelationships of industrial society.

Problems within the Marxist tradition stem from the inadequacy of Marx's analysis of revolution. His expectation of imminent revolution in the 1840s was tempered in his later writings. But he continued to argue that the establishment of communism would mark the end of coercive political institutions. The state, as an instrument of class rule, would wither away in a classless society. Marx was remarkably imprecise, however, about how the transition from capitalism to communism would occur. He recognized in *The Communist Manifesto* that temporary dictatorship would be essential in the ultimate triumph of the proletariat. The control and allocation of resources would require a coercive apparatus, akin to a bourgeois state, until such times as the last vestiges of bourgeois society have been eradicated.

The theme becomes more prominent in later writings. In Marx's short 'Critique of the Gotha Programme' (1875), for example, he insists that what communists have to deal with when they institute a new regime is not a society 'developed on its own foundations, but, on the contrary, just as it emerges from capitalist society; which is thus in every respect, economically, morally, and intellectually, still stamped with the birth marks of the old society from whose womb it emerges'.[248] It is to Marx's credit that he did not try to deduce detailed insurrectionary strategy from formal theory. Revolutionaries have to respond to contingent circumstances. Established interests can be expected to use all the resources at their disposal in their efforts to cling on to political power. Revolutionary violence is a mirror image of repression. Pure theory can contribute surprisingly little to the conduct of revolution and the consolidation of a regime.

Identifying the need for a temporary 'dictatorship of the proletariat' is thus an almost incidental feature of Marx's theory. The notion became much more important, however, in debates from the 1890s regarding the (so-called) crisis of Marxism. Advocates of a parliamentary road to socialism (such as Bernstein) seemed to many Marxists to be ignoring the central thrust of the theory of historical materialism. Marx had exposed the naivety of utopian socialist theory. In mobilizing opposition to an emerging social democratic strand in socialism, Marxists began to articulate a distinctively communist position.

Lenin's *What is to be Done?* (1902) is a characteristic and highly influential contribution to this debate. The text is driven by urgent practical considerations. The point of political debate is to mobilize a constituency. Argument is a political weapon alongside others, depending upon particular circumstances. There is no place, in this scheme of things, for balanced consideration of the views of opponents.

Lenin discounts the possibility of a parliamentary road to socialism, urging instead the need to form a vanguard party of the proletariat to assume the direction of affairs in order to raise the political consciousness of workers and peasants. Lenin objects, in particular, to the various species of reformism inspired by Bernstein's defence of evolutionary socialism. If workers are encouraged to play the bourgeois parliamentary game, they will merely find that their interests will be subordinated to the bourgeoisie. Skilled workers might profit as individuals, but that will necessarily be at the expense of the masses. There is no middle ground here, no scope for a discursive settlement of apparently opposed perspectives. Lenin sees himself as an orthodox Marxist, while recognizing that effective politics depends upon tactical flexibility. He takes the materialist analysis of the generation of ideas very seriously indeed. In Lenin's view, 'there can be no talk of an independent ideology' that miraculously reconciles antithetical class interests.[249] He asserts categorically that 'in a society torn by class antagonisms' a 'non-class or above-class ideology' is conceptually inconceivable: workers will support either 'bourgeois or socialist ideology'.[250] The point of polemic is precisely to rid them of self-deception.

Lenin steers a tortuous path between what he styles 'economism' on the one hand and 'terrorism' on the other.[251] 'Economism' offers passive explanation of the way in which ideological perspectives are shaped by class interest. As a political strategy, however, it is seriously limited, since (as a matter of fact) workers have shown a remarkable capacity to endorse 'false' ideological positions. The attractions of 'bourgeois' reformism or various species of nationalism have effectively split the working class movement, with catastrophic consequences for the political mobilization of the interests of workers. Workers have been duped into supporting the political positions of their class enemies, as should have been clear to close readers of Marx's writings.

Disenchantment with 'passive' class analysis could lead workers to embrace 'terrorism' as a political tactic. Violent confrontation might shake both workers and authorities out of their complacency, sharpening the real class divisions that would shape political conflict in the future. Violence as a symbolic and mobilizing strategy was defended by Georges Sorel in *Reflections on Violence* (1908), and would resonate across the political spectrum in Europe in the 1920s. In Lenin's view, however, the impact of 'terrorism' as a strategy on the working-class movement would be disastrous. Detached from sustained theoretical analysis, political energies would be dissipated, effectively fragmenting the political organization of the working class and leaving them an easy target for their enemies.

Lenin champions working-class interests in a broader context of classes whose emancipation from the constraints of a bourgeois state would be achieved only with the overthrow of capitalism. Crucially, however, awareness of the need for a vanguard party is not a spontaneous product of experience of class conflict under capitalism. The working classes require a certain kind of political leadership before they can be expected to grasp the revolutionary potential of their class position. Working-class experience itself is not sufficient. Lenin is adamant on this point. 'Class political consciousness', he insists, 'can be brought to the workers *only from without*, that is, only from outside the economic struggle, from outside the sphere of relations between workers and employers.'[252] This is a strong plea for the priority of theory over practice, with fateful consequences for prospects for political freedom under communist party leadership. An elite is authorized to lead in the name of the working class, but not through the perspective of working-class values and culture. Propaganda is required to mould attitudes. And given the urgency of the situation, and the need to take full advantage of revolutionary opportunities, quiet persuasion and measured argument are likely to be ineffective. Lenin's version of Marxist theory can thus justify ruthless manipulation.

The very idea of a parliamentary road to socialism is a contradiction in terms in Lenin's view. He pictures class conflict becoming more intense as capitalism nears its final crisis. In order to be an effective political force, a communist party in these circumstances has to be geared to the demands of insurrection, manipulation and control. Democratic politics is a luxury that a revolutionary party cannot afford. In *The State and Revolution*, a polemical text written in haste shortly before the revolution in Russia in 1917, Lenin scathingly dismisses democracy as a bourgeois obsession. All it amounts to in a capitalist context is 'democracy for an insignificant minority, democracy for the rich'.[253] Capitalist democracy 'is inevitably narrow and stealthily shoves aside the poor'.[254] Given that it is predicated upon political exclusion, it is 'pervasively hypocritical and false'.[255] Nor can it be assumed that there will be a 'progressive development . . . towards ever greater democracy', as Bernstein and others had argued.[256] The structures of capitalism will not disappear overnight. An initially successful political revolution will need to be followed by ruthless elimination of the remnants of capitalism. Lenin is emphatic on this issue. A temporary 'dictatorship of the proletariat' will be required to break 'the resistance of the exploiter-capitalists'.[257] There is no ambiguity in Lenin's language, any more than there can be any temporizing in a revolutionary situation. The previous oppressors of the poor cannot be expected to endorse the perspective of the proletariat. They will resist revolution, and 'their resistance must be crushed by force'.[258] Just as revolution imposes its own organizational demands, so institutional reconstruction after revolution must focus on the pressing problems to hand. If resistance is to be suppressed and coercion is necessary, Lenin is clear that there can be 'no freedom and no democracy'.[259]

It is a vexed question in Leninist theory precisely how long the dictatorship of the proletariat will be necessary. Lenin assumes that the state will 'wither away' in an unspecified future.[260] But he insists that this will be a gradual process, finally coming to fruition once 'habit' has accustomed people 'to observing the necessary rules of social intercourse'.[261] A great deal hinges, of course, on what the 'necessary rules of social intercourse' might amount to, and (more importantly perhaps) who will be authorized to declare what they should be. Lenin envisages a utopian future in which 'there is nothing that rouses indignation, nothing that calls forth protest and revolt and creates the need for suppression'.[262] But we cannot read these passages with any confidence if we harbour the suspicion that human needs might be controversial. Lenin does not allow his utopianism about the (more or less distant) future to distract him from the more immediate task of consolidating the 'transition from capitalism to communism'.[263] Institutional mechanisms will continue to be required to suppress exploiters and free riders. He simply presupposes that breaches of the 'necessary rules of social intercourse' are caused by poverty and deprivation. This is not an empirical proposition for Lenin. It follows from his analysis of the generation of conflict. It is similarly axiomatic that the state will 'wither away' simply because it is (by definition) an organ of class oppression. State-like functions will need to be fulfilled only so long as the remnants of class oppression persist. And they cannot persist indefinitely. There is no need to specify a time-scale.

Lenin was always much more specifically focused on the strategic demands of revolution than Marx. Two of his most widely read works, *The State and Revolution* and *Imperialism, the Highest Stage of Capitalism* (1917), attempt to analyse the contemporary situation with a view to maximizing the revolutionary potential of a manifest crisis in Europe.[264] It would be a mistake, however, to treat either work as mere propaganda. The latter, in particular, is a sophisticated attempt to apply Marxian economic analysis to the international political context, effectively extending and revising Marx's discussion of imperialism in the posthumously published third volume of *Capital*.[265] Few years in modern European history have been quite so dramatic as 1917. Europe was involved in a war which, within two years, would precipitate revolutionary transformation in Russia and a chaotic dismemberment of the Austro-Hungarian Empire. Two of the principal pillars of European geo-political order would have been swept away. And for the first time, the United States would emerge as a major player in the international politics of Europe.

Lenin continues to insist that Europe's crisis is structural, and not simply a matter of foolish political management on the part of the great powers. War itself he sees as a product of the imperialist adventures that major states have embarked upon as they seek to weather the crises of capitalism. Lenin tells a story linking the Spanish-American War (1898), the Anglo-Boer War (1899–1902) and the dramatic consequences of the European war that broke out in 1914. As Lenin wrote *Imperialism, the Highest Stage of Capitalism*, war in Europe was continuing, with long-term results that could not be confidently predicted. What is certain, though, is that questions of domestic and international order were inextricably interlinked. Lenin tries to explain these connections in theoretical terms, though his discussion remains highly contentious and deeply charged.

Lenin specifically sees imperialism as 'the eve of the social revolution of the proletariat'.[266] Capitalism had effectively 'internationalized' the class struggle, in ways that had taken socialists throughout Europe by surprise in 1914. For most socialists, the thought that workers would enlist for a capitalist war was anathema. The appeal of nationalism had proved to be far stronger than class solidarity. Yet close readers of Marx could extend discussions of demagogic populism within states to the ease with which political leaders managed to persuade workers to pit their lives against fellow workers in neighbouring states.

In Lenin's analysis, as capitalist competition becomes more deadly economically, so states try to maximize their resources by exploiting cheap labour and raw materials overseas. This inevitably leads to conflict as states find themselves locked in struggles for empire. War itself also changes economies dramatically, leading 'directly to the most comprehensive socialisation', dragging 'the capitalists, against their will and consciousness, into some sort of a new social order, a transitional one from complete free competition to complete socialisation'.[267] Thus at both elite and popular levels, transformations are afoot that make a straightforward resumption of parliamentary politics and market-based capitalism deeply problematic when states have fought themselves to exhaustion.

Lenin supplies a wealth of detail to explain the causal link between what he styles 'monopoly capitalism' and imperialism.[268] What this highlights in both economic and political terms is a concentration of decision making in ever fewer hands. Under monopoly conditions, decisions about production, distribution and exchange have already become so thoroughly centralized that market criteria cease to operate in the fashion envisaged by classical economists. Lenin, of course, sees no problem with this, anticipating a wholly different distributive principle once communism is finally attained. Relative scarcity would no longer be a relevant factor in the allocation of resources; hence individual and collective decision making would not be informed by calculations of marginal utility. In such a situation, decision making would reflect Marx's dictum: 'From each according to his ability, to each according to his need.'[269] The allocation of roles, responsibilities and rewards is unlikely to be contentious in conditions of plenty. Yet administrative decisions will have to be made. Here, at least, we may assume that questions of marginal utility will continue to be relevant.

Utopia, however, is a prospect for a (more or less) distant future in Lenin's writings. Revolution in the name of communism will not bring its immediate fulfilment. The conquest of the state by communists actually obliges them to use the state ruthlessly for their own ends. In the aftermath of revolution, argues Lenin, socialists will 'demand the *strictest* control by society *and by the state* over the measure of labour and the measure of consumption'.[270]

How long such structures would have to remain in place is a matter of fine judgement. Lenin's expectation in 1917 was that revolution in Russia would trigger wider upheavals in the more developed European states. The outcome was in fact very different. Though there were other revolutionary disturbances, successful revolution was accomplished only in Russia. The Soviet Union was left trying to consolidate itself in hostile circumstances both domestically and internationally. A bitter civil war saw massive administrative dislocation and chronic food shortages. If rigid centralization of decision making was necessary in revolution, it became even more imperative in the face of institutional implosion. The temporary dictatorship of the proletariat was transformed into the permanent dictatorship of the Communist Party, informed by the daunting (and finally catastrophic) project of reshaping a culture in its entirety.

Dictatorship of the proletariat has now become a synonym for tyranny. Marx's original usage, however, presupposed that capitalism could actually solve the problem of scarcity and that the vestiges of the bourgeois state's coercive functions would only be necessary in the transition period in which the ruling communist party needed to exploit the skills and services of individuals accustomed to the practices of the old regime. Marx's analysis of scarcity was mistaken. But so too was Lenin's assumption that a wider series of revolutions were imminent. Instead, isolated in a precarious international environment, government in the Soviet Union had to focus resources on defence of the revolution. An elaborate coercive apparatus was regarded as essential. Under Stalin the regime was finely tuned for both mass mobilization and oppression. It proved incapable, however, of responding to the domestic needs of its people.

Controversy still rages about just how far the Soviet Union should be regarded as a Marxist (or even Leninist) state. Lenin's was very much a theory of the state in revolution. His followers (down to Gorbachev) often tried to distance his theory from the form the Soviet Union assumed under Stalin. There is no doubt, though, about Lenin's deep-seated hostility to autonomous institutions within the sphere of civil society. His rejection of pluralism was complete, on both theoretical and political grounds. In his view, difference amounts to deviation from an appropriate path. Lenin assumes that such a path can be theoretically specified. That, in itself, is a controversial, though not necessarily sinister, position. What makes his doctrine so chilling is the easy shift to a view of theoretical opponents as necessarily political enemies. Here are grounds for political paranoia, without invoking the idea of a paranoid personality such as Stalin. Even the most doctrinaire of us can tolerate theoretical opponents if we regard them as benign or irrelevant. Class analysis of theoretical disagreement raises the stakes significantly. If class division is the root cause of differences of political view, then there is no scope for discursive agreement. Hypothetical 'bridging' positions are not available. A regime governed according to these assumptions may be more or less brutal; but it could not be an open society. In this scheme of things, the gap between theoretical conviction and political cynicism is very narrow indeed.

The Soviet Union managed to withstand military onslaught from Nazi Germany in remarkable circumstances. In the post-war period, however, the regime became increasingly bureaucratic. Central direction of the economy proved to be inefficient, leading to major problems as administrative, political and military costs grew. Attempts to reform the system by Gorbachev after 1985 precipitated a dramatic collapse in 1991.

Communism as an ideology should not be identified exclusively with the Soviet Union. Western European communist parties in the 1950s and 1960s, particularly in Italy, Spain, Portugal and France, sought to fashion distinctively national roads to socialism, distancing themselves from Soviet policy and defending political alliances with wider groups as a means of fostering structural reform. With the demise of Soviet communism, however, the entire movement was dealt a decisive blow. Some parties sought to refashion themselves in order to bolster their parliamentary credentials. In doing so they largely severed their connections with the movement identified with Marx and Lenin, without necessarily establishing a clear ideological profile within their national traditions. For the moment, the communist chapter in modern European political history appears to be closed, though it is certain that radically egalitarian ideologies will re-emerge in other guises.

Fascism

Fascism is the most deeply problematic of modern ideologies, in both political and theoretical terms. It is very much a product of the twentieth century, emerging as it did in its various forms in the reaction to the perceived threat to all parliamentary democracies posed by the Russian Revolution of 1917. It was widely assumed, especially in elite business circles, that governments in parliamentary systems would not be robust enough to resist the ruthless advance of Bolshevik parties. Political weakness in (often recent and precarious) democracies, coupled with the catastrophic impact of the economic crisis of 1929, left many influential groups and sectors yearning for a 'third way' that would combine industrial modernization with strong government.

The roots of fascist doctrine, however, are deeper than the immediate political and economic crisis. The dominant progressive ideologies of the nineteenth century, which both drew upon the Enlightenment belief in the historical emergence of a rationally defensible political order, could barely account for the horrors of the First World War. A technology that could lead to the slaughter of thousands for the sake of a few hundred metres of territory did not look like the apogee of progress. Certainly elites that had sacrificed troops on this scale found their authority shaken.

Europe's political and economic traumas in the opening decades of the twentieth century are obvious enough. Yet, at a deeper level, philosophers, psychologists, novelists and commentators more broadly had begun to question the conception of the individual that had informed the development of liberalism in particular. Liberal stress on rationality and individual responsibility was challenged by a range of sceptical theories. From the 1880s, the disturbing prospect was raised that all our actions might be rationalizations of fundamental drives. Standard assumptions about impartiality and objectivity began to seem highly questionable. Nietzsche and others raised the prospect that all judgements might be expressions of partial perspectives.[271] While Freud and an emerging school in psychology identified the subconscious as a source of action and decision, relegating moral precepts to a problematic status.

These theories had disturbing implications for the very idea of a discursive politics. Debate between groups holding distinctive positions is at the heart of parliamentary government. We can readily accept that political programmes and ideas may well support certain interests rather than others, but the thought that they merely reflect those interests significantly narrows the scope for principled agreement. Marxist class analysis focuses on this specific point. If the factors that drive political argument are broadened, embracing national, ethnic or racial identity, struggles for power or status or personality clashes, then principled justifications of specific forms of political order begin to look precarious. When parliamentary politics is going well, these concerns will not dominate everyday perceptions of public life. We can comfortably think of parliamentary politics as (among other things) a competition between elites in good times. Authorities begin to look exposed, however, if nothing else is felt to be at stake than the spoils that power confers.

This is precisely the move that Vilfredo Pareto made in his *Socialist Systems* (1902). He focuses specifically on the humbug (as he sees it) at the heart of socialism. Far from offering people a prospect of liberation from class-inspired government, Pareto treats socialist parties as just another emerging elite struggling to dominate a political order. It is axiomatic for him that all political competition is simply 'the struggle between one aristocracy and another'.[272] Ideology is irrelevant here. A democratic context will make popular appeal a key factor in political success. Political leaders will be encouraged to project themselves as champions of the people. Propaganda will be fashioned to meet the demands of the problem to hand. Politicians may believe they are acting from principle, but in fact they will be trying to mobilize resources that had previously proved to be beyond the reach of political competitors. An entrenched elite will grow decadent, corrupt and finally ineffective. A rising elite will expose obvious political shortcomings in the name of an ideal or programme. We can take the sorry comedy at face value, or opt for a more compelling analysis. Political conflict (everywhere and always) is merely a competition between elites based on perceived advantage. Pareto accepts that there are apparent changes of government, dressed up sometimes as radical breaches with old habits and customs. All that happens, in fact, is that one aristocracy is replaced by another. A new elite, for a time, may be more vigorous and effective. It will not help to have lofty ideals. Politics is (potentially deadly) struggle. The point is to be victorious, at whatever cost.

Pareto endorses much of the Marxian critique of parliamentary representation, while categorically rejecting the Marxian solution. In his view, parliamentary deliberation is inevitably a species of horse trading among private (perhaps predominantly class) interests. His point, however, is that a congeries of private interests cannot mobilize sufficient support around the basic goals that states have to accomplish. A state needs to be strong in relation to potential competitors. Indeed, the satisfaction of the private interests within a state cannot be guaranteed if governments simply try to broker a line of least resistance between interests. Weak government will ultimately undermine private interests. The state would ultimately be a prey to internal and external forces, unable to pursue consistent policies. Pareto's is a plea to free the state from the constraint of representative interests.

Pareto gives no clear indication in his writings as to how strong government might be attained, though towards the end of his life he was sympathetic to the rise of Mussolini and the fascists in Italy. He interprets parliamentary government as the end of a natural cycle. He describes the modern parliamentary system as 'the effective instrument of demagogic plutocracy'.[273] Writing in 1921, two years before his death, he could not envisage democratic politics of any kind surviving what he terms the 'vicissitudes of plutocracy'.[274] Government in organized societies, he argues, is 'regulated in the main by two agencies: consent and force'.[275] He felt he was witnessing the end of an era of consent, to be followed inevitably by a sustained period of authoritarian government.

Theory began to catch up with practice as authoritarian politics made headway throughout Europe. Italian fascism, in particular, announced itself as a thoroughly modern phenomenon, unlike earlier authoritarian regimes and difficult to locate on the political spectrum. Exploiting language drawn from Sorel and revolutionary syndicalism, the movement could appeal to critics of capitalism whose previous sympathies had been with the left. Mussolini himself had for a time used Marxist language, before the question of Italian involvement in the First World War led to a splintering and reorientation of anti-capitalist thinking. Contrasting conceptions of the state finally clarified ideological positions, with fascists of all stripes urging governments to use force to impose order on a potentially chaotic world.

Matters came to a head in Italy between 1919 and 1922. The success of the Russian Revolution in 1917 had shaken the confidence of establishments throughout Europe. Revolutionary turmoil in Italian factories brought the prospect of Bolshevism closer, precipitating (what many may have regarded as) an unholy alliance of defenders of capitalism and implacable critics of liberalism and parliamentary politics. The middle ground that liberals and reformist socialists had previously occupied lost all credibility in the space of two years. The spectacle of liberal political leaders encouraging Mussolini to form a government illustrates just how far a preoccupation with order had come to dominate political debate.

From the perspective of the right, just as from the left, parliamentary politics appeared to be collapsing under its own weight. Liberalism was seen as the flaw at the heart of the system, undermining the foundations of any conceivable political order. What had happened in Italy in 1922 was regarded as a foretaste of the fate of other parliamentary regimes. The choice appeared to be between Bolshevism or a species of explicit authoritarianism. On this view of things, there is no scope for limited government or a merely instrumental conception of the state as a means to serve the interests of society. Political order is seen to be a necessary condition for any other satisfactions that human beings might collectively attain. And it has to be imposed by force.

These are not new ideas. They have been a feature of European political thought since Hobbes's *Leviathan* (1651). What is novel, however, is the administrative and technical capacity of the state in a modern context. Total control and surveillance of society was simply not an option in the seventeenth century. It remains a moot point, of course, whether it is theoretically conceivable at all. It was nevertheless clear by the early twentieth century that populations could be mobilized and manipulated in unprecedented ways. Temptations were available to elites that looked irresistible in the light of the perceived weakness of the liberal constitutional state.

These arguments were drawn together with devastating effect in Carl Schmitt's *The Concept of the Political* (1927).[276] Schmitt is a controversial figure, not least because he joined the National Socialist Party in Germany in 1933 and for a time presented himself as something of an apologist for the Nazi regime. His ideas, however, capture the crisis of the 1920s with ruthless clarity, and remain disturbing to us precisely because we no longer feel we can take the normative foundation of our societies for granted. Like Pareto, Schmitt based his theoretical critique of liberalism on close study of parliamentary politics in practice.[277] He was haunted by the erosion of a specifically public sphere by the multifarious interests of society. He felt government had been reduced to service status, ministering to the needs of powerful private interests. In the process, the liberal distinction between public and private realms is effectively undermined. Private interests are in a position to dominate public debate so thoroughly that it is no longer possible to distinguish their preferences from the wider good of the state. The relationship between the 'general will' and the 'will of all' in Rousseau's analysis has been effectively inverted, such that a public interest cannot properly be characterized at all.[278] Liberal theory, in Schmitt's view, portrays society as a plurality of interests, more or less compatible, with no prospect of an encompassing good that might bind a society together.

Schmitt's basic premise is that social order is always under threat, from either internal dissension or external powers. This predicament is a limiting condition for any viable politics. It will not lose its relevance as societies become more sophisticated or interdependent. Liberal theories are built upon a progressive conception of history, picturing a future in which social and economic values predominate. Schmitt dismisses such views as naively (and finally dangerously) utopian. Organized societies never cease to define themselves in opposition to one another. In political terms, this reduces to an existential confrontation between 'friend and enemy'.[279] We can describe human relationships in all sorts of other ways. We may want to focus on the contrasting values that individuals or communities may profess, their different conceptions of beauty, their capacities to exploit and manage human and natural resources. These different criteria can connect us in all manner of cross-cutting ways; but they cannot overcome or replace the basic need to impose order on a territory. Note that Schmitt does not discuss the normative criteria that may distinguish political 'friends' from political 'enemies'. His point is more basic. We cannot think of communities at all unless we picture them locked in territorial competition and opposition. We cannot persuade communities to endorse our values or to subscribe to a common cause unconditionally. They may (contingently) support us on this or that issue. Yet nothing can guarantee *our* continuance as a community unless *we* resolve to defend ourselves and assert ourselves against others.

The point to stress, for Schmitt, is that political order must be considered as a good in itself. Within a political order we may be conditionally attached to a variety of goods. We may temporarily devote our energies and resources to certain objectives rather than others, secure in the knowledge that political order gives us the space to make choices. Our attachment to political order itself, however, should be beyond choice. Where we can agree to join a private association on certain terms, our allegiance to the state must be unconditional. Without that commitment, none of our enjoyments would be secure. While it might make sense to regard our endorsement of particular policies as conditional (Schmitt is cautious on this point), we cannot treat political order as a possible good alongside others.

In this view, liberalism and democracy are both based upon conceptual confusion. Extra-legal values are invoked to judge the legitimacy of political order. We may regard liberalism (or democracy) as the best political means to attain humanitarian policies or maximal wealth. For these values to work politically, all right-thinking people would have to endorse them. And that can be discounted. Schmitt argues forcefully that political order cannot be a lowest common denominator of views in a pluralist society. No such common factor exists. Political order needs to be imposed precisely because opinions in a society will naturally fragment. Consensus cannot be deep enough to function politically. In its absence, a community must use the force at its disposal to shape the parameters of a shared life.

Schmitt uses extreme cases to highlight the concept of the state and the political. Liberalism, in his view, had tried to domesticate politics by focusing on the civil practices of moral and economic exchange. Instead of recognizing force and conflict as inescapable phenomena among human beings, liberals translate these notions into 'competition in the domain of economics and discussion in the intellectual realm'.[280] These activities, however, presuppose the existence of an established political order. Liberals, here as elsewhere, get the cart before the horse, treating the fruits of political order as instances of properly political activity. Yet only force (or the threat of force) can create and maintain political order. In quiet, comfortable and prosperous times we can forget this hard truth. But we also know that only states can declare war on each other. And when this happens, we cannot choose (as individuals) not to be at war. We are committed, no matter how deep our reservations may be. We can be compelled by the state to kill complete strangers and to put ourselves in harm's way. Nothing in the repository of liberal political concepts can quite prepare us for this extremity. It is an existential fate rather than a choice. In an important sense, for Schmitt, liberalism is an anti-politics. It should not surprise us that a politics so conceived would appear to be ineffective.

Schmitt's is a harsh view of politics, committing everyone to take sides unconditionally. Within these terms of reference, it should not surprise us that Schmitt (as a German patriot) felt that he had to support the Nazi state. Between 1933 and 1936, indeed, he enjoyed status and authority through the Nazi regime, though after 1936 he became an object of suspicion in some Nazi circles and progressively withdrew from public life. His political theory, however, must be read as a body of ideas distinct from the regime. There is no doubt that it inclined him to support Hitler and his coterie, though in later life he was anxious to distance himself from the more odious aspects of the regime. Schmitt's political entanglements do him no credit. Yet he has provided a defence of authoritarian politics that demands attention, fitted to the exigencies of a mass-based society. Whether we like it or not, an authoritarian strand persists in the European political tradition. In some guises it is compatible with democratic politics, and it is certainly appealing to electorates in times of crisis. It has to be grasped theoretically, both as a response to circumstances and as a normative body of ideas.

The fascist preoccupation with order led to the formulation of a theory of the totalitarian state. We owe the term in its modern form to Giovanni Gentile. A philosopher of genuine distinction, Gentile was a prominent figure, along with Benedetto Croce, in the resurgence of interest in philosophical idealism that flourished in Italy in the early decades of the twentieth century. As a philosophical school, idealists opposed materialism and positivism. There was no pretension among them to present a shared political position. Gentile and Croce, for example, who enjoyed a rich philosophical collaboration before 1922, actually split with the advent of fascism. Instructively, though, Croce, who presented himself for most of his life as a vigorous champion of political liberalism, had initially been guardedly sympathetic to Mussolini and the fascists, as a possible means of imposing order and effective government in face of the chaos and corruption that marked the immediate post-First World War years in Italy. Croce denounced fascism after the regime-inspired assassination of Matteotti, a socialist parliamentary deputy who had been an outspoken critic of the fascists in government, in 1924. The crisis sparked by the assassination was a defining moment in the development of a distinctively fascist state. Thereafter the fascist government progressively dispensed with the parliamentary trappings that had brought Mussolini to power. Croce responded by styling himself a public critic of fascism, albeit through the printed page rather than active involvement in political resistance. Gentile, by contrast, embraced the regime, serving as Minister of Education in Mussolini's first cabinet until 1924, and generally providing intellectual justification for a regime that professed to be inaugurating a radically new order in Italy.

Gentile was thus always close to the fascist regime. Though fascist doctrine shifted between 1922 and 1943, not always in ways that Gentile welcomed, he enjoyed authoritative status as the regime's 'official' philosopher. This, to be sure, is a dubious privilege. It has done little to enhance Gentile's philosophical reputation. He remains a tainted source, despite wide appreciation of his philosophical range and originality. His historical significance, however, is beyond dispute. He was not only a major influence on Mussolini, but also the actual author of some of the writings on fascism that appeared under Mussolini's name.[281] Political scientists examining fascism as a phenomenon have been reluctant to take it seriously as a body of ideas. To some extent this is understandable, since fascism prided itself as a philosophy of life and action, rather than as a narrow political theory or ideology, drawing eclectically from movements that challenged liberalism and socialism in a variety of guises. Yet Gentile's conception of totalitarianism is a distinctively fascist contribution to political theory. For all that the concept remains deeply troubling, it clearly has a resonance beyond the fascist era.

Gentile's political philosophy exploits standard objections to theories focused on the individual, but with a novel twist. He accepts, with Hegel and the nationalists, that individuals are in an important sense products of their communities. But where Hegel stressed established social structures, and nationalists a primordial culture or ethnic community, Gentile highlights the active role of the state, creating unity rather than passively reflecting it. It is not enough to value the traditions and practices that have shaped a way of life. Citizens have to identify with the organized projection of those values by the state, treating the state as the public embodiment of their personalities. Thus, where liberalism had sought to contain the state through constitutional procedures in the interest of the freedom of individuals, Gentile invites individuals to see their personal interests and values as inseparable from the state. There is no room for a distinction between public and private spheres in this scheme of things. Everything that we may value as individuals is evanescent, vulnerable to accident and misfortune; but the state can elevate the ordinary things we do to a higher status, permanently involved with the collective political life of fellow citizens over continuing generations.

The potential for a properly organized state to mould the attitudes of citizens is thus limitless. In an important essay of 1929 (*Origins and Doctrine of Fascism*) that continues to frame discussions of fascist theory, Gentile stresses the mobilizing role of the state as the distinctive feature of fascist doctrine.[282] Above all, he insists on the 'totalitarian character' of fascism, concerning itself 'not only with political order and direction of the nation, but with its will, thought and sentiment'.[283] The state, for Gentile, can fashion any aspect of a way of life. It does not have to match a preconceived theoretical model in order to be regarded as legitimate. The state creates the attitudes and values that enable citizens to assess their public life. The idea of a political or social construction, newly fashionable in contemporary political theory, is taken by Gentile to an extreme. If, epistemologically, there is nothing outside the mind by which it can be judged, it follows that political orders must establish their own terms of reference.[284] They may be more or less successful, but they cannot be illegitimate.

Gentile explores the implications of the priority of the state ruthlessly. Because 'the state is conceived as prior to the individual', individuals cannot possibly be in a position to lay down criteria for the proper pursuit of public objectives.[285] They cannot 'contract', actually or hypothetically, to institute a state. The status of being an 'individual' is conferred on citizens by the state. They have neither capacities nor concepts of themselves outside that political and social framework. Gentile terms the relationship between 'state' and 'individual' in fascist theory a 'necessary synthesis'.[286] Neither is conceivable without the other, but (specific) individuals necessarily fulfil a subordinate role. Individuals are integral components of a wider social and political entity. Taken in isolation, they are of no significance whatever. Each of us can be replaced, our roles and responsibilities assumed by others. The state, however, is irreplaceable, in both phenomenological and normative terms.

The significance of political leadership is stressed throughout Gentile's political writings, in terms that are sometimes difficult to take seriously. The role of the *Duce*, for example, embodying the will of the people, giving direction and significance to people's lives, is intelligible only in the heady political atmosphere of the 1920s and 1930s. We should hesitate, however, before congratulating ourselves on our good sense. Democratic politics, even in stable parliamentary contexts, has often elevated the personal qualities of leaders unrealistically, using the personality of a leader to convey a style or set of priorities. Modern political campaigning invites voters to identify with leaders. Leaders are also expected to set agendas. These are very much political practices adapted to the peculiar demands of mass politics, where electorates (taken in the round) cannot be assumed to have the time or expertise to pass considered judgements on policies. We expect politics to be driven by elites, for better or worse. Fascist theory and rhetoric had grasped the significance of leadership in mass contexts long before liberalism and socialism. Gentile, in particular, was happy to see a strong leader adapting policy to circumstances, even at the cost of apparent contradiction. It is precisely the responsibility of a leader to make those adjustments. Leaders cannot wait upon elaborate discussions and brokerage between groups and factions. Politics is not simply a matter of grasping opportunities, but of creating them, imposing a style. Fascist political ambition far exceeds the bounds of modern elite leadership, but the role of the citizen remains passive in both contexts.

Gentile's philosophy of politics and the state is most fully worked out in *Genesis and Structure of Society* (1943), completed shortly before his assassination in 1944. What emerges is a powerful defence of the priority of the political over any other attachments. In language adapted from Hegel's *Philosophy of Right*, he describes the state as 'the universal common aspect of the will'.[287] Other spheres of organized social life – the economy and religion, for example – assume significance in relation to criteria that are finally political in origin. Outside political life, institutions and practices are inconceivable. Gentile goes so far as to portray religious sentiment as 'immanent in serious political action'.[288] In this world of ideas, everything is subsumed under politics, not least because politics creates and sustains a structure of order that is a necessary condition for human flourishing of any kind.

Political order is here conceived in the broadest possible terms, epitomized in a speech of Mussolini's given on 28 October 1925 that became notorious in fascist propaganda: 'Everything for the state; nothing against the state; nothing outside the state.' In *Genesis and Structure of Society*, Gentile is more subtle. Again following Hegel, he treats human personality as intrinsically tied to a conception of institutional order. Rights are conferred on individuals by the state, just as the development of social capacities and self-awareness is dependent upon an array of complex social institutions and practices. In Gentile's phrase. 'the concept of an individual' is immanent in 'the concept of society'.[289] At one level we can accept this thought, as Hegel did, without endorsing the idea of a totalitarian state. What is missing in Gentile's account is precisely Hegel's elaborate discussion of civil society in the *Philosophy of Right*, leaving individuals conceptually unadorned in relation to an all-embracing idea of the state.

The institutional detail of a totalitarian state need not detain us here. From a theoretical perspective, the point to stress is that state and society are treated as indivisible entities, demanding central management and control. Liberal theory, in particular, had adapted to the demands of mass society with immense difficulty. Fascism embraced that challenge, and was able to present itself as a vibrant movement shaking tired cultures out of their complacency. The appeal in contexts of economic and international crisis is now too obvious to ignore. The political experiment, of course, was disastrous. Yet a challenge had been thrown down to political theory in the most dramatic circumstances. Worrying numbers of citizens in liberal and democratic states had welcomed a political doctrine that insisted on their permanent subordination to wielders of power. This was a challenge to entrenched assumptions in European political thought. Raw politics had been resurrected, with all its frightening implications.

10

Liberal Democracy

In 1939 Europe was plunged into war again after a respite of barely twenty years. Precipitating circumstances looked significantly different from 1914, with stark ideological divisions superimposed on traditional balance-of-power rivalries. Obsessions with order in some states had made peace in Europe more vulnerable, in the process threatening the stability (and even existence) of specific states. The response to the political and economic crises of the 1920s and 1930s had made public and economic life throughout the continent more problematic than ever. If stability and order are regarded as necessary conditions for human flourishing, then states had failed at the most basic level.

From a broader perspective, the two world wars of the first half of the twentieth century are best seen as failures of the European system of states, rather than straightforward consequences of aberrant policies. Neither parliamentary politics nor capitalist economics could be taken for granted. Europe as a continent had been structurally (and perhaps permanently) weakened. Superpower confrontation between the United States and the Soviet Union dictated the alignment of states, with far-reaching consequences for the day-to-day conduct of politics in both Western and Eastern Europe. European political elites had been shaken out of their complacency in the most brutal fashion.

Peace in Europe in 1945 appeared to divide the continent along stark ideological lines. Fascism had been defeated, but broadly liberal-democratic states confronted a communist bloc that used Marxist-Leninist language to legitimize one-party rule. The reality, however, was significantly different. In both contexts there had been a marked retreat from the apocalyptic politics and language of the 1920s and 1930s. The Soviet Union behaved in international politics like a conventional great power, while liberal-democratic states sought to fashion a working 'contract' between state and citizens that would serve as a buffer against political extremism of both left and right. With the collapse of the Soviet empire in 1989–91, liberal democracy was (rashly) proclaimed as the only form of political organization fitted to meet the demands of the modern world.[1]

In the immediate aftermath of war, political expectations were drastically scaled down. In their different ways, communism and fascism had both treated ordinary political activity as a problem to be solved, offering satisfactions to citizens that could not be attained in a world of compromise, bargaining and accommodation. With the benefit of hindsight, however, the cost of utopia looked unacceptably high to citizens who had variously experienced war, the Holocaust and drastic reductions in civic freedoms, all in the pursuit of an 'ideal' way of life. The politics of total transformation soon lost its appeal. Conventional politics might be a muddle; but it must be treated as a muddle that cannot be qualitatively transcended. The great ideological projects of left and right were now regarded by growing numbers of theorists and citizens as mere pretexts for authoritarian rule. Above all, there was deep suspicion of the idea of a theoretical blueprint that could replace the various compromises that shape politics in practice. Utopia was rejected on both theoretical and practical grounds.

The retreat from a politics of high confrontation and mobilization in liberal democracies repays careful attention. Arguments against utopia were variously couched. Karl Popper, the distinguished philosopher of science, was inspired by the political catastrophe in Europe to try to rebut the very idea of a perfect society. Two highly polemical books, *The Open Society and its Enemies* (1945) and *The Poverty of Historicism* (1957, previously published in article form in 1944–5), focused on two flaws at the heart of utopian thought.[2] Popper rejects the claims, central to the doctrines of Hegel and Marx as he understood them, that theoretical analysis of the course of historical developments yields any grounds for predictions regarding the future. He accepts, of course, that we can test economic, social and political hypotheses at a micro-level, specifying relevant conditions in which particular outcomes could be anticipated. But he denies that sweeping historical change can ever be an appropriate topic for theoretical prediction. Coupled with this, he counters the idea that society as a whole can be an object of study. In Popper's view, a society is an aggregation of individuals pursuing various goals from specific perspectives. The interaction of such individuals will lead to complex outcomes, which can be studied in determinate circumstances, but not from the standpoint of society as an entity. In this account, the idea of a society is a theoretical fiction, more or less useful (or more or less useless). The proper focus for a social science should rather be individuals in their diversity.

These are contentious views, which arouse controversy to this day. Popper's attempted refutation of historicism, the view that there are specific laws of historical development, has a logical simplicity and power that still demand attention. In a preface to *The Poverty of Historicism* he reduces a complex argument to five principal propositions. He claims, in the first place, that 'the course of human history is strongly influenced by the growth of human knowledge'.[3] Even Marxists, insisting that ideas are the products of material conditions, would have to accept this point if Marxism is to be considered any sort of contribution to knowledge. Secondly (and crucially) Popper argues that 'we cannot predict, by rational or scientific methods, the future growth of our scientific knowledge'.[4] This would amount to claiming to 'anticipate today what we shall know only tomorrow'.[5] It follows from this (thirdly) that 'we cannot, therefore, predict the future course of history'.[6] This means (fourthly) 'that we must reject the possibility of a *theoretical history*', and (fifthly) that 'the fundamental aim of historicist methods is . . . misconceived'.[7]

Popper saw this as a devastating and irrefutable argument. The political implications are clear. Any elite that set itself up in authority because it had grasped a theoretical truth about the development of history could be dismissed as bogus. No such expertise is possible. Nor could an elite close off avenues of theoretical or practical research in the name of knowledge claims entrenched in a political ideology. These knowledge claims could only be regarded as provisional, useful for the moment in the light of experience, but with no pretensions to permanence or certitude. We could indeed have confidence in knowledge claims only if we left open the possibility that they might in fact be refuted. Knowledge, in any sphere, should be regarded as provisional and conditional. Recognizing these limits commits us to an open and tentative politics.

Popper's development of these ideas in *The Open Society and its Enemies* is deeply problematic. The book is conceived as a critique of totalitarianism, focusing on the doctrines that have been used to buttress different styles of totalitarian regime. Popper endorses the theoretical position he had advanced in *The Poverty of Historicism*, adding sustained criticism of historical figures who have contributed in any measure to the emergence of what might be described as a collectivist politics. These are not necessarily defences of totalitarianism in its modern forms, barely conceivable before the advent of mass-based industrial societies, but theoretical positions that justify the logical or normative priority of society (or groups of any kind) to the individual.

Popper singles out Plato, Hegel and Marx for special treatment. His scholarship (it must be said) is not always careful, and he admits that he adopted a harsher and more emotional tone than we would normally expect to find in a historical treatment of political ideas.[8] That Plato, who created a style of philosophical criticism that is still indispensable to political theory, should be castigated as a proto-totalitarian seemed preposterous to some scholars. Others objected to the reduction of Marx's rich analysis of the relationship between ideas and economic context to a series of historical prophecies that have turned out to be false. Popper's criticism of Hegel is even more dismissive, attributing direct responsibility for totalitarianism to Hegel's doctrines. He asserts without qualification that 'the formula of the fascist brew is in all countries the same: Hegel plus a dash of nineteenth-century materialism'.[9] Scholars have deplored the selective quotation and failure to engage constructively with Hegel's complex discussion of the logical and historical presuppositions of individual agency. To describe Hegel as an advocate of a 'new tribalism' does scant justice to his subtle account of the interdependence of state and civil society.[10] The fact remains, however, that Popper touches raw nerves in collectivist theory. The modern debate between (so-called) liberals and communitarians has gone beyond Popper's terms of reference.[11] Yet it is recognizably a reiteration of a debate that Popper had contributed to in the bitter aftermath of the Holocaust and war.

Popper focused specifically on the folly at the heart of any theory that seeks to mobilize populations around the idea of a collective good. *The Open Society and its Enemies* can be read as a direct rebuttal of totalitarianism in all its forms, with little to say about the style of parliamentary politics that seemed to be vindicated in the post-war settlement. Hayek, however, adopted a broader strategy, treating totalitarian thinking as an incipient threat to the practice of parliamentary politics itself. An economist by background and training, Hayek uses the idea of a market as a model for social co-ordination among strangers. Shifts in prices reflect changing relationships between supply and demand. Individuals make their choices in terms of their own priorities, with no need for authoritative agencies (such as governments) to intervene in a process that actually has no ideal outcomes. Preferences change, prices adapt, suppliers respond. The model is simple. Governments, of course, have a role. Free markets are not *natural* products. They depend upon a legal framework, transparent flows of information, a balanced money supply, a means of seeking redress for wrongdoing, and many other practices and institutions. What governments cannot do, in this scheme of things, is to specify priorities for individuals. The market as a mechanism presupposes a wide area of individual discretion and freedom. Governments have a vital (but limited) role in maintaining appropriate conditions.

It is easy to appreciate the implications of Hayek's individualist philosophy for totalitarianism. What is more disturbing to the conventional wisdom in parliamentary democracies, however, is Hayek's analysis of the way in which liberal opinion has absorbed so many of the collectivist assumptions that had informed socialism. In *The Road to Serfdom* (1944) Hayek focuses on the threat to freedom from even notionally benign intervention by governments.[12] Attempts to maintain a 'just price' or 'fair wage' within the context of a competitive economic system, for example, actually involve distortions of the market in line with the preferences of planners.[13] But these preferences enjoy no special status. They are simply the priorities of a select group who happen to be in positions of power and authority. There is no 'ideal' distribution of benefits and rewards in a complex society. In democratic contexts, politicians are under pressure from voters, producers and consumers. Interested parties will have very specific views about the levels of governmental support their activities deserve. They will focus their efforts on influencing key decision-makers however they can. The outcome is a politically expedient rather than a rational decision, responsive to vested interests rather than the demands of justice.

Planning requires bureaucracies. And in bureaucracies the quality of decision making depends upon the flow of information up and down a hierarchy. As information flows, so it is sifted. Members of a professional bureaucracy will have their own interests and axes to grind. They will be exposed to personal and professional pressures, striving to please and flatter some key players and to marginalize others. They will also be exposed to wider pressures, much as politicians are. Nobody has a dispassionate or detached perspective in this process. Far from constituting a preferable alternative to the (perceived) anarchy of a market, Hayek sees planning as a necessarily distorted process, loaded in favour of the interests of entrenched groups. These are not problems that more (rational?) planning can resolve. Experts may be called in, but they will have their own pet projects and views. Information flows will continue to be distorted, generating an ever more cumbersome administrative apparatus with increased opportunities to shape policy, formally and informally.

We can assume that a decision-making process of this kind would be slow. It would also be unlikely to reflect the interests of citizens. Co-ordination from the centre presupposes authorization for activities that are radically devolved in market systems. Authorization takes time. By the time it is granted, circumstances may have changed. Typically, bureaucracies bring last year's conventional wisdom to tackle this year's problems.

The unintended consequences of decisions will also take time to work through the system. Anomalies will arise, demanding more attention and further distortions. Citizens (we can assume) will soon recognize the shortcomings of the system and try to devise their own means of managing what may well appear to them to be absurd situations. Formal planning generates black markets. Clientele networks develop, along with a cynical line in political humour.

Elaborate welfare states, in Hayek's view, though well-intentioned, contain the seeds that might later develop into full-blown totalitarianism. In *The Road to Serfdom* Hayek sounds a warning shot, striving to alert a complacent political generation to the perils they are drifting towards. He recognized that conventional wisdom tended in precisely the opposite direction. One reading of the political disasters of the 1920s and 1930s suggests that elites have to take good care of the working masses in order to stave off any flirtation with political extremism. Hayek opposes such thinking, on both political and economic grounds. Persistent government intervention (micro-management) would, in his view, ratchet up public spending over successive business cycles, leading to an inexorable rise in inflation. At the same time, the scope for individual initiative would be progressively narrowed, effectively undermining the source of the dynamism of Western political cultures. Hayek thus combines the economics of Adam Smith with the classical liberalism of Constant and Tocqueville to forge a potent political doctrine, specifically adapted to meet the challenge of mid-century mass-based politics.

Hayek's fullest statement of his position is in *The Constitution of Liberty* (1960).[14] In this text he defends liberal (and limited) politics from first principles. He sets schemes of political co-ordination and control in the broad context of the survival of social orders in uncertain contexts. All societies face open futures, with neither the power nor the resources to guarantee their continued flourishing. A political order may be seen (among other things) as a problem-solving device, designed to maximize the co-operative potential of strangers. Note that strangers cannot be expected to subscribe to common goals. We do not know what is most important to them. Nor should we assume that their values will be stable over time. An elite may try to mould a society in its own image, but only by incurring immense economic and political costs. The attempt to micro-manage an entire society is actually self-defeating. The more we try to focus the energy and initiative of citizens on prescribed goals, the less flexible society as a whole will become. Hayek sees the economic, technical and political dominance of Europe from the early modern period as a product of a set of practices that had enlarged the scope for individuals to address their own problems. The Renaissance, Reformation and Enlightenment thus constitute a complex series of interconnected (but specifically unpredictable) processes. No one could have planned a sequence of development on this scale, though with hindsight we can grasp something of the way it has emerged. If individual initiative is seen as the dynamic core of this activity, then political steps to channel that initiative could have dire consequences. Hayek's cardinal assumption is that individuals (and societies) face unpredictable (and potentially threatening) futures. We simply do not know (and cannot know) what problems we will have to confront in the future. It follows, on this view, that as individuals (and societies) we should endorse institutions and practices that enable us to be maximally responsive. In evolutionary terms, an open society is far more likely to maintain itself and flourish over the long term than a society organized around a set of centrally imposed values.

Hayek treats liberty as a grounding assumption, on both moral and prudential grounds. He accepts the Kantian idea that individuals should be treated as ends in themselves, rather than as means towards some other good, but also contends that we have strong practical incentives to enlarge the sphere of freedom whenever possible. What this might require in legislative terms will depend upon circumstances. Hayek is at his most perceptive in discussions of the relationship between liberalism and democracy. He is unhappy with the conventional idea that we just happen to live in 'liberal democracies', as if no conceptual problems were involved in running the two doctrines together. The 'doctrinaire democrat', for Hayek, is a principled advocate of 'popular sovereignty'.[15] Democrats believe in majority rule, thus enabling a minority of potential voters to speak for the people as a whole. Hayek has no problems with pragmatic recourse to majority decisions, provided limits are specified to the range of issues that might be so decided. Majority rule as a free-standing principle, however, is 'unlimited and unlimitable'.[16] If the 'people' (always a mysterious entity) have expressed their 'will' according to a democratic decision procedure, then nothing (in pure democratic theory) could justify resistance or opposition. Majorities, of course, are arbitrary, shifting with fashion and circumstance. Hayek's fear is that the 'ideal of democracy' leads to 'the justification of a new arbitrary power'.[17] With the benefit of hindsight (and experience of elaborate and costly electoral campaigns aimed at voters whose direct involvement with political issues is limited), this is an open invitation to elites to mobilize popular opinion for their own ends. Democrats, in this view, may (or may not) be attached to the principle of individual liberty. We simply do not know how political opinions and fortunes will develop over time. In mass-based democracies, elites may offer electorates more than governments can reasonably provide in order to gain popular support. The upshot could well be that liberty will be sacrificed for welfare, as Tocqueville had earlier feared. In modern democratic contexts, Hayek accepts that we cannot dispense with popular elections. He insists, however, that if democracy is to function effectively, it must be limited by liberal principles. Without such a limiting condition in place, popular democracy is but a short step away from what we might style 'soft' totalitarianism, preferable (no doubt) to earlier brutal versions, but none the less a deadly threat to liberty and all that goes with it.

Institutional and policy details need not detain us unduly here. In broad terms Hayek tries to maintain a distinction between the state as a framework of rules and government as a means of pursuing specific objectives. He accepts that the state is (always and necessarily) a coercive apparatus, and strives accordingly to limit its activities to matters that are indispensable to individuals in the pursuit of substantive goals, whatever they might be. In this view, it is certainly not a proper use of the state to direct individuals to particular objectives rather than others. For Hayek it is of paramount importance that an individual should be 'subject only to the same laws as all his fellow citizens . . . immune from arbitrary confinement and free to choose his work', and that he should be 'able to own and acquire property'.[18] Interference by the state in these spheres would necessarily be coercive; and since the substantive priorities that individuals set themselves cannot be assessed against an ideal criterion, any attempt to use the resources of the state to persuade individuals to accommodate their interests to collective goals would be unjustified.

Coercion can, of course, be justified in order to maintain a framework of public rules. Without a legal order, strangers cannot co-operate together, individuals cannot plan their future activities with a reasonable assurance that procedures and practices will be honoured, and each of us would have to devote time and resources to security matters that would always remain beyond our control. Life would be an uphill struggle. Public trust (what modern theorists have described as 'social capital') would be eroded. This would not necessarily amount to a 'state of nature'; but certainly we would be loath to look beyond family and friends for services that could not be provided immediately. Coercion to sustain a viable public order actually enlarges the scope for individual activities, provided a line is drawn between rules and procedures on the one side and substantive goals on the other.

Hayek is best known as a staunch defender of economic liberalism in its modern form, arguing for the withdrawal of government from market activities wherever possible. Indeed he became a highly influential figure in Britain and the United States in the 1970s, as conservative governments sought to limit the role of the state and to 'privatize' key functions. His political philosophy, however, should be considered in broader perspective. His conception of limited government is driven by normative criteria. He combines scepticism about the normative status of substantive preferences and choices with a strong commitment to the conditions that would have to be satisfied for individuals to exercise their discretion and talents optimally. To be sure, maintaining a distinction between formal and substantive criteria is not without its own difficulties. But without some such distinction, it is easy to see how the state might engulf all social and civil arenas. Simply by recognizing moral and cultural diversity, we commit ourselves to limiting the way in which the state may be used to buttress certain values rather than others. Governments have both carrots and sticks at their disposal to focus the minds of citizens. Either way, though, government would be intruding on individual conduct with no conceivable theoretical warrant. In these circumstances, in fact, government policy would be fashioned to suit the interests of the influential and powerful, much as Marx had argued. Yet, for Hayek, the Marxist remedy is worse than the liberal disease. A properly liberal theory of the state would not be exposed to the same objections. Whether political elites and electorates would accept these constraints is quite another matter.

For all their polemical zeal, Popper and Hayek set themselves modest political goals. In different ways, they sought to expose the hubris at the heart of the rationalist follies of the first half of the twentieth century. They had distinctive views of the style and scope of a balanced politics, embracing diversity within certain (more or less closely specified) parameters. From a philosophical point of view, however, the focus of their work was largely negative, creating the critical space for a modest and reasonable politics that citizens could embrace once political illusions had been dispelled.

In some quarters it was accepted that normative political philosophy in the classical style was neither possible nor desirable. Indeed the death of political philosophy was proclaimed by political theorists themselves.[19] In reality normative theory continued, though it was conducted in a cautious (sometimes narrowly academic) style. Citizens and elites had largely accepted that 'high' politics was a dangerous game. Attention switched instead to a 'low' political agenda, focused on distribution, rights and provision of opportunities for citizens to fashion their lives.

Political priorities ranged across a narrower spectrum. Isaiah Berlin, for example, in a classic inaugural lecture at Oxford in 1958, insisted on a distinction between 'positive' and 'negative' liberty.[20] The focus of the essay is on the way in which the idea of liberty has been used and abused within and beyond the liberal tradition in political theory. Drawing very much on Constant's critique of Rousseau, Berlin argues that the diversity of views in any conceivable society in modern times precludes the pursuit of a 'common good' for citizens. Citizens may (or may not) favour redistributive policies for the poor, they may be more (or less) comfortable with a state that celebrates a unique cultural or religious heritage, more (or less) enthusiastic about the subordination of their personal interests to the perceived needs of the wider polity. These may be worthy goals, but they are contentious. Right-thinking people will come down on different sides in any dispassionate consideration of their merits. It certainly cannot be supposed that differences on these issues are consequences of malice or folly.

Berlin objects (specifically) to the idea that rational reflection can (in principle) resolve these disputes, thus (indirectly) authorizing the state to be used in all manner of ways to encourage us to endorse the appropriate positions. The thought that 'real' freedom should be identified with the pursuit of substantive goals is anathema to him. The state can, of course, intervene coercively in order to achieve certain objectives. But it would not thereby make us more free. Freedom, for Berlin as for Constant, is the absence of constraint, the space to pursue our ends, whatever they may be. This freedom can be abused. It is perfectly proper to constrain felons of various kinds. In these circumstances we restrict freedom as a means of attaining other goals. Whether this is justifiable in a given context is a matter of judgement. But it is always a restriction of freedom.

The priority of liberty was broadly accepted in the affluent parliamentary democracies in the second half of the twentieth century, though it was sometimes defended on terms very different from Berlin's. John Rawls, for example, in his magisterial *A Theory of Justice* (1971), treats liberty as a fundamental starting point for any serious discussion of political philosophy.[21] But that commitment, set in isolation from other values, gives us very little to work with when we consider the ordinary problems that arise in the business of managing a life. Broad acceptance of the priority of liberty leaves other conflicts of value unresolved. The path was thus clear for theorists to direct their attention to more substantive questions of rights and welfare.

Rawls himself holds that liberty outside a context of equal citizenship would be a very poor thing indeed. He is concerned with what we can make of our lives in a concrete sense, not simply on the notion that we have to be free to make choices. Lives are blighted by very tangible circumstances: poverty, ill-health and sheer bad luck. And these constraints will always be with us. As political philosophers, however, we can picture social and political arrangements that make these constraints more or less manageable. The thought here is that none of us deserve our good or bad luck; but as reflective agents we can think about practices and procedures that enable us to mitigate (at least some of) the ills that might befall us.

Rawls couches his argument in abstract terms that sometimes seem remote from ordinary experience. Yet he is guided throughout his discussion by basic intuitions that he supposes will be familiar to all of us. We all know what it is like to feel committed to incompatible goals. When we are not sure what to do next, we think hard. We are aware that our personal flourishing depends upon other people and wider circumstances that we cannot control. But we are not utterly powerless. We can mould (at least some of) these circumstances for ourselves. We are practical agents thoroughly familiar with various schemes of social co-operation. Rawls asks us to focus on the wider implications of the intuitions that inform our ordinary conduct.

A Theory of Justice sparked a resurgence of interest in normative theory, and continues to be hugely influential, especially in Anglo-American political philosophy. Rawls deploys Kantian contractualist argument in order to justify the broad redistributive provisions of a welfare state. He uses the idea of a hypothetical 'original position' to model terms of co-operation that individuals would accept if they were unaware of the role or status they would enjoy in a society.[22] Rawls's supposition is that none of us would be prepared to risk our liberty for the possible enjoyment of other goods. But we would nevertheless recognize that we could not flourish at all if we were not guaranteed access to 'primary social goods', construed as resources we need no matter what specific goals we might seek in life.[23] Thus we could all accept that we need some measure of education and welfare, though we might continue to argue about the appropriate distribution of such resources.

Rawls places his own work within a very clear tradition of liberal political philosophy. His conception, which he describes as 'justice as fairness', 'generalizes and carries to a higher level of abstraction the familiar theory of the social contract as found, say, in Locke, Rousseau, and Kant'.[24] Indeed, in a set of posthumously published lectures, he treats the figures who have contributed to the development of his own ideas in sympathetic detail.[25] What is distinctive in Rawls's position, however, is the close attention he devotes to redistributive principles and priorities. He insists (firstly) that 'each person is to have an equal right to the most extensive basic liberty compatible with a similar liberty for others'; and (secondly) that 'social and economic inequalities are to be arranged so that they are both (a) reasonably expected to be to everyone's advantage, and (b) attached to positions and offices open to all'.[26]

These 'two principles of justice' serve as a touchstone for the resolution of complex dilemmas.[27] The first principle specifies broad rights in a con- stitutional order. The second, the (so-called) 'difference principle', has proved to be much more controversial.[28] Decisions on redistribution are often seen as products of bargaining and compromise in liberal democra- tic polities. This is not enough for Rawls. Bargaining favours vested inter- est, in liberal (as in any other) polities. Rawls is anxious that the sheer luck of being well placed in a bargaining situation should not lead to dispro- portionate advantages in the allocation of life chances. It is a cardinal assumption for him that all citizens should enjoy the benefits of political order, though not necessarily in equal degree. It is vital, however, that where inequalities exist, they should be seen to work for the benefit of the least fortunate in a society. We all benefit from high-class surgery; and training costs. Incentives for surgeons are part of the price we pay for competence. It is not obvious that we benefit in the same measure from some of the other inequalities in our society. Where principled justification is lacking, Rawls asks us to think again about what we are prepared to tolerate.

Rawls assumes from the outset that we are each free and equal persons. Whatever terms of social co-operation we might deem acceptable would have to be compatible with that status for each and every one. How far this injunction should apply, whether to all human beings on the planet or merely to fellow citizens in a democratic state, was a matter that occupied Rawls in later developments of his thought.[29] The point to stress here, however, is that Rawls (in normative terms) will not allow us to treat fellow human beings simply as means in the pursuit of our ends. Whatever fortuitous advantages we may enjoy, we are obliged to take into account the free and equal status of the people we deal with on a day-to- day basis. We may employ them on mutually agreeable terms, though not enslave them. We must assume that they have priorities in their lives, just as we have. Whenever we limit their options, it must be in terms of social benefits which they can regard as necessary or appropriate to continued (mutual but not necessarily equal) enjoyment of a scheme of social co- operation.

In Rawls citizen interests are paramount. Arguments among theorists centre on what a politics that respects basic intuitions would look like. Yet basic intuitions are a notoriously ambiguous guide to normative language. The priority of liberty, for example, vigorously defended by Rawls, could lead politics away from questions of redistribution altogether. Nozick, in *Anarchy, State, and Utopia* (1974), developed an elaborate political theory from the simple premise that individuals have rights, challenging specifi- cally the welfare commitments that were central to the political consensus of the 1960s.[30] In Nozick's argument, government expenditure beyond basic security functions is based on the coercive appropriation of resources accumulated by citizens in the course of their work. Intriguingly, Nozick, like Rawls, can appeal to the authority of Locke, but he derives very different conclusions from the *Two Treatises of Government*. Nozick focuses specifically on (what might be called) Locke's labour theory of value. If, as Locke claimed, we acquire a title to property through our work, then (according to Nozick) the state has no business depriving us of resources without our consent through taxation. If we want education and health care for ourselves and our families, suggests Nozick, we should buy it. The political priorities of governments may be very distant from our own concerns. Liberal advocates of 'negative' freedom thus confront welfare liberals in terms that look every bit as ideological as the arguments between earlier generations of liberals and socialists.

The liberal-democratic political consensus also disguises significant differences regarding grounding assumptions. The conception of the individual at the heart of liberal-democratic theory is challenged by communitarians who see the 'liberal' individual as a product of contingent social and cultural circumstances.[31] In this view, arguments about rights simply tell us how we happen to see ourselves, they cannot be used to support binding commitments that we should properly see ourselves in certain ways.

The communitarian position is not new. In its modern form, it derives specifically from Hegel, though not all communitarians are happy to endorse Hegel's view of the state.[32] The common theme in modern communitarian writings is a rejection of the narrowness of an individualist theory. A calculating utility maximizer might properly be portrayed in a (hypothetical) 'original position', but the image itself would not be relevant in cultures where social roles are more prominent in discussions of rights and responsibilities. In this view, individualism is the specific cultural outcome of a complex history. Whether we like it or not, it is nothing more than one culture's view of itself. The argument, however, is sometimes pushed further. The simple (empirical?) claim that individuals are social products is seen by some theorists as a decisive argument against a dominant style of liberal theory.

Liberal political positions are not necessarily challenged, but liberal debate is treated as a parochial exploration of self-understandings within predominantly liberal cultures. Some see no prospect of escape from the obvious circularity of political argument. Rorty, for example, defends a shift away from philosophical argument to rhetorical persuasion.[33] As a matter of effective politics, this might very well make sense. Yet there is deep disquiet in some liberal quarters that our cultural starting points should somehow be beyond critical scrutiny.[34]

The conception of community at the heart of communitarian theory has always looked vulnerable. The idea that we can identify discrete cultural units is as unhistorical as liberal assumptions about the calculations of *homo economicus*. Once the discursive construction of community is factored in, we have a much more rewarding debate about precisely how individuals come to assume specific views of themselves in the first place. This obliges theorists to take raw politics into account. Cultural power becomes a crucial factor in the way individual identities are formed. Cultural power can be abused, quite as much as political or economic power. Yet if normative argument is treated simply as a projection of identity, we are left ill equipped to address questions of coercion and control in principled terms. The challenge here strikes beyond liberal theory to the wider status of political philosophy. The charge that argument is merely a rationalization of interest (of whatever kind) invites us to look again at earlier versions of this highly contentious position. The global context of contemporary debate, however, forces us beyond the conventional terms of reference of liberal theory.

11

Global Politics

At the end of the twentieth century the political world looked more uncertain than at any time since 1945. The dramatic fall of the Berlin Wall (1989) symbolized the end of an era. The ideological rhetoric that underpinned superpower confrontation seemed anachronistic in a world dominated by a single hegemon. Theorists talked (yet again) about the end of ideology. Francis Fukuyama pictured a world which would progressively endorse a liberal democratic consensus in politics and capitalist relations in economics.[1] The reality, however, proved to be much more fragmented.

The global economic context certainly constrains all political actors in the modern world more obviously and directly than in any previous era. Economic interdependence ('globalization') is a fact of life for all states. Economic elites have always looked beyond frontiers for opportunities; but governments have also had to temper the management of their economies to meet competitive challenges that are largely beyond their control. No state is exempt from these constraints, though vulnerability is not equally shared.

The global economy presents the spectre of highly integrated financial markets in cosmopolitan cities, surrounded by hinterlands that are becoming ever more conscious of their distinctive identities in relation to wider national cultures. Integration and disintegration are continuing apace, often in adjacent communities. Received terms of political discourse barely reflect the changes taking place. A state built around a conception of a 'common good' cannot accommodate the array of groups and cultures contending for political, economic and social space in given territories. Political and economic hubs no longer coincide so readily. Governments do not even enjoy the illusion of economic control, as almost instantaneous capital flows threaten to overwhelm even the best-placed treasuries. A global economic system has emerged without corresponding institutions to manage effectively the vagaries of economic co-operation across the planet.

Political elites strive to manage complex interdependence as best they can, with no guarantees that the myriad participants will respect the concerns of others. No political power has the resources to impose its will unilaterally. And weaker players are barely able to make their voices heard. For all the optimistic rhetoric that marked the end of the (so-called) cold war, the political world seems dangerously out of control. States have found that their effective power and autonomy is severely restricted, at a time when democratic electorates are becoming ever more demanding in a multitude of (often incompatible) ways.[2] Some theorists even claim that the era of the nation-state has run its course, to be replaced by a new and uncertain system of global politics.[3]

Just how far states have changed their nature is a much disputed issue that cannot be pursued further here. What is clear, however, is that the focus of political discussion has shifted significantly. Interests of various kinds would traditionally channel their energies towards key decision makers in various spheres, often grouped together as a more or less closely integrated network. It made sense to speak in terms of a 'power elite', gathered in and around government. With the dispersal of power, informal networks have become more important, extending beyond political borders. Theories of democratic accountability in these circumstances are rendered deeply problematic, not least because democratically elected politicians are not in a position to dominate relevant agendas. We continue to use a traditional political language and work through a façade of institutions. Politicians are elected, laws are framed, but governments increasingly operate in a world removed from electorates. The idea of a political manifesto looks touchingly naïve. Who could be held accountable for a political programme that could not (in principle) be put into practice? Governments are integral parts of wider discursive networks. No one calls the shots.

Michel Foucault developed the subversive implications of a stress on discursive contexts most forcefully.[4] In wide-ranging studies of disciplines, discourses and social practices, Foucault focuses on the contingent assumptions that inform various spheres of activity. Conceptions of the person and mental illness, for example, change over time, leading to radically different strategies for dealing with specific aspects of human conduct. These strategies are often justified in terms of scientific or other authoritative views, enshrining truths about human beings and their relationships with one another. In reality, for Foucault, the 'disciplinary' foundations of various social practices reflect, rather, a complex network of social and cultural power relations. Discourse, in this view, projects a conception of the way things stand ('the order of things') that effectively buttresses certain interests rather than others.

The implications for minority groups can be devastating. Practices at the heart of certain minority cultures may be treated as folly, madness or sheer wickedness by establishments. And given the economics of the propagation of knowledge, marginal cultures may be more or less invisible, failing even to register in the range of concerns on public agendas.

Gender, racial and sexual issues have historically been evaded by main-stream (male-dominated) establishment discourses, at best relegated to a 'private' sphere beyond public attention, at worst ignored. But the designation of something as a public or private matter cannot be decided in normatively neutral terms. A normative language will be a product of a hegemonic discourse. It can be challenged, but not from the perspective of 'truth'. Groups and cultures will have different views on these questions. Whichever prevails in public discourse will be a matter of politics and power.

Foucault diagnoses abuses of power, but is much less clear about what should replace 'constrained' social relations. We cannot picture complex social relations without a dynamic of power. A 'frictionless' society is undesirable in theory and barely conceivable in practice. We cannot fix any set of practices in concrete. Contingency frames all our activities. Change in any society is unpredictable, hitting the interests and values of groups and individuals in ways too complex to calculate. We cannot have a theory of how things will change or how we should respond to change. Foucault focuses, instead, on the damage done to groups and individuals at the margins, seeking to undermine the theoretical constraints that prevent them from articulating their interests effectively. This, to be sure, is a normative engagement, though it does not require elaborate theoretical defence. We should not ask Foucault for a theory of the 'good life', because it would inevitably amount merely to a conception of the good viewed from a particular perspective.

Foucault takes the fragmentation of politics seriously. He breaks down concepts like 'state' and 'society' into the discursive networks that sustain sets of practices. His theory reflects the prominence of civil society in a modern context, where associations of various kinds contend for space and shape the character of public life. Where traditional political theory and political science would focus on government as an institutional structure, Foucault talks in terms of 'governmentality', the deeper social and psychological practices that enable structures of power and authority to work.[5] In important respects, authoritative networks are more intrusive even than the totalitarian state. Individuals are socialized to see themselves in specific terms, internalizing moral and social ideas that make them amenable to the requirement of hegemonic groups. The idea of 'conscience', for example, enables individuals to 'police' their own activities, reinforcing values and practices that effectively prevent them from advancing subversive ideas and proposals.

Foucault thus defends a politics of resistance, but not in the name of a specific doctrine or ideology. He disdains political mobilization precisely because it depends for its success on the imposition of views from a notional centre, encouraging passivity and conformism. If power is dispersed in modern contexts, so, too, is protest. Foucault is acutely aware of the threat to individuality and diversity stemming from bogus moral and political solidarity. His critique of political ideologies is aimed at both right and left.

A politics of dispersed resistance runs the real risk of being politically ineffective. In a late newspaper article, Foucault accepts that we might all have an obligation to confront governments, though we cannot urge their permanent replacement by an alternative scheme as a remedy for the myriad misfortunes of being governed.[6] At a minimal level, however, he maintains that we should 'speak out against every abuse of power', not least because 'we are all members of the community of the governed'.[7] Governments presume to concern themselves with the 'welfare of societies', yet set themselves up as the judges of what that might involve.[8] Foucault insists that we have 'an absolute right to stand up and speak to those who hold power', though he is deeply sceptical of the traditional language of rights. We are all (as he puts it) 'just private individuals', but we cannot allow governments to speak for us, 'to reserve a monopoly for themselves' of authoritative pronouncement.[9] This amounts to a minimal exercise of 'international citizenship', despite the obvious absence of an international polity.[10]

Foucault's appeal to a right to judgement for 'private individuals' is intriguing in light of his celebrated critique of the self. No one has argued more forcefully that the self is a social product. The fact that we make personal judgements is not an issue (what else could we do?). But why should we attach normative authority to judgements that are framed and determined by contingent factors? The perspective from which we make our judgements is just one among many others. We may be repelled by the values and choices of others, but what normative significance should we attribute to that reaction? These matters take us to the heart of problems that have bedevilled normative theory for the last 300 years. In different ways theorists have confronted the status of normative judgements, treating them as products of historical circumstances or economic relations or as mere preferences. What Foucault challenges is the very idea of a self that could make authoritative judgements. Yet he also shows vividly that they are inescapable.

Postmodern theorists (drawing extensively on Foucault and Nietzsche) accept that the paradox cannot be resolved. Grand theory is treated as a species of myth, more or less comforting, but with no epistemological or moral status. Human beings simply tell themselves stories. Sometimes they take them very seriously indeed, presuming to impose their stories on others. Intellectual establishments devote time, effort and resources to narrative plausibility, striving to buttress a specific view of the world with whatever imaginative materials are to hand. Political philosophy, from this perspective, is an elaborate narrative game, with possibly serious political consequences. Imposing a set of stories on a whole population is necessarily intrusive. Assuming that the stories themselves have a special status affords a pretext for more drastic measures, moulding populations to fit the requirements of hegemonic groups. From a Foucauldian (or post-modern) position, however, these are not illusions that can be dispelled. A theory of discourse cannot replace discourse. We simply have to accept that we are story-tellers. Our political options are limited. Recognizing the contingency of our stories might encourage us not to impose them on others. But even that strategy presupposes that we can distance ourselves from narrative messages. We may not be disposed to listen to everything that people may be inclined to tell us. Yet how do we draw lines?

Postmodern theory allows only an exiguous role for theory. Theory can highlight what is going on in normative argument, without privileging any substantive arguments. A theoretical warrant for any particular choice or preference is actually ruled out. What we are left with, instead, is raw politics itself. Theorists may favour an inclusive rather than an exclusive politics, without having anything authoritative to say on any given issue. Postmodern theory provides a strategy for reading normative argument, rather than engaging in normative controversy. We are given procedural grounds for preferring an open politics, but very little help when we actually confront hard cases.

Conventional normative theory has thus been assailed in recent decades by a variety of objections to the very idea of a theoretical foundation to discursive politics. The core idea, shared by postmodernists, communitarians and multiculturalists, is that a critical vocabulary and reflective capacity are embedded in a specific social and cultural context. Terms of reference are construed as culturally circumscribed. They cannot be accorded status or authority beyond a given cultural world.

Everything hinges in these discussions on the way cultural identities are characterized. A stock objection to some versions of communitarianism has been that the conception of culture doing the work is a theoretical abstraction, reflecting a yearning for cultural and moral coherence that (so it is often claimed) has been lost in the modern world. The argument may be that human flourishing depends upon feeling at home in the world (in a Hegelian or Aristotelian sense), and that typically liberal ways of characterizing social co-operation underplay the significance of the cultural preconditions for the initiation of co-operative projects in the first place. In essence this is a conceptual reworking of certain standard objections to social contract theory (typically, but misleadingly, associated with Hegel).[11]

If we focus, instead, on the way cultures are actually constituted, the picture looks significantly different. Cultures, like traditions, are the product of bewilderingly complex (and necessarily open-ended) interactions. Sociologists and anthropologists argue fiercely among themselves about the process of culture formation. Yet political philosophers defending communitarian positions sometimes seem inclined to invoke a conception of culture as if it were uncontentious. Some of the most influential figures (Charles Taylor, for example) adopt an expressivist view of culture, stemming originally from Herder, that would be rejected out of hand as a piece of romantic nonsense by most modern sociologists.[12] Yet conceptions of culture are actually rhetorical devices in complex normative situations. The idea of 'culture' or 'community' can no more be taken as a foundation for argument and judgement than the 'individual' or 'self'. These terms may be treated as political trumps in polemical contexts, but they are always open to challenge.

In the 1990s 'identity' began to enjoy the prominence in political debate accorded to 'class' in earlier decades. A resurgence of interest in nationalism in Eastern Europe was an understandable response to years of Soviet hegemony. But in Western Europe, too, identity politics flourished, challenging the self-understandings of citizens in solidly established states. In the United Kingdom, for example, citizens in Scotland and Wales were increasingly uncomfortable with the easy assumption that England should dominate British public life, while in Italy the terms on which the state had been unified in the nineteenth century to reflect a proclaimed Italian national culture began to look strained.[13]

Identity politics thus enjoyed a variety of forms. The implosion of the Soviet empire triggered a round of state-building in difficult circumstances that made the nineteenth-century idea of the nation-state almost irresistible to elites that found themselves exposed without theoretical or rhetorical resources. Paradoxically, the 'triumph' of liberal capitalism at a global level was not matched by a liberal consensus in reconfigured states. Instead, liberal reformers were often marginalized, as programmes of structural institutional and economic reform encountered problems.[14]

The emergence of strong normative arguments in defence of minority cultures was more challenging to the conventional idea of a nation-state. Kymlicka (among others) champions the concept of 'ethno-cultural justice', urging a liberal case for the recognition of diverse cultures as a key to individual fulfilment and well-being.[15] Conventional liberal theory has no problem with the thought that we all require cultural resources in order to flourish. What is more disconcerting (at least to liberals with a strong commitment to equal citizenship) is the claim that hegemonic cultures in nation-states seldom accord adequate space or resources to the distinctive development of minority groups. In this light, the French revolutionary ideal of the 'liberty, equality, fraternity' of all citizens could look decidedly awkward (say) to cultures that distinguish sharply between male and female roles or view the state as a means of advancing specific religious goals. While liberals traditionally defend a concept of the state as a neutral arbiter between contending groups and cultures, advocates of 'ethno-cultural justice' argue, to the contrary, that political elites will always distribute resources in a partial fashion, even when they are sensitized to the interests of minorities. Cultural elites decide detailed questions of language policy, curriculum design, schedules of public holidays, etc., which inevitably marginalize groups that do not have ready access to the media and authoritative bureaucratic channels.

Responses to this dilemma are complex. Brian Barry has argued force-fully that the attempt to merge liberal and communitarian positions is con-ceptually flawed, effectively discounting liberal decision procedures in contexts where they may be regarded as contentious.[16] We appeal to liberal principles precisely when values clash. Crucially, liberal principles are not treated as 'values', but as formal means of resolving complex issues from a (notionally) neutral perspective. It is not fatal to the liberal position if in fact liberal elites display cultural bias. They can be alerted to this and urged to try harder. But it makes little sense to try to treat cultural (or other) groups 'fairly' if the concept of 'fairness' has been rejected at the outset as an independent principle.

It is now a vexed question even among liberals whether principles enjoy an independent status at all. The foundational arguments that were once the stock-in-trade of liberal theory are now regarded with profound suspicion. Rawls's defection from foundationalism in his later work is the most cele-brated (and arresting) case of a phenomenon which is wider and deeper, going to the heart of what we might mean by normative political philoso-phy.[17] Rawls continues to espouse a comprehensive liberal doctrine, but he is anxious to show that terms of political co-operation can be defended inde-pendently of the particular comprehensive doctrine he happens to endorse.

Other theorists – Rorty and Gray have been prominent here – defend the institutions and values they happen to have grown up with, but for purely contingent reasons.[18] Rorty's liberal ironist can delight in the cultural diversity that confronts him, enriching the heritage through complex description rather than analysis. Sentimental stories may be said to enhance possibilities for self-understanding. They do not furnish rules to live by. Rules which purport to be theoretically defensible are in fact simply arbitrary conventions that facilitate mutual enjoyment. But they do not facilitate everybody's enjoyment. The pretence that arbitrary conven-tions are necessary conditions for a just society is one of the principal foun-dational illusions that the liberal ironist is concerned to dispel.

Gray's position (at least in his more recent writings) is more straight-forward. He simply asserts that attachment to liberalism is a function of loyalty to a (purely contingent) national tradition. Liberals may express their loyalty in terms of doctrinal commitments. But once they recognize the fragility of the assumptions they have made (regarding progress, ratio-nality, personal autonomy and so on), they are bound to accept that the sources of their attachment are cultural rather than philosophical. There may well be decisive practical reasons for endorsing liberal institutions and practices as the best means of preserving and developing the advan-tages that accrue from flourishing civil societies. Yet such a defence could never be more than conditional, and certainly could not assume the guise of a deontological theory.

Far from helping to resolve difficult cases, political philosophy con-ducted in a certain style is being portrayed here as an integral part of the problem. At one level, arguments against normative theory look very strong indeed. If terms of reference differ radically, arguments across cultures simply miss their mark. The point can be pressed further. Arguing for the priority of values over arguments commits us to the stronger position that arguments framed by radically divergent values are 'incommensurable'.[19]

It is never quite clear what precisely is being claimed in these discussions. Conflicts of value make mutual comprehension difficult. Some commitments are mutually exclusive. It is difficult to be a soldier and a pacifist at the same time. Individuals balance their commitments in relation to their values, and recognize the necessary loss in some of the choices they make. They also revise their choices in the light of experience. Something further is being claimed, however, when it is suggested that values are 'incommensurable'. From the simple fact that we cannot understand or accommodate a position now, it does not follow that we might not do much better next week or next year. Problems arise, demand attention and may be more or less successfully resolved. There are no guarantees. But it is simply not an option to argue that theory has nothing to contribute in these cases, though it would be naïve to assume that theory alone will ever be sufficient to address our ills. Theory is dangerous when it overreaches itself; but that is not a warrant for giving up on theory altogether. We know that acute conflicts of value can lead to a breakdown in discursive politics. It would be quite another matter to claim that at certain points discursive politics will break down everywhere and always.

The political implications are profound. Advocates of 'strong' identity politics discount the possibility of building effective discursive or institutional 'bridges' between cultures. Within this view of the world, there is little scope for elites to engage in constructive dialogue internationally. Huntington's influential *The Clash of Civilizations and the Remaking of World Order* (1996) stresses the deep fissures between major cultures that condemn states to a policy of containment.[20] Essentially, Huntington offers a conceptual and ideological defence of a 'realist' view of international politics. He assumes from the outset that 'civilizations' are beyond significant discursive amendment. We are thus placed in situations where we simply have to take sides. In the aftermath of the catastrophe in New York on 11 September 2001, it is easy to see how appealing this language is to politicians and citizens confronting new styles of conflict. Yet it is also a counsel of despair, suggesting that this is an existential dilemma that can only be endured.

The situation is also complex in multicultural states. Groups may assert unique claims for special treatment, based on heightened awareness of the things that make them different from dominant cultures. Arguments are couched in terms not of universal justice or entitlement, but rather of practices that matter to 'us' but may be anathema to others. What can liberals make of demands that women should be circumcised or forced into virtual seclusion? Are governments obliged to recognize and support faith-based schools irrespective of the practical tenets of the faith in question? Clearly lines have to be drawn, but it is difficult to specify limits that will be acceptable to all cultures.

Where does this leave us as we confront political problems on a global scale, yet within systems that are fragmented both within and between states? To some citizens and commentators the challenges seem too daunting for constructive thought. Parekh, for example, claims that 'multicultural societies throw up problems that have no parallel in history'.[21] Yet there is nothing new about striving to reconcile 'the legitimate demands of unity and diversity'.[22] Long-standing empires have done it effectively, though not without incurring political costs that we are no longer prepared to pay. The nineteenth-century ideal of a homogeneous culture underpinning a state has made the task more difficult. But it can hardly be claimed that we are in uncharted territory. Parekh himself gives a nuanced account of the resources of the various traditions on which we can draw. He is right to suggest that 'no political doctrine or ideology can represent the full truth of human life'.[23] No system of ideas, of whatever kind, could embrace everything that mattered to us. Certainly political ideologies are poor creatures. Parekh insists that we cannot work exclusively within liberal (or any other specific) terms of reference. Yet the arguments he deploys come largely from liberal theory sensitized to cultural diversity. What he is trying to do is political philosophy of a rather traditional kind. It really does not matter whether we call it liberal, post-liberal or whatever. The point is that he cannot avoid the normative arguments that modern liberals typically address.

Note, for example, Parekh's frank acknowledgement that a multicultural society must maintain certain normative standards if it is to flourish. 'No multicultural society can be stable and vibrant unless it ensures that its constituent communities receive both just recognition and a just share of economic and political power.'[24] The point could have come straight out of Rawls. What 'just recognition' might amount to is not specified, though it would not be misleading presumably to think in terms of the social bases of self-respect. Similarly, a claim to 'a just share of economic and political power' could invoke Rawls's 'difference principle' or something like it. In relation to this book it is not necessary to defend any particular conception of justice in these cases, but only to insist that a conception of justice must be assumed if we are to make any sense of the ordinary business of co-operating in complex situations. We cannot defend pluralism on *any* terms. The good sense that is filtered through political cultures will be sufficient for most purposes. But 'good sense' is a product of practical reason exercised on myriad occasions by countless individuals. Sometimes, with the best will in the world, we are unsure how we should respond, what we should do next. On these occasions, as agents, we have to think harder. As philosophers, we may be encouraged to model what is going on when difficult choices are made. We do not put philosophy into practice in any straightforward sense; yet practical life throws up dilemmas that oblige us to think philosophically.

Multicultural politics shifts our focus of attention, but we are not doing anything qualitatively different. Parekh stresses the need for a dialogue between cultures. We can deepen our personal experience by taking seriously other possible ways of living. All this is unexceptionable. Yet dialogue will only be constructive if it is conducted on reasonable terms. We can hold conversations behind the barrel of a gun. We can also charmingly allow people to give vent to their feelings and then blithely carry on doing what we were minded to do anyway. Dialogue can be loaded, token, dishonest or serious. How we approach dialogue tells us a great deal about the way we regard others. It may be seen as an indicator of what we suppose we owe them. And, indeed, sometimes we will not be sure precisely what we do in fact owe them. Dialogue is a charged term. We need to think about its appropriate limits. How these should be specified, whether in terms of categorical rules or ideal situations, is much less important in the context of this book than simple acknowledgement that normative criteria apply.

Attention to the dynamics of social interaction within societies complicates matters further. Cultures, no matter how we style them, are not self-contained entities. They are products of social engagement over time and are always contested. Claiming and characterizing an identity is (among other things) a move in complex political contestation. Public arenas may be dominated by men, marginalizing options for women. Not everyone can speak for a group with the same authority. Establishing whose voice should be heard is both a political and normative issue. In a real sense, 'culture' is no less a theoretical abstraction than 'community', 'society', 'class' or 'state'. How these terms are understood will reflect a balance of normative and political argument.[25]

In relation to Kymlicka's notion of 'ethno-cultural justice', for example, great care needs to be taken in specifying the relevant territorial or cultural space. Groups and individuals may defend that space in radically divergent ways. The language issue has been especially explosive. To identify a shared language as a key component in cultural membership, as Kymlicka often does, makes it extremely difficult to treat minority language users as full citizens if the legitimacy of the state is identified in ethno-cultural terms. Safeguards can be built into a notion of ethno-cultural justice, defending basic rights, mobility and so forth, but citizens will not be able to identify equally with the dominant culture. Hungarian speakers in Romania can readily be portrayed as a threat to the legitimacy of the unitary Romanian state if they demand the right to educate their children in their native language. And, of course, this issue resonates powerfully in some Western European polities, not least in Wales.

Absence of (even an idea of) transcultural justice leaves the distribution of burdens and benefits to the unpredictable outcome of political discussion and conflict among variously placed groups. Establishments (as Foucault has shown) have formal and informal resources to marginalize awkward and intransigent voices. Power remains an issue in any normative theory. And we can all accept that (no matter how it is measured) it will never be distributed equally. In these circumstances, it is imperative that distributive decisions are based on more than raw convictions. What might count as a fair and attainable principle will remain a contentious matter. To assume that any such principle could reflect only the values of specific groups, however, undermines prospects for a distribution that could be regarded as reasonably acceptable to all interested parties. The point is not that we can easily establish strict neutrality or impartiality but, rather, that giving up on any transcultural distributive principle as a regulative ideal damages the interests of the worst-placed groups.[26]

These are modern variations on time-honoured themes. Plato's argument with Protagoras was precisely about the status of principled judgements. In one form or another, Protagoras's contention ('man is the measure of all things') has been presented in a variety of guises (community, class, nation, state, culture etc. supplying the relevant criteria) as a fall-back position if we give up on principles altogether. Yet despite our (often well-founded) scepticism about particular principles, we are left with the tangled business of making judgements in problematic contexts. We find ourselves on the horns of a paradoxical dilemma: we recognize the fragility of principles, but manifestly cannot do without them as we strive to sustain a decent social and political life.

Modern feminism illustrates the predicament aptly. It can hardly be doubted that mainstream political thought has been written largely from a male perspective. The commitment to free and equal citizenship, for example, reflects a generalizing mentality that filters out (often significant) variety in particular cases. Attention to women's actual experience yields insights that are lost in the dominant (largely liberal) public discourse. In a ground-breaking study, Carol Gilligan combined normative argument with developmental psychology to show in detail how women simply approach issues in a distinctive way.[27] Feminists can use the language of 'difference' (just as multicultural theory has) to highlight a particular and gender-specific scale of values. Co-operation rather than conflict may be regarded as 'natural' to women, encouraging an inclusive and consensual decision-making culture. The merits of this approach are clear. Procedural practices in institutions can be shown to exclude women, despite liberal legislation enshrining the principle of equality of opportunity. And liberal insistence on (at least some form of) distinction between public and private spheres makes it profoundly difficult to remedy social and institutional values through orthodox legislative means.

Yet perceptions of women's roles remain highly contested and socially constructed. We can alert ourselves to traditional male dominance in the specification of roles, without extricating women from complex webs of social power relations. How 'selves' are formed and framed continues to be controversial and varies historically and culturally.[28] If likely outcomes for women are intrinsically uncertain, the need to appeal to formal principles is unavoidable in hard cases. Notions of agency and autonomy, for sure, need to be adapted to gender-specific circumstances. But a political or cultural consensus will never be a sufficient guarantee of reasonable treatment for women. It is precisely reliance upon 'common sense' and conventional politics that has warranted the historical exclusion of women from public life. Enfranchising women goes some way towards shifting priorities in public debate. It would be naïve, however, to assume that democratic politics will always yield normatively defensible outcomes. Paradoxically, the harshest critics of liberal politics reinforce the indispensability of a style of normative theorizing usually associated with liberalism.

The political theory of multiculturalism gets entangled in similar difficulties. A modern city is a microcosm of global politics. We embrace pluralism as a matter of course, aware that the political cost of eradicating cultural difference is insupportable. But we do not tolerate everything and anything. Where we draw lines is a matter of justice. The conceptions we invoke are likely to be very much thinner than those portrayed in the political theory canon. The logic of argument, however, takes us back to positions that were advanced in vastly different cultural and historical circumstances.

For all the problems we encounter trying to characterize normative argument, we all employ it at one level or other in our practical engagements. Traditional political philosophy distinguishes government and state as a relevant focus for issues affecting a whole community. Yet (as we have seen) it can no longer be assumed that the state enjoys the kind of institutional supremacy attributed to it in orthodox theory. As sites of power are dispersed, so the challenge to effective political argument and persuasion among citizens becomes more demanding and tortuous. Formal political institutions and roles may lose some of their authority. One response among citizens may be to seek alternative routes for expressing normative concerns. Single-issue movements have arisen as umbrella ideologies look ever more remote from the interests of citizens.

An alternative is to treat the changed nature of the state as an opportunity for political assertion and mobilization across a wider range of institutions. The idea of 'civil society' has enjoyed renewed prominence since the 1990s, highlighting the autonomous institutional networks that impinge most directly on citizens and constrain the formal options of political elites. To be sure, this is a highly demanding style of politics, presupposing knowledge and resources distributed in specialized concentrations throughout a society. David Held (among others) has argued for democratic political theory to be adapted to the very different demands of global order, empowering individuals and groups to articulate positions and hold elites to account on broader fronts.[29] In this scheme of things, the politics of profession or work-place fills a void left by the conventional politics of a governmental hierarchy. Significantly, a politics so conceived must be cosmopolitan in scope, reflecting the interdependence of states, cultures and economies.

The theoretical wheel moves full circle. Confident predictions that the 'Enlightenment project' has run its course, that the very idea of justification is redundant in a postmodern epoch, that a whole cycle in political philosophy has closed, fracture on the hard reality of the need to orchestrate collaborative projects among distant strangers in a global context. Traditional political ideologies may well seem less compelling, sometimes even barely relevant to the circumstances of people's lives. But the contrast between coercion and consent remains. We are still bound to try to fashion reasonable terms of social co-operation, though our theoretical resources may well be stretched in modern contexts.

Dissatisfaction with the way the world is remains, along with unalloyed enjoyment of myriad possibilities. Philosophies of public life (in the broadest sense) have been exposed, but largely in terms of counter-positions that have been developed over the last 300 years. The *Communist Manifesto*, for example, looks like a decidedly dated text to some modern readers. Yet it has been used by Hardt and Negri as a model for the analysis of empire as a phenomenon in the contemporary world.[30] The terms of reference here are intriguing. Exposing humbug is a necessity for us as theorists and citizens. Faced with a cacophony of conflicting voices, we have to try to discriminate. If state-based ideologies look stale to some eyes, there is a clear imperative to think in global terms. The globalization of markets furnishes evidence that would not have surprised Marx himself, though the scale and speed of connections doubtless adds dimensions that could not have been anticipated in 1848. The simple thought that we cannot understand national economies without invoking a global capitalist context has been accepted almost universally. The constraints on political elites are as obvious now as they were to Marx, though we may analyse the interdependence of capitalism differently. These are very much variations on familiar themes, rather than brave new beginnings in uncharted territory.

The global context certainly presents new challenges to political theory. Political mobilization beyond borders is notoriously difficult. Even the most powerful interests have limited purchase in a bewilderingly interconnected world. The empirical exploration of interconnection can help us to focus our thinking. The way of the world, however, will not tell us what we should do. We are driven back to normative argument, despite our recognition of the contingency that frames our lives.

From a historical perspective, we may view political philosophy and theory as a series of (more or less effective) attempts to model our experience of normative argument. A lot is at stake for all of us. Life chances hinge on the authority of certain views. We all press our views, however, as interested parties, anxious to present our own pet projects as somehow ideally desirable. Normative argument (and political theory with it) is thus 'tainted' by the variety of perspectives we ordinarily encounter. But it remains indispensable. In one sense it simply follows from the thought that things could go better or worse for us. We cannot give up on this idea without incapacitating ourselves as critical agents. Yet we also have very good grounds for doubting the credentials of a whole series of arguments that have been habitually advanced.

Normative argument presupposes two distinct claims. One is the logical point that thinking involves presuppositions which we may regard as foundational. They will be relatively stable and abstract, compatible with a variety of argumentative moves. It would be misleading, however, to equate 'foundations' with values. We can all recognize the contingency of values. Yet, if we treat thinking itself as contingent, we make it unintelligible as an engagement. Thinking hard presupposes that our next argumentative moves are not arbitrary.

The second claim is that thinking hard about moral or political questions can clarify our predicament, even if we are sceptical about the capacity of practical reason to transform our basic situation. We are 'thrown' into circumstances that demand a theoretical response. Despite our (eminently justified) reservations about our intellectual resources, we still have to think hard in some contexts. There is nothing mysterious about this engagement. We all find ourselves doing it on occasion, no matter how ill-equipped we might feel we are. A minimal role for theory is to model what is going on in these situations.

In practice no one disputes that normative dilemmas arise. There is a temptation in contemporary theory, though, to explain the dilemmas away, as if our failure to agree on normative matters could be treated as a necessary limit to our powers of practical reason. Yet we can imagine better and worse ways of modelling normative dilemmas. Equating all choices with personal preferences is unlikely to be helpful when we are really in a fix, struggling to balance contending (and possibly incompatible) demands.

The point here is to take seriously the perspective of the troubled agent, rather than to retreat to a more detached vantage point. The thought is not that theory can resolve the agent's dilemma, but that the dilemma can be modelled in ways that convey the seriousness of what is at stake. Modelling is not neutral. Different ways of framing a context of decision and choice will filter out certain argumentative strategies as unhelpful or redundant. But there is no suggestion that we can deduce options from first principles.

The principles in question here are necessarily 'thin', embracing a range of widely different (yet sustainable) ways of life. And if they are described as 'foundational', it must be clear that the foundation is too weak to sustain thick institutional detail. Thin principles may nevertheless be robust enough to do normative work for us. Rawls gives us an intriguing glimpse of what may be involved in the concluding paragraph of the introduction to the paperback edition of *Political Liberalism*. He sets his own work in the context of the 'extreme violence and increasing destructiveness' of the twentieth century, 'culminating in the manic evil of the Holocaust', and asks himself (in the light of that catastrophe) 'whether political relations must be governed by power and coercion alone'.[31] Here, if anywhere, the ineffectiveness of a reflective politics had been most dramatically illustrated. Note that Rawls is not concerned simply with the fact that politics had gone so horribly wrong. His wider worry is the very possibility that 'a reasonably just society that subordinates power to its aims' might be discounted.[32]

This takes us to the heart of an issue that has dominated political thought. On one side we have the thought that 'people are largely amoral, if not incurably cynical and self-centred'.[33] If this is the case, asks Rawls, following Kant, would it be 'worthwhile for human beings to live on the earth'?[34] It is not clear how we should take this question. We are lumbered with human beings on the face of the earth, 'thrown' into situations that are often deeply precarious and threatening. Yet Rawls is remarkably robust. 'We must start', he says, 'with the assumption that a reasonably just society is possible, and for it to be possible, human beings must have a moral nature, not of course a perfect such nature, yet one that can understand, act on, and be sufficiently moved by a reasonable political conception of right and justice to support a society guided by its ideals and principles.'[35] We should focus here on the force of the sentence. Rawls says that we *must* make these commitments, not merely that we *should* (all things considered). Without these commitments, we cannot begin to think normatively, and we have already granted that normative thinking is unavoidable.

Rawls's position, of course, is one among many. But he highlights forcefully the need to invoke broad conceptions of what is possible for human beings before we go on to look at more specific questions. Rawls is emphatic on this issue. He is assuming that a society is a system of social co-operation (more or less fair) extending over a complete life. He is also assuming that the agents involved in such schemes of social co-operation are aware of themselves and their dealings with others, though they may articulate that involvement in all manner of intriguing ways. No matter how agents conceive of themselves, however, we must assume that they have 'a capacity for a sense of justice and a capacity for a sense of the good'.[36] We have to assume that all human beings have these 'two moral powers', and not simply the citizens of polities such as our own.[37] Of course, human beings may not always conceive of themselves in these ways. They may suppose that they are marionettes in God's hands or the products of strictly demarcated property relations. These notions may comfort them and make various aspects of their lives more or less intelligible. But they disguise the fact that they are exercising the 'burdens of judgement' in conditions of uncertainty, anxious to preserve social co-operation on at least minimally sustainable terms. In order to understand what they are thinking and doing, we actually have to construe their engagements in another idiom. We would not want to accuse them of being victims of false consciousness because we all filter our experience through symbols and myths. Where we differ from them is in invoking the constructive symbolism of the social world. Our disenchantment changes things radically for us. They think they are doing God's will, and we think they are doing the best they can for themselves in determinate circumstances. We can take a permissive view of the way social experience is construed in different contexts. But we cannot avoid meta-ethical assumptions about the 'burdens of judgement' and the 'circumstances of justice'.

The history of political thought is very much a series of (often starkly contrasting) responses to this basic dilemma. Even if the contingency of values and institutions is granted, we are still left with the problem of explaining what it means to make hard choices in contexts where binding decisions have to be made. For the most part, we can accept that reasons which are regarded as compelling within a culture may have little purchase beyond it. But cultures are not self-contained. It is precisely when terms of reference are challenged that more basic forms of justification are called for. In these cases, we have to give reasons for our choices that extend beyond the values we happen to have. We do not have to presuppose that stark moral or theoretical dilemmas can always be resolved, only that we have to appeal to (something like) practical reason whenever we are asked to give a public justification of our preferences.

Theorists carry on asking the standard question ('What do we owe to each other?'), but it is less clear who the question is addressed to.[38] Specifying what should count as politically relevant difference significantly complicates the original liberal theory of citizenship. Gender and culture are seen as prisms that render universal principles deeply problematic. Yet criteria still have to be specified for access to public goods. As groups challenge the distortion implicit in hegemonic discourse, they still have to justify their claims in public arenas. Normative theory has to answer the charge that in a profound sense we simply cannot understand each other. If that is held to be the case, there is a real risk that power will replace right as a legitimate distributive criterion. Normative theory remains indispensable to a decent politics. Its grounding principles, however, are more contentious than ever.

Doing political philosophy (from where we stand) is necessarily a tentative engagement. There are severe limits on what we can presume (even hypothetically) to control. What remains is a burden of normative responsibility that simply cannot be relinquished. How that burden has been exercised in the past informs our thinking and acting in profound ways. We are inescapably historical creatures. Terms of reference change, but not beyond recognition. This is unfinished work, done best in full awareness of a rich practical tradition.

Notes

2. Nature and Convention

1 Aristotle, *The Politics*, ed. Stephen Everson (Cambridge: Cambridge University Press, 1988), p. 3.

2 See Homer, *The Odyssey*, trans. Walter Shewring (Oxford: Oxford University Press, 1980); and Homer, *The Iliad*, trans. A. T. Murray (Cambridge, Mass.: Harvard University Press, 1924–5, 2 vols).

3 See Aristotle, *Metaphysics*, trans. Hippocrates G. Apostle (Bloomington: Indiana University Press, 1966), pp. 17, 191, 198; G. W. F. Hegel, *Lectures on the History of Philosophy*, trans E. S. Haldane and Frances H. Simson (London: Routledge and Kegan Paul, vol. 1, 1892), pp. 166–349; and Terence Irwin, *Classical Thought* (Oxford: Oxford University Press, 1989), pp. 20–42.

4 See Herodotus, *The Histories*, trans. Robin Waterfield (Oxford: Oxford University Press, 1998).

5 Aeschylus, *Oresteia*, trans. Christopher Collard (Oxford: Oxford University Press, 2002).

6 Hugh Lloyd-Jones, ed., *Sophocles* (Cambridge, Mass.: Harvard University Press, 1994), vol. II, p. 127.

7 Plato, 'Theaetetus', in *The Collected Dialogues of Plato*, ed. Edith Hamilton and Huntington Cairns (Princeton: Princeton University Press, 1961), p. 866 [160d].

8 See G. B. Kerferd, *The Sophistic Movement* (Cambridge: Cambridge University Press, 1981); W. K. C. Guthrie, *The Sophists* (Cambridge: Cambridge University Press, 1971); and Peter Nicholson, 'The Sophists', in David Boucher and Paul Kelly, eds, *Political Thinkers: From Socrates to the Present* (Oxford: Oxford University Press, 2003), pp. 23–39.

9 Plato, 'Meno', in *The Collected Dialogues of Plato*, p. 379 [95c].

10 Plato, 'Protagoras', in ibid., p. 320 [322c].

11 Plato, 'Theaetetus', in ibid., p. 873 [167c].

12 See Plato, 'Protagoras', in ibid., pp. 318–24 [320c-328d].

13 See Cynthia Farrar, *The Origins of Democratic Thinking: The Invention of Politics in Classical Athens* (Cambridge: Cambridge University Press, 1988), pp. 44–98.

14 Plato, 'Republic', in *The Collected Dialogues of Plato*, p. 588–9 [338c, 339a].
15 See ibid., pp. 605–10 [357a-363e].
16 Ibid., pp. 606–7 [359a-b].
17 See Plato, 'Crito', in ibid., pp. 35–8 [49e-53d].
18 Plato, 'Republic', ibid., p. 740 [505a].
19 See ibid., p. 746 [511c].
20 Ibid., p. 747 [511e].
21 Ibid., p. 658 [414b].
22 Aristotle, *The Politics*, p. 21.
23 Ibid., p. 21.
24 Ibid., p. 21.
25 Ibid., p. 3.
26 Aristotle, *The Nicomachean Ethics*, trans. David Ross (Oxford: Oxford University Press, 1998), p. 266.
27 Aristotle, *The Politics*, p. 3.
28 Ibid., p. 3.
29 Ibid., p. 3.
30 Ibid., p. 4.
31 Ibid., p. 4.
32 Ibid., p. 4.
33 See Aristide Tessitore, ed., *Aristotle and Modern Politics: The Persistence of Political Philosophy* (Notre Dame, Ind.: University of Notre Dame Press, 2002).
34 See Thucydides, *History of the Peloponnesian War*, trans Rex Warner (Harmondsworth: Penguin Books, 1972), pp. 143–51.
35 Aristotle, *The Politics*, p. 5.
36 Ibid., p. 6.
37 Ibid., p. 7.
38 Ibid., p. 7.
39 Ibid., p. 57.
40 Ibid., p. 53.
41 Ibid., p. 61.
42 Ibid., p. 62.
43 Ibid., p. 55.

3. Law

1 See Thucydides, *History of the Peloponnesian War*, especially pp. 143–51.
2 See G. W. F. Hegel, *Phenomenology of Spirit*, trans. A. V. Miller (Oxford: Clarendon Press, 1977), pp. 119–38.
3 See St Augustine, *The City of God*, trans. Henry Bettenson (Harmondsworth: Penguin Books, 1972). See below, pp. 47–62.
4 See Diogenes Laertius, *Lives of Eminent Philosophers* (Cambridge, Mass.: Harvard University Press, 1925, 2 vols).
5 Ibid., pp. 673–5.

6 Ibid., p. 675.

7 Ibid., p. 675.

8 Ibid., p. 675.

9 Ibid., p. 675.

10 Dio Chrysostom, *Discourses*, trans. J. W. Cohoon (Cambridge, Mass.: Harvard University Press, 1932), vol. 5, p. 61.

11 Ibid., p. 61.

12 See ibid., p. 61.

13 Ibid., p. 85.

14 See F. E. Adcock, *Roman Political Ideas and Practice* (Ann Arbor: The University of Michigan Press, 1959).

15 Among classic sources see Titus Livy, *The Early History of Rome*, trans. Aubrey de Selincourt (Harmondsworth: Penguin Books, 2002); Titus Livy, *Rome and Italy*, trans. Betty Radice (Harmondsworth: Penguin Books, 1982); Titus Livy, *The War with Hannibal*, trans. Aubrey de Selincourt (Harmondsworth: Penguin Books, 1974); Titus Livy, *Rome and the Mediterranean*, trans. Henry Bettenson (Harmondsworth: Penguin Books, 1976); Cornelius Tacitus, *The Histories*, ed. D. S. Levene, trans. W. H. Fyfe (Oxford: Oxford University Press, 1999); Cornelius Tacitus, *The Annals of Imperial Rome*, trans. Michael Grant (Harmondworth: Penguin Books, 1973); Sallust, *The Histories*, trans. Patrick McGushin (Oxford: Oxford University Press, 1992); and for discussion Ronald Mellor, *The Roman Historians* (London: Routledge, 1999).

16 Cicero, *The Republic and the Laws*, trans. Niall Rudd (Oxford, Oxford University Press, 1998), p. 111.

17 Ibid., p. 112.

18 Ibid., p. 112.

19 Ibid., p. 112.

20 See Donald R. Kelley, *Foundations of Modern Historical Scholarship: Language, Law and History in the French Renaissance* (New York: Columbia University Press, 1970); and Peter Burke, *The Renaissance Sense of the Past* (London: Edward Arnold, 1969).

21 See *The Institutes of Gaius*, trans. W. M. Gordon and O. F. Robinson (London: Duckworth, 1988).

22 See *The Institutes of Justinian*, ed. J. A. C. Thomas (Cape Town: Juta and Company, 1975).

23 Ibid., p. 1.

24 Ibid., p. 1.

25 Ibid., p. 1.

26 Ibid., p. 2.

27 See Peter Stein, *Roman Law in European History* (Cambridge: Cambridge University Press, 1999).

28 See *The Institutes of Justinian*, pp. 2–6.

29 See Hans Kelsen, *General Theory of Law and State*, trans. Anders Wedberg (Cambridge, Mass.: Harvard University Press, 1945); and H. L. A. Hart, *The Concept of Law* (London: Oxford University Press, 1961).

30 *The Institutes of Justinian*, p. 4.
31 Ibid., p. 4.
32 Ibid., p. 5.
33 Ibid., p. 6.
34 See *Cicero's Letters to his Friends*, trans. D. R. Shackleton Bailey (Harmondsworth: Penguin, 1978, 2 vols); and *Cicero's Letters to Atticus*, trans. D. R. Shackleton Bailey (Harmondsworth: Penguin, 1978).
35 See Cicero, *Pro Caecina*, trans. H. Grose Hodge (Cambridge, Mass.: Harvard University Press, 1927).
36 Ibid., p. 171.
37 Ibid., pp. 169–71.
38 Ibid., p. 171.
39 Ibid., pp. 171–3.
40 See Cicero, *On Duties*, trans. Walter Miller (Cambridge, Mass.: Harvard University Press, 1913).
41 Ibid., pp. 247–9.
42 Ibid., p. 249.
43 Ibid., p. 249.
44 Ibid., p. 253.
45 Ibid., p. 255.
46 Ibid., p. 259.
47 Ibid., pp. 259–61.
48 Ibid., p. 261.
49 Ibid., p. 261.
50 See Giambattista Vico, *Opere giuridiche*, ed. Paolo Cristofolini (Florence: Sansoni, 1974); and for discussion Bruce Haddock, *Vico's Political Thought* (Swansea: Mortlake Press, 1986), pp. 72–112.
51 Ibid., p. 101. Vico's felicitous phrase is 'certum est pars veri'.
52 See ibid., pp. 26, 38, 60, 96, 100, 170, 220, 288, 690.
53 I am grateful to Rex Martin for this observation.
54 Giambattista Vico, *Opere giuridiche*, p. 101.
55 See H. L. A. Hart, *The Concept of Law* (London: Oxford University Press, 1961).
56 See Ludwig Wittgenstein, *Philosophical Investigations*, trans. G. E. M. Anscombe (Oxford: Blackwell, 1968); and Peter Winch, *The Idea of a Social Science* (London: Routledge and Kegan Paul, 1958).
57 H. L. A. Hart, *The Concept of Law*, pp. 245, 107.
58 See ibid., pp. 97–8.
59 See H. F. Jolowicz and Barry Nicholas, *Historical Introduction to the Study of Roman Law* (Cambridge: Cambridge University Press, 1972, third edition), pp. 108–18.
60 See H. L. A. Hart, *The Concept of Law*, pp. 77–96.
61 Ibid., p. 89.
62 Ibid., p. 91.

4. The Earthly City

1 See St Augustine, *The City of God*, trans. Henry Bettenson (Harmondsworth: Penguin Books, 1972). For biographical details, see Peter Brown, *Augustine of Hippo: A Biography* (London: Faber and Faber, 1967). Augustine's own account of his intellectual and spiritual development is also invaluable. See St Augustine, *Confessions*, ed. R. S. Pine-Coffin (Harmondsworth: Penguin Books, 1961).
2 St Augustine, *The City of God*, p. 72.
3 Ibid., p. 73.
4 Ibid., p. 73.
5 Ibid., p. 75.
6 Ibid., p. 42.
7 Ibid., p. 176.
8 Ibid., p. 205.
9 Ibid., p. 212.
10 Ibid., pp. 212–13.
11 Ibid., p. 190.
12 Ibid., p. 191.
13 Ibid., p. 195.
14 Ibid., p. 454.
15 Ibid., p. 568.
16 Ibid., p. 568.
17 Ibid., p. 552.
18 Ibid., p. 589.
19 Ibid., p. 430.
20 Ibid., p. 593.
21 Ibid., p. 593.
22 Ibid., p. 593.
23 Ibid., p. 831.
24 Ibid., p. 139.
25 Ibid., p. 139.
26 Ibid., p. 874.
27 Ibid., p. 876.
28 In his writings against the Donatist schism and the rebellion of the Circumcellions, Augustine specifically set aside his earlier his earlier reservations about confounding the spiritual mission of the Church through association with the secular power of the civil authorities. He now felt able to justify coercion both as an incentive to right thinking among waverers ('compel them to come in') and as a defence of civil order.
29 Ibid., p. 877.
30 Ibid., p. 877.
31 Ibid., p. 877.
32 Ibid., p. 73.
33 Ibid., p. 881.

34 Ibid., p. 890.
35 Augustine extends his theory of authority even to the Church. In his anti-Donatist writings he was concerned to counter the contention that the authority of a bishop depended upon the moral and spiritual purity of his character. For Augustine, it was not the man, but the office, which conferred authority. In both the secular and spiritual spheres, the social means to desirable ends are all-important. Institutional procedures serve as a necessary corrective to the impotence and frailty of individual judgement and will.
36 For wider discussion see Etienne Gilson, *Reason and Revelation in the Middle Ages* (New York: Scribner, 1938).
37 St Thomas Aquinas, *Faith, Reason and Theology*, translated by Armand Maurer (Toronto: Pontifical Institute of Mediaeval Studies, 1987), p. 48.
38 *The Summa Theologica of St Thomas Aquinas*, translated by the Fathers of the English Dominican Province (London: Burns Oates and Washbourne, 1942, 22 vols), vol. 1, p. 13.
39 Ibid., p. 13
40 Ibid., p. 14.
41 St Thomas Aquinas, 'On Princely Government', in *Aquinas: Selected Political Writings*, ed. A. P. D'Entrèves (Oxford: Blackwell, 1965), p. 3.
42 St Thomas Aquinas, *Treatise on Law*, ed. Ralph McInerny (Washington, DC: Regnery Publishing, 1996).
43 Ibid., p. 10.
44 Ibid., p. 12.
45 Ibid., p. 15.
46 Ibid., p. 15.
47 Ibid., pp. 15–6.
48 Ibid., p. 16.
49 Ibid., p. 19.
50 Ibid., p. 19.
51 Ibid., p. 33.
52 Ibid., p. 78.
53 Ibid., p. 79.
54 For full discussion see John Finnis, *Aquinas: Moral, Political, and Legal Theory* (Oxford: Oxford University Press, 1998).
55 St Thomas Aquinas, 'On Princely Government', p. 5.
56 See Marsilius of Padua, *The Defender of the Peace*, ed. and trans. Annabel Brett (Cambridge: Cambridge University Press, 2005).

5. The State

1 See Niccolò Machiavelli, *The Prince*, ed. Quentin Skinner and Russell Price (Cambridge: Cambridge University Press, 1988); and Niccolo Machiavelli, *The Discourses*, ed. Bernard Crick (Harmondsworth: Penguin Books, 1970).

2 Machiavelli, *Discourses*, p. 97.
3 Machiavelli, *The Prince*, p. 54.
4 Ibid., p. 54.
5 Ibid., p. 54.
6 Ibid., p. 54.
7 Ibid., p. 55.
8 Ibid., p. 57.
9 Ibid., p. 58.
10 Ibid., p. 59.
11 Ibid., p. 61.
12 Ibid., p. 61.
13 Ibid., p. 61.
14 Ibid., p. 61.
15 Ibid., p. 61.
16 Ibid., p. 62.
17 Ibid., p. 87.
18 Ibid., p. 87.
19 Ibid., p. 85.
20 Ibid., p. 31.
21 Ibid., p. 31.
22 Ibid., p. 23.
23 Ibid., p. 26.
24 Machiavelli, *Discourses*, p. 105.
25 Ibid., p. 105.
26 Ibid., p. 105.
27 Ibid., p. 124.
28 See ibid., pp. 128–31.
29 Ibid., p. 128.
30 Ibid., p. 129.
31 Ibid., p. 164.
32 Ibid., p. 164.
33 Ibid., p. 514.
34 Ibid., p. 515.
35 Ibid., p. 515.
36 Machiavelli, *The Prince*, p. 87.
37 See Jean Bodin, *On Sovereignty*, ed. Julian H. Franklin (Cambridge: Cambridge University Press, 1992). The text consists of four chapters drawn from *The Six Books of the Commonwealth*.
38 Ibid., p. 1.
39 Ibid., p. 3.
40 Ibid., p. 13.
41 Ibid., p. 14.
42 See Sir Robert Filmer, *Patriarcha and Other Writings*, ed. Johann P. Sommerville (Cambridge: Cambridge University Press, 1991).
43 Ibid., p. 1.

44 Ibid., p. 3.
45 Ibid., p. 3.
46 Ibid., p. 12.
47 Ibid., p. 34.
48 Ibid., p. 35.
49 Ibid., p. 35.
50 See King James VI and I, 'The Trew Law of Free Monarchies', in his *Political Writings*, ed. Johann P. Sommerville (Cambridge: Cambridge University Press, 1994).
51 Ibid., p. 74.
52 Ibid., p. 74.
53 Ibid., p. 75.
54 Ibid., p. 75.
55 Ibid., p. 76.
56 See Thomas Hobbes, *Leviathan*, ed. Richard Tuck (Cambridge: Cambridge University Press, 1991).
57 Ibid., p. 491.
58 Ibid., p. 39.
59 Ibid., p. 44.
60 Ibid., p. 46.
61 Ibid., p. 46.
62 Ibid., p. 62.
63 Ibid., p. 70.
64 Ibid., pp. 86–7.
65 Ibid., p. 88.
66 Ibid., p. 89.
67 Ibid., p. 89.
68 Ibid., p. 89.
69 Ibid., p. 89.
70 Ibid., p. 89.
71 Ibid., p. 89.
72 Ibid., p. 90.
73 Ibid., p. 90.
74 Ibid., p. 91.
75 Ibid., p. 91.
76 Ibid., p. 91.
77 Ibid., p. 92.
78 Ibid., p. 92.
79 Ibid., p. 96.
80 Ibid., p. 101.
81 Ibid., p. 9.
82 Ibid., p. 147.
83 Ibid., p. 184.
84 Ibid., p. 153.
85 Ibid., p. 153.

6. Rights

1 Hugo Grotius, *On the Law of War and Peace*, trans. Francis W. Kelsey (Oxford: Clarendon Press, 1925).
2 Ibid., p. 11.
3 Ibid., p. 11.
4 Ibid., p. 11.
5 Ibid., p. 12.
6 Ibid., pp. 12–13.
7 Ibid., p. 13.
8 Ibid., p. 13.
9 Ibid., p. 13.
10 Ibid., p. 15.
11 Ibid., p. 15.
12 Ibid., p. 17.
13 Ibid., p. 17.
14 Ibid., p. 17.
15 Ibid., p. 17.
16 Ibid., p. 23.
17 Ibid., p. 23.
18 Ibid., pp. 23–4.
19 Ibid., p. 24.
20 See David Hume, *A Treatise of Human Nature*, ed. Ernest C. Mossner (Harmondsworth: Penguin Books, 1969), p. 521.
21 Hugo Grotius, *On the Law of War and Peace*, p. 343.
22 Ibid., p. 346.
23 Ibid.,p. 348.
24 Ibid., p. 351.
25 Ibid., p. 352.
26 Ibid., p. 352.
27 See Quentin Skinner, *The Foundations of Modern Political Thought* (Cambridge: Cambridge University Press, 1978, 2 vols), vol. 2, pp. 189–358.
28 See Craig L. Carr, ed., *The Political Writings of Samuel Pufendorf*, trans. Michael J. Seidler (Oxford: Oxford University Press, 1994).
29 See Samuel Pufendorf, *On the Duty of Man and Citizen According to Natural Law*, ed. James Tully (Cambridge: Cambridge University Press, 1991).
30 Ibid., p. 35.
31 Ibid., p. 35.
32 Ibid., p. 35.
33 Ibid., p. 35.
34 Ibid., p. 36.
35 Ibid., p. 77.
36 Ibid., p. 77.
37 Ibid., p. 79.
38 Ibid., p. 79.

39 Ibid., p. 79.
40 Ibid., p. 118.
41 Ibid., p. 118.
42 Ibid., p. 119.
43 Ibid., p. 119.
44 Ibid., p. 136.
45 Ibid., p. 136.
46 Ibid., p. 138.
47 Ibid., p. 139.
48 Ibid., p. 146.
49 *The Politics of Johannes Althusius*, ed. Frederick S. Carney (London: Eyre and Spottiswood, 1964).
50 Ibid., p. 12.
51 Ibid., p. 22.
52 Ibid., p. 23.
53 Ibid., p. 28.
54 Ibid., pp. 28–9.
55 Ibid., p. 29.
56 Ibid., p. 35.
57 Ibid., p. 35.
58 Ibid., p. 34.
59 Ibid., p. 62.
60 Ibid., p. 76.
61 Ibid., p. 76.
62 Ibid., p. 76.
63 See John Locke, *Two Treatises of Government*, ed. Peter Laslett (New York: Mentor Books, 1965).
64 See Laslett's introduction to the *Two Treatises* for full discussion of context.
65 Ibid., p. 176.
66 Ibid., p. 178.
67 Ibid., p. 257.
68 Ibid., p. 309.
69 Ibid., p. 309.
70 Ibid., p. 311.
71 Ibid., p. 311.
72 Ibid., p. 312.
73 Ibid., p. 312.
74 Ibid., p. 315.
75 Ibid., p. 318.
76 Ibid., p. 321.
77 Ibid., p. 316.
78 See ibid., pp. 327–44. An influential neo-Marxist account of Locke on property is advanced in C. B. Macpherson, *The Political Theory of Possessive Individualism* (Oxford: Clarendon Press, 1962).
79 John Locke, *Two Treatises of Government*, pp. 327, 333.

80 Ibid., p. 328.
81 See Robert Nozick, *Anarchy, State, and Utopia* (New York: Basic Books, 1974).
82 John Locke, *Two Treatises of Government*, p. 329.
83 Ibid., p. 329.
84 Ibid., p. 327.
85 Ibid., p. 332.
86 Ibid., p. 332.
87 Ibid., p. 335.
88 Ibid., p. 374.
89 Ibid., p. 375.
90 Ibid., p. 395.
91 Ibid., p. 396.
92 Ibid., p. 396.
93 Ibid., p. 397.
94 Ibid., p. 399.
95 Ibid., p. 372.
96 Ibid., p. 375.
97 Ibid., p. 411.
98 Ibid., p. 409.
99 Ibid., p. 409.
100 Ibid., p. 409.
101 Ibid., p. 409.
102 Ibid., p. 409.
103 See ibid., pp. 454–77.
104 Ibid., p. 466.
105 Ibid., p. 454.
106 Ibid., p. 455.
107 Ibid., p. 459.
108 Ibid., p. 459.
109 Ibid., p. 476.
110 Ibid., p. 476.
111 Ibid., p. 392.
112 Ibid., p. 392.
113 Ibid., p. 392.
114 Ibid., p. 392.

7. Enlightenment

1 See Baruch Spinoza, *Ethics*, trans. Andrew Boyle (London: Dent, 1970).
2 Ibid., pp. 63–4.
3 Ibid., p. 63.
4 Ibid., p. 63.
5 Ibid., p. 126.
6 Ibid., p. 187.
7 Ibid., p. 187.

8 See Benedict de Spinoza, *The Political Works*, ed. A. G. Wernham (Oxford: Clarendon Press, 1958).

9 See Bruce Haddock, *An Introduction to Historical Thought* (London: Edward Arnold, 1980) for further discussion.

10 Benedict de Spinoza, *The Political Works*, pp. 124–47.

11 Ibid., p. 125.

12 Ibid., p. 127.

13 Ibid., p. 127.

14 Ibid., p. 129.

15 Ibid., p. 129.

16 Ibid., p. 131.

17 Ibid., p. 131.

18 Ibid., p. 133.

19 Ibid., p. 133.

20 Ibid., p. 133.

21 Ibid., p. 133.

22 Ibid., p. 137.

23 Ibid., p. 137.

24 Ibid., p. 441.

25 Ibid., p. 441.

26 Ibid., p. 261.

27 Ibid., p. 261.

28 Ibid., p. 261.

29 Ibid., p. 263.

30 See Francis Bacon, *The Advancement of Learning*, ed. G. W. Kitchin (London: Dent, 1973).

31 See Pierre Bayle, *Historical and Critical Dictionary*, ed. Richard H. Popkin (Indianapolis: The Bobbs-Merrill Company, 1965).

32 Ibid., p. 49.

33 See Montesquieu, *The Spirit of the Laws*, ed. Anne M. Cohler, Basia C. Miller and Harold S. Stone (Cambridge: Cambridge University Press, 1989).

34 Ibid., p. xliii.

35 Ibid., p. 21.

36 See ibid., pp. 156–66.

37 See David Hume, *A Treatise of Human Nature*, ed. Ernest C. Mossner (Harmondsworth: Penguin Books, 1969).

38 Ibid., p. 521.

39 Ibid., p. 521.

40 Ibid., p. 521.

41 Ibid., p. 521.

42 Ibid., p. 462.

43 David Hume, *Enquiries Concerning the Human Understanding and the Principles of Morals*, ed. L. A. Selby-Bigge (Oxford: Clarendon Press, 1966), p. 188.

44 Ibid., p. 195.

45 David Hume, *A Treatise of Human Nature*, p. 578.
46 Among many works by Voltaire see, *Political Writings*, ed. David Williams (Cambridge: Cambridge University Press); *Philosophical Letters*, ed. Ernest Dilworth (Indianapolis: Bobbs-Merrill, 1961); *The Age of Louis XIV*, trans. Martyn P. Pollack (London; Everyman, 1961); and *Candide, or Optimism*, trans. Theo Cuffe (Harmondsworth: Penguin Books, 2006).
47 See Diderot, *Political Writings*, ed. John Hope Mason and Robert Wokler (Cambridge: Cambridge University Press); and Jean Le Rond d'Alembert, *Preliminary Discourse to the Encyclopedia of Diderot*, trans. Richard N. Schwab (Indianapolis: Bobbs-Merrill, 1963).
48 See Immanuel Kant, 'An Answer to the Question: What is Enlightenment?', in his *Practical Philosophy*, ed. Mary J. Gregor (Cambridge: Cambridge University Press, 1996), pp. 15–22.
49 Ibid., p. 18.
50 Ibid., p. 18.
51 Ibid., p. 18.
52 Ibid., p. 17.
53 See Immanuel Kant, *Critique of Pure Reason* (London: Macmillan, 1929); 'Critique of Practical Reason', in Immanuel Kant, *Practical Philosophy*; and Immanuel Kant, *The Critique of Judgement*, trans. J. C. Meredith (Oxford: Clarendon Press, 1953).
54 Immanuel Kant, *Critique of Pure Reason*, p. 25.
55 See Immanuel Kant, 'Groundwork of the Metaphysics of Morals', in his *Practical Philosophy*, pp. 41–108.
56 Ibid., p. 83.
57 Ibid., p. 73.
58 Ibid., p. 83.
59 Ibid., p. 83.
60 See Immanuel Kant, 'Toward Perpetual Peace: A Philosophical Project', in his *Practical Philosophy*, pp. 315–51.
61 Ibid., p. 324.
62 Ibid., p. 322.
63 Ibid., p. 322.
64 Ibid., p. 325.
65 See Immanuel Kant, 'The Metaphysics of Morals', in his *Practical Philosophy*, pp. 363–603.
66 Ibid., p. 387.
67 Ibid., p. 393.
68 Ibid., p. 393.
69 See Jean-Jacques Rousseau, *The Social Contract*, trans. Maurice Cranston (Harmondsworth: Penguin Books, 1968).
70 Ibid., p. 49.
71 See Jean-Jacques Rousseau, *The Social Contract and Discourses*, trans. G. D. H. Cole (London: Dent, 1968), pp. 143–229.
72 Ibid., p. 192.

73 Jean-Jacques Rousseau, *The Social Contract*, p. 53.
74 Ibid., p. 53.
75 Ibid., p. 60.
76 Ibid., p. 60.
77 Ibid., p. 59.
78 Ibid., p. 64.
79 Ibid., p. 65.
80 Ibid., p. 65.
81 Ibid., p. 63.
82 Ibid., p. 64.
83 Ibid., p. 64.
84 Ibid., p. 64.
85 Ibid., p. 72.
86 Ibid., p. 72.
87 Ibid., p. 72.
88 Ibid., p. 75.
89 See John Rawls, *A Theory of Justice* (Oxford: Oxford University Press, 1972), p. 9.
90 Jean-Jacques Rousseau, *The Social Contract*, p. 77.
91 Ibid., p. 80.
92 Ibid., p. 80.
93 Ibid., p. 80.
94 Ibid., p. 81.
95 Ibid., p. 83.
96 Ibid., p. 83.
97 Ibid., p. 49.
98 Ibid., p. 84.
99 Ibid., p. 88.
100 Ibid., p. 84.
101 Ibid., p. 49.
102 Ibid., pp. 84–5.
103 Ibid., p. 85.
104 Ibid., pp. 86–7.
105 Ibid., p. 124.
106 Ibid., p. 149.
107 Ibid., p. 174.
108 Ibid., p. 174.
109 Ibid., p. 174.
110 See ibid., pp. 176–87.

8. Revolution

1 Alexander Hamilton, James Madison and John Jay, *The Federalist, with Letters of 'Brutus'*, ed. Terence Ball (Cambridge: Cambridge University Press, 2003), no. 1, p. 1.

2 The text of the *Declaration* is reproduced in Thomas Paine, *Rights of Man*, ed. Henry Collins (Harmondsworth: Penguin Books, 1969), pp. 132–4. The quotation is from p. 132.

3 Ibid., p. 132.

4 Ibid., p. 132.

5 Ibid., p. 132.

6 Ibid., p. 132.

7 Ibid., p. 132.

8 Ibid., p. 132.

9 Ibid., p. 132.

10 See Emmanuel Joseph Sieyes, *What is the Third Estate?*, ed. S. E. Finer (London: Pall Mall Press, 1963).

11 Ibid., p. 53.

12 Ibid., p. 53.

13 Ibid., p. 57.

14 Ibid., p. 119.

15 Ibid., p. 121.

16 Ibid., p. 121.

17 Ibid., p. 122.

18 Ibid., p. 122.

19 Ibid., p. 124.

20 Ibid., p. 124.

21 Ibid., p. 128.

22 Ibid., p. 135.

23 Ibid., p. 136.

24 Thomas Paine, *Common Sense*, ed. Isaak Kramnick (Harmondsworth: Penguin Books, 1976), p. 65.

25 Ibid., p. 65.

26 Thomas Paine, *Rights of Man*, p. 187.

27 See Edmund Burke, *Reflections on the Revolution in France*, ed. A. J. Grieve (London: Dent, 1967); and the discussion below, pp. 188–93.

28 For discussion see Ruth Scurr, *Fatal Purity: Robespierre and the French Revolution* (London: Chatto and Windus, 2006); and George Klosko, *Jacobins and Utopians: The Political Theory of Fundamental Moral Reforms* (Notre Dame: University of Notre Dame Press, 2003), especially pp. 89–120.

29 Cited in ibid., p. 99.

30 Ibid., p. 104.

31 Ibid., p. 105.

32 Ibid., p. 105.

33 See *The Federalist*, pp. 40–6.

34 Ibid., p. 41.

35 Ibid., p. 43.

36 Ibid., p. 43.

37 Ibid., p. 44.

38 Ibid., p. 46.

39 Ibid., p. 46.
40 Ibid., p. 46.
41 Ibid., p. 252.
42 Ibid., p. 252.
43 Ibid., p. 252.
44 Ibid., p. 252.
45 Ibid., p. 254.
46 Ibid., p. 35.
47 Ibid., p. 126.
48 See Saul Cornell, *The Other Founders: Anti-Federalism and the Dissenting Tradition in America, 1788–1828* (Chapel Hill: University of North Carolina Press, 1999).
49 See below, pp. 188–93.

9. The Age of Ideologies

1 See G. W. F. Hegel, *Philosophy of Right*, ed. and trans. T. M. Knox (Oxford: Clarendon Press, 1952).
2 See G. W. F. Hegel, *Phenomenology of Spirit*, trans. A. V. Miller (Oxford: Clarendon Press, 1977).
3 Hegel, *Philosophy of Right*, p. 11. References to the preface of the *Philosophy of Right* are to page numbers; references to the rest of the text are to the numbered paragraphs of the Knox edition, with an 'R' or 'A' appended to indicate respectively 'remarks' and 'additions'.
4 Ibid., p. 11.
5 Ibid., p. 11.
6 Ibid., p. 10.
7 Ibid., para. 2.
8 Ibid., para. 4.
9 See ibid., para. 4A.
10 Ibid., para. 4.
11 See G. W. F. Hegel, *Philosophy of Mind*, trans. A. V. Miller (Oxford: Clarendon Press, 1971). The text is part 3 of the 1830 edition of the *Encyclopaedia of the Philosophical Sciences*.
12 Hegel, *Philosophy of Right*, para. 5.
13 Ibid., para. 5R.
14 Ibid., para 5A.
15 Ibid., para. 5R.
16 Ibid., para. 6.
17 Ibid., para. 7.
18 Ibid., para. 7.
19 See ibid., paras. 34–104.
20 Ibid., para. 36.
21 Ibid., para. 41.
22 Ibid., para. 51.

23 Ibid., para. 71R.
24 Ibid., para. 71.
25 See ibid., paras. 84–6.
26 Ibid., para. 87.
27 See ibid., para. 92.
28 See ibid., para 99.
29 See ibid., para. 104.
30 See ibid., paras. 105–41.
31 See ibid., paras. 117–8.
32 See ibid., para. 119.
33 See ibid., para. 123.
34 See ibid., para. 125.
35 See ibid., para. 128.
36 Ibid., para, 129.
37 See ibid., para. 132.
38 Ibid., para. 133.
39 Ibid., para. 135R.
40 See Immanuel Kant, 'Groundwork of the Metaphysics of Morals', in his *Practical Philosophy*, p. 73.
41 Hegel, *Philosophy of Right*, para. 135R.
42 Ibid., para. 135R.
43 See ibid., para. 136.
44 See ibid., para. 137.
45 See ibid., para. 138.
46 See ibid., para. 139.
47 See ibid., para. 149.
48 Ibid., para. 147.
49 Ibid., paras. 150–3.
50 See ibid., paras. 142–360.
51 See ibid., para. 158.
52 See ibid., paras. 162, 173–5, 181.
53 See ibid., paras. 182–3.
54 See ibid., paras. 189–208.
55 See ibid., paras. 189R, 201.
56 See ibid., paras. 202–5.
57 See ibid., paras. 211–18.
58 See ibid., paras. 219–29.
59 Ibid., para. 183.
60 See ibid., paras. 213–45.
61 Ibid., para. 245.
62 Ibid., paras. 246–9.
63 See ibid., paras. 250–2.
64 See ibid., para. 253.
65 See ibid., para. 256.
66 Ibid., para. 257.

67 Ibid., para. 260.
68 Ibid., para. 260.
69 See ibid., para. 211R.
70 See ibid., paras. 275–320.
71 Ibid., para. 258.
72 Ibid., para. 325.
73 See Benjamin Constant, 'The Liberty of the Ancients Compared with that of the Moderns', in his *Political Writings*, ed. and trans. Biancamaria Fontana (Cambridge: Cambridge University Press, 1988), pp. 307–28.
74 Ibid., p. 326.
75 See ibid., pp. 310–11.
76 See Alexis de Tocqueville, *Democracy in America and Two Essays on America*, trans. Gerald E. Bevan (London: Penguin Books, 2003).
77 Ibid., p. 17.
78 Ibid., p. 15.
79 See above, pp. 156–68.
80 Tocqueville, *Democracy in America*, p. 16.
81 Ibid., p. 17.
82 Ibid., p. 16.
83 Ibid., p. 23.
84 Ibid., p. 97.
85 Ibid., pp. 700, 640, 493.
86 See ibid., pp. 130–200.
87 Ibid., p. 778.
88 Ibid., p. 16.
89 Ibid., p. 18.
90 Jeremy Bentham, 'An Introduction to the Principles of Morals and Legislation', in *A Fragment on Government with an Introduction to the Principles of Morals and Legislation*, ed. Wilfred Harrison (Oxford: Blackwell, 1967), p. 125.
91 Ibid., p. 125.
92 Jeremy Bentham, 'A Fragment on Government', ibid., p. 3.
93 John Stuart Mill, 'Utilitarianism', in his *On Liberty and Other Essays*, ed. John Gray (Oxford: Oxford University Press, 1991), p. 138.
94 Ibid., p. 139.
95 Ibid., p. 140.
96 Ibid., p. 141.
97 Ibid., p. 142.
98 Ibid., p. 142.
99 Ibid., p. 142.
100 John Stuart Mill, 'On Liberty', in ibid., pp.13–4.
101 Ibid., p. 14.
102 Ibid., p. 14.
103 Ibid., p. 14.
104 See ibid., pp. 20–61.

105 See John Stuart Mill, *Autobiography* (London: Longman, 1873).
106 John Stuart Mill, 'On Liberty', in his *On Liberty and Other Essays*, p. 15.
107 Ibid., p. 15.
108 Ibid., p. 65.
109 Ibid., p. 63.
110 Ibid., p. 63.
111 Ibid., p. 17.
112 Ibid., p. 105.
113 Ibid., p. 105.
114 Ibid., pp. 105–6.
115 Ibid., p. 108.
116 Ibid., p. 108.
117 Ibid., p. 108.
118 Ibid., p. 120.
119 Ibid., p. 120.
120 Ibid., p. 120.
121 Ibid., p. 120.
122 Ibid., p. 121.
123 See Thomas Hill Green, *Lectures on the Principles of Political Obligation*, ed. A. D. Lindsay (London: Longman, 1941).
124 Hobhouse was especially critical of the neo-Hegelian Bernard Bosanquet. See L. T. Hobhouse, *Liberalism and Other Writings*, ed. James Meadowcroft (Cambridge: Cambridge University Press, 1994); and Bernard Bosanquet, *The Philosophical Theory of the State* (London: Macmillan, 1965).
125 See François Furet, *Interpreting the French Revolution*, trans. Elborg Forster (Cambridge: Cambridge University Press, 1981).
126 See Edmund Burke, *Reflections on the Revolution in France*, ed. A. J. Grieve (London: Dent, 1967).
127 See Michael Oakeshott, *Rationalism in Politics and Other Essays* (London: Methuen, 1962).
128 See Edmund Burke, 'Speech on American Taxation' (19 April 1774) and 'Speech on Conciliation with the Colonies' (22 March 1775), in B. W. Hill, ed., *Edmund Burke on Government, Politics and Society* (London: Fontana, 1975), pp. 121–55 and 159–87.
129 Burke, *Reflections on the Revolution in France*, pp. 15–16.
130 Ibid., pp. 14–15.
131 Ibid., p. 18.
132 Ibid., p. 19–20.
133 Ibid., p. 20.
134 Ibid., p. 20.
135 Ibid., p. 56.
136 Ibid., p. 56.
137 Ibid., p. 56.
138 Ibid., p. 56.
139 Ibid., p. 57.

140 Ibid., p. 57.
141 Ibid., p. 57.
142 Ibid., p. 57.
143 Ibid., p. 57.
144 Ibid., p. 57.
145 Ibid., p. 58.
146 Ibid., p. 58.
147 Ibid., p. 58.
148 Ibid., p. 58.
149 Ibid., p. 58.
150 Ibid., p. 58.
151 Ibid., p. 59.
152 Ibid., p. 59.
153 Ibid., p. 59.
154 Ibid., p. 28.
155 Ibid., p. 28.
156 Ibid., p. 28.
157 Ibid., p. 84.
158 Ibid., p. 84.
159 Ibid., p. 84.
160 Ibid., p. 84.
161 Ibid., pp. 36–7.
162 See Joseph de Maistre, *Considerations on France*, trans. Richard A Lebrun (Montreal: McGill-Queen's University Press, 1974).
163 Ibid., p. 23.
164 Ibid., p. 51.
165 Ibid., p. 62.
166 Ibid., p. 65.
167 Ibid., p. 71.
168 Ibid., p. 71.
169 Ibid., p. 73.
170 Ibid., p. 135.
171 Ibid., p. 144.
172 Ibid., p. 145.
173 Ibid., p. 169.
174 Ibid., p. 169.
175 Michael Oakeshott, *Rationalism in Politics and other Essays* (London: Methuen, 1962), preface.
176 In *Rationalism in Politics* Oakeshott presupposes the sophisticated view of knowledge and experience he had elaborated in *Experience and its Modes* (Cambridge: Cambridge University Press, 1933), which focuses on knowledge as a *factum* rather than a *datum*, dependent on specific and incommensurable assumptions in the distinct spheres of practice, history and science.
177 For Oakeshott's treatment of key thinkers and issues in the classic tradition of political philosophy, see his influential, posthumously published *Lectures on*

the History of Political Thought, ed. Terry Nardin and Luke O'Sullivan (Exeter: Imprint Academic, 2006).

178 See Oakeshott, *Rationalism in Politics and Other Essays,* pp. 80–110.

179 Ibid., p. 89.

180 Ibid., p. 90.

181 Ibid., p. 110.

182 Ibid., p. 8.

183 Ibid., p. 4.

184 Ibid., p. 22.

185 Ibid., p. 25.

186 Ibid., p. 31.

187 Ibid., p. 31.

188 Ibid., p. 128.

189 Ibid., p. 128.

190 See Michael Oakeshott, *On Human Conduct* (Oxford: Oxford University Press, 1975), pp. 108–84.

191 Ibid., p. 121.

192 Ibid., p. 121.

193 See Ricard Rorty, *Contingency, Irony and Solidarity* (Cambridge: Cambridge University Press, 1989).

194 J. G. Herder, 'Journal of my Voyage in the Year 1769', in *Herder on Social and Political Culture,* ed. and trans. F. M. Barnard (Cambridge: Cambridge University Press, 1969), pp. 85–6.

195 J. G. Herder, 'Yet Another Philosophy of History', in ibid., p. 182.

196 Ibid., p. 184.

197 Ibid., p. 217.

198 Ibid., pp. 191–2.

199 Ibid., p. 194.

200 See Bruce Haddock, 'Italy: Independence and Unification without Power', in Bruce Waller, ed., *Themes in Modern European History 1830–90* (London: Unwin Hyman, 1990), pp. 67–98.

201 See Giuseppe Mazzini, 'Carlo Botta e I romantici' and 'D'una letteratura europea', in his *Scritti editi ed inediti,* ed. L. Rave et al. (Imola: Galeati, 1906–40, 98 vols), vol. 1.

202 Ibid., p. 218.

203 Ibid., p. 219.

204 Giuseppe Mazzini, 'Manifesto della *giovine Italia*', in his *Scritti editi ed inediti,* vol. 2, p. 76.

205 Giuseppe Mazzini, 'Istruzione generale per gli affratellati nella *giovine Italia*', in ibid., p. 46.

206 Ibid., p. 46.

207 Ibid., p. 47.

208 Giuseppe Mazzini, 'Dei doveri dell'uomo', in his *Scritti politici,* ed. Terenzio Grandi and Augusto Comba (Turin: Unione tipografico-editrice torinese, 1972), p. 910.

209 Ibid., p. 910.

210 Ibid., p. 910.

211 See Denis Mack Smith, ed., *Il Risorgimento italiano* (Bari: Laterza, 1987), p. 422; Giuseppe Mazzini, *Scritti editi ed inediti*, vol. 58, pp. 42–4; and E. J. Hobsbawm, *Nations and Nationalism since 1780: Programme, Myth, Reality* (Cambridge: Cambridge University Press, 1990), pp. 31–2.

212 See Jules Michelet, *The People*, ed. J. P. Mckay (Urbana: University of Illinois Press, 1973).

213 See Bruce Haddock, *An Introduction to Historical Thought*, pp. 90–105.

214 See Giorgio Candeloro, *Storia dell'Italia moderna* (Milan: Feltrinelli, 1956–86, 11 vols), vol. 2, pp. 224–42 and 371–84; and Giuseppe Mazzini, *Note autobiografiche*, ed. Mario Menghini (Florence: Le Monnier, 1943), pp. 248–50 and 261. Note that Mazzini had in fact opposed the expedition of the Bandiera brothers.

215 See J. G. Fichte, 'The Closed Commercial State', in Hans Reiss, ed., *The Political Thought of the German Romantics* (Oxford: Blackwell, 1955), pp. 86–102; and J. G. Fichte, *Addresses to the German Nation*, trans. R. E. Jones and G. H. Turnbull (Chicago: Open Court Publishing Company, 1922).

216 See Robert Owen, *A New View of Society*, ed., Gregory Claeys (Harmondsworth: Penguin Books, 1991); and Ghita Ionescu, ed., *The Political Thought of Saint-Simon* (Oxford: Oxford University Press, 1976).

217 See, in particular, Karl Marx, 'Critique of Hegel's Doctrine of the State' and 'A Contribution to the Critique of Hegel's Philosophy of Right', in his *Early Writings*, ed. Lucio Colletti (Harmondsworth: Penguin Books, 1975), pp. 57–198 and 243–57.

218 Karl Marx and Frederick Engels, *Collected Works* (London: Lawrence and Wishart, 1976), vol. 5, p. 31.

219 Ibid., p. 32.

220 Ibid., p. 59.

221 Ibid., p. 62.

222 See Karl Marx and Frederick Engels, 'Manifesto of the Communist Party', in Karl Marx, *The Revolutions of 1848*, ed. David Fernbach (Harmondsworth: Penguin Books, 1973), pp. 62–98.

223 Ibid., p. 67.

224 See ibid., pp. 94–7.

225 Ibid., p. 79.

226 Ibid., p. 87.

227 Ibid., p. 81.

228 Ibid., pp. 83–4.

229 Ibid., p. 83.

230 Ibid., p. 83.

231 Karl Marx and Frederick Engels, *Selected Works* (London: Lawrence and Wishart, 1968), p. 182.

232 Ibid., pp. 182–3.

233 Hegel, *Philosophy of Right*, p. 11.

234 Karl Marx, *Capital: A Critique of Political Economy*, trans. Ben Fowkes (Harmondsworth: Penguin Books, 1976).

235 See ibid., pp. 258–69.

236 See ibid., pp. 492–639.

237 See ibid., pp. 126–8.

238 Karl Marx and Frederick Engels, 'The German Ideology', in *Collected Works*, vol. 5, p. 47.

239 Ibid., p. 47.

240 Both are available in Karl Marx, *Surveys from Exile*, ed. David Fernbach (Harmondsworth: Penguin Books, 1973).

241 Ibid., p. 239.

242 Ibid., p. 35.

243 See Eduard Bernstein, *Evolutionary Socialism*, trans. E. C. Harvey (London: Independent Labour Party, 1909).

244 Karl Marx and Frederick Engels, 'Manifesto of the Communist Party', p. 98.

245 See Antonio Labriola, *La concezione materialistica della storia*, ed. Eugenio Garin (Bari: Laterza, 1965); and Benedetto Croce, *Materialismo storico ed economia marxista* (Bari: Laterza, 1941).

246 See Georges Sorel, *La Décomposition du marxisme* (Paris: Marcel Riviere, 1907); Georges Sorel, *Les Illusions du progrès* (Paris: Marcel Riviere, 1927); and Georges Sorel, *Reflections on Violence*, trans. T. E. Hulme (London: Allen and Unwin, 1925).

247 See Philippe Buonarotti, *La Conspiration de Babeuf* (Paris: Editions sociales, 1957).

248 Karl Marx, 'Critique of the Gotha Programme', in his *Selected Writings*, ed., David McLellan (Oxford: Oxford University Press, 2000), p. 614.

249 V. I. Lenin, 'What is to be Done?', in his *Selected Writings* (Moscow: Progress Publishers, 1963), vol. 1, p. 121.

250 Ibid., pp. 121–2.

251 See ibid., pp. 149–52.

252 Ibid., p. 152.

253 V. I. Lenin, *The State and Revolution*, trans. Robert Service (London: Penguin Books, 1992), p. 79.

254 Ibid., p. 79.

255 Ibid., p. 79.

256 Ibid., p. 79.

257 Ibid., p. 79.

258 Ibid., p. 80.

259 Ibid., p. 80.

260 Ibid., p. 80.

261 Ibid., p. 80.

262 Ibid., p. 80.

263 Ibid., p. 81.

264 See V. I. Lenin, 'Imperialism, the Highest Stage of Capitalism', in his *Selected Works*, vol. 1, pp. 634–731.

265 See Karl Marx, *Capital: A Critique of Political Economy*, vol. 3, ed. Frederick Engels (Chicago: Kerr, 1909).

266 Lenin, 'Imperialism, the Highest Stage of Capitalism', p. 640.

267 Ibid., p. 649.

268 See ibid., pp. 442–53.

269 Lenin, *The State and Revolution*, p. 86.

270 Ibid., p. 87; Lenin's italics.

271 See Friedrich Nietzsche, *On the Genealogy of Morals*, ed. Keith Ansell Pearson (Cambridge: Cambridge University Press, 1994).

272 Vilfredo Pareto, 'Les systèmes socialistes', in Adrian Lyttelton, ed., *Italian Fascisms: From Pareto to Gentile* (London: Jonathan Cape, 1973), p. 78.

273 Vilfredo Pareto, 'Trasformazioni della democrazia', in ibid., p. 92.

274 Ibid., p. 92.

275 Ibid., p. 93.

276 See Carl Schmitt, *The Concept of the Political*, ed. George Schwab (Chicago: University of Chicago Press, 1996).

277 See Carl Schmitt, *The Crisis of Parliamentary Democracy*, ed., Ellen Kennedy (Cambridge, Mass.: MIT Press, 1988).

278 See ibid., p. 26.

279 Schmitt, *The Concept of the Political*, p. 26.

280 Ibid., p. 71.

281 See Benito Mussolini, 'The Doctrine of Fascism', in Lyttelton, ed., *Italian Fascisms*, pp. 39–57.

282 See Giovanni Gentile, *Origins and Doctrine of Fascism*, trans. A. James Gregor (New Brunswick, NJ: Transaction Publishers, 2002).

283 Ibid., p. 21.

284 See Giovanni Gentile, *The Theory of Mind as Pure Act*, trans. H. Wildon Carr (London: Macmillan, 1922).

285 Giovanni Gentile, *Origins and Doctrine of Fascism*, p. 25.

286 Ibid., p. 25.

287 Giovanni Gentile, *Genesis and Structure of Society*, trans. H. S. Harris (Urbana: University of Illinois Press, 1960), p. 121.

288 Ibid., p. 152.

289 Ibid., p. 98.

10. Liberal Democracy

1 See Francis Fukuyama, 'The End of History?', *The National Interest*, 16 (1989), pp. 3–18; and Fukuyama's extended defence of the position in his *The End of History and the Last Man* (Harmondsworth: Penguin Books, 1992).

2 K. R. Popper, *The Open Society and its Enemies* (London: Routledge and Kegan Paul, 1945, 2 vols); and *The Poverty of Historicism* (London: Routledge, 1991).

3 Popper, *The Poverty of Historicism*, p. vi.

4 Ibid., pp. vi-vii.

5 Ibid., p. vii.

6 Ibid., p. vii.

7 Ibid., p. vii, Popper's italics.

8 Popper, *The Open Society and its Enemies*, vol. 1, p. viii.

9 Ibid., vol. 2, p. 57.

10 Ibid., vol. 2, p. 25.

11 See Stephen Mulhall and Adam Swift, *Liberals and Communitarians* (Oxford: Blackwell, 1996).

12 See F. A. Hayek, *The Road to Serfdom* (London: Routledge, 2001).

13 Ibid., p. 115.

14 See F. A. Hayek, *The Constitution of Liberty* (London: Routledge and Kegan Paul, 1960).

15 Ibid., p. 106.

16 Ibid., p. 106.

17 Ibid., p. 106.

18 Ibid., p. 20.

19 See Peter Laslett, ed., *Politics, Philosophy and Society* (Oxford: Blackwell, 1956).

20 See Isaiah Berlin, 'Two Concepts of Liberty', in his *Four Essays on Liberty* (London: Oxford University Press, 1969), pp. 118–72.

21 See John Rawls, *A Theory of Justice* (Oxford: Oxford University Press, 1972).

22 See ibid., pp. 118–92.

23 See ibid., pp. 90–95.

24 Ibid., p. 11.

25 See John Rawls, *Lectures on the History of Political Philosophy*, ed. Samuel Freeman (Cambridge, Mass: Harvard University Press, 2007).

26 Rawls, *A Theory of Justice*, p. 60.

27 See ibid., pp. 60–5.

28 See ibid., pp. 75–83.

29 See John Rawls, *Political Liberalism* (New York: Columbia University Press, 1996); and John Rawls, *The Law of Peoples* (Cambridge, Mass: Harvard University Press, 1999).

30 See Robert Nozick, *Anarchy, State, and Utopia* (Oxford: Blackwell, 1974).

31 See Alasdair MacIntyre, *After Virtue* (London: Duckworth, 1985, second edition); Michael J. Sandel, *Liberalism and the Limits of Justice* (Cambridge: Cambridge University Press, 1982); and Charles Taylor, *Sources of the Self* (Cambridge: Cambridge University Press, 1989).

32 See Charles Taylor, *Hegel* (Cambridge: Cambridge University Press, 1975).

33 See Richard Rorty, *Contingency, Irony and Solidarity* (Cambridge: Cambridge University Press, 1989).

34 See Bruce Haddock, 'Liberalism and Contingency'; and Bruce Haddock and Peter Sutch, eds, *Multiculturalism, Identity and Rights* (London: Routledge, 2003).

11. Global Politics

1 See Francis Fukuyama, *The End of History and the Last Man*.

2 See Susan Strange, *The Retreat of the State: The Diffusion of Power in the World Economy* (Cambridge: Cambridge University Press, 1996).

3 See Jean-Marie Guehénno, *The End of the Nation-State*, trans. Victoria Elliott (Minneapolis: University of Minnesota Press, 1995).

4 See Michel Foucault, *Madness and Civilization*, trans. R. Howard (New York: Pantheon, 1965); idem, *The Birth of the Clinic*, trans. A. Sheridan (New York: Vintage, 1973); idem, *The Order of Things: An Archaeology of the Human Sciences*, trans. A. Sheridan (London: Routledge, 2002); and idem, *The Archaeology of Knowledge*, trans. A. Sheridan (London: Routledge, 2002).

5 See Michel Foucault, 'Governmentality', in his *Power*, ed. James D. Faubion (London: Penguin, 2000), pp. 201–22.

6 See Michel Foucault, 'Confronting Governments: Human Rights', in ibid., pp. 474–5.

7 Ibid., p. 474.

8 Ibid., p. 474.

9 Ibid., pp. 474–5.

10 Ibid., p. 474.

11 See Bruce Haddock, 'Hegel's Critique of the Theory of Social Contract', in David Boucher and Paul Kelly, eds, *The Social Contract from Hobbes to Rawls* (London: Routledge, 1994), pp. 147–63.

12 See Charles Taylor, *Hegel* (Cambridge: Cambridge University Press, 1975), pp. 3–50.

13 See Gino Bedani and Bruce Haddock, eds, *The Politics of Italian National Identity* (Cardiff: University of Wales Press, 2000).

14 See Bruce Haddock and Ovidiu Caraiani, 'Nationalism and Civil Society in Romania', *Political Studies*, 47 (1999), pp. 258–74; idem, 'Legitimacy, National Identity and Civil Association', in Lucian Boya, ed., *Nation and National Ideology: Past, Present and Future* (Bucharest: New Europe College, 2002), pp. 377–89.

15 Will Kymlicka, 'Western Political Theory and Ethnic Relations in Eastern Europe', in Will Kymlicka and Magda Opalski, eds, *Can Liberal Pluralism be Exported? Western Political Theory and Ethnic Relations in Eastern Europe* (Oxford: Oxford University Press, 2001), p. 48.

16 See Brian Barry, *Culture and Equality: An Egalitarian Critique of Multiculturalism* (Cambridge: Polity, 2001).

17 See John Rawls, *Political Liberalism*.

18 See Richard Rorty, *Contingency, Irony and Solidarity* (Cambridge: Cambridge University Press, 1989); John Gray, *Enlightenment's Wake* (London: Routledge, 1995); and idem, *Endgames: Questions in Late Modern Political Thought* (Cambridge: Polity, 1997).

19 See Joseph Raz, *The Morality of Freedom* (Oxford: Clarendon Press, 1986), pp. 321–66; W. B. Gallie, 'Essentially Contested Concepts', *Proceedings of the Aristotelian Society*, 66 (1955–6), pp. 167–98; and John Gray, 'Political Power, Social Theory and Essential Contestability', in D. Miller and L. Siedentop, eds, *The Nature of Political Theory* (Oxford: Oxford University Press,), pp. 75–101.

20 See Samuel P. Huntington, *The Clash of Civilizations and the Remaking of World Order* (New York: Simon and Schuster, 1996).

21 Bikhu Parekh, *Rethinking Multiculturalism: Cultural Diversity and Political Theory* (Basingstoke: Macmillan, 2000), p. 343.

22 Ibid., p. 343.

23 Ibid., p. 338.

24 Ibid., p. 343.

25 See Seyla Benhabib, *The Claims of Culture: Equality and Diversity in the Global Era* (Princeton: Princeton University Press, 2002).

26 See Paul Kelly, 'Identity, Equality and Power: Tensions in Parekh's Political Theory of Multiculturalism', in Bruce Haddock and Peter Sutch, eds, *Multiculturalism, Identity and Rights* (London: Routledge, 2003), pp. 94–110.

27 See Carol Gilligan, *In a Different Voice* (Cambridge, Mass.: Harvard University Press, 1982).

28 See Seyla Benhabib, *Situating the Self* (Cambridge: Polity, 1992).

29 See David Held, *Democracy and the Global Order: From the Modern State to Cosmopolitan Governance* (Cambridge: Polity, 1995).

30 See Michael Hardt and Antonio Negri, *Empire* (Cambridge, Mass.: Harvard University Press, 2000).

31 Rawls, *Political Liberalism*, p. lxii.

32 Ibid., p. lxii.

33 Ibid., p. lxii.

34 Ibid., p. lxii.

35 Ibid., p. lxii.

36 Ibid., p. 19.

37 Ibid., p. 19.

38 The phrase is adapted from T. M. Scanlon, *What We Owe to Each Other* (Cambridge, Mass.: Harvard University Press, 1998).

Suggestions for Further Reading

Good studies covering the range of texts and thinkers in the history of political thought abound. David Boucher and Paul Kelly (eds), *Political Thinkers: From Socrates to the Present* (Oxford: Oxford University Press, 2003), deals clearly with major figures and is helpful on further reading. Murray Forsyth and Maurice Keens-Soper (eds), *The Political Classics: A Guide to the Essential Texts from Plato to Rousseau* (Oxford: Oxford University Press, 1992), Murray Forsyth, Maurice Keens-Soper and John Hoffman (eds), *The Political Classics: Hamilton to Mill* (Oxford: Oxford University Press, 1993), and Murray Forsyth and Maurice Keens-Soper (eds), *The Political Classics: Green to Dworkin* (Oxford: Oxford University Press, 1996), focus instead on specific texts. Janet Coleman, *A History of Political Thought: From Ancient Greece to Early Christianity* (Oxford: Blackwell, 2000) and *A History of Political Thought: From the Middle Ages to the Renaissance* (Oxford: Blackwell, 2000), provides sure guidance on classical through to Renaissance political thought. Iain Hampsher-Monk, *A History of Modern Political Thought: Major Political Thinkers from Hobbes to Marx* (Oxford: Blackwell, 1992), is also a sound introduction to selected theorists. J. S. McClelland, *A History of Western Political Thought* (London: Routledge, 1996), is wider-ranging and patchy, but written in a lively and accessible style. Terence Ball, *Reappraising Political Theory: Revisionist Studies in the History of Political Thought* (Oxford: Oxford University Press, 1995), includes sensitive discussion of recent methodological debates. Quentin Skinner's seminal 'Meaning and Understanding in the History of Ideas', *History and Theory*, 8 (1969), sparked a generation of debate on the relationship between theory and history. David Boucher, *Texts in Context: Revisionist Methods for Studying the History of Ideas* (Dordrecht: Martinus Nijhof, 1985), addresses key contributions to the debate. Major figures exploring the history of political thought are always rewarding. See, in particular, John Rawls, *Lectures on the History of Political Philosophy*, ed. Samuel Freeman (Cambridge, Mass.: Harvard University Press, 2007), and Michael Oakeshott, *Lectures in the History of Political Thought*, ed. Terry

Nardin and Luke O'Sullivan (Exeter: Imprint Academic, 2006). Among older studies, Sheldon Wolin, *Politics and Vision* (Boston: Little Brown, 1960), John Plamenatz, *Man and Society: A Critical Examination of Some Important Social and Political Theories from Machiavelli to Marx*, 2 vols (London: Longman, 1963), and R. N. Berki, *The History of Political Thought: A Short Introduction* (London: Dent, 1977), continue to be rewarding. Students coming to political theory for the first time should perhaps begin with Peri Roberts and Peter Sutch, *An Introduction to Political Thought: A Conceptual Toolkit* (Edinburgh: Edinburgh University Press, 2004), or John Morrow, *The History of Political Thought: A Thematic Introduction* (Basingstoke: Macmillan, 1998).

Standards of scholarship in Greek political thought are very high indeed. For important background material see Cynthia Farrar, *The Origins of Democratic Thinking: The Invention of Politics in Classical Athens* (Cambridge: Cambridge University Press, 1988), and Dean Hammer, *The Iliad as Politics: The Performance of Political Thought* (Norman: University of Oklahoma Press, 2002). A good collection of early texts can be found in Michael Gagarin and Paul Woodruff (eds), *Early Greek Political Thought from Homer to the Sophists* (Cambridge: Cambridge University Press, 1995). For the sophists, W. K. C. Guthrie, *The Sophists* (Cambridge: Cambridge University Press, 1971), and G. B. Kerford, *The Sophistic Movement* (Cambridge: Cambridge University Press, 1981), remain indispensable. Terence Irwin, *Classical Thought* (Oxford: Oxford University Press, 1989), is a good broad survey.

Among general studies of Plato's thought, the following can be strongly recommended: George Klosko, *The Development of Plato's Political Theory* (London: Methuen, 1986); Robert W. Hall, *Plato* (London: George Allen and Unwin, 1981); G. C. Field, *The Philosophy of Plato* (Oxford: Oxford University Press, 1969); Angela Hobbs, *Plato and the Hero: Courage, Manliness, and the Impersonal Good* (Cambridge: Cambridge University Press, 2000); R. M. Hare, *Plato* (Oxford: Oxford University Press, 1982); Terence Irwin, *Plato's Moral Theory: The Early and Middle Dialogues* (Oxford; Clarendon Press, 1977); and Gregory Vlastos, *Plato's Universe* (Seattle: University of Washington Press, 1973).

For Plato's political philosophy, specifically (but not exclusively) the *Republic*, see Julia Annas, *An Introduction to Plato's Republic* (Oxford: Clarendon Press, 1981); C. D. C. Reeve, *Philosopher-Kings: The Argument of Plato's Republic* (Princeton: Princeton University Press, 1988); and Malcolm Schofield, *Plato: Political Philosophy* (Oxford: Oxford University Press, 2006).

Richard Kraut (ed.), *The Cambridge Companion to Plato* (Cambridge: Cambridge University Press, 1992) and Hugh H. Benson (ed.), *A Companion to Plato* (Oxford: Blackwell, 2006), are good collections of critical essays.

There are many good general studies of Aristotle, though they often deal with technical aspects of his thought that may seem remote from the interests of students of political philosophy and theory. However Jonathan Barnes, *Aristotle: A Very Short Introduction* (Oxford: Oxford University Press, 2000), is highly accessible. Anthony Kenny, *Aristotle on the Perfect Life* (Oxford: Clarendon Press, 1992) and Jonathan Lear, *Aristotle: The Desire to Understand* (Cambridge: Cambridge University Press, 1988), should also be helpful. Jonathan Barnes (ed.), *The Cambridge Companion to Aristotle* (Cambridge: Cambridge University Press, 1995), a wide-ranging collection of essays covering the gamut of Aristotle's thought, can be thoroughly recommended.

For Aristotle's political philosophy see R. G. Mulgan, *Aristotle's Political Theory* (Oxford: Clarendon Press, 1977); Fred D. Miller, *Nature, Justice and Rights in Aristotle's Politics* (Oxford: Clarendon Press, 1995); John B. Morrall, *Aristotle* (London: George Allen and Unwin, 1977); Bernard Yack, *The Problems of a Political Animal: Community, Justice, and Conflict in Aristotelian Political Thought* (Berkeley: University of California Press, 1993); Stephen G. Salkever, *Finding the Mean: Theory and Practice in Aristotelian Political Philosophy* (Princeton: Princeton University Press, 1990); Richard Kraut, *Aristotle: Political Philosophy* (Oxford: Oxford University Press, 2002); Peter Simpson, *A Philosophical Commentary on the Politics of Aristotle* (Chapel Hill: University of North Carolina Press, 1998); and Curtis N. Johnson, *Aristotle's Theory of the State* (London: Macmillan, 1990). David Keyt and Fred D. Miller (eds), *A Companion to Aristotle's Politics* (Oxford: Blackwell, 1991) and Aristide Tessitore (ed.), *Aristotle and Modern Politics: The Persistence of Political Philosophy* (Notre Dame, Ind.: University of Notre Dame Press, 2002), are good collections of critical essays.

For the stoics and the later Greek period see Andrew Erskine, *The Hellenistic Stoa: Political Thought and Action* (Ithaca: Cornell University Press, 1990); Malcolm Schofield, *The Stoic Idea of the City* (Chicago: University of Chicago Press, 1991); and Brad Inwood, *Ethics and Human Action in Early Stoicism* (Oxford: Clarendon Press, 1985). Christopher Rowe and Malcolm Schofield (eds), *The Cambridge History of Greek and Roman Political Thought* (Cambridge: Cambridge University Press, 2000), is an invaluable collection of essays addressing thinkers and themes throughout the classical period.

Roman law is hugely important for the development of European political thought and practice. Much of the scholarship, however, is highly technical and makes daunting reading for beginners in political philosophy. Barry Nicholas, *An Introduction to Roman Law* (Oxford: Clarendon Press, 1962), repays careful reading. David Johnston, *Roman Law in Context* (Cambridge: Cambridge University Press, 1999), is also very helpful. Among more advanced studies, H. F. Jolowicz and Barry Nicholas, *Historical Introduction to the Study of Roman Law* (Cambridge: Cambridge University Press, 1973, third edition), is richly informative. For wider views of the impact of Roman law see Peter Stein, *Roman Law in European*

History (Cambridge: Cambridge University Press, 1999), and Donald R. Kelley, *The Human Measure: Social Thought in the Western Legal Tradition* (Cambridge, Mass.: Harvard University Press, 1990).

F. E. Adcock, *Roman Political Ideas and Practice* (Ann Arbor: The University of Michigan Press, 1959), remains a good brief introduction to the wider Roman picture. Cicero is the pre-eminent Roman source for political and legal ideas. See Neal Wood, *Cicero's Social and Political Thought* (Berkeley: University of California Press, 1988); David Stockton, *Cicero: A Political Biography* (London: Oxford University Press, 1971); and R. E. Smith, *Cicero: The Statesman* (Cambridge: Cambridge University Press, 1966). For Cicero's more narrowly legal thought see Bruce W. Frier, *The Rise of the Roman Jurists: Studies in Cicero's Pro Caecina* (Princeton: Princeton University Press, 1985), and Jonathan Powell and Jeremy Paterson (eds), *Cicero the Advocate* (Oxford: Oxford University Press, 2004). Advanced students will recognize a continuing preoccupation with Roman terms of reference in modern jurisprudence. See Lon L. Fuller, *The Morality of Law* (New Haven: Yale University Press, 1969); H. L. A. Hart, *The Concept of Law* (Oxford: Clarendon Press, 1961); and James Gordley, *The Philosophical Origins of Modern Contract Doctrine* (Oxford: Clarendon Press, 1991).

Among broad overviews of medieval political thought, Walter Ullmann, *A History of Political Thought: The Middle Ages* (Harmondsworth: Penguin, 1965), and John B. Morrall, *Political Thought in Medieval Times* (London: Hutchinson, 1960), are helpful, in addition to the two volumes by Janet Coleman cited above. J. H. Burns, *The Cambridge History of Medieval Political Thought c. 350 – c. 1450* (Cambridge: Cambridge University Press, 1988), is an invaluable collection of wide-ranging essays.

Students coming to Augustine for the first time should begin with Henry Chadwick, *Augustine* (Oxford: Oxford University Press, 1986). The definitive biography is Peter Brown, *Augustine of Hippo: A Biography* (London: Faber and Faber, 1967). Eleonore Stump and Norman Kretzman (eds), *The Cambridge Companion to Augustine* (Cambridge: Cambridge University Press, 2001), is a good collection of recent essays. For historical background see A. Momigliano (ed.), *The Conflict between Paganism and Christianity in the Fourth Century* (Oxford: Clarendon Press, 1963); E. R. Dodds, *Pagan and Christian in an Age of Anxiety* (Cambridge: Cambridge University Press, 1965); C. N. Cochrane, *Christianity and Classical Culture* (Oxford: Clarendon Press, 1940); Peter Brown, *Religion and Society in the Age of Saint Augustine* (London: Faber and Faber, 1972); and Carol Harrison, *Augustine: Christian Truth and Fractured Humanity* (Oxford: Oxford University Press, 2000).

On Augustine's use of his sources see Harald Hagendahl, *Augustine and the Latin Classics* (Stockholm: Almquist and Wiksell International, 1967). Augustine's debt to Cicero on a detailed issue is dealt with in Neal Wood, '*Populares* and *Circumcelliones*: The Vocabulary of 'Fallen Man' in Cicero and St Augustine', *History of Political Thought*, 7 (1986). Far and away Augustine's most important source, however, is the Bible. Students with only a cursory knowledge of the text should read (at least) the Pauline Letters.

The surest guide to Augustine's intellectual biography is his own *Confessions*, ed. R. S. Pine-Coffin (Harmondsworth: Penguin, 1961). But the importance of the *Confessions* extends far beyond the development of his mind. Students intimidated by Augustine's technical theological discussions can grasp the rudiments of his doctrine of grace from the *Confessions*.

Augustine's wider views on history and society are also crucial for an understanding of his political thought. See R. A. Markus, *Saeculum: History and Society in the Thought of St Augustine* (Cambridge: Cambridge University Press, 1970). On a specific theological issue which students of political theory should not neglect, see G. R. Evans, *Augustine on Evil* (Cambridge: Cambridge University Press, 1982). More specifically on Augustine's political thought, the most comprehensive account is Herbert A. Deane, *The Political Ideas of St Augustine* (New York: Columbia University Press, 1963). Rex Martin, 'The Two Cities in Augustine's Political Philosophy', *Journal of the History of Ideas*, 33 (1972), considers the central distinction in the *City of God*. William E. Connolly, *The Augustinian Imperative: A Reflection on the Politics of Morality* (Newbury Park: Sage, 1993), engages with wider implications of Augustine's thought. Of older studies, students will still profit from J. N. Figgis, *The Political Aspects of St Augustine's 'City of God'* (London: Longmans, Green, 1921), and Norman H. Baynes, *The Political Ideas of St Augustine's 'De Civitate Dei'* (London: The Historical Association, 1936).

The best short introduction to the range of Aquinas's thought is Anthony Kenny, *Aquinas* (Oxford: Oxford University Press, 1980). F. C. Copleston, *Aquinas* (Harmondsworth: Penguin, 1991), can also be thoroughly recommended. Eleonore Stump, *Aquinas* (London: Routledge, 2003), is more comprehensive and thoroughly rewarding. John Finnis, *Aquinas: Moral, Political, and Legal Theory* (Oxford: Oxford University Press, 1998), is the best study of the political philosophy. D. J. O'Connor, *Aquinas and Natural Law* (London: Macmillan, 1967), and Anthony J. Lisska, *Aquinas's Theory of Natural Law* (Oxford: Clarendon Press, 1996), are good discussions of a key theme. For biography see James A. Weisheipl, *Friar Thomas d'Aquino: His Life, Thought and Works* (Oxford: Blackwell, 1975). Norman Kretzman and Eleonore Stump (eds), *The Cambridge Companion to Aquinas* (Cambridge: Cambridge University Press, 1993), is a good collection of essays covering the range of Aquinas's thought.

Among studies of later developments in medieval political thought, Anthony Black, *Political Thought in Europe, 1250–1450* (Cambridge: Cambridge University Press, 1992), provides a good overview. See also Brian Tierney, *Foundations of Conciliar Theory: The Contribution of the Medieval Canonists from Gratian to the Great Schism* (Cambridge: Cambridge University Press, 1955); Paul E. Sigmund, *Nicholas of Cusa and Medieval Political Thought* (Cambridge, Mass.: Harvard University Press, 1963); and

Alan Gewirth, *Marsilius of Padua and Medieval Political Philosophy* (New York: Columbia University Press, 1951). Otto von Gierke, *Political Theories of the Middle Age*, trans. F. W. Maitland (Cambridge: Cambridge University Press, 1900), remains a classic.

Historical background for late-medieval, Renaissance and early-modern political thought is admirably covered in Quentin Skinner, *The Foundations of Modern Political Thought* (Cambridge: Cambridge University Press, 1978, 2 vols). J. H. Burns (ed.), *The Cambridge History of Political Thought, 1450–1700* (Cambridge: Cambridge University Press, 1991), is a good collection of wide-ranging essays.

For Machiavelli, Quentin Skinner, *Machiavelli* (Oxford: Oxford University Press, 1981), is a clear introduction. Roberto Ridolfi, *The Life of Niccolo Machiavelli*, trans. Cecil Grayson (London: Routledge and Kegan Paul, 1963), is a sound biography. Among studies which are very strong on historical context see Sydney Anglo, *Machiavelli: A Dissection* (London: Gollancz, 1969); Felix Gilbert, *Machiavelli and Guicciardini: Politics and History in Sixteenth-century Florence* (Princeton: Princeton University Press, 1965); and Federico Chabod, *Machiavelli and the Renaissance*, trans. David Moore (New York: Harper and Row, 1965). For more specialized focus on the political thought, see Maurizio Viroli, *Machiavelli* (Oxford: Oxford University Press, 1998); Joseph V. Femia, *Machiavelli Revisited* (Cardiff: University of Wales Press, 2004); Leo Strauss, *Thoughts on Machiavelli* (Seattle: University of Washington Press, 1958); Peter S. Donaldson, *Machiavelli and Mystery of State* (Cambridge: Cambridge University Press, 1988); Hanna Pitkin, *Fortune is a Woman: Gender and Politics in the Thought of Machiavelli* (Chicago: University of Chicago Press, 1999); Ruth W. Grant, *Hypocrisy and Intensity: Machiavelli, Rousseau, and the Ethics of Politics* (Chicago: University of Chicago Press, 1997); and Gisela Bock, Quentin Skinner and Maurizio Viroli (eds), *Machiavelli and Republicanism* (Cambridge: Cambridge University Press, 1990).

Good treatments of patriarchal political thought can be found in James Daly, *Sir Robert Filmer and English Political Thought* (Toronto: University of Toronto Press, 1979), and Gordon J. Schochet, *Patriarchalism in Political Thought: The Authoritarian Family and Political Speculation especially in Seventeenth-Century England* (Oxford: Blackwell, 1975). For a broader survey see J. P. Sommerville, *Politics and Ideology in England, 1603–40* (London: Longman, 1886). Sommerville's introductions to King James VI and I, *Political Writings* (Cambridge: Cambridge University Press, 1994), and Robert Filmer, *Patriarcha and Other Writings* (Cambridge: Cambridge University Press, 1991), are also very helpful. Stuart Clark, *Thinking with Demons: The Idea of Witchcraft in Early Modern Europe* (Oxford: Oxford University Press, 1997), highlights fascinating insights from an alternative perspective.

The secondary literature on Hobbes is very strong indeed. Richard Tuck, *Hobbes* (Oxford: Oxford University Press, 1989), A. P. Martinich,

Hobbes (London: Routledge, 2005), Richard Peters, *Hobbes* (Harmondsworth: Penguin, 1967), and Tom Sorrell, *Hobbes* (London: Routledge and Kegan Paul, 1986), provide good introductions. Noel Malcolm, *Aspects of Hobbes* (Oxford: Clarendon Press, 2002), is a wealth of information, especially on biographical matters. Tom Sorrell (ed.), *The Cambridge Companion to Hobbes* (Cambridge: Cambridge University Press, 1996), is an excellent collection of essays on the range of Hobbes's writings. Among more specialized studies, the following can be strongly recommended: Jean Hampton, *Hobbes and the Social Contract Tradition* (Cambridge: Cambridge University Press, 1986); Michael Oakeshott, *Hobbes on Civil Association* (Oxford: Blackwell, 1975); Deborah Baumgold, *Hobbes's Political Theory* (Cambridge: Cambridge University Press, 1988); J. W. N. Watkins, *Hobbes's System of Ideas: A Study in the Political Significance of Philosophical Theories* (London: Hutchinson, 1973); M. M. Goldsmith, *Hobbes's Science of Politics* (New York: Columbia University Press, 1966); David P. Gauthier, *The Logic of Leviathan: The Moral and Political Theory of Thomas Hobbes* (Oxford: Clarendon Press, 1969); Howard Warrender, *The Political Theory of Hobbes: His Theory of Obligation* (Oxford: Clarendon Press, 1957); Leo Strauss, *The Political Philosophy of Hobbes*, trans. Elsa M. Sinclair (Oxford: Clarendon Press, 1936); Quentin Skinner, *Reason and Rhetoric in the Philosophy of Hobbes* (Cambridge: Cambridge University Press, 1996); Gabriella Slomp, *Thomas Hobbes and the Political Philosophy of Glory* (Basingstoke: Macmillan, 2000); C. B. Macpherson, *The Political Theory of Possessive Individualism: Hobbes to Locke* (Oxford: Clarendon Press, 1962); and Richard E. Flathman, *Thomas Hobbes: Skepticism, Individuality, and Chastened Politics* (Newbury Park: Sage, 1993).

The literature on seventeenth-century rights theory is vast. Among broad surveys, Knud Haakonssen, *Natural Law and Moral Philosophy: From Grotius to the Scottish Enlightenment* (Cambridge: Cambridge University Press, 1996), and Richard Tuck, *Natural Rights Theories: Their Origin and Development* (Cambridge: Cambridge University Press, 1979), are exceptionally clear guides to complex technical issues. Stephen Buckle, *Natural Law and the Theory of Property: Grotius to Hume* (Oxford: Clarendon Press, 1991), sheds light on a more specific issue. J. N. Figgis, *Studies of Political Thought from Gerson to Grotius: 1414–1625* (Cambridge: Cambridge University Press, 1907), is still useful. David Boucher, *Political Theories of International Relations: From Thucydides to the Present* (Oxford: Oxford University Press, 1998), has good discussions of rights theory. On specific thinkers, see Edward Dumbauld, *The Life and Legal Writings of Hugo Grotius* (Norman: University of Oklahoma Press, 1969); Knud Haakonssen, 'Hugo Grotius and the History of Political Thought', *Political Theory*, 13 (1985); Hedley Bull, Benedict Kingsbury and Adam Roberts (eds), *Hugo Grotius and International Society* (Oxford: Clarendon Press, 1990); Renee Jeffrey, *Hugo Grotius in International Thought* (New York: Palgrave Macmillan, 2006); Leonard Krieger, *Pufendorf and the Acceptance of Natural Law*

(Chicago: University of Chicago Press, 1965); J. B. Schneewind, 'Pufendorf's Place in the History of Ethics', *Synthese*, 72 (1987); Michael Nutkiewicz, 'Samuel Pufendorf: Obligation as the Basis of the State', *Journal of the History of Philosophy*, 21 (1983); and Thomas Mautner, 'Pufendorf's Place in the History of Rights Concepts', in Timothy O'Hagan (ed.), *Revolution and Enlightenment in Europe* (Aberdeen: Aberdeen University Press, 1991).

The following are good introductory treatments of Locke: John Dunn, *Locke* (Oxford: Oxford University Press, 1984); Geraint Parry, *John Locke* (London: Allen and Unwin, 1978); J. D. Mabbott, *John Locke* (London: Macmillan, 1973); and E. J. Lowe, *Locke* (London: Routledge, 2005). Locke's intellectual development is admirably covered in Ian Harris, *The Mind of John Locke: A Study of Political Theory in its Intellectual Setting* (Cambridge: Cambridge University Press, 1998). Peter Laslett's introduction to his edition of the *Two Treatises of Government* (New York: Mentor, 1965) is also a mine of information. For detailed historical treatment of the text, see John Dunn, *The Political Thought of John Locke: An Historical Account of the Argument of the 'Two Treatises of Government'* (Cambridge: Cambridge University Press, 1969). Richard Ashcraft, *Revolutionary Politics and Locke's 'Two Treatises of Government'* (Princeton: Princeton University Press, 1986), is an important contribution to our understanding of the immediate context. For wider issues in Locke's political thought, see Ruth W. Grant, *John Locke's Liberalism* (Chicago: University Chicago Press, 1987), J. W. Gough, *John Locke's Political Philosophy: Eight Studies* (Oxford: Clarendon Press, 1950), Michael P. Zuckert, *Launching Liberalism: On Lockean Political Philosophy* (Lawrence: University of Kansas Press, 2002), and Richard H. Cox, *Locke on War and Peace* (Oxford: Clarendon Press, 1960). Among more specialized studies, James Tully, *A Discourse on Property: John Locke and his Adversaries* (Cambridge: Cambridge University Press, 1980), Jeremy Waldron, *God, Locke, and Equality: Christian Foundations of John Locke's Political Thought* (Cambridge: Cambridge University Press, 2002), and A. John Simmons, *The Lockean Theory of Rights* (Princeton: Princeton University Press, 1992), are rewarding.

Among overviews of the Enlightenment, the following are especially useful for students of political thought: Peter Gay, *The Enlightenment: An Interpretation* (London: Weidenfeld and Nicolson, 1967, 2 vols); Ernst Cassirer, *The Philosophy of the Enlightenment*, trans. Fritz C. A. Koelln and James P. Pettegrove (Princeton: Princeton University Press, 1979); Jonathan I. Israel, *Radical Enlightenment: Philosophy and the Making of Modernity, 1650–1750* (Oxford: Oxford University Press, 2002); Jonathan I. Israel, *Enlightenment Contested: Philosophy, Modernity, and the Emancipation of Man, 1670–1752* (Oxford: Oxford University Press, 2006); and Louis Dupre, *The Enlightenment and the Intellectual Foundations of Modern Culture* (New Haven: Yale University Press, 2004).

Spinoza is a challenging and controversial figure, whose technical philosophy will prove demanding for beginners. His importance, however, as a bridge between the seventeenth-century rationalists and the Enlightenment, is indisputable. Two clear introductions will prove helpful: Roger Scruton, *Spinoza* (Oxford: Oxford University Press, 1986), and Stuart Hampshire, *Spinoza* (Harmondsworth: Penguin Books, 1988), reprinted in his *Spinoza and Spinozism* (Oxford: Clarendon Press, 2005). For biography, see Steven Nadler, *Spinoza: A Life* (Cambridge: Cambridge University Press, 2001). Don Garrett (ed.), *The Cambridge Companion to Spinoza* (Cambridge: Cambridge University Press, 1996), is a good collection of essays. For Spinoza's political thought, see Robert J. McShea, *The Political Philosophy of Spinoza* (New York: Columbia University Press, 1968), Steven B. Smith, *Spinoza, Liberalism and the Question of Jewish Identity* (New Haven: Yale University Press, 1998), and Etienne Balibar, *Spinoza and Politics*, trans. Peter Snowden (London: Verso, 1998).

Elisabeth Labrousse, *Bayle*, trans. Denys Potts (Oxford: Oxford University Press, 1983), is the most accessible introduction to Bayle. For the wider context of sceptical philosophy in the early-modern period, see Richard H. Popkin, *The History of Scepticism: From Savonarola to Bayle* (Oxford: Oxford University Press, 2003).

Montesquieu is best approached initially through Judith N. Shklar, *Montesquieu* (Oxford: Oxford University Press, 1987). For the life, see Robert Shackleton, *Montesquieu: A Critical Biography* (London: Oxford University Press, 1961). Good studies of Montesquieu's politics include: Thomas L. Pangle, *Montesquieu's Philosophy of Liberalism: A Commentary on 'The Spirit of the Laws'* (Chicago: University of Chicago Press, 1974), Mark Waddicor, *Montesquieu and the Philosophy of Natural Law* (The Hague: Kluwer Academic Publishers, 1970), and Mark Hulliung, *Montesquieu and the Old Regime* (Berkeley: University of California Press, 1976). Norman Hampson, *Will and Circumstance: Montesquieu, Rousseau and the French Revolution* (London: Duckworth, 1983), and Maurice Cranston, *Philosophers and Pamphleteers: Political Theorists of the Enlightenment* (Oxford: Oxford University Press, 1986), place Montesquieu helpfully in the wider context of Enlightenment thought.

Studies of Hume abound. A. J. Ayer, *Hume* (Oxford: Oxford University Press, 1980), is a good introduction to the philosophy. For biography, see Ernest Campbell Mossner, *The Life of David Hume* (Oxford: Clarendon Press, 1980). David Fate Norton (ed.), *The Cambridge Companion to Hume* (Cambridge: Cambridge University Press, 1993), is a valuable collection of essays. An earlier collection edited by V. C. Chappel, *Hume* (New York: Doubleday, 1966), is still useful. For the moral philosophy, see Anthony Flew, *David Hume: Philosopher of Moral Science* (Oxford: Blackwell, 1986), Paul Russell, *Freedom and Sentiment: Hume's Way of Naturalizing Responsibility* (Oxford: Oxford University Press, 2002), Jonathan Harrison, *Hume's Moral Epistemology* (Oxford: Clarendon Press, 1976), J. L. Mackie, *Hume's Moral Theory* (London: Routledge, 1980), and Sophie Botros, *Hume, Reason and Morality: A Legacy of Contradiction* (London: Routledge, 2006).

Duncan Forbes, *Hume's Philosophical Politics* (Cambridge: Cambridge University Press, 1975), David Miller, *Philosophy and Ideology in Hume's Political Thought* (Oxford: Clarendon Press, 1981), and John B. Stewart, *The Moral and Political Philosophy of David Hume* (New York: Columbia University Press, 1963), are excellent studies of the political theory.

Peter Gay, *Voltaire's Politics: The Poet as a Realist* (Princeton: Princeton University Press, 1959), is informative and accessible. For biography, see Theodore Besterman, *Voltaire* (Oxford: Blackwell, 1969). Peter France, *Diderot* (Oxford: Oxford University Press, 1983), is a clear introduction. For biography, see Arthur M. Wilson, *Diderot* (Oxford: Oxford University Press, 1983).

There is a wealth of literature on Kant's moral and political thought, often written from a technical philosophical perspective. For Kant's life, Ernst Cassirer, *Kant's Life and Thought*, trans. James Haden (New Haven: Yale University Press, 1981), is a model of clarity. For a more recent treatment, see Manfred Kuehn, *Kant: A Biography* (Cambridge: Cambridge University Press, 2002). Allen W. Wood, *Kant* (Oxford: Blackwell, 2005), is a balanced and perceptive introduction to the gamut of Kant's work. Andrew Ward, *Kant: The Three Critiques* (Cambridge: Polity, 2006), can also be thoroughly recommended. For the moral philosophy, Allen W. Wood, *Kant's Ethical Thought* (Cambridge: Cambridge University Press, 1999), is painstaking and demanding, but richly rewarding. Beginners may prefer to start with Roger J. Sullivan, *An Introduction to Kant's Ethics* (Cambridge: Cambridge University Press, 1994). For Kant's politics, see Howard Williams, *Kant's Political Philosophy* (Oxford: Blackwell, 1983), Kimberley Hutchings, *Kant, Critique and Politics* (London: Routledge, 1996), Jeffrie G. Murphy, *Kant: The Philosophy of Right* (London: Macmillan, 1970), Elisabeth Ellis, *Kant's Politics: Provisional Theory for an Uncertain World* (New Haven: Yale University Press, 2005), Allen D. Rosen, *Kant's Theory of Justice* (Ithaca: Cornell University Press, 1993), and Howard Williams, *Kant's Critique of Hobbes: Sovereignty and Cosmopolitanism* (Cardiff: University of Wales Press, 2003). *Perpetual Peace* is the focus of Georg Cavallar, *Kant and the Theory and Practice of International Right* (Cardiff: University of Wales Press, 1999). More advanced students should not neglect the engagement of contemporary philosophers with Kant's ethics. See Barbara Herman, *The Practice of Moral Judgement* (Cambridge, Mass.: Harvard University Press, 1993), Onora O'Neill, *Constructions of Reason: Explorations of Kant's Practical Philosophy* (Cambridge: Cambridge University Press, 1989), and John Rawls, *Lectures on the History of Moral Philosophy*, ed. Barbara Herman (Cambridge: Mass.: Harvard University Press, 2000).

Rousseau has always been a controversial figure. The most accessible short introduction is Robert Wokler, *Rousseau* (Oxford: Oxford University Press, 1995). Nicolas Dent, *Rousseau* (London: Routledge, 2005), is also very helpful. For biography, see the two volumes by Maurice Cranston: *Jean-Jacques: The Early Life and Work of Jean-Jacques Rousseau, 1712–1754*

(Harmondsworth: Penguin, 1987), and *The Noble Savage: Jean-Jacques Rousseau, 1754–1762* (London: Allen Lane, 1991). Patrick Riley (ed.), *The Cambridge Companion to Rousseau* (Cambridge: Cambridge University Press, 2001), is an excellent collection of essays. For Rousseau's complex relationship with mainstream Enlightenment thinkers, see Mark Hulliung, *The Autocritique of Enlightenment: Rousseau and the Philosophes* (Cambridge, Mass.: Harvard University Press, 1994), and Graeme Garrard, *Rousseau's Counter-Enlightenment: A Republican Critique of the Philosophes* (Albany: State University of New York Press, 2003). For Rousseau's impact on the theory and practice of revolution, see Carol Blum, *Rousseau and the Republic of Virtue: The Language of Politics in the French Revolution* (Ithaca: Cornell University Press, 1986), and James Swenson, *On Jean-Jacques Rousseau: Considered as one of the first authors of the Revolution* (Stanford: Stanford University Press, 2000). For Rousseau's social and political theory, see Maurizio Viroli, *Jean-Jacques Rousseau and the 'Well-Ordered Society'*, trans. Derek Hanson (Cambridge: Cambridge University Press, 1988), Judith N. Shklar, *Men and Citizens: A Study of Rousseau's Social Theory* (Cambridge: Cambridge University Press, 1969), Ronald Grimsley, *The Philosophy of Rousseau* (London: Oxford University Press, 1973), Roger D. Masters, *The Political Philosophy of Rousseau* (Princeton: Princeton University Press, 1968), and John Charvet, *The Social Problem in the Philosophy of Rousseau* (Cambridge: Cambridge University Press, 1974). Among older studies, Ernst Cassirer, *The Question of Jean-Jacques Rousseau*, trans. Peter Gay (New York: Columbia University Press, 1954), and Alfred Cobban, *Rousseau and the Modern State* (London: Allen and Unwin, 1934), are still very much worthwhile.

An understanding of modern political thought requires some familiarity with arguments and issues raised in the French Revolution. William Doyle, *The French Revolution: A Very Short Introduction* (Oxford: Oxford University Press, 2001), is admirably clear. Other standard studies include William Doyle, *The Oxford History of the French Revolution* (Oxford: Oxford University Press, 1989), François Furet, *Revolutionary France: 1770–1870* (Oxford: Oxford University Press, 1992), and Simon Schama, *Citizens: A Chronicle of the French Revolution* (London: Viking, 1989). François Furet, *Interpreting the French Revolution*, trans. Elborg Forster (Cambridge: Cambridge University Press, 1981), illustrates the pivotal nature of the Revolution in emerging ideological debates. Geoffrey Best (ed.), *The Permanent Revolution: The French Revolution and its Legacy, 1789–1989* (London: Fontana, 1988), is exceptionally useful for students primarily interested in political theory. J. L. Talmon, *The Origins of Totalitarian Democracy: Political Theory and Practice during the French Revolution and Beyond* (Harmondsworth: Penguin Books, 1982; first published 1952), is a polemical critique of the revolutionary tradition, which is now attracting renewed attention. Slovoj Zizek's introduction to Maximilien Robespierre, *Virtue and Terror*, ed. Jean Ducange, trans. John Howe (London: Verso,

2007), is a spirited contribution to the debate. On specific theorists, see Murray Forsyth, *Reason and Revolution: The Political Thought of the Abbe Sieyes* (Leicester: Leicester University Press, 1987), and Murray Forsyth, 'Emmanuel Sieyes: *What is the Third Estate?'*, in Murray Forsyth, Maurice Keens-Soper and John Hoffman (eds), *The Political Classics: Hamilton to Mill*.

For the history and politics of the American Revolution, see Edmund S. Morgan, *The Birth of the Republic, 1763–89* (Chicago: Chicago University Press, 1992), Colin Bonwick, *The American Revolution* (Basingstoke: Palgrave Macmillan, 2005), and Gordon S. Wood, *The American Revolution: A History* (London: Weidenfeld and Nicolson, 2003). For broader theoretical background to the thinking of the revolutionary period, see J. G. A. Pocock, *The Machiavellian Moment: Florentine Political Thought and the Atlantic Republican Tradition* (Princeton: Princeton University Press, 1975), Morton White, *The Philosophy of the American Revolution* (Oxford: Oxford University Press, 1978), and Gordon S. Wood, *The Radicalism of the American Revolution* (New York: Vintage Books, 1993). Hannah Arendt's parallel reading of the American and French revolutions, *On Revolution* (London: Faber, 1963), is provocative and challenging. Among studies focused more specifically on the *Federalist Papers*, see Morton White, *Philosophy, 'The Federalist' and the Constitution* (Oxford: Oxford University Press, 1987), David F. Epstein, *The Political Theory of the Federalist* (Chicago: University of Chicago Press, 1986), and Saul Cornell, *The Other Founders: Anti-Federalism and the Dissenting Tradition in America, 1788–1828* (Chapel Hill: University of North Carolina Press, 1999).

Developments in political thought in the nineteenth century must be seen in relation to wider currents of thought. The emergence of historical awareness, in particular, is crucial. See Bruce Haddock, *An Introduction to Historical Thought* (London: Edward Arnold, 1980), Maurice Mandelbaum, *History, Man and Reason: A Study in Nineteenth-Century Thought* (Baltimore: Johns Hopkins University Press, 1971), and Hayden White, *Metahistory: The Historical Imagination in Nineteenth-Century Europe* (Baltimore: Johns Hopkins University Press, 1973). For the cult of science in the nineteenth century, see W. M. Simon, *European Positivism in the Nineteenth Century: An Essay in Intellectual History* (Ithaca: Cornell University Press, 1963). The optimistic current in French thought is covered in Frank E. Manuel, *The Prophets of Paris* (Cambridge, Mass.: Harvard University Press, 1962). Wider cultural currents are vividly portrayed in J. W. Barrow, *The Crisis of Reason: European Thought, 1848–1914* (New Haven: Yale University Press, 2000).

There is a vast literature on the emergence of modern political ideologies. Good short introductions are Michael Freeden, *Ideology* (Oxford: Oxford University Press, 2003), and David McLellan, *Ideology* (Milton Keynes: Open University Press, 1986). Beginners will find Terence Ball and Richard Dagger, *Political Ideologies and the Democratic Ideal* (New York:

Harper Collins, 1991), a helpful guide to positions and ideas. Michael Freeden, *Ideologies and Political Theory: A Conceptual Approach* (Oxford: Clarendon Press, 1996), is a rigorous defence of the wider significance of ideological thinking. Andrew Vincent, *Modern Political Ideologies* (Oxford: Blackwell, 1992), gives a comprehensive account of controversies across the ideological spectrum. John B. Thompson, *Studies in the Theory of Ideology* (Cambridge: Polity, 1984), is a good analysis of recent methodological debates.

Hegel gives us the most detailed philosophical account of the emergence of the modern state in the early nineteenth century, but he remains a difficult and controversial thinker. The Knox edition of the *Philosophy of Right* has been used in this book. Allen W. Wood's edition of the text, *Elements of the Philosophy of Right* (Cambridge: Cambridge University Press, 1991), can also be strongly recommended. Peter Singer, *Hegel* (Oxford: Oxford University Press, 1983), and Raymond Plant, *Hegel* (London: Allen and Unwin, 1973), are clear introductory accounts. Frederick Beiser, *Hegel* (London: Routledge, 2005), is more detailed and extremely useful for more advanced students. For Hegel's life, see Terry Pinkard, *Hegel: A Biography* (Cambridge: Cambridge University Press, 2000). Among critical studies, see Allen W. Wood, *Hegel's Ethical Thought* (Cambridge: Cambridge University Press, 1991); Michael Hardimon, *Hegel's Social Philosophy: The Project of Reconciliation* (Cambridge: Cambridge University Press, 1994); Manfred Riedel, *Between Tradition and Revolution: The Hegelian Transformation of Political Philosophy* (Cambridge: Cambridge University Press, 1984); Shlomo Avineri, *Hegel's Theory of the Modern State* (Cambridge: Cambridge University Press, 1972); Alan Patten, *Hegel's Idea of Freedom* (Oxford: Oxford University Press, 1999); Robert Pippin, *Idealism as Modernism: Hegelian Variations* (Cambridge: Cambridge University Press, 1997); Charles Taylor, *Hegel* (Cambridge: Cambridge University Press, 1975); Frederick Neuhouser, *Foundations of Hegel's Social Theory: Actualizing Freedom* (Cambridge, Mass.: Harvard University Press, 2000); Fred R. Dallmayr, *G. W. F. Hegel: Modernity and Politics* (Newbury Park: Sage, 1993); Ian Fraser, *Hegel and Marx: The Concept of Need* (Edinburgh: Edinburgh University Press, 1998); Robert R. Williams, *Hegel's Ethics of Recognition* (Berkeley: University of California Press, 1997); Mark Tunick, *Hegel's Political Philosophy: Interpreting the Practice of Legal Punishment* (Princeton: Princeton University Press, 1992); and Herbert Marcuse, *Reason and Revolution: Hegel and the Rise of Social Theory* (London: Routledge and Kegan Paul, 1955). Frederick C. Beiser (ed.), *The Cambridge Companion to Hegel* (Cambridge: Cambridge University Press, 1993), is a wide-ranging collection of essays. Useful collections of essays focused more specifically on Hegel's political philosophy include: Robert R. Williams (ed.), *Beyond Liberalism and Communitarianism: Studies in Hegel's Philosophy of Right* (Albany: State University of New York Press, 2001); Z. A. Pelczynski (ed.), *Hegel's Political Philosophy: Problems and Perspectives*

(Cambridge: Cambridge University Press, 1971); and Z. A. Pelczynski (ed.), *The State and Civil Society: Studies in Hegel's Political Philosophy* (Cambridge: Cambridge University Press, 1984).

Among broad treatments of liberalism, Guido de Ruggiero, *The History of European Liberalism*, trans. R. G. Collingwood (Boston: Beacon Press, 1959), remains outstanding. Pierre Manent, *An Intellectual History of Liberalism*, trans. Rebecca Balinski (Princeton: Princeton University Press, 1995), is also thoroughly stimulating. Nancy L. Rosenblum, *Another Liberalism: Romanticism and the Reconstruction of Liberal Thought* (Cambridge, Mass.: Harvard University Press, 1987), explores a neglected dimension in the liberal tradition. Beginners will find John Gray, *Liberalism* (Milton Keynes: Open University Press, 1986), useful. See also John Gray, *Two Faces of Liberalism* (Cambridge: Polity, 2000), for a challenging statement of the deep divisions in liberal thought. Contemporary themes are expertly covered in Paul Kelly, *Liberalism* (Cambridge: Polity, 2005). For a good overview see Mark Evans (ed.), *The Edinburgh Companion to Contemporary Liberalism* (Edinburgh: Edinburgh University Press, 2001).

There is a wide literature on specific liberal figures. For Constant's life, see Dennis Wood, *Benjamin Constant: A Biography* (London: Routledge, 1993). Stephen Holmes, *Benjamin Constant and the Making of Modern Liberalism* (New Haven: Yale University Press, 1984), is a vigorous defence of Constant's case for a modern constitutional state. Biancamaria Fontana, *Benjamin Constant and the Post-Revolutionary Mind* (New Haven: Yale University Press, 1991), is helpful on context. See also George Armstrong Kelly, *The Humane Comedy: Constant, Tocqueville and French Liberalism* (Cambridge University Press, 1992).

There has been a renaissance of interest in Tocqueville's thought among both historians and political theorists. For the life, see André Jardin, *Tocqueville: A Biography*, trans. Lydia Davis and Robert Hemenway (Baltimore: Johns Hopkins University Press, 1998), and Hugh Brogan, *Alexis de Tocqueville: Prophet of Democracy in the Age of Revolution* (London: Profile Books, 2006). Sheldon S. Wolin, *Two Worlds: The Making of a Political and Theoretical Life* (Princeton: Princeton University Press, 2001), is characteristically subtle and wide-ranging, combining careful reading of the gamut of Tocqueville's writings and papers with critical engagement with his ideas. Larry Siedentop, *Tocqueville* (Oxford: Oxford University Press, 1994), is a short but stimulating introduction. The following can also be thoroughly recommended: Cheryl Welch, *De Tocqueville* (Oxford: Oxford University Press, 2001); James T. Schleifer, *The Making of Tocqueville's Democracy in America* (Chapel Hill: University of North Carolina Press, 1980); Jack Lively, *The Social and Political Thought of Alexis de Tocqueville* (Oxford: Clarendon Press, 1962); and Roger Boesche, *The Strange Liberalism of Alexis de Tocqueville* (Ithaca: Cornell University Press, 1987). Cheryl B. Welch (ed.), *The Cambridge Companion to Tocqueville* (Cambridge: Cambridge University Press, 2006), is a good collection of essays.

For Bentham, see P. J. Kelly, *Utilitarianism and Distributive Justice: Jeremy Bentham and the Civil Law* (Oxford: Clarendon Press, 1990); David Manning, *The Mind of Jeremy Bentham* (London: Longman, 1968); Frederick Rosen, *Jeremy Bentham and Representative Democracy: A Study of the Constitutional Code* (Oxford: Clarendon Press, 1983); Ross Harrison, *Bentham* (London: Routledge, 1983); Douglas G. Long, *Bentham on Liberty: Jeremy Bentham's Idea of Liberty in Relation to his Utilitarianism* (Toronto: University of Toronto Press, 1977); and John Dinwiddy, *Bentham* (Oxford: Oxford University Press, 1989).

John Stuart Mill remains a staple figure for political theorists, attracting consistently high levels of scholarship. William Thomas, *Mill* (Oxford: Oxford University Press, 1985), and Alan Ryan, *J. S. Mill* (London: Macmillan, 1975), are clear introductions. From a vast literature, see J. C. Rees, *John Stuart Mill's On Liberty*, ed. G. L. Williams (Oxford: Oxford University Press, 1985); John Gray, *Mill on Liberty: A Defence* (London: Routledge, 1983); Roger Crisp, *Mill on Utilitarianism* (London: Routledge, 1997); Joseph Hamburger, *John Stuart Mill on Liberty and Control* (Princeton: Princeton University Press, 1999); C. L. Ten, *Mill on Liberty* (Oxford: Oxford University Press, 1980); John Skorupski, *John Stuart Mill* (London: Routledge, 1989); Alan Ryan, *The Philosophy of John Stuart Mill* (Basingstoke: Macmillan, 1987); Fred R. Berger, *Happiness, Justice and Freedom: The Moral and Political Philosophy of John Stuart Mill* (Berkeley: University of California Press, 1984); John M. Robson, *The Improvement of Mankind: The Social and Political Thought of John Stuart Mill* (London: Routledge, 1968); and Georgios Varouxakis, *Mill on Nationality* (London: Routledge, 2002). John Skorupski (ed.), *The Cambridge Companion to Mill* (Cambridge: Cambridge University Press, 1998), is an invaluable collection of essays covering the range of Mill's work.

Conservatism has attracted much less attention from theorists as a body of ideas, though thoughtful work is available. Robert Nisbet, *Conservatism: Dream and Reality* (Milton Keynes: Open University Press, 1986), is a good introduction. Roger Eatwell and Noel O'Sullivan (eds), *The Nature of the Right: European and American Politics and Political Thought since 1789* (London: Pinter, 1989), is a useful collection of essays. Roger Scruton, *The Meaning of Conservatism* (Harmondsworth: Penguin, 1980), and Lincoln Allison, *Right Principles: A Conservative Philosophy of Politics* (Oxford: Blackwell, 1984), are vigorous defences. E. H. H. Green, *Ideologies of Conservatism: Conservative Political Ideas in the Twentieth Century* (Oxford: Oxford University Press, 2002), is a thoroughly reliable guide. Anthony Quinton, *The Politics of Imperfection: Religious and Secular Traditions of Conservative Thought in England from Hooker to Oakeshott* (London: Faber, 1978), covers a remarkable amount of ground within a short compass.

Burke's specific reaction to the French Revolution has always attracted attention. For the life, see Isaac Kramnick, *The Rage of Burke: Portrait of an Ambivalent* (New York: Basic Books, 1977), and Conor Cruise O'Brien, *The*

Great Melody: A Thematic Biography and Commented Anthology (London: Sinclair-Stevenson, 1992). C. B. Macpherson, *Burke* (Oxford: Oxford University Press, 1980), is a perceptive introduction. For critical studies, see Michael Freeman, *Edmund Burke and the Critique of Political Radicalism* (Oxford: Blackwell, 1980); Frank O'Gorman, *Edmund Burke: His Political Philosophy* (London: Allen and Unwin, 1973); Alfred Cobban, *Edmund Burke and the Revolt against the Eighteenth Century* (London: Allen and Unwin, 1960); Charles Parkin, *The Moral Basis of Burke's Political Thought* (Cambridge: Cambridge University Press, 1956); Burleigh Taylor Wilkins, *The Problem of Burke's Political Philosophy* (Oxford: Clarendon Press, 1967); and Peter J. Stanlis, *Edmund Burke and the Natural Law* (Ann Arbor: University of Michigan Press, 1965).

For Joseph de Maistre, Richard A. Lebrun has made a massive contribution. See his *Throne and Altar: The Political and Religious Thought of Joseph de Maistre* (Ottawa: University of Ottawa Press, 1965), *Joseph de Maistre: An Intellectual Militant* (Kingston: McGill-Queen's University Press, 1988), and his edited collection, *Joseph de Maistre's Life, Thought and Influence: Selected Studies* (Montreal: McGill-Quenn's University Press, 2001). See also Cara Camcastle, *The More Moderate Side of Joseph de Maistre: Views on Political Liberty and Political Economy* (Montreal: McGill-Queen's University Press, 2005), and Domenico Fisichella, *Il pensiero politico di De Maistre* (Bari: Laterza, 1993).

Interest in Oakeshott has grown apace in recent years. See Paul Franco, *The Political Philosophy of Michael Oakeshott* (New Haven: Yale University Press, 1990); W. H. Greenleaf, *Oakeshott's Philosophical Politics* (London: Longman, 1966); Terry Nardin, *The Philosophy of Michael Oakeshott* (University Park, Pa.: Pennsylvania State University Press, 2001); Efrain Podoksik, *In Defence of Modernity: Vision and Philosophy in Michael Oakeshott* (Exeter: Imprint Academic, 2003); Kenneth B. MacIntyre, *The Limits of Politics: Oakeshott's Philosophy of Civil Association* (Exeter: Imprint Academic, 2004); and the special issue of *European Journal of Political Theory*, 4 (2005), number 1.

There has been a proliferation of studies of nationalism in recent years. From a vast literature, see John Hutchinson and Anthony Smith (eds), *Nationalism* (Oxford: Oxford University Press, 1994); John Hutchinson, *Modern Nationalism* (London: Fontana, 1994); Ernest Gellner, *Nations and Nationalism* (Oxford: Blackwell, 1983); Peter Alter, *Nationalism* (London: Edward Arnold, 1989); Benedict Anderson, *Imagined Communities: Reflections on the Origin and Spread of Nationalism* (London: Verso, 1991); Liah Greenfield, *Nationalism: Five Roads to Modernity* (Cambridge, Mass.: Harvard University Press, 1992); E. J. Hobsbawm, *Nations and Nationality since 1780: Programme, Myth, Reality* (Cambridge: Cambridge University Press, 1990); Anthony D. Smith, *Nations and Nationalism in a Global Era* (Cambridge: Polity, 1995); David Miller, *On Nationality* (Oxford: Oxford University Press, 1995); David Miller, *Citizenship and National Identity*

(Cambridge: Polity, 2000); Margaret Canovan, *Nationhood and Political Theory* (Cheltenham: Edward Elgar, 1996); and Andrew Vincent, *Nationalism and Particularity* (Cambridge: Cambridge University Press, 2002).

Individual nationalist theorists have attracted less attention. On Herder, see F. M. Barnard, *Herder's Social and Political Thought: From Enlightenment to Nationalism* (Oxford: Oxford University Press, 1965); Isaiah Berlin, *Vico and Herder: Two Studies in the History of Ideas* (London: Hogarth Press, 1976); and Robert T. Clark, Jr., *Herder: His Life and Thought* (Berkeley: University of California Press, 1969).

For Mazzini we have Denis Mack Smith, *Mazzini* (New Haven: Yale University Press, 1994), for the life. Gaetano Salvemini, *Mazzini*, trans. I. M. Rawson (London: Cape, 1956), is a spirited reconstruction of the burden of Mazzini's thought. See also Nadia Urbinati, 'A Common Law of Nations: Giuseppe Mazzini's Democratic Nationality', *Journal of Modern Italian Studies*, 1 (1996); C. E. Vaughan, 'Mazzini', in his *Studies in the History of Political Philosophy before and after Rousseau* (Manchester: Manchester University Press, 1925), vol. 2; and Bruce Haddock, 'State and Nation in Mazzini's Political Thought', *History of Political Thought*, 20 (1999). For wider context, see Bruce Haddock, 'State, Nation and Risorgimento', in Gino Bedani and Bruce Haddock (eds), *The Politics of Italian National Identity: A Multidisciplinary Perspective* (Cardiff: Cardiff University Press, 2000).

Leszek Kolakowski, *Main Currents of Marxism*, trans. P. S. Falla (Oxford: Oxford University Press, 1978, 3 vols), is a masterly guide to the socialist tradition. R. N. Berki, *Socialism* (London: Dent, 1975), Michael Newman, *Socialism: A Very Short Introduction* (Oxford: Oxford University Press, 2005), and Anthony Wright, *Socialisms: Theories and Practices* (Oxford: Oxford University Press, 1987), are clear introductory surveys. Donald Sassoon, *One Hundred Years of Socialism: The West European Left in the Twentieth Century* (London: Fontana, 1997), is richly informative, but accessible. For discussion and controversy, see Leszek Kolakowski and Stuart Hampshire (eds), *The Socialist Idea: A Reappraisal* (London: Weidenfeld and Nicolson, 1974); John Dunn, *The Politics of Socialism: An Essay in Political Theory* (Cambridge: Cambridge University Press, 1984); Gavin Kitching, *Rethinking Socialism: A Theory for a better Practice* (London: Methuen, 1973); and Norberto Bobbio, *Which Socialism?: Marxism, Socialism and Democracy*, trans. Roger Griffin, ed. Richard Bellamy (Cambridge: Polity, 1987).

The literature on Marx is vast, but patchy in quality. Isaiah Berlin, *Karl Marx: His Life and Environment* (Oxford: Oxford University Press, 1978), remains highly accessible and perceptive. David McLellan, *Karl Marx: His Life and Thought* (London: Macmillan, 1973), is a solid guide to the range of Marx's writings. Among other introductory studies see, Peter Singer, *Marx* (Oxford; Oxford University Press, 1980); Jon Elster, *An Introduction to Marx* (Cambridge: Cambridge University Press, 1986); John Sanderson, *An*

Interpretation of the Political Ideas of Marx and Engels (London: Longmans, 1969); Michael Evans, *Karl Marx* (London: Allen and Unwin, 1975); and John Higgins, *Karl Marx* (London: Routledge, 2007). For the complex relationship between Marx and Engels, see Terrell Carver, *Marx and Engels: The Intellectual Relationship* (Brighton: Wheatsheaf, 1983). More advanced students will find John Torrance, *Karl Marx's Theory of Ideas* (Cambridge: Cambridge University Press, 1995), and Jon Elster, *Making Sense of Marx* (Cambridge: Cambridge University Press, 1985), deeply rewarding. The most rigorous philosophical study of Marx's theory of history is G. A. Cohen, *Karl Marx's Theory of History: A Defence* (Oxford: Oxford University Press, 1978). On Marx's politics, see Shlomo Avineri, *The Social and Political Thought of Karl Marx* (Cambridge: Cambridge University Press, 1968); Bertell Ollman, *Alienation: Marx's Critique of Man in Capitalist Society* (Cambridge: Cambridge University Press, 1971); Terrell Carver, *Marx's Social Theory* (Oxford: Oxford University Press, 1982); and Steven Lukes, *Marxism and Morality* (Oxford: Clarendon Press, 1985). Terrell Carver (ed.), *The Cambridge Companion to Marx* (Cambridge: Cambridge University Press, 1988), is an excellent collection of essays.

Communism and its legacy is a deeply controversial topic in political thought. Robert Service, *Comrades! A History of World Communism* (Cambridge, Mass.: Harvard University Press, 2007), is a comprehensive study. Richard Pipes, *Communism: A Brief History* (London: Weidenfeld and Nicolson, 2001), is a lucid survey. R. N. Carew Hunt, *The Theory and Practice of Communism* (Harmondsworth: Penguin, 1969), remains useful on technical issues. Advanced students will profit from Claude Lefort, *Complications: Communism and the Dilemmas of Democracy* (New York: Columbia University Press, 2007). For the final crisis of communist regimes, see Gale Stokes, *The Walls Came Tumbling Down: The Collapse of Communism in Eastern Europe* (Oxford: Oxford University Press, 1994), and Stephen White, *Communism and Its Collapse* (London: Routledge, 2000). François Furet, *The Passing of an Illusion: The Idea of Communism in the Twentieth Century*, trans. Deborah Furet (Chicago: University of Chicago Press, 1999), is a sustained polemic against communist theory and practice.

For Lenin, see Neil Harding, *Lenin's Political Thought* (London: Macmillan, 1977–81, 2 vols); Robert Service, *Lenin: A Biography* (Cambridge, Mass.: Harvard University Press, 2000); A. J. Polan, *Lenin and the End of Politics* (London: Methuen, 1984); and Kevin Anderson, *Lenin, Hegel, and Western Marxism* (Urbana: University of Illinois Press, 1995). For broader impact and influence, see Neil Harding, *Leninism* (Basingstoke: Macmillan, 1996).

Fascism is the most problematic of modern ideologies from the perspective of political thought, and many of the secondary studies are controversial. Kevin Passmore. *Fascism: A Very Short Introduction* (Oxford: Oxford University Press, 2002), is a dispassionate guide for beginners. Martin Blinkhorn, *Fascism and the Right in Europe, 1919–45* (London:

Longman, 2000), and Richard Thurlow, *Fascism* (Cambridge: Cambridge University Press, 1999), are also very helpful. Roger Eatwell, *Fascism: A History* (London: Pimlico, 2003), and Stanley G. Payne, *A History of Fascism* (Madison: University of Wisconsin Press, 1995), give sure accounts of tortuous developments. Roger Griffin, *The Nature of Fascism* (London: Pinter, 1991), has been particularly influential. See also Robert O. Paxton, *The Anatomy of Fascism* (Harmondsworth: Penguin, 2005); Richard Wolin, *The Seduction of Unreason: The Intellectual Romance with Fascism* (Princeton: Princeton University Press, 2004); and Roger Griffin, *Modernism and Fascism: The Sense of a Beginning Under Mussolini and Hitler* (Basingstoke: Palgrave Macmillan, 2007). Roger Griffin (ed.), *Fascism* (Oxford: Oxford University Press, 1995), and Adrian Lyttelton (ed.), *Italian Fascisms: From Pareto to Gentile* (London: Jonathan Cape, 1973), are good collections of sources.

The concept of totalitarianism is crucial for an understanding of both fascism and communism. The most arresting study of the phenomenon in relation to political ideas is Hannah Arendt, *The Origins of Totalitarianism* (London: George Allen and Unwin, 1967, third edition). For broader discussion, see Simon Tormey, *Making Sense of Tyranny: Interpretations of Totalitarianism* (Manchester: Manchester University Press, 1995). Margaret Canovan, *Hannah Arendt: A Reinterpretation* (Cambridge: Cambridge University Press, 1992), is the best guide to Arendt's thought.

Thinkers associated with fascism have been treated with deep suspicion by political theorists. Carl Schmitt, in particular, remains a troubling figure, though his critique of liberalism touches a nerve in modern political theory. See Joseph W. Bendersky, *Carl Schmitt: Theorist for the Reich* (Princeton: Princeton University Press, 1983); Renato Cristi, *Carl Schmitt and Authoritarian Liberalism: Strong State, Free Economy* (Cardiff: Cardiff University Press, 1997); Paul Gottfried, *Carl Schmitt: Politics and Theory* (Westport, Conn.: Greenwood Press, 1990); John P. McCormick, *Carl Schmitt's Critique of Liberalism: Against Politics as Technology* (Cambridge: Cambridge University Press, 1997); and David Dyzenhaus (ed.), *Law as Politics: Carl Schmitt's Critique of Liberalism* (Durham, NC: Duke University Press, 1998).

H. S. Harris, *The Social Philosophy of Giovanni Gentile* (Urbana: University of Illinois Press, 1960), did most to sustain Gentile's reputation as a serious political philosopher in the English-speaking world. A. James Gregor, *Giovanni Gentile: Philosopher of Fascism* (New Brunswick, NJ: Transaction Publishers, 2001), is a shorter, and less rigorous, introduction.

Philosophers and political theorists contributing to the consolidation of liberal democracy in the post-war period are readily accessible. For critical consideration of figures discussed in this book, see Bryan Magee, *Popper* (London: Fontana, 1973); Jeremy Shearmur, *The Political Thought of Karl Popper* (London: Routledge, 1996); Geoffrey Stokes, *Popper: Philosophy, Politics and Scientific Method* (Cambridge: Polity, 1998);

Malachi Haim Hacohen, *Karl Popper: The Formative Years, 1902–1945* (Cambridge: Cambridge University Press, 2002); John Gray, *Hayek on Liberty* (Oxford: Blackwell, 1986); Norman P. Barry, *Hayek's Social and Economic Philosophy* (London: Macmillan, 1979); Andrew Gamble, *Hayek: The Iron Cage of Liberty* (Cambridge: Polity, 1996); Chandran Kukathas, *Hayek and Modern Liberalism* (Oxford: Oxford University Press, 1989); Alan Ebenstein, *Friedrich Hayek: A Biography* (Chicago: University of Chicago Press, 2003); John Gray, *Berlin* (London: HarperCollins. 1995); Claude J. Galipeau, *Isaiah Berlin's Liberalism* (Oxford: Clarendon Press, 1994); and George Crowder, *Isaiah Berlin: Liberty and Pluralism* (Cambridge: Polity, 2004).

John Rawls has been the focus of more discussion than any other contemporary theorist, in terms of both exegesis and critical engagement. A clear introduction is Chandran Kukathas and Philip Pettit, *A Theory of Justice and its Critics* (Cambridge: Polity, 1990). Brian Barry, *The Liberal Theory of Justice* (Oxford: Clarendon Press, 1973), is a sustained critical analysis of leading ideas from *A Theory of Justice*. Michael J. Sandel, *Liberalism and the Limits of Justice* (Cambridge: Cambridge University Press, 1982), is a close criticism of Rawls from a communitarian perspective. Samuel Freeman, *Rawls* (London: Routledge, 2007), is a comprehensive overview. Catherine Audard, *John Rawls* (Stocksfield: Acumen, 2007), and Thomas Pogge, *John Rawls: His Life and Theory of Justice* (Oxford: Oxford University Press, 2007), are also very useful. Samuel Freeman, *Justice and the Social Contract: Essays on Rawlsian Political Philosophy* (Oxford: Oxford University Press, 2007), is a set of closely argued studies which together highlight Rawls's central position in contemporary liberal theory. Thomas Pogge, *Realizing Rawls* (Ithaca: Cornell University Press, 1989), pursues implications in the wider international arena. Samuel Freeman (ed.), *The Cambridge Companion to Rawls* (Cambridge: Cambridge University Press, 2003), is an excellent collection of essays covering all aspects of Rawls's thought. Rex Martin and David Reidy (eds), *Rawls's Law of Peoples: A Realistic Utopia?* (Oxford: Blackwell, 2006), focuses on the international dimension.

Students coming to analytical political theory for the first time would do well to begin with broader texts. See Will Kymlicka, *Contemporary Political Philosophy* (Oxford: Oxford University Press, 1990); Jonathan Wolff, *An Introduction to Political Philosophy* (Oxford: Oxford University Press, 1996); Andrew Vincent, *The Nature of Political Theory* (Oxford: Oxford University Press, 2004); Raymond Plant, *Modern Political Thought* (Oxford: Blackwell, 1991); and Jean Hampton, *Political Philosophy* (Boulder: Westview Press, 1997).

The presuppositions of normative theory have been challenged most forcefully by Foucault. Good introductions include Gary Gutting, *Foucault: A Very Short Introduction* (Oxford: Oxford University Press, 2005); Lois McNay, *Foucault: A Critical Introduction* (Cambridge: Polity, 1994); J.

G. Merquior, *Foucault* (London: Fontana, 1991); and Sara Mills, *Michel Foucault* (London: Routledge, 2003). Among more specialized studies, see Jon Simons, *Foucault and the Political* (London: Routledge, 1995); Michael Clifford, *Political Genealogy after Foucault: Savage Identities* (London: Routledge, 2001); John S. Ransom, *Foucault's Discipline: The Politics of Subjectivity* (Durham, NC: Duke University Press, 1997); Roy Boyne, *Foucault and Derrida: The Other Side of Reason* (London: Unwin Hyman, 1990); Barry Hindess, *Discourses of Power: From Hobbes to Foucault* (Oxford: Blackwell, 1996); Wolfgang Detel, *Foucault and Classical Antiquity: Power, Ethics, and Knowledge*, trans. David Wigg-Wolf (Cambridge: Cambridge University Press, 2005); Johanna Oksala, *Foucault on Freedom* (Cambridge: Cambridge University Press, 2005); and Michele Barrettt, *The Politics of Truth: From Marx to Foucault* (Cambridge: Polity, 1991). Gary Gutting (ed.), *The Cambridge Companion to Foucault* (Cambridge: Cambridge University Press, 1994), is an excellent collection of essays covering the range of Foucault's writings.

For broader themes in twentieth-century political thought, see Terence Ball and Richard Bellamy (eds), *The Cambridge History of Twentieth-Century Political Thought* (Cambridge: Cambridge University Press, 2003), and Alan Finlayson (ed.), *Contemporary Political Thought: A Reader and Guide* (Edinburgh: Edinburgh University Press, 2003). Jonathan Glover, *Humanity: A Moral History of the Twentieth Century* (London: Pimlico, 2001), and Mark Mazower, *Dark Continent: Europe's Twentieth Century* (London: Allen Lane, 1998), provide striking accounts of the shifting context of debate. The problematic impact of intellectuals is covered in Mark Lilla, *The Reckless Mind: Intellectuals in Politics* (New York: New York Review of Books, 2001). Allan Bloom's controversial treatment of these issues in relation to universities, *The Closing of the American Mind* (New York: Simon Schuster, 1987), still touches a raw nerve.

What is perhaps most marked in the contemporary literature on the status of normative argument is a failure to engage across disciplines. One of the major attractions of approaching normative argument through history of political thought is precisely that theory and history are brought together. The recent literature on multiculturalism has also forced a dialogue between disciplines, though results have not always been encouraging. Tariq Modood, *Multiculturalism: A Civic Idea* (Cambridge: Polity, 2007), is a balanced introduction for political theorists. Bhiku Parekh, *Rethinking Multiculturalism: Cultural Diversity and Political Theory* (Basingstoke: Macmillan, 2000), and Will Kymlicka, *Multicultural Citizenship: A Liberal Theory of Minority Rights* (Oxford: Clarendon Press, 1995), have been influential. Will Kymlicka (ed.), *The Rights of Minority Cultures* (Oxford: Oxford University Press, 1995), is a valuable collection of essays. Responses to Brian Barry, *Culture and Equality* (Cambridge: Polity, 2000), highlight the striking implications of contemporary theory. See Paul Kelly (ed.), *Multiculturalism Reconsidered* (Cambridge: Polity, 2002), and

Bruce Haddock and Peter Sutch (eds), *Multiculturalism, Identity and Rights* (London: Routledge, 2003). These are contemporary examples of long-standing arguments between universalists and particularists. And there is no end in sight.

Index